W9-BUL-842

Life's Ultimate Questions

Some Other Books by Ronald Nash

The Concept of God

Faith and Reason: Searching for a Rational Faith

Worldviews in Conflict

Is Jesus the Only Savior?

When a Baby Dies

Why the Left Is Not Right: The Religious Left—Who They Are and
What They Believe

The Summit Ministry Guide to Choosing a College

The Gospel and the Greeks

Poverty and Wealth: Why Socialism Doesn't Work

The Closing of the American Heart: What's Really Wrong with America's
Schools

The Word of God and the Mind of Man

Freedom, Justice and the State

The Light of the Mind: St. Augustine's Theory of Knowledge

The Meaning of History

Life's Ultimate Questions

An Introduction to Philosophy

Ronald H. Nash

GRAND RAPIDS, MICHIGAN 49530

ZONDERVAN™

Life's Ultimate Questions
Copyright © 1999 by Ronald H. Nash

Requests for information should be addressed to:

Zondervan, *Grand Rapids, Michigan 49530*

Library of Congress Cataloging-in-Publication Data

Nash, Ronald H.
    Life's ultimate questions : an introduction to philosophy / Ronald H. Nash.
        p.   cm.
    Includes bibliographical references and index.
    ISBN: 0-310-22364-4 (alk. paper)
    1. Christianity—Philosophy. 2. Philosophy Introductions. I. Title.
BR100.N27 1999
   190—dc21   99-26079

Interior design by Sherri L. Hoffman

Printed in the United States of America

This edition printed on acid-free paper.

---

08 09 10 11 • 20 19 18 17 16 15 14 13 12

CONTENTS

PREFACE

I took my first philosophy course during my senior year in college. When I left the classroom after those first sixty minutes, I said, "Wow! Where has this stuff been all my life?" I decided to stay for another year to complete a philosophy major before beginning graduate studies at Brown University. I taught my first philosophy class in 1957, and I've been teaching the subject ever since: forty-one years and still kicking. I estimate I have taught more than fifteen thousand students at the bachelor's, master's, and doctor's levels.

During many of those forty-one years, I had difficulty finding a satisfactory textbook for my Introduction to Philosophy courses. All of the books I examined and many that I used seemed to have been written not for students but for a relatively small group of philosophers. Now that it's finished, this book is the kind of text I wish I'd had when I began teaching.

This book represents a synthesis of three distinct approaches: a section that deals with important philosophical problems and issues; another section dealing with six major systems in the history of philosophy; and a section that relates approaches in the first two sections to worldview thinking. This book differs from other beginning texts in the emphasis it gives to the notion of a worldview.

I have written this book with several kinds of readers in view: the college and seminary students who will be using the book as a text; their professors, who will use it as a teaching tool; and readers outside of any academic community who want to know more about philosophy and its relevance for their lives and their own worldview. I had at least five objectives in writing this book:

—To show that many of life's problems can be illuminated by philosophy. In fairness, I must also admit that some philosophers produce more darkness than light on the subjects they discuss.
—To help students think more clearly about the problems and philosophers discussed in this book.
—To introduce readers to several important philosophical tools, including logic and ways of developing an argument.
—To introduce readers to examples of conceptual analysis. Many centuries ago, Socrates noted how often human arguments contain an implicit appeal to some concept or term that few people

seemed able to define. Twenty-five hundred years of philosophy have not diluted the wisdom of Socrates' judgment.

—To introduce readers to worldview thinking. Conceptual analysis deals with individual ideas or concepts. Sooner or later we have to combine separate concepts into patterns of thought that this book calls worldviews.

Chapter 1 introduces the reader to the idea of a worldview, to the importance of worldviews, and to their place in philosophy. It also serves as an introduction to the book. One of the more important things that a study of philosophy ought to do is acquaint the reader with the role that worldviews play in every person's thought and conduct. I want readers to advance their understanding of their own worldview. I would like to think that by the time readers have finished the book, their worldview will have undergone some changes and will be better because of those changes. I trust many readers will have eliminated inconsistent or inadequate beliefs from their worldviews. In chapter 1, I introduce some of the elements of any reasonably complete worldview and discuss the tests by which we can evaluate these beliefs. One such test is the law of non-contradiction, a topic I cover in chapter 8.

Part 1 of the book covers six important systems from the history of philosophy. The content of part 1 is significant for several reasons. For one thing, knowing the fundamental ideas of thinkers like Plato, Aristotle, Augustine, and Aquinas used to be a vital part of what it meant to be an educated person. Moreover, the study of these six systems will enable us to tap into formative discussions of life's ultimate questions at different stages of their development.

Why, many will ask, are the conceptual systems of no philosophers after Aquinas included? For one thing, this is not a textbook in the history of philosophy. I would like to think that many of my readers will want some day to take a history course that will introduce them to the systems of Descartes, Spinoza, Leibniz, Locke, Berkeley, Hume, Kant, Hegel, and others. This book is intended for beginners. There will be plenty of opportunities later in life to explore the intricacies of modern and contemporary philosophy. Moreover, part 2 of this book covers a number of issues that have gained prominence in recent centuries and that owe much to the work of modern and contemporary philosophers.

Who can complain about my decision to include the systems of Plato, Aristotle, Augustine, and Aquinas in part 1? I added the system of Plotinus because it marks a brilliant synthesis of the work of Plato and Aristotle and also because it played a major role in the development of the systems of Augustine and Aquinas. Only someone unfamiliar with the importance of Plotinus would object. Then, to provide balance and to close a major gap, I included the materialistic and naturalistic beliefs of such ancient thinkers as Democritus, Epicurus, and Lucretius. Part 1 begins with the chapter on naturalism because most of the core beliefs of ancient naturalism were opposed by Plato and Aristotle. Naturalism continues to be an influential worldview, even though many of its modern formulations appear to be more sophisticated than the ancient opinions I examine.

Part 2 introduces readers to a number of important philosophical problems and topics (see the table of contents). It begins with a short examination of the law of noncontradiction and then moves to a topic that has gained prominence only in the last thirty years or so, namely, the doctrine of possible worlds (chap. 9). In my judgment, when this material in chapter 9 is taught properly, students find it interesting and exciting. When it is taught badly, however, many students will think their professor needs a week off in either an asylum or a monastery. I considered placing this material in part 1 but decided students could handle it better after completing their study of the six conceptual systems. The study of possible worlds comes near the beginning of part 2 because students grounded in the subject will find much of the material in the topical chapters easier to understand. Professors are welcome, of course, to tackle the chapters in part 2, including chapter 9, in any order they please.

The book contains more material than any one-semester course could possibly cover. I think most professors will appreciate this fact. It affords them the opportunity to vary the topics, thus allowing for some freshness each time they teach the course. Professors who wish to include topics, issues, and questions not covered in this book are free to supplement it with other readings. It is always the professor's option not to cover some sections of some chapters in class. If I have done my job well, most students will be able to grasp the major details of such omitted material through their own study.

It is important, I believe, for students to have the opportunity to do some reading in primary sources. These should include Plato's *Phaedo, Republic* (books 6 and 7), and if time permits, possibly the *Euthyphro* and *Meno*. Selections from Aristotle's *Nichomachean Ethics,* Plotinus's *Enneads,* Augustine's *Confessions* plus selections from other examples of Augustine's works, along with selections from Aquinas's *Summa Theologiae,* should also be considered.

I have written this book from a perspective for which I have great sympathy. However, I do not belabor this perspective and believe that my approach leaves open the possibility of this text being adopted by philosophers who may disagree with some of its content but who nonetheless will welcome the organization and clarity of the book, along with its usefulness as a teaching tool. Many philosophy professors have used textbooks at variance with their own convictions, finding them a foil for their lectures. My book may well function in a similar way for an open-minded teacher who disagrees with some of its opinions. Why should a theistic perspective in such a book preclude its adoption by someone who is not a theist, especially at a time in history when so many scholars claim to be tolerant with respect to worldviews different from their own?

I am painfully aware of the fact that I have had to omit material that some readers and professors might hope to find in the book. Some of this content was excluded because the book could not exceed a preassigned page limit. Other material was omitted because, in my judgment, it is too difficult for beginners. This is supposed to be an introduction to philosophy, not a doctoral-level thesis or monograph. Many favorite topics of a generation ago have become passé. Nothing prevents professors from covering other issues and thinkers in supplementary texts.

I owe a word of thanks to several friends who read an early draft of the book and made many helpful comments. They include Dr. Frank Beckwith of Trinity International University, Dr. Paul Boling of Bryan College, Dr. Carlton Fisher of Houghton College, Dr. Stephen Parrish of William Tyndale College, Dr. J. P. Moreland of Biola University, Dr. Roger Nicole of Reformed Theological Seminary, Joseph Stanford Goss of Chicago, and Kevin Bywater of Colorado Springs. I also wish to acknowledge the splendid work of Linda Triemstra in editing the manuscript.

INTRODUCTION

The chapter that makes up the introduction to the book deals with material that is basic to the rest of the book. Chapter 1 introduces the reader to the notion of a worldview and to its importance and place in philosophy. Readers of this book already have a worldview, even though many are unaware of this fact. Many people are also uninformed about the content of their worldview, along with whatever strengths and weaknesses it might have. Chapter 1 will get you started on the task of identifying and evaluating your own worldview.

Chapter One

Worldview Thinking

Fifty years ago, a California gangster named Mickey Cohen shocked people on both sides of the law when he went forward in a Billy Graham crusade and made a profession of faith. After several months, however, people began to notice that Cohen's life showed no sign of the changes that should have been apparent in the life of a genuine convert. During an interview, Cohen made it clear that he had no interest in abandoning his career as a gangster. He explained his position in a novel way. Since we have Christian movie stars and Christian politicians, Cohen noted, he wanted to be known as the first Christian gangster.

Until recently, most Americans, regardless of their competence in religious matters, would have expressed their dismay at Cohen's behavior. Religious converts, people used to say, are supposed to live better lives than they did before their conversion. I suspect that many Americans today would find nothing unusual in Cohen's attempt at self-justification.

One purpose of this chapter is to explain these odd happenings. Cohen displayed a defective understanding of the cognitive and moral demands of what this chapter will call the Christian worldview. If someone considers himself a Christian, he is supposed to think and act like a Christian. The fact that so many Americans no longer think that way is indication of a major shift in their worldview.

One thing students can learn from philosophy is the nature, importance, and influence of worldviews. If one is serious about getting somewhere in the study of philosophy, it is helpful to examine the bigger picture, namely, the worldviews of the thinkers whose theories have become a large part of what philosophers study.

The Importance of Worldview Thinking

A worldview contains a person's answers to the major questions in life, almost all of which contain significant philosophical content. It is a conceptual framework, pattern, or arrangement of a person's beliefs. The best worldviews are comprehensive, systematic, and supposedly true views of life and of the world. The philosophical systems of great thinkers such as Plato, Aristotle, Plotinus, Augustine, and Thomas Aquinas delineate their worldviews. Of course, many worldviews suffer from incompleteness, inconsistencies, and other failings. Few of the pieces of such worldviews fit together.

Most people have no idea what a worldview is, or even that they have one. People like this are unlikely to know much about the specific content of their own worldview. Nonetheless, achieving a greater awareness of our own worldview is one of the most important things we can do; insight into the worldviews of others is essential to understanding what makes them tick. One thing we can do for others is to help them achieve a better understanding of their worldview. We can also help them to improve it, which means eliminating inconsistencies and providing new information that will fill gaps and remove errors in their conceptual system. A worldview, then, is a conceptual scheme that contains our fundamental beliefs; it is also the means by which we interpret and judge reality.

Worldviews function much like eyeglasses. The right eyeglasses can put the world into clearer focus, and the correct worldview can do something similar. When people look at the world through the wrong worldview, reality doesn't make sense to them. Putting on the right conceptual scheme, that is, viewing the world through the correct worldview, can have consequences for the rest of a person's thinking and acting. The *Confessions* of Augustine provides ample support for this claim.

Most of us know people who seem incapable of seeing certain points that are obvious to us; perhaps those people view us as equally thickheaded or stubborn. They often seem to have a built-in grid that filters out information and arguments and that leads them to place a peculiar twist on what seems obvious to us. Such obstinacy is often a consequence of their worldview.

The study of philosophy can help us realize what a worldview is, assist us in achieving a better understanding of our worldview, and aid us in improving it. Another thing the study of philosophy can teach us is that some worldviews are better than others. Even though Plato and Aristotle got some things, perhaps many things wrong, chances are their worldviews will generally get higher marks than will those of students reading this book. The fact that some worldviews are better than others suggests the need for tests or criteria by which worldviews can be evaluated. This chapter will identify some of these criteria.

Five Central Worldview Beliefs

Worldviews contain at least five clusters of beliefs, namely, beliefs about God, metaphysics (ultimate reality), epistemology (knowledge), ethics, and human nature.[1] While worldviews may include other

---

1. One important area of human knowledge that could be added to our list is history. I have devoted a book to representative theories about history. See Ronald H. Nash, *The Meaning of History* (Nashville: Broadman and Holman, 1998).

beliefs that need not be mentioned at this point, these five usually define the most important differences among competing conceptual systems.

God

The crucial element of any worldview is what it says or does not say about God. Worldviews differ greatly over basic questions: Does God exist? What is God's nature? Is there but one God? Is God a personal being, that is, is he the kind of being who can know, love, and act? Or is God an impersonal force or power? Because of conflicting views about the nature of God, such systems as Buddhism, Hinduism, and Shintoism are not only different religions but also different worldviews. Because Christianity and Judaism are examples of theism, conservative adherents of these religions hold to worldviews that have more in common with each other than they do with dualistic religions (two deities), polytheistic faiths (more than two deities), and pantheistic systems that view the world as divine in some sense. One essential component, then, of any worldview is its view of God.

Metaphysics

A worldview also includes answers to such questions as these: What is the relationship between God and the universe? Is the existence of the universe a brute fact? Is the universe eternal? Did an eternal, personal, and all-powerful God create the world? Are God and the world co-eternal and interdependent beings?[2] Is the world best understood in a mechanistic (that is, a nonpurposeful) way? Or is there purpose in the universe? What is the ultimate nature of the universe? Is the cosmos material, spiritual, or something else? Is the universe a self-enclosed system in the sense that everything that happens is caused by and thus explained by other events within the system? Or can a supernatural reality (a being beyond nature) act causally within nature? Are miracles possible? Though some of these questions never occur to some people, it is likely that anyone reading this book has thought about most of these questions and holds beliefs about some of them.

Epistemology

A third component of any worldview is a theory of knowledge. Even people not given to philosophical pursuits hold some epistemological beliefs. The easiest way to see this is to ask them if they believe that knowledge about the world is possible. Whether they answer yes or no

---

2. Advocates of what is known as process theology answer this question in the affirmative. For a detailed analysis of this increasingly influential position, see Ronald H. Nash, *The Concept of God* (Grand Rapids: Zondervan, 1983).

to this question, their reply will identify one element of their epistemology. Other epistemological questions include the following: Can we trust our senses? What are the proper roles of reason and sense experience in knowledge? Do we apprehend our own states of consciousness in some way other than reason and sense experience? Are our intuitions of our own states of consciousness more dependable than our perceptions of the world outside of us? Is truth relative, or must truth be the same for all rational beings? What is the relationship between religious faith and reason? Is the scientific method the only or perhaps the best method of knowledge? Is knowledge about God possible? If so, how can we know God? Can God reveal himself to human beings? Can God reveal information to human beings? What is the relationship between the mind of God and the human mind?[3] Even though few human beings think about such questions while watching a baseball game on television (or during any normal daily activities), all that is usually required to elicit an opinion is to ask the question. All of us hold beliefs on epistemological issues; we need only to have our attention directed to the questions.

Ethics

Most people are more aware of the ethical component of their worldview than of their metaphysical and epistemological beliefs. We make moral judgments about the conduct of individuals (ourselves and others) and nations. The kinds of ethical beliefs that are important in this context, however, are more basic than moral judgments about single actions. It is one thing to say that some action of a human being like Adolf Hitler or of a nation like Iran is morally wrong. Ethics is more concerned with the question of why that action is wrong. Are there moral laws that govern human conduct? What are they? Are these moral laws the same for all human beings? Is morality subjective, like some people's taste for squid, or is there an objective dimension to moral laws that means their truth is independent of our preferences and desires? Are the moral laws discovered in a way more or less similar to the way we discover that seven times seven equals forty-nine, or are they constructed by human beings in a way more or less similar to what we call human customs?[4] Is morality relative to individuals, cultures, or historical periods? Does it make sense to say that the same action may be right for people in one culture or historical epoch and wrong for others? Or does morality transcend cultural, historical, and individual boundaries?

---

3. My answers to many of these questions can be found in Ronald H. Nash, *The Word of God and the Mind of Man* (Phillipsburg, N.J.: Presbyterian and Reformed, 1992).
4. Examples would include the ways men in our society used to open doors for women or walk on the street side of their female companion.

Anthropology

Every worldview includes a number of beliefs about the nature of human beings. Examples of relevant questions include the following: Are human beings free, or are they merely pawns of deterministic forces? Are human beings only bodies or material beings? Or were all the religious and philosophical thinkers correct who talked about the human soul or who distinguished the mind from the body? If they were right in some sense, what is the human soul or mind, and how is it related to the body? Does physical death end the existence of the human person? Or is there conscious, personal survival after death? Are there rewards and punishment after death? Are humans good or evil?

An Important Qualification

I do not want to suggest that adherents of the same general worldview will agree on every issue. Even Christians who share beliefs on all essential issues may disagree on other major points. They may understand the relationship between human freedom and the sovereignty of God in different ways. They may disagree over how some revealed law of God applies to a current situation. They may squabble publicly over complex issues like national defense, capital punishment, and the welfare state, to say nothing about the issues that divide Christendom into different denominations.

Do these many disagreements undercut the case I've been making about the nature of a worldview? Not at all. A careful study of these disagreements will reveal that they are differences within a broader family of beliefs. When two or more Christians, let us say, argue over some issue, one of the steps they take (or should take) to justify their position and to persuade the other is to show that their view is more consistent with basic tenets of their worldview.

However, it is also necessary to recognize that disagreement on some issues should result in the disputants' being regarded as people who have left that family of beliefs, however much they desire to continue to use the Christian name. For example, many theological liberals within Christendom continue to use the label of *Christian* for views that are clearly inconsistent with the beliefs of historic Christianity. Whether they deny the Trinity, the personality of God, the doctrine of creation, the fact of human depravity, or the doctrine of salvation by grace, they make clear that the religious system they espouse is a different worldview from what has traditionally been called Christianity. Much confusion could be eliminated if some way could be found to get people to use labels like *Christianity* in a way that is faithful to their historic meaning.

Conclusion

Whether we know it or not—whether we like it or not—each of us has a worldview. These worldviews function as interpretive conceptual schemes to explain why we see the world as we do, why we think and act as we do. Competing worldviews often come into conflict. These clashes may be as innocuous as a simple argument between people or as serious as a war between two nations. It is important, therefore, that we understand the extent to which significant disagreements reflect clashes between competing worldviews.

Worldviews are double-edged swords. An inadequate conceptual scheme can hinder our efforts to understand God, the world, and ourselves. The right conceptual scheme can suddenly bring everything into proper focus.

Worldview Thinking and Religion

Worldview thinking has important links to religious belief. Take the Christian faith as an example. Instead of viewing Christianity as a collection of theological bits and pieces to be believed or debated, individuals should approach it as a conceptual system, as a total world-and-life view. Once people understand that both Christianity and its competitors are worldviews, they will be in a better position to judge the relative merits of competing systems. The case for or against Christian theism should be made and evaluated in terms of total systems. The reason why many people reject Christianity is not due to their problems with one or two isolated issues; their dissent results rather from the fact that the anti-Christian conceptual scheme of such people leads them to reject information and arguments that for believers provide support for their worldview. One illustration of this claim lies in people's differing approaches to the central place that miracles occupy in the Christian faith. Religious believers who affirm the reality of such miracles as the resurrection of Jesus Christ need to understand how one's general perspective on the world (that is, one's worldview) controls one's attitude toward miracle claims. People who disagree about the reality of miracles often find themselves talking past each other because they do not appreciate the underlying convictions that make their respective attitudes about miracles seem reasonable to them.

Christianity then is not merely a religion that tells human beings how they may be forgiven. It is a world-and-life view. The Christian worldview has important things to say about the whole of human life. Once we understand in a systematic way how challenges to Christianity are also worldviews, we will be in a better position to rationally justify our choice of the Christian worldview.

The Unavoidability of Religious Concerns

Religious faith is not one isolated compartment of a person's life—a compartment that we can take or leave as we wish. It is rather a dimension of life that colors or influences everything we do and believe. John Calvin taught that all human beings are "incurably religious." Religion is an inescapable given in life. All humans have something that concerns them ultimately, and whatever it is, that object of ultimate concern is that person's God. Whatever a person's ultimate concern may be, it will have an enormous influence on everything else the person does or believes; that is one of the things ultimate concerns are like.

This view was shared by the late Henry Zylstra, who wrote:

> To be human is to be scientific, yes, and practical, and rational, and moral, and social, and artistic, but to be human further is to be religious also. And this religious in man is not just another facet of himself, just another side to his nature, just another part of the whole. It is the condition of all the rest and the justification of all the rest. This is inevitably and inescapably so for all men. No man is religiously neutral in his knowledge of and his appropriation of reality.[5]

No human is religiously neutral, Zylstra states. Whether the person in question is an atheistic philosopher offering arguments against the existence of God, or a psychologist attributing belief in God to cognitive malfunction, or an American Civil Liberties Union lawyer attempting another tactic to remove religion from the public square, no human is religiously neutral. The world is not composed of religious and nonreligious people. It is composed rather of religious people who have differing ultimate concerns and different gods and who respond to the living God in different ways. Each human life manifests different ways of expressing a person's allegiances and answers to the ultimate questions of life. All humans are incurably religious; we manifest different religious allegiances.

This point obliterates much of the usual distinction between sacred and secular. A teacher or a politician who pretends to be religiously neutral is not thinking very deeply. Secular humanism is a religious worldview as certainly as are Christianity and Judaism. It expresses the ultimate commitments and concerns of its proponents.

Other Considerations

The Role of Presuppositions

The philosopher Augustine (354–430) noted that before humans can know anything, they must believe something. Whenever we think, we take some things for granted. All human beliefs rest upon other beliefs

---

5. Henry Zylstra, *Testament of Vision* (Grand Rapids: Eerdmans, 1958), 145.

that we presuppose or accept without support from arguments or evidence. As philosopher Thomas V. Morris explains,

> The most important presuppositions are the most basic and most general beliefs about God, man, and the world that anyone can have. They are not usually consciously entertained but rather function as the perspective from which an individual sees and interprets both the events of his own life and the various circumstances of the world around him. These presuppositions in conjunction with one another delimit the boundaries within which all other less foundational beliefs are held.[6]

Even scientists make important epistemological, metaphysical, and ethical assumptions. They assume, for example, that knowledge is possible and that sense experience is reliable (epistemology), that the universe is regular (metaphysics), and that scientists should be honest (ethics). Without these assumptions that scientists cannot justify within the limits of their methodology, scientific inquiry would soon collapse.

Basic assumptions or presuppositions are important because of the way they often determine the method and goal of theoretical thought. They can be compared with a train running on tracks that have no switches. Once people commit themselves to a certain set of presuppositions, their direction and destination are determined. An acceptance of the presuppositions of the Christian worldview will lead a person to conclusions quite different from those that would follow a commitment to the presuppositions of naturalism.[7]

Paradigms

One purpose of this book is to help the reader recognize overlooked, unseen patterns of thinking that operate in and control much human thinking, including many of the philosophical theories we'll examine. I have talked about worldviews and the impact that presuppositions have upon such conceptual systems. Another relevant factor is sometimes discussed under the label of *paradigms*. A paradigm is a habitual way of thinking. In a sense, every worldview is composed of many smaller paradigms. A worldview, in other words, is a collection of paradigms.

Paradigms provide boundaries. They act as filters that screen data, namely, data that do not meet expectations connected with the paradigm. Paradigms filter information produced by our experiences. They admit data that fit the paradigm and filter out data that conflict with the para-

---

6. Thomas V. Morris, *Francis Schaeffer's Apologetics* (Grand Rapids: Baker, 1987), 109.

7. This claim assumes that the parties involved think and act consistently. We all know professing Christians whose judgments and conduct conflict with important principles of their faith. Many nontheists, often unconsciously, appear to draw back from positions that their presuppositions seem to entail.

digm. The outdated Ptolemaic model of the solar system[8] functioned as a paradigm for centuries. Copernicus's new model placing the sun at the center of our solar system met enormous opposition at first. Much of that opposition came from the power that the old way of thinking, the old paradigm, had over the minds of many influential people.

Of course, not all paradigms are as big as our model of the solar system. People are subject to the influence of many kinds of paradigms in matters of race, religion, and other areas of life and thought.[9]

Personal Considerations

It is hard to ignore the personal dimension that is often present in the acceptance and evaluation of worldviews. It would be foolish to pretend that human beings always handle such matters impersonally and objectively, without reference to considerations rooted in their psychological makeup. Many people demonstrate that they are often incapable of thinking clearly about their worldview. Most of us have met people or read the writings of people who appear so captive to a paradigm that they seem incapable of giving a fair hearing to any argument or piece of evidence that appears to threaten their system. This is true of both theists and nontheists.

Sometimes people have difficulty with competing claims and systems because of philosophical presuppositions. But often people's theoretical judgments seem inordinately affected by nontheoretical factors. This is the case, for example, when racial prejudice causes people to hold untrue beliefs about those who are objects of their prejudice. Sometimes these factors are rooted in that person's history. Some writers have suggested that another type of nontheoretical influence affects our thinking. According to such writers, human thoughts and actions have religious roots in the sense that they are related to the human heart, the center or religious root of our being.[10] Human beings are never neutral with regard to God. Either we worship God as Creator and Lord, or we turn away from God. Because the heart is directed either toward God or against God, theoret-

---

8. If any readers need reminding, this is the creation of the ancient Greek astronomer Ptolemy, who taught that the earth was the center of our solar system.

9. My use of the word *paradigm* in this book must not be confused with its meaning in Thomas Kuhn's *The Structure of Scientific Revolutions*, 2d ed. (Chicago: University of Chicago Press, 1970). Kuhn did not invent the term; he took the word from the English language, redefined it, and turned into a technical term. The lack of a suitable alternative forces me to use the word *paradigm* even though my usage of the term differs from Kuhn's in at least two ways. Kuhn's "paradigm" refers primarily to the way a dominant theory in the sciences tends to blind people to a new, better, and more adequate theory. Kuhn's usage also contains a heavy dosage of relativism. He often seems disinterested in questions about the truth of conflicting paradigms.

10. For example, see Herman Dooyeweerd, *In the Twilight of Western Thought* (Philadelphia: Presbyterian and Reformed, 1960).

ical thinking is never as pure or autonomous as many would like to think. While this line of thinking raises questions that cannot be explored further in this book, it does seem that some people who appear to reject Christianity on what they regard as rational theoretical grounds are acting under the influence of nonrational factors, that is, more ultimate commitments of their hearts. People should be encouraged to dig below the surface and uncover the basic philosophical and religious presuppositions that appear to control their thinking.

Two Challenges

The Contemporary Philosophical Assault on Conceptual Systems

Midway through the twentieth century, large numbers of younger philosophers in the English-speaking world became hostile toward philosophical system building. To people familiar with the history of philosophy, this repudiation of conceptual systems as the most important task of philosophers made some sense. Even the more famous and distinguished systems of philosophy, such as those of Plato and Aristotle, contained problems for which no solutions seemed possible. Things worsened in the nineteenth century, when philosophers like Hegel built conceptual systems that seemed less like attempts to understand reality than efforts to squeeze the world into artificial and arbitrary pigeonholes. Consequently, many British and American philosophers turned away from system building and focused their efforts on achieving a better understanding of small, isolated issues, problems, and puzzles.

Corliss Lamont, one of the more famous American humanists in my lifetime, admitted that "there has been some justifiable reaction against philosophic 'systems'" and then noted how "contemporary philosophers have tended to confine themselves to certain circumscribed problems and areas rather than striking out boldly toward a comprehensive world-view or *Weltanschauung*." Nonetheless, he counseled, analytic or linguistic philosophers like this "cannot really escape from the responsibility of endeavoring to provide a systematic answer concerning the main issues in philosophy, however unfinished and tentative their conclusions may be. Over-specialization within the field of philosophy is a convenient way of avoiding major controversial questions."[11] On this issue, at least, Lamont was correct.

During my master's and doctor's studies in philosophy, I took many courses from such analytic philosophers. I remember spending one semester examining a single sentence from the writings of David Hume. I spent another semester exploring the two-word expression "I can." I look back

---

11. Corliss Lamont, *The Philosophy of Humanism*, 6th ed. (New York: Frederick Ungar, 1982), 6.

with admiration at the creativity of the professors, even though I remember many days in which I felt certain there were better ways to spend my time.

Imagine such a clever and intelligent philosopher who spends several decades studying the meaning of a few key words or concepts. Are we to believe that this philosopher holds no larger view of things, that his or her intellectual life contains only tiny pieces of information (important though they may be) that have no relationship to a larger picture? What if such a philosopher has reached a point of certainty about thirty individual beliefs? But what if the content of some of those beliefs logically contradicts other beliefs held by that person? What would we think about someone who fails to notice or care about such inconsistencies?

Let me make it clear that philosophical or conceptual or linguistic analysis is important, and several examples of it will show up later in this book. A well-formed worldview must be composed of something, and the separate pieces of the worldview ought to represent clear thinking about many smaller issues. No one in his or her right mind, I think, believes that the choice between a conceptual system and philosophical analysis is an either/or situation.

Imagine a person who enters a room and finds a large table where someone has dumped hundreds of pieces from a picture puzzle. What would an observer conclude if this person examined individual pieces with no display of interest in putting those pieces together? Or what would we think if this person laboriously managed to connect three or four pieces and then put them aside with no further interest in seeing how various groupings of pieces fit together in some pattern? Aristotle began one of his books with these words, "By nature, all men desire to know." Are analytic philosophers an exception to Aristotle's wise words? I think not. Sometimes I imagine that in various graduate departments of philosophy there may exist secret societies for analytic philosophers, a kind of parallel to Alcoholics Anonymous, where analytic thinkers receive help in overcoming their natural desire to see the bigger picture. The letters of such a society might well be "AA," meaning Analytics Anonymous.

I maintain, therefore, that the public philosophical assaults against worldviews that once were so fashionable may well have suffered from a degree of self-deception. All of those analytic philosophers had worldviews, whether they knew it or not, whether they were willing to admit it or not. And so, we are not going to allow the missteps of the old analytic philosophers to turn us aside from the legitimate task of worldview thinking.

A Second Challenge

As we approach the start of a new millennium, a new obstacle to getting people to think in terms of worldviews or conceptual systems has reared up, like Godzilla rising from the deep. Writing in *First Things,* Richard

Mouw, a former student of mine who is now president of Fuller Theological Seminary, recalls once observing two conflicting symbols in a car he was following. In the rear window of the auto was a Playboy bunny decal while on the dashboard was a plastic statue of the Virgin Mary. At the time Mouw saw the symbols, he interpreted their odd juxtaposition as a possible conflict between a devoutly Roman Catholic wife and a carnal husband. In his 1998 essay, Mouw leans in a new direction, namely, "that these symbols were indeed incompatible and yet were held simultaneously and sincerely by the same person."[12]

Mouw regards these conflicting symbols as a disturbing sign of a serious problem in American culture. Not too long ago, he writes, it was possible for Christians to argue for the truth of their faith by placing a "strong emphasis on the coherence of a Christian view of reality. The biblical perspective was shown to tie things together, to answer adequately more questions than other worldviews. Such an approach challenged students to make a clear choice between Christianity and, say, a naturalistic or an Eastern religious perspective."[13] However, Mouw believes (mistakenly, I think), that the day when this approach might have worked seems to have passed. Today's students, Mouw continues,

> don't seem to put much stock in coherence and consistency. They think nothing of participating in an evangelical Bible study on Wednesday night and then engaging in a New Age meditation group on Thursday night, while spending their daily jogging time listening to a taped reading of *The Celestine Prophecy*—without any sense that there is anything inappropriate about moving in and out of these very different perspectives on reality [worldviews].[14]

In short, many people are confused, and what makes the situation even more depressing is the inability of these people to see how confused they are.

Mouw then recounts a debate he had once with a theologically liberal church leader on a radio show in southern California. Mouw was there to defend the historicity of Jesus' resurrection from the dead, while the liberal attacked the reliability of the New Testament accounts of the resurrection. The radio program was a call-in show where listeners were invited to air their opinions; one of the first callers was a young woman identifying herself as Heather from Glendale who offered the following comments:

> I'm not what you would call, like, a Christian.... Actually, right now I am sort of into—you know, witchcraft and stuff like that? But I agree with the

---

12. Richard Mouw, "Babel Undone," *First Things* (May 1998), 9.
13. Ibid.
14. Ibid.

guy from Fuller Seminary. I'm just shocked that someone would, like, say that Jesus wasn't really raised from the dead![15]

Mouw reports that he was taken aback by Heather's way of offering support for his belief in the resurrection of Christ. The more he thought about what Heather said, the more worried he became about what she embodies about contemporary culture. "I am concerned," Mouw writes,

> about the way she seems to be piecing together a set of convictions to guide her life. While I did not have the opportunity to quiz her about the way in which she makes room in her psyche for an endorsement of both witchcraft and the Gospel's resurrection narratives, I doubt that Heather subscribes to both views of reality, Wicca and Christianity, in their robust versions. She is placing fragments of worldviews side by side without thinking about their incompatibility. And it is precisely the fact that these disconnected cognitive bits coexist in her consciousness that causes my concern. . . . Here is a sense in which Heather is a microcosm—or a microchaos—of the larger culture.[16]

Indeed she is; and that is bad news about American culture and that of other western nations. What steps can be taken to help confused people like Heather from Glendale? I believe the answers lie in the specifics of this chapter. We must help the Heathers of the world to achieve consciousness of how well or how badly the pieces of their conceptual system fit. We must help them understand the indispensability of thinking and behaving in a logically consistent way, so that when they finally become cognizant of their incoherent beliefs, they will begin the task of tossing many of them aside. In other words, we should strive to do what many Christians under the influence of postmodernism have ceased to do.

Many people, acting under a false sense of tolerance, are reluctant to disagree with the opinions of other people, no matter how patently false those opinions may be. It is only natural that many who think this way will adopt a kind of worldview relativism. In this way of thinking, all worldviews apparently are created equal, whether their creators happen to be Mother Teresa or Adolf Hitler. When this mantra is put into words, it comes out as "You have your worldview, and I have mine." For such people, one worldview is as good as another.

Worldviews should be evaluated according to several tests. In fact, I contend, there are four such tests. They are the test of reason; the test of outer experience; the test of inner experience; and the test of practice.

Evaluating a Worldview

---

15. Ibid., 10.
16. Ibid.

The Test of Reason

By the test of reason I mean logic or, to be more specific, the law of non-contradiction. Since most of chapter 8 is devoted to an analysis of this test, I can be brief. Attempts to define the law of noncontradiction seldom induce much in the way of excitement, but I offer a definition anyway. The law of noncontradiction states that *A,* which can stand for anything, cannot be both *B* and non-*B* at the same time in the same sense. For example, a proposition cannot be true and false at the same time in the same sense; an object cannot be both round and square at the same time and in the same sense.

The presence of a logical contradiction is always a sign of error. Hence, we have a right to expect a conceptual system to be logically consistent, both in its parts (its individual propositions) and in the whole. A conceptual system is in obvious trouble if it fails to hang together logically. Logical incoherence can be more or less fatal, depending on whether the contradiction exists among less central beliefs or whether it lies at the center of the system.[17]

Worldviews should always be submitted to the test of the law of non-contradiction. Inconsistency is always a sign of error, and the charge of inconsistency should be taken seriously.

For all its importance, however, the test of logical consistency can never be the only criterion by which we evaluate worldviews. Logic can be only a negative test. While the presence of a contradiction will alert us to the presence of error, the absence of contradiction does not guarantee the presence of truth. For that, we need other criteria.

The Test of Outer Experience

Worldviews should pass not only the test of reason but also the test of experience. Worldviews should be relevant to what we know about the world and ourselves. My brief account of the test of experience will be divided into two parts: the test of the outer world (this section) and the test of the inner world. The human experience that functions as a test of worldview beliefs includes our experience of the world outside us. It is proper for people to object when a worldview claim conflicts with what we know to be true of the physical universe. This is one reason why no reader of this book believes that the world is flat or that the earth is the center of our solar system.

As part of the test of outer experience, we have a right to expect worldviews to touch base with our experience of the world outside us.

---

17. It is fair to raise questions about supposed contradictions within the Christian faith. I consider one of these in the appendix to chapter 4.

The worldview should help us understand what we perceive. A number of worldview beliefs fail this test, including the following:

Pain and death are illusions.
All human beings are innately good.
Human beings are making constant progress toward perfection.

No worldview deserves respect if it ignores or is inconsistent with human experience.

The Test of Inner Experience

As we have seen, worldviews should fit what we know about the external world. It does appear, however, that many who urge objective validation fail to give proper credit to the subjective validation provided by our consciousness of our inner world.[18] Worldviews also need to fit what we know about ourselves. Examples of this kind of information include the following: I am a being who thinks, hopes, experiences pleasure and pain, believes, and desires. I am also a being who is often conscious of moral right and wrong and who feels guilty and sinful for having failed to do what is right. I am a being who remembers the past, is conscious of the present, and anticipates the future. I can think about things that do not exist. I can plan and then execute my plans. I am able to act intentionally; instead of merely responding to stimuli, I can will to do something and then do it.[19] I am a person who loves other human beings. I can empathize with others and share their sorrow and joy. I know that someday I will die, and I have faith that I will survive the death of my body.

No matter how hard it may be to look honestly at our inner self, we are right in being suspicious of those whose defense of a worldview ignores or rejects the inner world. Worldviews that cannot do justice to an internalized moral obligation or to the guilt we sense when we disobey

---

18. My language in this section should not be understood in a way that suggests I view the human being as some kind of ghost in a machine. Phrases like "outer world," "inner world," and "the world outside us" are metaphors that come naturally to all of us who are not, at the moment, reading a paper to a philosophy seminar. My language is not intended to imply any particular metaphysical theory (for example, an opinion with regard to the mind-body problem) or epistemological view (such as a representative theory of sense perception). My language is *phenomenological language*, that is, it describes the way different things appear to us. My experience of my typewriter at this moment is of an object that appears to exist outside of and independent of my consciousness or awareness of the typewriter. My consciousness of my mental states (expressible in propositions like "I am hungry") is of something that most people can describe comfortably as belonging to their inner world. As long as the language is understood in a nonliteral way, there is no problem.

19. It would be a mistake to think that this sentence implies anything with regard to what we commonly refer to by the expression "free will." See chapter 15 in part 2.

such duties or to the human encounter with genuine love are clearly defective when compared with the biblical worldview.

The Test of Practice

Worldviews should be tested not only in the philosophy classroom but also in the laboratory of life. It is one thing for a worldview to pass certain theoretical tests (reason and experience); it is another for the worldview to pass a practical test, namely, can people who profess that worldview live consistently in harmony with the system they profess? Or do we find that they are forced to live according to beliefs borrowed from a competing system? Such a discovery, I suggest, should produce more than embarrassment.

This practical test played an important role in the work of the Christian thinker Francis Schaeffer. As Morris explains Schaeffer's thinking, the two environments in which humans must live include "the external world with its form and complexity, and the internal world of the man's own characteristics as a human being. This 'inner world' includes such human qualities 'as a desire for significance, love, and meaning, and fear of nonbeing, among others.'"[20]

This is a good time to see these various tests at work.

An Application of Our Four Tests

In September 1996, an American monthly magazine published an article in which the author, Kimberly Manning, told the story of her sojourn among several conflicting worldviews.[21] Mrs. Manning was reared in a Christian home in which, she reports, the "Christian values of love thy neighbor, personal morality, and strong faith were modeled constantly at home and reinforced by Anabaptist fundamentalists who set a very conservative tone for the community. Most significantly, I was raised with the old-fashioned idea that there is objective truth—that while there may be some gray areas in life, there is such a thing as definitive right and wrong."[22] But because no one ever explained to Manning how these val-

---

20. Morris, *Francis Schaeffer's Apologetics,* 21. In this paragraph, Morris is both paraphrasing and quoting Schaeffer.

21. See Kimberly Manning, "My Road from Gender Feminism to Catholicism," *New Oxford Review* (September 1996), 20–26. Gender feminism is the present subject only because it was the new worldview toward which Mrs. Manning gravitated. All of the descriptions and opinions offered about this worldview are those of Mrs. Manning. She has produced a remarkable testimony of the events and conditions that led her to embrace gender feminism and then to reject it. It seldom happens that people who become converts to a set of paradigms such as her gender feminism are able to achieve sufficient distance from their original commitment to recognize its intellectual difficulties. Even less frequently can we find someone like Mrs. Manning who can describe her sojourn in such an engaging manner. Mrs. Manning's story is an excellent example of the worldview tests identified earlier in this chapter.

22. Ibid., 21.

ues were connected to God and to a Christian worldview, she admits that it was easy for her to drift away from the beliefs and standards of her family. Over a period of several years, she slowly abandoned her Christian worldview and moved into the orbit of a worldview known as gender feminism.

Manning's abandonment of her parents' Christianity and her conversion to gender feminism were "a slow and insidious process. I use the word 'conversion' purposely, because I later came to see that gender feminism is a pseudo-religion in which all of the archetypal symbols are there in a twisted manner. 'Womyn' is deified, empowerment is the mantra, unborn children are the blood sacrifices in the ritual of abortion, and men are the scapegoats for our sins."[23] Keep in mind that Manning is describing beliefs she embraced as a substitute for her earlier Christian worldview. She was content with the beliefs she describes.

So long as she majored in science, nothing happened to move her toward gender feminism. Things changed, however, as soon as she changed her college major to social work. She tells of hearing "a lot of talk about 'woman's experience,' how it is the ultimate source of truth. It began to seem like an all-out attack on women was taking place in society, in the form of domestic abuse.... I began to read a lot about misogyny, considered by many feminists to be a deep psychological predisposition in all men."[24]

After graduation from college, Manning explored pantheism and added features of New Age thinking to her worldview. She became fascinated with theories that stressed subjectivism from a female perspective. "Psychology and spirituality were my passions," she writes, "and the left-brained world of critical thinking was now diagnosed as anal-retentive.[25] I became convinced of such nebulous notions as there is no evil (or good/evil/God are all the same), pain is an illusion, God is really a woman, if you don't get it right in this life you can always come back and try again, truth is whatever we make it for we are all creating our own realities, and all views and choices are of equal value. My highest virtue became tolerance, and I felt guilty if I in any way judged another's actions."[26] In other words, Manning's radical feminism embraced many features of what is often called New Age thinking.[27] She goes on to note

---

23. Ibid.

24. Ibid.

25. The term *anal-retentive* is becoming a common term in American discourse. People who use it to demean persons who differ from them seem to have in mind something like intellectual constipation.

26. Manning, "My Road from Gender Feminism to Catholicism," 21.

27. For a discussion of the New Age worldview, see Ronald H. Nash, *Worldviews in Conflict* (Grand Rapids: Zondervan, 1992).

that some feminists she read even described sex within marriage as rape.

Manning describes a view of history that she shared with others in her movement. She begins by talking about a time of peace and harmony on this planet. Humans held all things equally; violence did not exist. The major reason for the harmony and nonviolence was the fact that these cultures were ruled by women who wielded their power wisely. Given Manning's wholehearted commitment to her feminist paradigms, she was not troubled by the lack of any historical support for her theories.

Then, she writes, "It all came to a halt when men rose up and began to use force, rooted in misogyny, to bring women under their control. This was not some series of isolated uprisings, but a systematic reversal of world power and a subjugation of women which has left [the female] gender devastated. Rape was the first method used to subdue women, followed by the development of the institution of marriage; however, as time went on, more sophisticated mechanisms were employed to rob women of their power, both earthly and spiritual."[28] Manning is describing her beliefs at the time.

As she continues, Manning explains her growing hostility toward Christianity.

> The coup de grace in this destruction of matriarchal utopia was the development of Christianity. This patriarchal system, purposely dominated by men, would seek to destroy the last vestiges of the great goddess-centered religions by establishing the complete authority of males over females through its use of supposed sacred writings (the Bible) and masculine symbolism to describe God. The great peace-loving goddess religions[29] were no match for the brute force of a male dominated Christendom and so were decimated. The greatest blow was the Inquisition, in which millions of pagan women, many high priestesses, were burned at the stake, as the Catholic Church made its massive attempt finally to eradicate female power. Then came the witch hunts in the New World, while today such constructs as gender roles continue the assaults against feminine energy on the planet.[30]

Manning then deals with another dimension of her new worldview: "The evidence mounted in my mind: Men were simply evil, and governments and organized religion—specifically Christianity in America—were their weapons."[31] She next turns her attention to the day when gender feminism

---

28. Manning, "My Road from Gender Feminism to Catholicism," 20–21.

29. The ancient goddess religions included enormous amounts of violence, including self-castration. For information, see Ronald H. Nash, *The Gospel and the Greeks* (Richardson, Tex.: Probe, 1992), chap. 8.

30. Manning, "My Road from Gender Feminism to Catholicism," 21.

31. Ibid., 22.

ceased to be a collection of theories. It was the day of her "conversion," the day she had what she describes as her "click" experience, her paradigm shift, her rebirth as a gender feminist. She had begun working in a women's shelter when it struck her "that the cultural reality of my childhood did not exist. I realized in my moment of 'enlightenment' that *all* men were perpetrators and *all* women were victims."[32] "From that moment on," she says,

> for the next four years, I essentially abandoned the notion of objective truth and embraced the world view that all things are relative and truth is determined by the individual. This was a wholly right-brained approach to life in which one's personal experience and feelings at any given moment determine reality. Left-brained thinking patterns, such as critical analysis [i.e., logic] and skepticism, were deemed too rigid, too limiting, too male. I felt freed by the artistic approach to life [i.e., feelings] where everything is an open possibility."[33]

At this point, it would have been understandable for anyone familiar with Manning's commitment to her new worldview to feel confident that any return to the Christian faith of her parents was inconceivable. But problems arose for her subjective, relative view of truth. First, it clashed with her studies in science, especially when the women's shelter falsified data and used a defective statistical method. The relativity of truth did not extend to mathematics, at least so far. But then she had an "anti-click experience."

> One day it suddenly dawned on me that if I were to base my truth solely on my own personal experience, then I could not subscribe to the gender feminist model. After all, my experience [the test of outer experience] of my father, brother, and husband was that men were wonderfully kind and had the utmost respect for women. It was statistically impossible that I alone would have found the only three decent men in the entire world. So with that, gender feminism became a self-refuting proposition for me [the test of reason] and began to crumble before my eyes. That one such basic argument in logic could devastate my entire philosophy [i.e., worldview] was quite an embarrassing blow.[34]

After leaving gender feminism, Manning began to attend a church where the pastor "argued that Christianity is not some nebulous religion of blind faith. He spoke of Christianity as the source of objective truth, grounded in a real act that had occurred in a specific moment in human history."[35] The rest of Manning's story is bound to produce disagreements among those who wish to read it. Nonetheless her account is a fine

---

32. Ibid.
33. Ibid.
34. Ibid., 23.
35. Ibid.

example of the ways in which worldviews come to control our thinking, both for the good and for the bad. As Manning discovered, the right eyeglasses (in her case, the correct worldview) can put the world into clearer focus. The wrong worldview can lead one into serious error.

Though the influence of nontheoretical factors on people's thinking is often extensive, it is seldom total in the sense that it precludes life-altering changes. Even in the case of Saul of Tarsus—one of early Christianity's greatest enemies—where it might appear that a person was dominated by commitments that ruled out any possibility of a change or conversion, things may never be hopeless. People do change conceptual systems. Conversions take place all the time. People who used to be humanists or naturalists or atheists or followers of some competing religious faith have found reasons to turn away from their old conceptual systems and embrace Christianity. Conversely, people who used to profess allegiance to Christianity reach a point where they feel they can no longer believe. In spite of all the obstacles, people do occasionally begin to doubt conceptual systems they had accepted for years.

It does not seem possible to identify a single set of necessary conditions that are always present when people change a worldview. Many people remain blissfully unaware that they have a worldview, even though the sudden change in their life and thought resulted from their exchanging their old worldview for their new one. What does seem clear is that changes this dramatic usually require time along with a period of doubt about key elements of the worldview. Even when the change may appear to have been sudden, it was in all likelihood preceded by a period of growing uncertainty and doubt. In many cases, the change is triggered by an important event, often a crisis. But I have also heard people recount stories that lay out a different scenario. Suddenly, or so it seemed, one event or piece of information led these persons to begin thinking in terms of a conceptual scheme that was totally different for them or one that they were becoming conscious of for the first time. Quite unexpectedly, these people saw things they had overlooked before; or they suddenly saw things fit together in a pattern so that there was meaning where none had been discernible before. It seems foolish, therefore, to stipulate that life-transforming changes in a worldview must match some pattern. People change their minds on important subjects for a bewildering variety of reasons.

In keeping with this book's emphasis upon conceptual systems, the chapters in part 1 will deal with six of the most influential worldviews in the history of human thought. Even though these conceptual systems predate modern times, all of them continue to exercise a significant influence in our own day.

OPTIONAL WRITING ASSIGNMENT

Make a list providing as much detail as you can about your worldview at this time in your life. Use the five major parts of a worldview as headings for information about your major worldview beliefs. Can you identity any potential logical inconsistencies among these beliefs? Is your commitment to any elements in this list shaky? Save this list until your reading of the book is completed and the course for which this book is a text is finished. Then do this exercise again, and compare your two lists and note the changes.

FOR FURTHER READING

Norman L. Geisler and William D. Watkins, *Worlds Apart* (Grand Rapids: Baker, 1989).

C. S. Lewis, *Miracles* (New York: Macmillan, 1960).

Ronald H. Nash, *Faith and Reason* (Grand Rapids: Zondervan, 1988).

Ronald H. Nash, *Worldviews in Conflict* (Grand Rapids: Zondervan, 1992).

Gary Phillips and William E. Brown, *Making Sense of Your Worldview* (Chicago: Moody Press, 1991).

Richard L. Purtill, *Reason to Believe* (Grand Rapids: Eerdmans, 1974).

PART ONE

Six Conceptual Systems

Now that we have been introduced to the notion of a worldview or conceptual system, we are ready to apply that knowledge to six important worldviews from the ancient and medieval worlds.

In chapter 2, I explain the naturalistic worldview found in the writings of the ancient Greek atomist Democritus, the somewhat later Greek thinker Epicurus, and his Roman disciple Lucretius. The naturalistic worldview dates to the beginnings of western philosophy in ancient Greece. It continues to hold fascination for large numbers of people.

The chapters on Plato, Aristotle, Plotinus, Augustine, and Aquinas contain few surprises for readers familiar with the terrain. If this were a book on the history of philosophy, there would be differences in emphasis. But because I am primarily interested in the worldviews of each thinker, I am justified in paying less or no attention to certain aspects of their thinking. I am also interested in noting links between the systems I examine and facets of Christian belief.

In the case of Plato, for example, I will discuss his theory of the Forms and its relationship to his understanding of the human soul and human knowledge. In other words, I will use Plato's conceptual system as a way of introducing the student to some fundamental issues in metaphysics, epistemology, ethics, and anthropology as well as thinking about God. My selection of material is based on the following criteria: the importance of these ideas in the history of philosophy and the interest that thinking people within Christendom ought to have in some of these theories, such as the radical differences between Plato's understanding of creation and the Christian doctrine of *creation ex nihilo*. Each of the conceptual systems covered in part 1 sides with one of these views. The naturalists I discuss along with Aristotle and possibly Aquinas side with empiricism. Plato, Plotinus, and Augustine meet the qualifications for being rationalists.

Aristotle's writings are notorious for their difficulty. Even worse, many discussions of Aristotle's thought are boring. I have done my best to avoid these pitfalls, though with Aristotle no one can guarantee immunity from boredom. I will explain as clearly as I can how Aristotle's metaphysics, epistemology, and anthropology, particularly his view of the soul, differ from Plato's.

Even though Plotinus is the most important philosopher between Aristotle and Augustine, he is often ignored outside of history of philosophy courses. His writings are also difficult to understand unless one has the benefit of the kind of approach represented in this book. While Plotinus was not a Christian, his views played a role in the development of Augustine's thought. Eight hundred years later, Plotinus's beliefs were influencing the world of ideas in Aquinas's lifetime. Moreover, Plotinus is in some respects a forerunner of twentieth-century process philosophy. I will relate Plotinus's system both to Plato and Aristotle before him and to Augustine and Aquinas after him.

My treatment of the life and thought of Augustine will enable me to show how Augustine's Christian worldview provides a foundation from which we can look back and see the serious failings of the first four worldviews covered in part 1. Augustine was not a simpleminded Platonist. He transformed Plato's system in many significant ways as he developed his own worldview.

Even philosophers who are not followers of Thomas Aquinas find it easy to express admiration for his genius, along with appreciation for many elements of his system. Aquinas was not a simpleminded Aristotelian. I will explore the agreements and disagreements between Augustine and Aquinas and between Augustinians and Thomists. I will examine the strengths and weaknesses of the more important elements of Aquinas's system, including his thinking about God.

Chapter Two

Naturalism

IMPORTANT DATES IN ANCIENT ATOMISM

490–430 B.C.   Birth and death of Leucippus
460–360 B.C.   Birth and death of Democritus
341–271 B.C.   Birth and death of Epicurus
306 B.C.   Epicurus founds his university, the
                          Garden, in Athens
96–55 B.C.   Birth and death of T. Lucretius Carus

Why Begin with Naturalism?

If we accept the fairly widespread tradition that Democritus lived more than one hundred years (460–360 B.C.), his life overlapped the lives of Socrates, Plato, and Aristotle. This chapter helps set the stage for the following chapter's treatment of Plato's philosophy. This is so because Plato opposed every distinctive claim of naturalism, including the theories of Democritus that we will examine in this chapter.

Versions of the theories discussed in this chapter are still popular. It is important to recognize how much of contemporary naturalism is largely a restatement, however more sophisticated it may appear, of ideas known and opposed by all of the other systems discussed in chapters 3–7. Because naturalism is such a powerful and influential system, it makes sense to begin with a look at contemporary naturalism. Among other things, this will help establish a definition for the term. As dead as many ideas of the ancient naturalists may seem, the worldview they represented is alive.

Contemporary Metaphysical Naturalism

For much of the twentieth century, the worldview of naturalism has been the major antagonist of the Christian faith in those parts of the world described by the label of Christendom. The central claim of metaphysical naturalism is that nothing exists outside the material, mechanistic (that is, nonpurposeful), natural order. My discussion will focus on naturalists who are what we call *physicalists,* people who insist that everything that exists can be reduced to physical or material entities. But some thinkers reject physicalism (that is, they deny the physicalist's claim that all of reality can be reduced to material entities) yet are also naturalists because they deny the possibility of any divine intervention in the natural order. The famous deists of the eighteenth century were naturalists in this second sense. So too are certain liberal Christian theologians of the twentieth century such as Paul Tillich and Rudolf Bultmann. Because we live in a day when physicalists control the agenda, I am justified in concentrating on this first kind of naturalist.

A naturalist believes that the physical universe is the sum total of all that is. In the famous words of Carl Sagan (1934–1996), "The universe is all that is, or ever was, or ever will be." In the naturalist view of things, Christian supernaturalism is false by definition, as are miracles and the existence of the Judeo-Christian God. Since the matter that makes up the universe is eternal, any belief in a divine creation of the universe is false by definition.

One of the better accounts of contemporary naturalism can be found in a book by the British author C. S. Lewis:

> What the Naturalist believes is that the ultimate Fact, the thing you can't go behind, is a vast process in space and time which is *going on of its own accord.* Inside that total system every particular event (such as your sitting reading this book) happens because some other event has happened; in the long run, because the Total Event is happening. Each particular thing (such as this page) is what it is because other things are what they are; and so, eventually, because the whole system is what it is. All the things and events are so completely interlocked that no one of them can claim the slightest independence from "the whole show." None of them exists "on its own" or "goes on of its own" except in the sense that it exhibits at some particular place and time, that general "existence on its own" or "behaviour of its own accord" which belongs to "Nature," the great total interlocked event as a whole.[1]

For a naturalist, the universe is analogous to a sealed box. Everything that happens inside the box (the natural order) is caused by or is explicable in terms of other things that exist within the box. Nothing, including God, exists outside the box; therefore, nothing outside the box that we call the universe or nature can have any causal effect within the box. The resulting picture of metaphysical naturalism looks like this:

---

1. C. S. Lewis, *Miracles* (New York: Macmillan, 1960), 6–7.

Figure 2.1

NOTHING	NATURE (The Physical Universe)	NOTHING

It is important to notice that the box is closed and sealed tightly. Even if something did exist outside the box, it could not serve as the cause of any event that occurs within the box.

I must pause a moment to consider a possible objection or two to this picture. Some critics will point out that such early naturalists as Democritus and Epicurus believed the universe was infinitely large. Surely, my critics could say, you distort at least their version of naturalism by portraying their universe as a closed box. Other critics might complain that my analogy of the box distorts the naturalist's understanding of the universe by implying both an inside and an outside of the natural order, although for a true naturalist there is no outside. Nonetheless, the picture of the box has helped large numbers of naturalists to comprehend the essential features of their worldview, or so many have told me.

This is a good opportunity to clarify what my illustration is about. Whether the universe of a naturalist is infinite or finite, nothing exists that is independent of the natural order and its processes. We will see this clearly when we study ancient atomism, which taught that all of nature consists of eternal, indestructible, corporeal atoms moving through empty space. Nothing can exist that is not a result of some mechanistic, nonpurposeful combining of these eternal atoms. As we'll see, Epicurus believed in the existence of the Greek gods.[2] However, he taught, even the gods are composed of atoms; even the gods are contained within the box that is the natural order. Understood properly, my example of the closed box illustrates important features of naturalism.

Naturalists believe that everything that happens within nature has its cause in something else that exists within the natural order. As philosopher William Halverson explains, metaphysical naturalism claims

> that what happens in the world is theoretically explicable without residue in terms of the internal structures and the external relations of these material entities. The world is ... like a gigantic machine whose parts are so numerous and whose processes are so complex that we have thus far been able to achieve only a very partial and fragmentary understanding of how it works. In principle, however, everything that occurs

2. I am not suggesting that Epicurus believed in the Greek gods in the sense that modern-day Christians believe in God. But it seems clear that he believed that the ancient Greek gods did exist in some sense.

is ultimately explicable in terms of the properties and relations of the particles of which matter is composed.[3]

A metaphysical naturalist, then, believes the following propositions.

1. *Only nature exists.* By *nature* I mean (following Stephen Davis) "the sum total of what could in principle be observed by human beings or be studied by methods analogous to those used in the natural sciences."[4] Anyone who adopts a naturalist worldview holds that a supernatural God (that is, the kind of God found in theistic religions like Judaism and Christianity whose existence is independent of nature and whose creative activity brought the universe into existence from nothing) does not exist. By definition, anything that exists is part of the box.

2. *Nature is a materialistic system.* The basic components of existing things are material entities. This does not mean that metaphysical naturalists deny the existence of such things as human memories of the past and hopes for the future, or plans, intentions, and logical inferences. Whatever such things as thoughts, beliefs, and inferences are, they are either material things or reducible to or explainable in terms of material things or caused by something material.

3. *Nature is a self-explanatory system.* Anything that happens within the natural order must, at least in principle, be explainable in terms of other elements of the natural order. It is never necessary to seek the explanation for any event within nature in something beyond the natural order. In general, the naturalist holds that only the parts and not the whole require explanation in terms of something else (which brings us back to the brute factuality of the universe, whether it has an absolute beginning or not). It is neither necessary nor possible to seek an explanation in terms of something beyond the natural order. Even though naturalists insist that every individual and event in the system be explained, they deny both the necessity and the possibility of explaining the whole in terms of something else.

In this connection, it would be easy to assume that metaphysical naturalists must also believe that the natural order is eternal. But naturalism is more complex than this. It is true that many naturalists prefer to think of the universe as always existing in some state or other. However, many of them reserve the right to claim that even though the universe had a beginning, it sprang into existence uncaused. The naturalist position about the age of the natural order amounts to the claim that either the universe has always existed or it came into existence without a cause. It should be noted, however, that one does not need to be a theist to have

---

3. William H. Halverson, *A Concise Introduction to Philosophy,* 3d ed. (New York: Random House, 1976), 394.

4. Stephen T. Davis, "Is It Possible to Know That Jesus Was Raised from the Dead?" *Faith and Philosophy* 1 (1984): 154.

trouble understanding or accepting the belief that an uncaused universe sprang into existence from nothing.

4. *Nature is characterized by total uniformity.* This uniformity is apparent in the regularity of the natural order, something that scientists attempt to capture in the natural laws they formulate. Many philosophers at this point mistakenly infer that a belief in miracles is incompatible with the order and regularity of the natural order.

5. *Nature is a deterministic system.* Determinism is the belief that every event is made physically necessary by one or more antecedent causes. Because the metaphysical naturalism under consideration here is a kind of physicalism, those antecedent causes must be either matter or reducible to matter. In this view of things, there is no room for any theory of agency whereby either God or human beings acting apart from any totally determining causes can function as causes in the natural order.[5]

One of the most important benefits of responsible worldview thinking is recognizing the logical implications of one's major beliefs. How well does naturalism meet the tests of reason, outer experience, inner experience, and practice? Once naturalists commit to their naturalistic presuppositions, what implications are they obliged to accept, to live with?

Any persons in the grip of these naturalistic habits of mind could not be expected to believe in the existence of the personal, omnipotent God of Judaism and Christianity or in miracles, angels, conscious existence after death, or any other essential feature of the historic Christian faith. For such persons, evidence of putative miracles can never be persuasive. Since such persons believe that miracles are impossible, it is impossible that there should ever be convincing evidence for a miracle. Thus, no arguments on behalf of the miraculous can possibly succeed with a naturalist on the naturalist's own terms. The only proper way to address the naturalists' disbelief is to begin by challenging the elements of their naturalism.

One way for the reader to see important features of naturalism is to dwell in the mood and atmosphere of the following quotations from two naturalistic philosophers of the twentieth century, Corliss Lamont and Bertrand Russell. Lamont expresses clearly the naturalist's need to reject all forms of supernaturalism. "Humanism," he writes, "believes in a naturalistic metaphysics or attitude toward the universe that considers all forms of the supernatural as myth; and that regards Nature as the totality of being and as a constantly changing system of matter and energy which exists independently of any mind or consciousness."[6] Moreover, Lamont

---

5. Contemporary physics wrestles with so many apparent anomalies that it is possible for someone to be a naturalist and question both determinism and the uniformity of the natural order. But the comments in points 4 and 5 have been appropriate for too long to omit.

6. Corliss Lamont, *The Philosophy of Humanism,* 6th ed. (New York: Fredrick Ungar, 1982), 12–13.

continues, "Humanism, drawing especially upon the laws and facts of science, believes that man is an evolutionary product of the Nature of which he is part; that his mind is indivisibly conjoined with the functioning of his brain; and that as an inseparable unity of body and personality he can have no conscious survival after death."[7]

Two quotations from Bertrand Russell also provide important confirmation of my account of contemporary naturalism. In the first quote, Russell says:

> That man is the product of causes which had no prevision of the end they were achieving; that his origin, his growth, his hopes and fears, his loves and his beliefs are but the outcome of accidental collocations of atoms; that no fire, no heroism, no intensity of thought and feeling, can preserve an individual life beyond the grave; that all the labours of the ages, all the devotion, all the inspiration, all the noonday brightness of human genius, are destined to extinction in the vast death of the solar system, and the whole temple of Man's achievement must inevitably be buried beneath the debris of a universe in ruins—all these things, if not quite beyond dispute, are yet so nearly certain, that no philosophy which rejects them can hope to stand. Only within the scaffolding of these truths, only on the firm foundation of the unyielding despair, can the soul's habitation henceforth be safely built.[8]

In the second passage Russell is even gloomier:

> Brief and powerless is Man's life; on him and all his race the slow, sure doom falls pitiless and dark. Blind to good and evil, reckless of destruction, omnipotent matter rolls on its relentless way; for Man, condemned today to lose his dearest tomorrow, himself to pass through the gate of darkness, it remains only to cherish, ere yet the blow falls, the lofty thoughts that ennoble his little day.[9]

To Russell's credit, he was not reticent to reveal the practical outcome for life of the naturalistic worldview.

Ancient Atomism

Most of us know that prior to Albert Einstein and other scientists who effected the revolution in physics leading to the nuclear age, nineteenth-century science explained the physical universe as a collection of indivisible atoms that in various combinations made up everything that exists. Many students do not realize that a similar kind of atomism, simpler in specifics, existed in ancient Greece during the lifetimes of Socrates and Plato and was revived and modified by the school of philosophy known as Epicureanism.

---

7. Ibid., 13.

8. Bertrand Russell, *Mysticism and Logic* (London: Longmans, Green and Co., 1925), 47–48.

9. Ibid., 56–57.

Most of the philosophers who came before Socrates, Plato, and Aristotle are described as naturalists. One reason for this was their focus on nature, the physical universe. They were interested in the heavenly bodies they observed at night, and they wondered what the things they encountered in their experience were composed of. They tended to say comparatively little about such human issues as knowledge and ethics. One reason such thinkers were called naturalists is because they centered their attention on nature rather than on human problems. Naturalism in this pre-Socratic sense is rather benign, even though we might regret the narrow focus of these philosophers' work.[10]

But another sense of naturalism characterized early Greek thinkers, a sense that will occupy us in this chapter and several others. The early Greek thinkers often thought that the natural world or physical universe is the only reality that exists. One consequence of this was their denial that anything exists outside the bounds of the physical universe. I have already noted similar thinking in representatives of twentieth-century naturalism.

The two names associated with ancient Greek atomism were Leucippus (490–430 B.C.) and Democritus (460–360 B.C.). Since it may be impossible to separate their views and since Democritus is usually regarded as the more important of the two, I'll concentrate upon his work.

Democritus

Marble bust, Roman period

THE GRANGER COLLECTION, NEW YORK

Democritus

Democritus was the most accomplished of the early naturalists. To quote one historian of philosophy, "No one, even in modern times, has given a more classic expression to atomism or mechanism [than has Democritus]. The motivation of materialistic or mechanistic systems is to explain all phenomena in terms of mechanism; that is, the only original differences allowed to the elements are strictly geometrical, plus the motion in space necessary to alter their positions. For Democritus therefore two principles explain everything: atoms and empty space."[11]

Democritus proposed that the basic building blocks of the universe are tiny, indivisible material entities called atoms. (The word *atom* means that which cannot be divided.) Atomists explained every feature of the material world as varying combinations of an infinite number of atoms moving haphazardly through empty space. The atoms, we must understand, had no properties such as color, taste, or smell; they were neither hot nor cold, sweet nor sour. But every physical thing we encounter in

---

10. In the time of Socrates and Plato, the word *phusis* (nature) had begun to take on a wider meaning, so that it became more difficult to distinguish between issues pertinent to nonhuman nature and issues pertinent to humans.

11. Gordon H. Clark, *Thales to Dewey,* 2d ed. (Unicoi, Tenn.: The Trinity Foundation, 1989), 35.

our experience does have such qualities. The atomists explained such properties as the way things appear to us as a result of the chance linkage of the atoms that possess no such properties.

Atoms differ, the ancients taught, only in quantitative terms like size and shape, never in quality. Atoms are also uncreated and indestructible, which translates into their being eternal. They had no beginning and will have no end. According to the atomists, then, everything in the world can be explained as a chance combination of qualitatively identical atoms.

The Question That Has No Answer

Contemporary naturalists excel at posing problems for which they suppose there is no answer. But atomists and naturalists have their own questions for which they have no' answer. Why is there something (atoms) rather than nothing? Why do the atoms move rather than sit there? If you're an atomist, this is what you have to believe.

It is interesting to observe those important times when even antireligious thinkers like naturalists find it necessary to make leaps of faith. These leaps occur when their thinking leads them to questions for which their system has no answer. Usually they find it convenient to pretend the question doesn't exist. One such question is why atoms exist. Another is why atoms move.

One must never ask why atoms move. Their random movement is a given. Atoms move in all directions. Much like billiard balls on a pool table, the atoms collide with other atoms. These collisions may result in some atoms hooking up in new combinations, or a collision might cause an atom to ricochet in a new direction. The chance conjoining of atoms produces the many different things that exist in the world. The combinations of atoms finally break up, and when this happens, the individual thing that they composed ceases to exist. But the individual atoms exist forever.

So, according to Democritus, the truth about the physical universe can be summed up in two words, "atoms" and the "void." Everything in the universe is a result of qualitatively indistinguishable atoms moving around the universe, bouncing into other atoms, briefly linking up with other atoms. The taste of an orange, the color of a tulip, and the fragrance of a rose are reducible to the quantitatively different factors to which everything that exists can be reduced. All quality is an illusion. It is the way certain configurations of quantitatively different atoms appear to people.

The ancient atomists had another problem. Their universe was a machine, devoid of purpose and design. But the universe we live in is full of order. Consider two piles of apples and oranges. If we took the mechanistic, purposeless metaphysics of the ancient atomists literally, they had no explanation for why apple seeds don't produce orange trees. But that never happens in the real world. Not only did the atomists have difficulty explaining why there were atoms or why the atoms moved so conveniently, but also they seemed to have no way to explain the lawlike and orderly nature of the universe.

The world we perceive is rich with color, tastes, sounds, and other properties. But the world of the atomists is colorless, tasteless, and devoid of sound. As W. T. Jones explains, "When the atoms flung off by the pattern that we call a rose strike those other atoms that we call an eye, the former set up a motion in the latter (as a billiard ball flung into a group of stationary balls sets them in motion), and this motion, communicated to other atoms by way of the optic nerve (itself, of course, really another collection of atoms with another configuration), eventually produces the sensation that we know and experience as 'rose.'"[12]

The atomism of Democritus was a mechanistic view of the universe. It portrayed the universe as a machine, purring along in ways that seemed to produce order and design, but this view is without any ability to explain that order and design. Taken literally, the system encouraged people to expect not order but chaos. As we'll see, Plato opposed the mechanism of the atomistic worldview in favor of a teleological worldview, one requiring a source for order and design that transcends the physical world.

It is worth considering whether our contemporary understanding of DNA is good news or bad news for naturalists. Some have argued that a proper understanding of DNA requires as part of its explanation the positing of a power beyond the physical universe. And since this force would appear to explain what appear to be order, design, and intelligence (in the case of humans) in the universe, this transcendent cause might be a mind.

Epicureanism

Atomism reappeared in the philosophy of Epicurus (341–271 B.C.). Epicurus introduced some changes in atomistic theory that had the effect of creating new difficulties for the defenders of atomism.

In one important sense, Epicureanism was the search for a worldview that would deliver humans from their fear of death and the gods. This treatment of death still has appeal for secularists. According to Epicurus, we need not fear death because, in his words, "When death is, we are not and when we are, death is not."[13] The point is that as long as we are conscious, we are not dead, but when we are dead, we are no longer conscious of anything. There is no need therefore to fear what might happen after we are dead, because the atoms that made up our soul and body

---

12. W. T. Jones, *A History of Western Philosophy,* vol. 1, *The Classical Mind,* 2d ed. (New York: Harcourt Brace & World, 1969), 91.

13. Epicurus *Letter to Menoeceus.*

have broken apart. Nor should we grieve over the events that will follow our death. Rational persons do not grieve over the centuries that passed before their lives began; why then should we grieve over the centuries that will pass after we have ceased to exist?

The Epicureans tended to accept the existence of the traditional Greek gods. Does this not then disqualify them as naturalists, some might ask? Such finite deities are confined within the box and are therefore religiously, metaphysically, and ethically irrelevant, especially the latter.

Even though the materialistic, atomistic, mechanical system adopted by Epicurus denied purpose (teleology) in the world, it was not completely mechanical. Epicurus thought it important to free humans from mechanistic determinism, which he viewed as a threat to human happiness. In order to provide an argument freeing humans from the machine of the atomistic universe, he had to find a way to introduce indeterminism into the movement of the atoms. After all, humans are made of atoms. Therefore, in order for humans to be free, the movement of atoms must be undetermined—at least in some cases.

In order to make room for interdeterminism and human freedom, Epicurus introduced a significant change in atomistic metaphysics. As we've seen, Democritus's atoms moved helter-skelter, in all directions, through empty space. Epicurus added weight as a property of atoms, which he thought led to each atom falling downward in a straight line at the same speed. It is relatively easy to understand how the atoms of Democritus can bump into other atoms and join together. But picture an infinite number of atoms falling in a straight line in infinite space. We have a new question for which there is no answer: How do Epicurus's atoms collide and enter into combinations? Epicurus's convenient answer is what has been called the declination of the atom. Occasionally, in an unpredictable and inexplicable fashion, atoms swerve out of their straight downward path. Such deviations or swerves bring about collisions and vortices;[14] eventually some of these vortices become a world. The declination of the atoms became the device by which Epicurus attempted to guarantee some measure of human freedom.

The indeterministic twist Epicurus added to atomism allows humans to pursue pleasure, which for Epicurus was the highest good. The belief that pleasure is the highest good is known as hedonism. As Gordon H. Clark explains:

> Epicurus attempted to remove the three greatest, perhaps the three only, impediments to a happy life. The first obstacle is pessimism, which can result only in an unhappy consciousness. But freedom from mechanical

---

14. The vortex in view here is a kind of spinning motion in a group of atoms that pulls them together.

law, obtained by rejecting uniform causality, gives the feeling that our choices and endeavors count, and that life is worth living. . . . Second, by showing as Lucretius does at length, that all phenomena can be explained without recourse to divine providence, the fear of the gods with its superstition and attendant inquietude is removed.[15] It is under this heading that all the specifically scientific investigations must be placed. . . . The third great obstacle to happiness, strictly related to the other two, namely the fear of death, is overcome by the same methods. Death can cause us the pain of fear now while we are living only if it will cause us pain in an afterlife. Obviously it is unreasonable to fear a future event which will not pain us when it happens. And a thorough study of psychology shows this to be the case. Man is nothing but a collection of atoms; their motions are sufficient to explain animation, sensation, and thought. To be sure man has a soul and a spirit but they are neither immaterial nor immortal. Consequently, when death comes the atoms disperse, and man as a sensitive being no longer exists to suffer either the wrath of the gods or any other unknown evil.[16]

Another Question That Has No Answer

Earlier I introduced the notion of the question that has no answer. The first naturalistic question to which there is no answer is why the atoms exist. Why is there something rather than nothing? The second is why the atoms move. In one sense they have to move, because if they didn't move, nothing else, including naturalistic philosophers, would exist. But this is no answer to the question; it points to the atomist's situation from which the inexplicable motion of the atoms is his only escape. Epicurus now introduces us to another question that has no answer: Why do the atoms swerve? There is no reason, except that otherwise nothing else would exist.

In infinite space, we should notice, the words *up* and *down* have no meaning.[17] But Epicurus did use the word *falling,* and he implied that the atoms were falling down. Down toward what? The polite thing is not to ask. As Jones observes, "Why should an atom swerve—except to get the atomic theory out of an insoluble difficulty? Unfortunately, the doctrine of the swerve extricated the theory from one difficulty only by plunging it into another, equally grave."[18]

---

15. It is important at this point not to confuse the thinking of Lucretius on this issue with that of Epicurus.

16. Gordon H. Clark, *Selections from Hellenistic Philosophy* (New York: Appleton-Century-Crofts, 1940), Introduction, 6.

17. Plato had treated any discussion of up and down in infinite space as nonsense. See Plato *Timaeus* 62d.

18. Jones, *A History of Western Philosophy,* vol. 1, *The Classical Mind,* 87.

Figure 2.2

**Democritus's atoms (helter-skelter) vs.
Epicurus's (falling with swerve)**

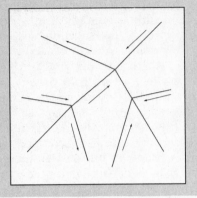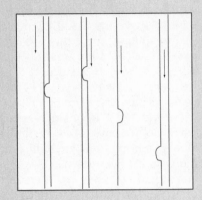

All of the ancient atomists rejected the possibility of a creation out of nothing. The atomists boasted of their ability to explain everything in completely mechanistic terms. Unfortunately, any spontaneous and arbitrary (uncaused) event such as even a single swerve is an event for which no explanation is possible. Atomism could not explain the most fundamental features of reality.

Lucretius

Lucretius (96–55 B.C.) presented Epicurean ideas in his poem *On the Nature of Things*. If Lucretius's work were evaluated solely in terms of new ideas, he would be an insignificant footnote in the history of ideas. But his poem presented Epicureanism in almost epic form; moreover, it was written in Latin, thus making the ideas of Greek atomism accessible to Romans. It remains the most complete extant work on atomism and Epicureanism. Lucretius assumed but never proved the uniformity of nature. He said little or nothing about such apparent irregularities in nature as unpredictable changes in the weather or volcanic eruptions or earthquakes.

**A Summary of
the Naturalist
Worldview**

The Gods

According to Epicurus, the gods of the Olympian religion exist because humans have mental pictures of them, especially while sleeping. Basic to Epicurus's belief is the assumption that all forms of consciousness are caused by atoms passing from an object to a sense organ. The pictures of the gods were explained in terms of images streaming from the bodies of the gods. The mental pictures of such beings are too strong and clear to be the product of any possible distortion of the stream of atoms. Epicurus believed the gods, who are also composed of atoms, dwell in perfect happiness in the empty spaces existing between worlds.

One difference between Lucretius and Epicurus lies in their different attitudes toward the gods. While Epicurus made the gods prominent in his system, Lucretius wanted to eliminate them from the world. Three of the more unfortunate developments in human life, he thought, are belief in the gods, immortality, and punishment. Religion is humankind's worst affliction, Lucretius thought. One reason for Lucretius's negative attitude toward the gods was his belief that the possibility of divine punishment for human acts could cause humans pain in the form of fear and distress. If Lucretius could show that the gods have no role in human lives, he could relieve humans from this distress.

Metaphysics

There is no need to repeat anything about the basics of Greek atomism.

Epistemology: Empiricism

The ancient atomists were empiricists, and nothing about this fact should surprise anyone. All knowledge depends on sensation. There is no room for innate ideas or intellectual intuitions in the atomistic worldview. All human knowledge has its start in sense experience. What is worth some comment is the way in which the atomists explained sensible information. In the obvious case of smell and sight, no direct physical contact is apparent. Epicurus assumes particles passing between the sensed object and the perceiver. Since everything that exists is made up of atoms, these things (combinations of atoms) are constantly sending out streams of atoms that eventually strike the sense organs (also combinations of atoms) of human beings (combinations of atoms), which, in ways too complex for us to explore here, produce an awareness of what we regard as sensible objects. The objects of sensible awareness are collections of atoms.

Epistemology: The Problem of the Human Perceiver

Democritus distinguished between the world as humans perceive it and the way it is. For Democritus, anything we perceive is an illusion. For every viewer, there is a different appearance. But who or what is this perceiver to whom the world appears? As Jones explains:

> A viewer turns out to be some particular sense organ, and a sense organ is a collection of atoms. So Democritus' position is that one set of atoms in motion out there appears as a rose to another set of atoms in motion over here. . . . But it is quite illegitimate to introduce a "we" that is supposedly doing the experiencing. There is no "we"; there are only atoms

in motion. Does it really make any sense to say that one set of atoms experiences another set as red, solid and extended?[19]

Do atomists have a right to use words like "perceiver," "viewer," or "self"? Does their illegitimate use of such words make their system appear more plausible than it is?

Humanity

Like everything else, a human being is a collection of indistinguishable, material, propertyless atoms. The human mind is as material as any physical organ. The major difference between a human being and a rock is the complexity of the collection of atoms making up the human. The reason why a rock does not perceive a tree or think about a tree is because the atoms making up the rock lack the special accumulation of atoms that make up a mind.

A human thought is a movement of atoms, different from other movements such as perception. It would appear that people whose worldview entails that only atoms and empty space exist must either deny the existence of thought or reduce it to atomistic motion in empty space; they cannot have it both ways.

Cyril Bailey views the question of human consciousness as the Achilles' heel of materialism. "Can the movement of insensible particles," he asks, "produce or account for consciousness?"[20] For the atomists, Bailey continues, "consciousness, sensation, thought, and will *are* the movements of the soul-atoms."[21] The problems atomists had with human consciousness will inevitably be difficulties for any purely materialistic system.

While the atomists used the law of noncontradiction,[22] laws of logic cannot be reduced to or equated with mechanical laws of motion. As Jones observes, "the logical relation between the premises and the conclusion of a valid argument is very different from the cause-and-effect relation that, according to the Atomists' theory, exists between successive states of mind-atoms. When the mind is reasoning well—when it is 'moving' from premises to a valid conclusion in accordance with the rules of logic—the order of the propositions that are successively before it is determined by considerations of logic, not by the mechanical motion of atoms."[23]

Reflect on any example of a sound deductive argument such as "All men are mortal; Socrates is a man; therefore, Socrates is mortal." Because

---

19. Ibid., 91.
20. Cyril Bailey, *The Greek Atomists and Epicurus* (Oxford: Clarendon, 1928), 436.
21. Ibid.
22. See Jones, *A History of Western Philosophy*, vol. 1, *The Classical Mind*, 96.
23. Ibid.

the two premises are true, the conclusion must be true. We accept the conclusion that Socrates is mortal because the premises entail the conclusion. We recognize the logically necessary relationship between the premises and the conclusion.[24]

Imagine yourself driving somewhere through Nevada and stopping for gas and a soft drink. While resting, you observe someone playing a slot machine. As different symbols show up on the screen, the person begins talking to the machine, using words like "true," "false," "valid," and "invalid." Purely mechanical processes do not and cannot produce valid inferences. Mental processes cannot be reduced to mechanical cause-effect relationships. Logical connections are nonmechanistic.

As we know, the Epicureans were interested in avoiding the mechanistic determinism of Democritus. They did this by introducing the swerve or declination of the atom into the system. But did this provide room for free will and choices? For Democritus, the feeling of freedom is an illusion. Human choices occur because when I decide to have wheat flakes for breakfast rather than corn flakes, the determining cause is the fact that at the moment of choice, the atoms making up my body and soul are arranged in one way and not another. My thoughts about the boxes of cereal in my kitchen at 6:00 A.M. are nothing but a particular set of atomic motions. If the motion and arrangement of the atoms were otherwise, so too would be my thoughts. Everything involved in what many of us regard as a free choice is nothing but movements of atoms, movements that in turn were caused by earlier jostlings of other sets of atoms, and so on to infinity. If one had the power to trace the movements of the relevant atoms back in infinite space and time, one would learn that the movement and placement of atoms at the time of your choice were made necessary by all of the atomic motions that preceded them. Free choice is as much an illusion as is the existence of the perceiver and what the perceiver perceives.

Followers of a worldview in which the universe is only a machine must admit that this universe proceeds in a blind and irresponsible manner. The universe cares not a whit either for us or our destiny. While Epicurus and Lucretius denigrated our cosmic fears as illusions, they should have gone on to say that our choices and hopes are also illusions. Life in such a worldview can have no significance.

Ethics

One plank of the Epicurean ethic was hedonism, the belief that pleasure is the highest good. Epicurus's view of pleasure was more sophisticated

---

24. The difference between something being logically necessary and being physically necessary will be discussed in more detail in chapter 9.

than anything we find in the surviving fragments of Democritus's writings. Moreover, the hedonism of Epicurus was different from the crude, sensual hedonism promoted by pre-Socratics like Aristippus. Aristippus urged his followers to seek the greatest physical pleasure obtainable in the present moment, while Epicurus urged people to consider the long-range consequences. Epicurus was willing to surrender short-lived physical pleasures of the present in order to attain longer-lasting mental pleasures over a lifetime. It does little good to say that pleasure is the highest good and then pursue actions that cannot help but produce more pain than pleasure.

The Case Against Naturalism

A careful analysis of naturalism reveals a problem so serious that it fails one of the major tests that rational persons should expect any worldview to pass.[25] In order to see how this is so, it is necessary first to recall that naturalism regards the universe as a self-contained and self-explanatory system. There is nothing outside the box we call nature that can explain or that is necessary to explain anything inside the box. Naturalism claims that every individual object or event can be explained in terms of something else within the natural order. This dogma is not an accidental or a nonessential feature of the naturalistic position. All that is required for naturalism to be false is the discovery of one thing that cannot be explained in the naturalistic way. Lewis sets up this line of argument:

> If necessities of thought force us to allow to any one thing any degree of independence from the Total System—if any one thing makes good a claim to be on its own, to be something more than an expression of the character of Nature as a whole—then we have abandoned Naturalism. For by Naturalism we mean the doctrine that only Nature—the whole interlocked system—exists. And if that were true, every thing and event would, if we knew enough, be explicable without remainder . . . as a necessary product of the system.[26]

With a little effort, we can quickly see that no thoughtful naturalist can ignore at least one thing. Lewis explains:

> All possible knowledge . . . depends on the validity of reasoning. If the feeling of certainty which we express by words like *must be* and *therefore* and *since* is a real perception of how things outside our minds really "must" be, well and good. But if this certainty is merely a feeling *in* our

---

25. As noted in chapter 1, these tests include reason or logical consistency, outer experience (conformity to what we know about the world around us), inner experience (conformity to what we know about things going on in the realm of our own consciousness), and practice (the claim that any respectable worldview ought to be a system we can live in our everyday life).

26. Lewis, *Miracles,* 12.

minds and not a genuine insight into realities beyond them—if it merely represents the ways our minds happen to work—then we have no knowledge. Unless human reasoning is valid no science can be true.[27]

And unless human reasoning is valid, no arguments by any metaphysical naturalist directed against Christian theism or offered in support of naturalism can be sound.

The human mind has the power to grasp contingent truths, that is, things that are the case though they might not have been the case. But the human mind also has the power to grasp *necessary connections,* that is, what must be the case. This latter power, the ability to grasp necessary connections, is the hallmark of human reasoning. What I am calling a necessary connection may be illustrated by the syllogism I cited earlier. If it is true that all men are mortal and if it is true that Socrates is a man, then it must be true that Socrates is mortal. Nearly anyone can see, even without special training in logic, that the conclusion, "Socrates is mortal," must be true if the other two propositions are true.

Naturalists must appeal to this kind of necessary connection in their own arguments for naturalism; indeed, in their reasoning about everything. But can naturalists account for this essential element of the reasoning process that they utilize in their arguments for their own position? Lewis thinks not, and for good reason. As Lewis sees it, naturalism "discredits our processes of reasoning or at least reduces their credit to such a humble level that it can no longer support Naturalism itself."[28] Why is that? Because

> no account of the universe [including metaphysical naturalism] can be true unless that account leaves it possible for our thinking to be a real insight. A theory which explained everything else in the whole universe but which made it impossible to believe that our thinking was valid, would be utterly out of court. For that theory would itself have been reached by thinking, and if thinking is not valid that theory would, of course, be itself demolished. It would have destroyed its own credentials. It would be an argument which proved that no argument was sound—a proof that there are no such things as proofs—which is nonsense.[29]

In the argument before us, Lewis is talking about the logical connection between a belief and the ground of that belief. It is one thing for a belief to have a nonrational cause; it is something else for a belief to have a reason or a ground. The ravings of a madman may have a cause but lack any justifying ground. The reasoning of a philosopher may have both

27. Ibid., 14.
28. Ibid., 15.
29. Ibid., 14–15.

a cause and a justifying ground.[30] What metaphysical naturalism does, according to Lewis, is to sever what should be unseverable: the link between conclusions and the grounds or reasons for those conclusions. As Lewis says, "Unless our conclusion is the logical consequent from a ground it will be worthless [as an example of a reasoned conclusion] and could be true only by a fluke."[31] Therefore, naturalism "offers what professes to be a full account of our mental behaviour; but this account, on inspection, leaves no room for the acts of knowing or insight on which the whole value of our thinking, as a means to truth, depends."[32]

By now the thrust of Lewis's argument against naturalism has become clear. By definition, metaphysical naturalism excludes the possible existence of anything beyond nature. But the process of reasoning requires something that exceeds the bounds of nature, namely, the laws of logical inference. (For help in understanding Lewis's argument, see chapter 9 of this book.)

A More Recent Attack on Metaphysical Naturalism

In a book first published in 1963, American philosopher Richard Taylor presented an argument pointing to an additional problem with metaphysical naturalism. Taylor introduced his argument with an example that bid his readers to imagine themselves in a coach on a British train. Looking out the window, the passengers see a large number of white stones on a hillside lying in a pattern that spells out the letters: THE BRITISH RAILWAYS WELCOMES YOU TO WALES. Should the passengers be in a reflective mood on such an occasion, they might begin to contemplate how those stones happened to be in that particular arrangement. It is possible that, without any intelligent being having anything to do with it, the stones rolled down the hillside over a period of many years and happened to end up in an arrangement that resembled the letters noted. However implausible we find this hypothesis, we must admit that such a thing is possible. Of course, Taylor says, the most natural reaction to seeing the stones would be a conviction that the arrangement of stones was brought about by one or more humans who intended it to communicate a message. And so there are at least two explanations for the arrangement of the stones: a natural, nonpurposive explanation, and an explanation in terms of the intentions of at least one intelligent being.

---

30. For example, a person suffering from a particular disorder might believe something because he hears an inner voice. We tend to judge such people as insane when their conclusions lack any justifying ground. The beliefs of the philosopher I describe may also have a cause, for example, something that happened in the philosopher's childhood. One would hope that persons aspiring to the title of philosopher would be able to produce grounds for their beliefs.

31. Lewis, *Miracles,* 16.

32. Ibid., 18.

Taylor's next step in the development of his argument is critical. Suppose, he suggests, that the passengers decide, solely on the basis of stones they see on the hillside, that they are in fact entering Wales. Taylor does not insist that the purposive account of the stones is the true one. His argument is purely hypothetical. If the passengers infer that the stones communicate a true message and that they are entering Wales, it would be inconsistent for them also to assume that the positioning of the stones was an accident. Once you conclude that the stones convey an intelligible message, Taylor continues,

> you would, in fact, be presupposing that they were arranged that way by an intelligent and purposeful being or beings for the purpose of conveying a certain message having nothing to do with the stones themselves. Another way of expressing the same point is that it would be *irrational* for you to regard the arrangement of the stones as evidence that you were entering Wales, and at the same time to suppose that they might have come to have that arrangement accidentally, that is, as the result of the ordinary interactions of natural or physical forces. If, for instance, they came to be so arranged over the course of time, simply by rolling down the hill, one by one, and finally just happening to end up that way, or if they were strewn upon the ground that way by the forces of any earthquake or storm or what-not, then their arrangement would in no sense constitute evidence that you were entering Wales, or for anything whatever unconnected with themselves.[33]

Taylor's analysis thus far seems correct. If I were a passenger and if I thought the arrangement of the stones were a result of chance, natural forces, there would be something bizarre about my also believing, solely on the evidence provided by the stones, that I was entering Wales. But if I concluded, solely on the evidence provided by the stones, that I was entering Wales, consistency would seem to require that I also believe the arrangement of the stones was not an accident.

What does this have to do with a human being's making an intelligent choice between theism and metaphysical naturalism? Taylor invites us to consider similar reasoning about our cognitive faculties:

> Just as it is possible for a collection of stones to present a novel and interesting arrangement on the side of a hill . . . so also it is possible for such things as our own organs of sense to be the accidental and unintended results, over ages of time, of perfectly impersonal, nonpurposeful forces. In fact, ever so many biologists believe that this is precisely what has happened, that our organs of sense are in no real sense purposeful things, but only appear so because of our failure to consider how they might have arisen through the normal workings of nature.[34]

---

33. Richard Taylor, *Metaphysics,* 2d ed. (Englewood Cliffs, N.J.: Prentice-Hall, 1974), 115.
34. Ibid., 116–17.

In the case of the stones, the fact that they exhibited a particular shape or pattern did not constitute proof that there was purpose or intention behind the arrangement. Likewise, Taylor observes, "the mere complexity, refinement, and seemingly purposeful arrangement of our sense organs do not, accordingly, constitute any conclusive reason for supposing that they are the outcome of any purposeful activity. A natural, nonpurposeful explanation of them is possible, and has been attempted—successfully, in the opinion of many."[35] It appears as though any metaphysical naturalist would have to pursue this kind of nonpurposeful account of human cognitive faculties.

Taylor then points to the problem in the naturalist's position. Even those persons who view their sense organs as the product of chance, natural, and nonpurposeful forces depend on them to deliver information about the world that they regard as true. "We suppose, without even thinking about it, that [our sense organs] reveal to us things that have nothing to do with themselves, their structures, or their origins."[36] Such people, Taylor thinks, are just as inconsistent as the person who derives a true message from a nonpurposeful arrangement of stones.

> It would be irrational for one to say *both* that his sensory and cognitive faculties had a natural, nonpurposeful origin and *also* that they reveal some truth with respect to something other than themselves, something that is not merely inferred from them. *If* their origin can be entirely accounted for in terms of chance variations, natural selection, and so on, without supposing that they somehow embody and express the purposes of some creative being, then the most we can say of them is that they exist, that they are complex and wondrous in their construction, and are perhaps in other respects interesting and remarkable. We cannot say that they are, entirely by themselves, reliable guides to any truth whatever, save only what can be inferred from their own structure and arrangement. If, on the other hand, we do assume that they are guides to some truths having nothing to do with themselves, then it is difficult to see how we can, consistently with that supposition, believe them to have arisen by accident, or by the ordinary workings of purposeless forces, even over ages of time.[37]

Naturalists seem caught in a trap. If they are consistent with their naturalistic presuppositions, they must assume that our human cognitive faculties are a product of chance, purposeless forces. But if this is so, naturalists appear inconsistent when they place so much trust in those faculties. But like the passengers on the train, if they assume that their

---

35. Ibid., 117.
36. Ibid., 117–18.
37. Ibid., 118–19.

cognitive faculties are trustworthy and do provide accurate information about the world, they seem compelled to abandon one of the cardinal presuppositions of metaphysical naturalism and conclude that their cognitive faculties were formed as a result of the activity of some purposeful, intelligent agent.[38]

It is difficult to see how metaphysical naturalism can provide an adequate reason why human reasoning can ever be valid or that our sense organs can be trusted. Why should we not conclude that naturalism is incompatible with attitudes of trust in either our rational or empirical faculties? We could think, following Richard Purtill, that naturalism destroys "our confidence in the validity of *any* reasoning—including the reasoning that may have led us to adopt [naturalistic] theories. Thus they [the naturalistic theories] are self-destructive, rather like the man who saws off the branch he is sitting on. The only cold comfort they [metaphysical naturalists] hold out is that some of our thought might happen to agree with reality."[39] But on naturalistic grounds, we can never know that it does. And when we are honest about the probabilities, it appears to be enormously improbable that such agreement would ever occur.

One of naturalism's major problems then is explaining how mindless forces give rise to minds, knowledge, sound reasoning, and moral principles that report how human beings ought to behave.[40] Not surprisingly, naturalists want the rest of us to think that their worldview, naturalism, is a product of their sound reasoning. All things considered, it is hard to see why naturalism is not self-referentially absurd. Before any person can justify his or her acceptance of naturalism on rational grounds, it is first necessary for that person to reject a cardinal tenet of the naturalist position. The only way a person can provide rational grounds for believing in naturalism is first to cease being a naturalist.

Concluding Comments About the Critique of Naturalism

---

38. For a still more recent exploration of a similar line of attack on metaphysical naturalism, see Alvin Plantinga, *Warrant and Proper Function* (New York: Oxford University Press, 1993), chaps. 11–12.

39. Richard L. Purtill, *Reason to Believe* (Grand Rapids: Eerdmans, 1974), 44.

40. While my earlier remarks did not discuss ethics, moral principles seem to be in as much difficulty in the worldview of metaphysical naturalists as are logical principles. Treating both adequately seems to force us to recognize the existence of things that transcend the purely natural order, that exist outside of the box.

OPTIONAL WRITING ASSIGNMENT

If you wish, examine the update on this chapter's criticism of naturalism in chapter 9. Then, without looking at your notes or the text, explain in your own words why naturalism is a logically self-defeating theory.

FOR FURTHER READING

Cyril Bailey, *The Greek Atomists and Epicurus* (Oxford: Clarendon, 1928).

John Burnet, *Early Greek Philosophy* (New York: The Meridian Library, 1957).

Frederick C. Copleston, *A History of Philosophy* (Westminster, Md.: Newman Press, 1962), vol. 1.

W. T. Jones, *A History of Western Philosophy,* vol. 1, *The Classical Mind,* 2d ed. (New York: Harcourt, Brace and World, 1969).

G. S. Kirk, J. E. Raven, and M. Schofield, *The Presocratic Philosophers,* 2d ed. (New York: Cambridge University Press, 1983).

Whitney J. Oates, ed. *The Stoic and Epicurean Philosophers* (New York: The Modern Library, 1940).

Philip Wheelwright, ed. *The Presocratics* (New York: Odyssey Press, 1966).

Chapter Three

Plato

No one, with the possible exception of Aristotle, comes close to challenging Plato's prominence in the history of philosophy. But since Aristotle was Plato's student, since much of Aristotle's work evolved as a reaction to Plato's theories, and since Aristotle's system as we know it would not have existed save for Plato, Plato's standing as valedictorian of the class of western philosophers seems secure.

Our best information suggests that Plato was born around 427 B.C. and died eighty years later, in 347 B.C. His parents were wealthy Athenian aristocrats. His birth name was Aristocles, and "Plato" seems to have been a nickname referring to his rather robust physical appearance.

Plato's Life and Writings

Plato showed little interest in philosophy until the execution of Socrates in 399 B.C. Many believe that the courage and honor that Socrates displayed at his death affected Plato greatly, resulting in a pursuit of philosophical knowledge similar to that modeled by Socrates. Dismay at Socrates' execution also led to Plato's voluntary exile from Athens for many years. While Plato may have spent time in Egypt, he seems to have settled in Greek colonies in what is today southern Italy. While in Italy,

Plato

From Fresco *The School of Athens* by Raphael, 1509–10

THE GRANGER COLLECTION, NEW YORK

he came in contact with the school of thought known as Pythagoreanism. Several features of Pythagoreanism appear prominently in Plato's mature thinking, including mind-body dualism, the immortality of the soul, and a keen interest in mathematics.

At the midpoint of his life,[1] tradition has Plato returning to Athens in 387 B.C. in order to found his great school, the Academy.[2] Plato seems to have made several trips to the city-state of Syracuse in Sicily in an effort to influence its leaders to enact some of his political ideas.[3]

Several different interpretations of Plato's thought exist. The technical details of such disputes lie beyond the scope of this book. For the most part this book presents the majority opinion of Plato's work. While approximately thirty-six writings are attributed to Plato, possibly six to ten of them are forgeries that may have been written by some of Plato's followers in the Academy. All of Plato's great writings, including the *Apology, Phaedo,* the *Euthyphro, Meno, The Republic, Timaeus,* and *The Laws* are authentic. Plato's earlier writings are generally shorter, concentrate on ethical questions, and are inconclusive in the sense that they raise rather than solve questions.[4] Plato's use of Socrates as the leading interlocutor in many of his dialogues was one way of honoring the great man who was responsible for his becoming a philosopher. In his earliest writings, such as the *Apology* and the *Crito,* Plato seems to present a faithful representation of Socrates' method and beliefs. In writings produced during his middle period, such as the *Phaedo, Meno,* and *Republic,* Plato often places his own beliefs into Socrates' mouth. Plato's later writings either drop any reference to Socrates or use him exclusively as a spokesman for theories the historical Socrates never entertained.

Seven Theories Opposed by Plato

Plato opposed seven prevalent beliefs of his day. Several years ago a student pointed out to me that these theories can be arranged as an acronym that forms a misspelled version of my middle name: HERMMAN.

H—Hedonism
E—Empiricism
R—Relativism
M—Materialism

---

1. This coincidence has led some scholars to question this chronology. The Greeks believed that the age of forty began the peak years of a philosopher's work.

2. The Academy continued to exist until A.D. 529, when the school closed at the order of the emperor Justinian. One should not think of the Academy along the lines of a modern college.

3. Much of the reliability of the traditional picture of Plato's journeys depends on the authenticity of a long autobiographical letter known as his seventh epistle.

4. For one scholar's chronology of Plato's writings, see Frederick C. Copleston, *A History of Philosophy* (Westminster, Md.: Newman Press, 1962), vol. 1, chap. 18.

M—Mechanism
A—Atheism
N—Naturalism

Hedonism

Hedonism is the belief that pleasure is the highest good. Materialists like Democritus, Epicurus, and Lucretius rejected the existence of objective, transcendent standards of right and wrong and reduced the good life to the pursuit of pleasure. Plato believed hedonism is falsified by the widespread human recognition that some pleasures are evil. If that is so, then it follows that pleasure and the good cannot be identical. And if this is so, then hedonism is false.

Empiricism

As we saw in chapter 2, empiricism is the belief that all human knowledge has its origin in human sense experience. Plato opposed empiricism throughout his writings, maintaining that it is impossible for the human senses to bring a human being to knowledge. I will have much to say about Plato's rejection of empiricism in his theory of knowledge.

Relativism

Plato opposed two kinds of relativism. The first, *ethical relativism,* is the belief that the same moral judgment, such as murder is wrong, is true for some people and false for others. The second kind of relativism, *epistemological relativism,* includes the belief that truth is relative.[5] Both types of relativism were propagated in ancient Athens by thinkers known as Sophists. Plato opposed the Sophists and proclaimed the existence of absolute and unchanging standards that preclude moral and epistemological relativism. Neither truth nor goodness is relative, Plato believed.

Materialism

As we saw in chapter 2, most Greek philosophers before Socrates and Plato were materialists.[6] The materialist strain of Greek philosophy is seen most clearly in the work of the atomists. In opposition to materialism, Plato argued for the existence of an immaterial or ideal world existing independently of the physical world we inhabit through our bodies.

---

5. Plato did recognize how people's sensible perceptions of things could differ. The temperature of the same body of water could seem warm to one person and cold to another. See the opening pages of Plato's *Thaeatetus*. Since sense experience is not knowledge in Plato's thinking, his comments in this connection do not entail any kind of epistemological relativism.

6. The Pythagorean school that existed in southern Italy seems to have been an exception.

Mechanism

Atomism also provides an excellent example of *mechanism,* the belief that everything happens according to laws and principles that operate mechanically without purpose or design. Plato's view of the universe was teleological in the sense that he believed that a divine intelligence and purpose is at work in the universe.

Atheism

Plato's view of God is hardly a model of clarity. What is clear, however, is Plato's rejection of atheism. Nonetheless, scholars continue to debate whether Plato believed in one god, or two, or more.

Naturalism

Naturalism is the belief that the natural, material universe is self-sufficient and self-explanatory. Given the time devoted to both ancient and modern versions of naturalism in chapter 2, it should be clear what issues are at stake in the naturalistic worldview. While Plato never compared naturalism's view of a closed universe with a box, his alternative can be described as the belief that outside the confines of the box, the natural order, there exists a world of eternal, transcendent, unchanging, and immaterial Forms or ideals.

Plato's Dualism

One helpful way to highlight several central elements of Plato's system is to think in terms of a fundamental dualism. Plato's philosophy is marked by three kinds of dualism: metaphysical, epistemological, and anthropological.

1. *The metaphysical dualism* of Plato's philosophy is seen in his distinction between two worlds, or two levels of reality—the imperfect, changing, temporal, material world of particular things over against the perfect, unchanging, nontemporal, nonmaterial world of the Forms.

2. *The epistemological dualism* of Plato is evident not only in his radical distinction between sense experience and reason but also in his claim that sense experience always falls short of producing knowledge. True knowledge is attainable only by reason and then only as human reason apprehends the Forms.

3. Plato's *anthropological dualism* is apparent in his radical distinction between body and soul. Just as there are two worlds (particular physical things and Forms) and two ways of apprehending these two worlds (sensation and reason), so humans are a composite of two parts (body and soul).

The heart of Plato's philosophy is his theory of Ideas, or Forms. Plato believed that human beings participate in two different worlds. One of these is the physical world that we experience through our bodily senses. Our contact with the lower world[7] comes through our bodily senses, as in seeing or touching particular things like rocks, trees, cats, and humans. The physical things that exist in the lower world exist in space and time.

The other world in which we participate is more difficult to describe, a fact that helps explain why Plato's teaching is so foreign to most of us. This higher world is composed of immaterial and eternal essences that we apprehend with our minds. Plato's ideal world (sometimes called the world of the Forms) is more real for Plato than is the physical world, inasmuch as the particular things that exist in the world of bodies are copies, or imitations, of their archetypes, the Forms.

Plato's Theory of Forms

Upper World —	Forms	— No Space or time
Lower World —	Particulars	— In Space and time

Figure 3.1

For Plato, a Form is an eternal, unchangeable, and universal essence. Some of Plato's Forms are relatively easy to understand. He believed that what we encounter in the physical world are imperfect examples of such unchanging absolutes as Goodness, Justice, Truth, and Beauty that exist in an ideal, nonspatial world. Plato also believed that the world of the Forms contains exemplars of such mathematical and geometrical entities as numbers and the perfect circle. The imperfect circles that we encounter in the physical world are copies of one perfect and eternal circle that we know through our minds. It would be a mistake to think that Plato believed these Forms exist only in people's minds. The point to his theory is that these Forms have an objective or extramental existence. They would exist even if no human being existed or were thinking of them. Truth, Beauty, Goodness, and the other Forms existed before there were any human minds. Only when human minds focus on the Forms does genuine human knowledge become possible.

Forms are also universals in the sense that they can be in several or many things at the same time. For example, greenness is a property that can be in grass, a sweater, and a piece of broccoli at the same time.

---

7. The language about higher and lower worlds does not appear in Plato's writings. I use it because many students find it helpful.

Significant human speech typically occurs in cases where the speaker or writer attributes some predicate to a subject. And so we can say that *A* (some particular human act) is just, *B* is just, *C* is just, and so on. The predicate *just* is applied to many different particular examples. Such predicates can be called *universal terms* because the one word is applied universally to a number of different particular subjects. Since the word *red* is applied to many particular things, it too is a universal term.

Plato explained this feature of human language by saying there is a universal redness (the Form of redness) that serves as a standard or a norm for all the particular examples and shades of red found in the physical world. When we encounter something in our experience that exemplifies universal terms like "round" or "red," we are justified in applying the universal term to that subject. We call things red or round when the subject in question has the property of redness or roundness.

Sometimes Plato wrote as though there were a Form, or an archetype, for every class of object in the physical world. This would mean that the world of the Forms contains a perfect dog, a perfect horse, and a perfect human, along with the other Forms already noted. The possibility of a perfect horse or dog raised some difficult questions for Plato, and some interpreters think he abandoned this position late in life.

Examples of Plato's Two Worlds

In the study of philosophy, there are times when it helps to approach difficult issues from different perspectives. The material in this section illustrates such a procedure. I will use various examples to help the reader understand Plato's theory of the Forms. If an example is difficult to grasp, drop it and move on to another.

Definitions Versus Examples

In many of his earlier writings, Plato is interested in finding the proper definition of such important terms as "justice," "piety," and "virtue." In the *Euthyphro,* Socrates asks the young Euthyphro to define the meaning of piety. Instead of providing a definition, Euthyphro offers examples of piety. A contemporary American in the same situation might provide such examples of piety in terms of going to church, reading the Bible, praying, and being a good neighbor. Socrates replies that he did not ask for examples of pious deeds; he wants to know instead what all of those examples have in common.

The relevant difference can be illustrated by ten or so vertical lines connected by one horizontal line. The vertical lines stand for different examples of the concept; the horizontal line represents the essence common to all of the examples. When he seeks a definition, Plato does not want examples (the vertical lines); he wants the common essence (the horizontal line). This universal element sought in definitions is an anticipation of Plato's universal Form, or essence. During our lifetime, each of us will presumably come into contact with many instances of such concepts as justice. But in each instance, there will be one essential element without which the particular act would not be an example of justice.

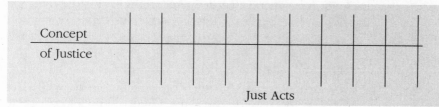

Figure 3.2

A Set (Class) Versus the Members of the Set

One can also approach Plato's theory of the Forms in terms of the difference between a set or class versus the particular things that make up that set. In some writings Plato seems to teach that every class of objects in the physical world has an archetype or a perfect pattern existing in the immutable, eternal, and immaterial world of the Forms.[8] Any class of objects can serve as an example. Consider the class or set of all dogs.[9] Suppose we use a circle to represent that class. Then think of a number of specific dogs that may include different breeds. We will indicate these particular dogs by x's inside the circle. What enables us to group all of these different particular animals into the same class? After all, there are significant differences between a collie and a mixed breed. Particular things are grouped into the same class if they possess similar essential properties. Utilizing this distinction, we come to recognize the difference between the class or set of all dogs (our circle) and the countless number of particular dogs that are members of that class (the x's inside the circle).

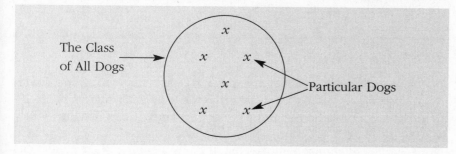

Figure 3.3

---

8. See book 10 of Plato's *Republic*. Plato recognized significant exceptions to this point. There are no perfect exemplars for such things as mud, hair, dirt, or cow dung. See the early pages of Plato's *Parmenides*.

9. Sometimes (as in book 10 of his *Republic*) Plato wrote as though there were a Form for every class of objects in the physical world.

Suppose we concede that the Form of a dog exists. Obviously, the Form of a dog does not exist in the physical world of particular things. The perfect dog (the Form) is a way of referring to the set of essential properties shared by all specific members of the set. Some people refer to this essence under the term *dogginess*. According to Plato, when we see a particular dog, we recognize in that imperfect specimen something that reminds us of the perfect Form. Similarly, we can think about horsiness, catness, and treeness.

Hence the circle represents some class or set, in this case the set of all dogs. The class concept exists in the world of the Forms while the particular members of the class exist in the lower world of particular things.

Mathematical Entities

As Plato's thought matured, he seems to have paid less attention to forms of physical objects. In fact, he sometimes seems to be embarrassed by his former talk about a perfect dog or horse.[10] Eventually, or so many think, this facet of his theory fades away. Of more permanent importance in his system is his belief in the existence of perfect standards of Truth, Beauty, and Goodness, as well as the kinds of eternal entities that we encounter in mathematics, such as the number one and the perfect circle. Plato believed that the disciplines of mathematics and geometry prove the need for and the existence of eternal, nonmaterial Forms. Suppose we focus on the apparently simple matter of a circle.

What is a circle? Consider the following examples.

Figure 3.4

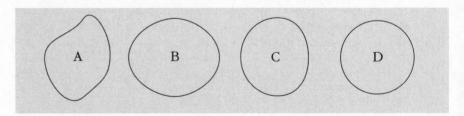

While no knowledgeable person would ever confuse A, B, and C with a perfect circle, it should be possible to see why such figures might be thought to resemble something we call circularity. I can imagine someone saying, "Figure B isn't really a circle, but it's closer to being a circle than A is." Such language implies that there is a concept of a perfect circle all parties to the discussion are familiar with in some way and that

10. Some interpreters believe this embarrassment shows up in the early pages of Plato's *Parmenides*. For a helpful discussion of this difficult dialogue, see Gordon H. Clark, *Thales to Dewey,* 2d ed. (Unicoi, Tenn.: The Trinity Foundation, 1989), 85–90.

the members of the group recognize that B comes closer to that ideal (Form) than A does. They would also concede that C is a better example than is B.

But now let us reflect a bit about D. Is it a circle? To see my point, consider the definition of a circle: A circle is an enclosed line every point on which is equidistant from a given fixed point that is its center. It follows that no figure we might encounter in the physical world is or can be a circle. A perfect circle would have to be bounded by a line that has only length and no width. The reason is that if the line of our circle has any width, that line segment moving from one side to the other would contain an infinite number of points. From which of those points do we measure the distance to the center of the circle? Lines that have length but no width do not exist in the physical universe, in what we have been calling the lower world. Neither do the kinds of points discussed in geometry. It then follows that no real or perfect circle can exist in the physical world; hence none of us can encounter such a circle through our bodily senses. See the illustration below:

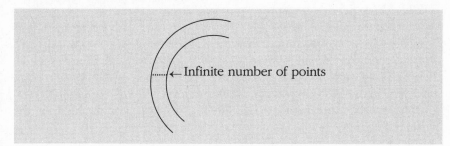

Figure 3.5

Whatever else may be true about the perfect circle, it must match our definition, namely, a line each point of which is equidistant from another point, the center. If there is no such thing as a perfect circle, any claim to the effect that some of our earlier examples like A, B, C, and D are better instances of circularity would be nonsense. Surely we do not want to pretend that two or more people can correctly have differing concepts of a perfect circle. We must never assent to a situation in which someone could say, "You have your idea of a perfect circle and I have mine." If there is a perfect circle, and there must be, it can exist only in a different kind of reality, a world of eternal and unchanging essences, a world that can be apprehended only by the mind, a world in which lines can have length and no width. The so-called circles that we encounter in our everyday experience can be only copies or imitations of a perfect circle that exists in another world. The circles that we encounter in the physical world are but representations of perfect, ideal entities existing in some other sphere of existence.

I don't wish to suggest that Plato's kind of reasoning cannot be challenged. It would be interesting to see if any challenge can be successful. As much as I might like to fill in some additional gaps in the Platonist's argument for the existence of the perfect circle, constraints upon the length of this book oblige me to leave the matter where it is and move on.

In the instance of circles, the real object of human thought is not the imperfect circles that appear on a blackboard or in a textbook. As Plato sees it, the true object of our reflection about circles is the ideal, perfect circle grasped by the mind. The imitations of circularity we encounter in this world of material, particular things cannot satisfy the definition of a circle. Unless there were an ideal circle that we already knew in some way, our concept or thought of a circle would be vacuous; it would have no referent. And since the perfect circle cannot exist in the physical world,[11] since it must exist somewhere, and since things exist in either the lower world or the higher world, the perfect circle must exist in the world of the Forms.

Other Forms

There is another class of Forms composed of normative ideals such as Goodness, Beauty, Truth, and Justice. For example, we apply the word *good* to many particular human acts. What grounds judgments such as these? Plato's answer is that we already have an idea of the Form or standard of Goodness in our minds. As we go through life we see acts conforming to the norm, and we judge human behavior in light of the standard.

A Summary

For Plato, a Form is an eternal, unchangeable, and universal essence. The Forms are archetypes or ideal patterns in the sense that the particular things that exist in the physical world imitate or copy them. An essence is the set of essential properties without which a particular thing like this squirrel or that tree would not exist as a squirrel or a tree. The Forms embody the essence that marks the similarities among members of a class and enables us to group them into a set or class.

Forms can never change. Equality itself (that is, the concept or standard of equality) can never change. If it ever did, Plato teaches, it would become inequality. The concept of oneness can never become twoness.

The Forms are also eternal. They existed before the physical world came into existence. They would continue to exist even if everything in the physical universe, the lower world, ceased to exist. Truth, Goodness,

---

11. Remember that the line marking the perimeter of the circle must have length but no width.

and Justice are eternal, timeless entities that do not depend for their existence upon the particular things that exist in this world.

Two errors common to beginning students of philosophy must be avoided. The first mistake is to assume that the physical world is more real than is the ideal world of the Forms. For Plato, the situation is the reverse. Just as the shadow cast by a tree is less real than the tree, so the physical world, which is only a reflection of the ideal world, must be less real than the world of the Forms.

The second error is to think that Plato viewed these Forms as existing only in people's minds. The whole point to his theory is that these essences have an objective existence. They would exist even if no human being were thinking of them. Truth, Beauty, Goodness, and the other Forms existed before there were any human minds. It does not follow, however, that the Forms exist independent of all minds. Many of Plato's followers have maintained that the eternal Forms exist as thoughts in the eternal mind of God. While Plato never entertained this possibility, Plotinus and Augustine did.[12]

Humans live in two different worlds: the world of many particular things that are constantly changing and that are apprehended through our bodily senses plus a perfect, unchanging, and timeless world known through our minds.

Epistemology is the technical name for the branch of philosophy that studies human knowledge. The first thing to note about Plato's epistemology is the intrinsic connection that exists between being (what is real) and knowing. How humans know is related to what is. We have already seen that for Plato there are two distinct kinds of reality: the world of particular things and the world of the Forms. Corresponding to these two kinds of reality are two distinct epistemological states: opinion and knowledge.

In order for a human being to have genuine knowledge (as opposed to some other epistemological state, such as a belief or an opinion), the object of that knowledge must be unchanging. One can have knowledge only of that which is unchanging. But Plato believed that immutability (unchangeability) is an exclusive property of the Forms. Every particular thing existing in the physical world constantly undergoes change. Since our bodily senses provide only an awareness of the changing particular things in the physical world, it follows for Plato that our senses can never give us knowledge. If the only possible objects of knowledge are the unchanging Forms and if the only way to apprehend the Forms is through our reason, it follows that knowledge must be a function of our minds.

Plato's Theory of Knowledge

---

12. See chapters 5 and 6.

The most that we can attain through our senses is opinion, not knowledge. Given Plato's analysis of the meaning of knowledge, sense experience fails the test. Only reason can give us knowledge.

Plato's Figure of the Divided Line

In book 6 of his *Republic,* Plato illustrates the difference between knowledge and opinion using a device called the figure of the divided line. Plato's account is abbreviated and open to different interpretations. In the figure of the divided line, Plato distinguishes four levels of awareness or cognition. His purpose is to help us understand that there are various levels of human awareness. In some of these cases, the use of the word *knowledge* is inappropriate.

Plato asks us to imagine an unevenly divided vertical line. The horizontal line that divides the top from the bottom distinguishes the world of sense experience from the world of reason. The lowest segment (A on the following diagram) contains images and shadows of physical objects. The next segment (B) contains the physical objects that are the causes of the shadows and reflections.

Plato describes the longer, lower part of the line as the realm of sense experience; he calls it opinion. He applies the term *knowledge* to the shorter, upper part of the line. The important distinction in this divided line is that between knowledge and opinion. For Plato, knowledge is a rational apprehension of the unchanging Forms, while opinion is a sensible awareness of changing particulars. The objects of opinion are the particular things that exist in the physical world; the proper objects of knowledge are the eternal and unchanging Forms that exist in Plato's ideal world. With regard to the means of apprehension, knowledge uses reason while opinion utilizes sense experience.

Plato then divides the line still further to illustrate two kinds or levels of knowledge (dialectic and understanding) and two levels of opinion (belief and conjecture) so that the entire divided line looks like the diagram:

Figure 3.6

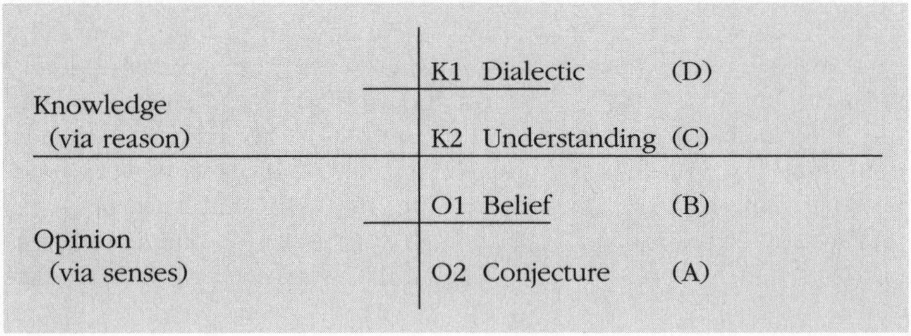

	K1 Dialectic	(D)
Knowledge (via reason)		
	K2 Understanding	(C)
	O1 Belief	(B)
Opinion (via senses)		
	O2 Conjecture	(A)

In the most literal interpretation, the difference between belief and conjecture is the difference between perceiving a particular thing under conditions that produce a fairly reliable belief and perceiving a shadow, a reflection, or an otherwise less reliable image of the sensible object. Seeing Lassie the dog would be an example of belief (B), whereas seeing her shadow or reflection in a mirror would be conjecture (A).[13]

Surely Plato was thinking of something more profound than this. When we reflect about our experience of the world, we can recognize that some experiences are more reliable, more dependable, than others. Our senses often mislead us; things are not always as they appear. Perhaps this is what Plato was trying to indicate in his distinction between belief and conjecture. Sometimes our sense perception seems so reliable that we have good grounds for holding a belief; at other times it makes any judgment risky at best, thus leaving us with conjecture.

Plato's distinction between the two levels of knowledge, understanding (C) versus dialectic (D), raises several other difficulties. He says that understanding, unlike dialectic, makes use of images and hypotheses. His reference to images could suggest that he has things like circles and squares in mind. He also relates understanding to conclusions drawn from hypotheses that might point to geometry and possibly scientific reasoning. Plato's hypotheses are not the tentative suppositions of a scientist but self-evident truths or axioms. By dialectic, Plato seems to mean a pure knowledge of the Forms, the highest knowledge available to humans. Whereas understanding is inferential knowledge, reasoning from hypotheses to a conclusion, dialectic is intuitive, that is, immediate knowledge not mediated by anything else.

Plato's Allegory of the Cave and the Ascent to the Good

One of the most important passages in all of Plato's writings, his famous allegory of the cave, is found in book 7 of his *Republic*. Once again Plato uses Socrates as a spokesman; he invites us to imagine a cave. At the back of the cave exists a group of prisoners who have been chained from birth in such a way that they can perceive only the back wall of the cave. They cannot look behind them or to either side.

Behind the prisoners, out of their line of vision, is a shallow trench before which a low wall has been built. Behind the wall and thus in the trench, people walk carrying statues that appear above the top of the wall. Still farther back in the cave, beyond the wall and the statues, is a fire large enough to cast shadows of the statues upon the back wall of the cave. Given the situation as Socrates describes it, the prisoners can know nothing about the fire, the wall, or the statues behind them. The only

---

13. A twentieth-century example of conjecture (A) would be viewing Lassie in a movie.

things they will have perceived during their entire lives will be the shadows cast by the statues on the back wall of the cave. These unfortunate people will naturally think that the shadows they perceive are the only world that exists; it is the only world they have ever experienced.

Suppose, Socrates suggests, that one of the prisoners gets free from his chains,[14] walks back in the cave, and sees the fire, the wall, and the statues. He would gradually begin to realize how mistaken he had been all of his life. The shadows he had perceived on the back wall of the cave were not the real world; there was another world that had been behind him. All he had to do was turn around and see the light.

Suppose further that the freed prisoner climbs out of the cave. To be sure, this ascent in total darkness turns out to be extremely difficult. There are times when it appears he will never escape the darkness of the cave. But finally he reaches the opening to the cave and suddenly exits to stand in the bright, blinding light of the sun. Because he has lived his entire life in the darkness of the cave, the prisoner's eyes require time to adjust to the light of the sun. But after a while he begins to see the world outside the cave more clearly. He is tempted to stay there and revel in the beauty of that world. But he remembers his former companions, the slaves who are still trapped in darkness. So he goes back into the cave to share his discoveries with them.

Figure 3.7

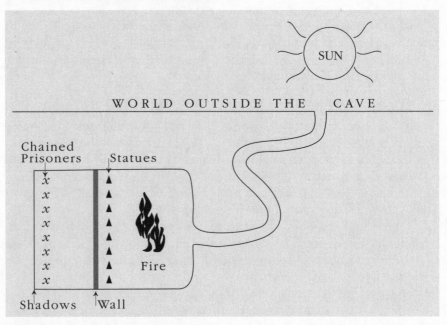

14. The male pronoun is necessary here because Plato uses it and because the freed prisoner represents a historical person.

After walking back into the darkness, he begins the arduous descent to the bottom of the cave. Since his eyes have grown adjusted to the light outside the cave, he has trouble seeing in the darkness. He stumbles; he appears awkward.

He begins talking to the other slaves, telling them what he has seen, trying to get them to see that the shadows they perceive are not the real world. Refusing to believe him, the chained prisoners kill the freed prisoner. They cannot stand to be told that their world is not real; they don't want their illusions shattered or their security threatened.

The Interpretation of the Allegory

The prisoners represent the human race, including the author and every reader of this book. From birth to death, human experience is limited to physical particulars. It is understandable that such prisoners would believe that the only world they have experienced (the shadows) is the only world that exists. The prisoners do not know that there is much more to reality than the shadow world on the back wall of the cave. They know nothing about a nonphysical world that is far more real and important than their shadow world. Like the prisoners chained in the cave, each human being perceives a physical world that is but a poor imitation of a more real world. But every so often, one of the prisoners gets free from the shackles of sense experience, turns around, and sees the light! Socrates (the murdered prisoner) did, as did Plato, along with a few others who have followed their lead down through the centuries.

Plato's allegory helps explain why so many humans have such difficulty appreciating Plato's doctrine of the ideal world. It clashes with one of humankind's most basic paradigms, that the world apprehended through our senses is the only world that exists. Suddenly someone tells them that the world of the senses is not real and that there is another, more real world behind and above them. But they cannot understand because they are slaves to their senses. And so they continue to live and think as though the only real world is the one they see, hear, touch, and smell.

In order to appreciate Plato's point about the existence of a higher world, a kind of philosophical conversion is necessary, a conversion that breaks the empiricist paradigm that enslaves the human race. We need to turn away from the objects of sensation (the shadows), turn to the light, and begin an ascent to the highest reality of all, that which Plato symbolizes under the figure of the sun.

I will for the moment ignore questions about the statues and bonfire inside the cave. It is obvious that the world outside the cave has everything to do with the world of the Forms. The sun represents Plato's highest Form, the Form of the Good.[15]

One purpose of the allegory of the cave is to show that there are different levels of human awareness, ascending from sense perception to a rational knowledge of the Forms and eventually to the highest knowledge of all, the knowledge of the Good. Only after humans, with great effort, leave the objects of sensation in the cave do they see the objects of knowledge such as the Forms of Truth, Beauty, and Justice. With persistence, it is possible that they will see the Light itself, that is, the Good.

The Divided Line and the Cave

Many interpreters of Plato conclude that there must be a perfect symmetry between the major points of the divided line and the allegory of the cave. But there is no compelling reason to accept this belief. There is some symmetry, but we should not be surprised to find some elements of one illustration that do not match some element in the other. The following diagram will illustrate my understanding of how the divided line and the cave are related:

Figure 3.8

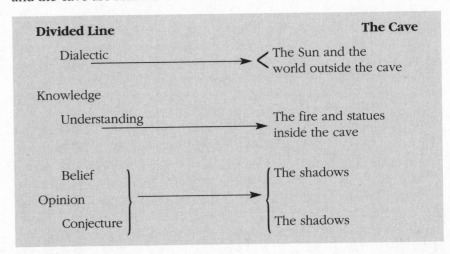

Some parallels between the two passages seem clear. The ascent of the freed prisoner into the world of the sun pictures the need of the human soul to climb from the realm of sense perception to the realm of the intellect. The arduous nature of the ascent out of the cave and the temporary blindness that follows illustrate the great difficulties that accompany the attainment of dialectic. The awareness attained by the prisoner outside the cave clearly represents the line's highest level, dialectic, the intuitive apprehension of the highest Forms.

15. See Plato *Republic* 7.517b–c.

It seems best to conclude that the prisoners and their shadowy world visible on the wall of the cave represent the realm of opinion. In other words, the allegory contains no distinction between belief and conjecture. The experience of the freed prisoner who turns and sees the statues that cast the shadows is most likely a reference to the lowest level of knowledge, that is, understanding. Just as the objects of understanding can be imaged, so, the allegory suggests, it is possible to form images, however imperfect, of the exemplars (such as the Form of the perfect circle) behind the copies (imperfect circles) that we find in the lower world.

One reason why it makes little sense to interpret the vision of the statues as belief is the significance Plato attaches to the prisoner getting free from his chains. The moment one is free from sense perception, he is already in the realm of knowledge. Plato attaches too much significance to the prisoner's gaining freedom from the chains for the vision of the statues to parallel the otherwise insignificant distinction between conjecture and belief. I contend that what the freed prisoner sees by the light inside the cave represents the human apprehension of a lower level of Forms; it is thus akin to the level of understanding.

To summarize, no precise correlation between the levels of the divided line and the levels found in the allegory of the cave can be drawn. The prisoners perceiving the shadows on the back wall of the cave represent the realm of opinion. The allegory does not contain any distinction between belief and conjecture. The freed prisoner's perception of the statues that cause the shadows should be interpreted as understanding, the lower level of knowledge. The fact that the statues cannot be seen until the prisoner is freed from his chains suggests that when the prisoner sees the statues, he has already moved beyond the realm of mere sense perception. But dialectic is not attained until the freed prisoner enters the world outside the cave, the world illumined by the bright light of the sun.

Plato's Three-Story Universe

Our effort to grasp the central features of Plato's philosophical system can advance a few steps further once we grasp Plato's belief that the universe exists hierarchically, in three major levels or stories. Picture a triangle divided into three levels or stories.

The lowest level of the triangle represents the world of particular things. It corresponds to the shadows in the cave and to the level of opinion in the divided line. It is the material world apprehended through our bodily senses.

In the middle of the illustrated triangle lies the second of Plato's three stories, the world of Forms. Plato seems to hint that there are two distinct levels of Forms, a point that appears in my illustration under the labels of higher forms and lower forms. The higher Forms, I suggest, include concepts that humans cannot image, such as the Forms of Truth,

Figure 3.9

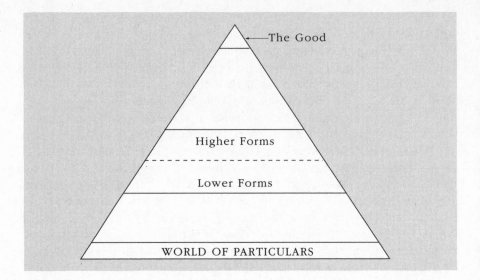

Beauty, and Justice. The lower level includes Forms that can be imaged, including geometrical entities like the perfect circle. There is reason to believe that this is also where Plato placed such Forms as the perfect dog, horse, and similar class concepts.[16] At the apex of Plato's universe, the highest level of his three stories, is the highest of all the Forms, the Form of the Good, about which much remains to be said.

What lessons can we learn from this? Both reality and human knowledge are structured hierarchically. The highest kind of knowledge is human knowledge of the Good. Below the Good exists a whole range of other things that humans should strive to know: Truth, Beauty, and Justice. But still lower levels of knowledge are possible, culminating in knowledge attainable through mathematics and geometry and finally in human knowledge of the Forms that correspond to classes of physical objects. The bottom layers of human awareness are related to sense experiences, which vary in reliability. Some types of sense experience are more reliable; some uses of reason are more important. Plato's message is to trust your reason rather than your senses; seek to know the Forms; strive to know the higher Forms; and seek knowledge of the highest Form of all, the Good.

Plato's Rationalism

Plato made at least three important contributions to the rationalist tradition. First, he taught that all human knowledge contains an unavoidable reference to a universal element that is known independently of sense experience; the technical term for this kind of knowledge

16. Keep in mind how Plato pictures men carrying statues of physical objects before the bonfire. I have already noted that as Plato grew older, he seemed to lose interest in Forms of all classes of physical objects.

is *a priori*.[17] Second, Plato argued that reason is superior to sense perception because sensation is powerless to provide the crucial universal and necessary element present in knowledge. And finally, the superiority of reason over sense experience led Plato to think in terms of a hierarchy of epistemological states with reason at the top and sense perception at the bottom.

Plato's *Phaedo,* one of his greatest achievements, contains what I regard as one of the most important passages in all of philosophical literature.[18] Even though the passage appears to focus on an argument for the immortality of the soul, its greatest significance is the contribution it makes to the debate between rationalism and empiricism. Even though Plato puts the argument into the mouth of the imprisoned Socrates as he awaits his execution, no serious student of Plato thinks that the historical Socrates advanced this argument. What seems more likely is that Plato borrowed the argument, along with much other material that appears in the *Phaedo,* from the Pythagoreans during his travels in southern Italy.

An Account of Plato's Argument

Plato has Socrates begin the argument by pointing out that people can only remember things they knew at some earlier time. If I can remember something in the present, then I must have known it sometime in the past. From this apparently innocent observation, Socrates goes on to argue that some kind of remembering exists in every act of knowing. To illustrate his point, Plato uses judgments of the form "*a* is equal to *b.*" Consider a case where we judge that two sticks or two line segments or two triangles are equal to each other. What conditions must be met before we can know that *a* is equal to *b?* We must have perceptual awareness of the two line segments. We must have seen *a* and then seen *b.* That is obvious. But, Plato insists, we must also have knowledge of something else that Plato calls the Equal itself. That is, in addition to particular things like sticks or lines on a paper that we apprehend with our senses, there is something else, namely, the standard or idea or Form of Equality, that must exist and be known before we can judge that two line segments are equal in length or that two triangles are equal in size and shape.

But this raises an obvious question: Where does our knowledge of the standard or Form of Equality come from? How is this knowledge acquired? Plato gives two answers to this question, his own and one that he rejects. It is interesting to note that the position he rejects is the

---

17. *A priori* knowledge is independent of sense experience. One example of such would be "three times four equals twelve." *A posteriori* knowledge is dependent upon sense information. The proposition "Some roses are red" is *a posteriori* while the proposition "Some red roses are red" is *a priori*.

18. The standard pagination for the passage is Plato *Phaedo* 72e–77a.

position proposed later by his pupil Aristotle.[19] It is the answer of classical empiricism.

According to the empiricist position, human beings first perceive through their senses several things that are similar[20] in a certain way. In this case, we perceive that the two line segments or the two triangles are equal in length or size. The line segments or triangles are instances of what Plato calls particular things. And, as we know, the only way humans can become conscious of particular things is through sense experience, such as seeing or touching.

From our perceptual awareness of these particular things (a and b), we then abstract an idea of the property or relation they share in common, namely, Equality or Similarity. It should be easy to see how the position Plato rejects approximates the empiricist thesis that all human knowledge arises from sense experience.[21] Universals or Forms like Equality can be in the mind only after particular examples are apprehended in sensible objects. Only then does the mind through abstraction or some other means grasp the universal.[22]

Plato offered two objections to what I have called the empiricist or Aristotelian theory that human beings come to know the eternal Forms by abstracting a universal element from data supplied by the senses. First, Plato argued that it is absurd to believe that one first knows that a is equal to b, that c is equal to d, and then from these judgments about equal particulars derives the more general knowledge of what Equality is. One could not know that a and b were equal unless he already knew the standard, the Equal itself. Knowledge of the universal is logically prior to knowledge of the particular. But since the awareness that a and b are equal is impossible without a logically prior knowledge of the form or universal (Equality or Sameness or Similarity), the empiricist thesis that all human knowledge arises from sense experience is false. Either the rationalist thesis that at least some human knowledge does not arise from sense experience is true, or else no human knowledge is possible.

---

19. I have sometimes wondered if the young Aristotle did not happen to challenge Plato's teaching by offering this line of thought. But since empiricism tends to be an opinion held by the majority of humans, anyone could have verbalized this position. Nonetheless, as I will explain in my discussion of Aristotle, the position rejected by Plato resembles Aristotle's empiricism.

20. The notion of similarity is very important here, because it is the basic notion present in the idea of equality. To say that a is equal to b is another way of saying that a is similar to b.

21. See the appendix to this chapter.

22. I must interpose a footnote that may not make sense until after we finish the chapter on Aristotle. No comfort can be found in the fact that Aristotle distinguished between a passive and an active aspect of the human intellect. It is obvious that the active intellect mentioned in some of Aristotle's writings is useless until given sensible information to act upon.

In his second objection, Plato argued that no particular thing or group of particular things is ever sufficient to provide a notion of the universal. Universals always have properties that can never be found in the earthly particulars that exemplify them. Particular things are always imperfect copies of the exemplars, the Forms. It is impossible, for example, to obtain an idea of the perfect circle by contemplating examples of imperfect circles. Any circle that might be encountered in the physical world is imperfect. Since the concept of Equality could not be derived from the senses and since we began to use these senses the moment we were born, our knowledge of the Equal itself must have been acquired independently of sense perception. Plato went on to explain *a priori* knowledge of the Forms in terms of a theory of preexistence. Students of Plato differ as to whether Plato meant that theory to be taken literally or only offered it as a myth or likely story. For an account of how the mature Augustine modified Plato's position into his own theory of divine illumination, see chapter 6 of this book.

An Outline of Plato's Argument

A simple outline of Plato's argument will place his words in the proper context.

(1) All knowing presupposes a prior knowledge of some Form, rule, or standard.

Comment: In order to know that *a* is equal to *b,* one must have not only perceptual awareness about the particular things in question but also a concept or idea of the standard or concept of Equality. The same is true with respect to judgments about Goodness, Beauty, Truth, Justice, and so on. This raises the question dealt with in (2) as to how humans acquire their knowledge of these rules, standards, or Forms.

(2) Human knowledge of the Form, rule, or standard cannot be acquired through the senses (that is, it cannot be acquired in this life).

Comment: The senses only bring humans into contact with particular things. Just as there is an obvious difference between a Form like the Equal itself and two or more particular things that are equal or alike or similar, it is obvious that humans can never encounter the Form of Equality through their senses. We may see this or that particular instance of Equality, but we can never see with our physical eyes the standard or concept of the Equal itself.

(3) Therefore, human knowledge of the Forms is acquired in an earlier existence.

Comment: Since our knowledge of any Form cannot be acquired through sense experience, we cannot attain such knowledge during our present physical life. This entails a doctrine of reincarnation, that is, the preexistence of the soul.

(4) Therefore, the human soul is immortal.

Surely step (4) does not follow from (3). Even if we agree that (3) is true, that the soul existed in one or more earlier lives, that claim hardly justifies the inference that human beings will never die in any future existence, which is the point in the claim that humans possess immortality. Even if my soul has survived several or even many bodily deaths in my past, that does not prove that my soul will continue to live the next time I die. In such matters, past performance is no guarantee of future performance. Therefore, Plato's inference from step (3) to (4) fails.

Equally important is the fact that nothing Plato says provides logical support for step (3), that is, for his assertion of preexistence. Even if steps (1) and (2) are true (and I believe they are), they do not ground the inferences to steps (3) and (4). They do not constitute a proof for the preexistence of the soul. The reason for this is that there is at least one other explanation for the claims made in (1) and (2). There is a far more plausible account of why all knowing presupposes a prior knowledge of a Form (1) and why this Form cannot be known through sense experience or in this life (2 and 3).

Even if we took Plato's appeal to the preexistence of the soul seriously, the important consequence remains the same: This preexistent knowledge could not have been acquired through the senses since it is a necessary condition for anything that human beings can know. In chapter 6 of this book, we will return to this argument and examine the remarkable use to which Augustine puts Plato's theorizing. Nonetheless, Plato's argument reveals the fundamental flaw of empiricism and the basic strength of rationalism. If humans can attain even one item of knowledge apart from or prior to sense experience, then empiricism is false and rationalism is true. As Plato shows, there are abundant examples of such knowledge, all of them related to universals.

Plato's View of Human Beings: Mind-Body Dualism, Immortality, and Reincarnation

According to Plato, the ultimate objective of the human soul is to know eternal truth that is found only in the realm of eternal forms. The human body is a hindrance to the attainment of such truth. The physical senses impede the advance of the soul toward truth. Death will free the soul from this hindrance and make it possible for the philosopher to achieve what he has sought, knowledge of absolute truth. Even though the philosopher should welcome death, he should not push open the door or hasten the process through suicide. The soul of the philosopher is directed away from the things of the body toward the things of the soul. For such a person, death can only mean the realization of what the philosopher has sought for years.

The Christian New Testament does not teach the kind of radical body-soul dualism advanced by Plato. While Plato viewed the human body as a useless, incidental, and bothersome home for the soul, the New Testament teaches that the human body is both good and important to our humanness. For Plato, immortality is the soul's continuing existence apart from the body, while in the New Testament, survival after death is an existence in a resurrected body. The hope of the Christian believer, according to the New Testament, is not the disembodied existence of a Platonic soul but the resurrection of the body at the end of the world (see 1 Corinthians 15). The New Testament doctrine of bodily resurrection shows an intellectual environment totally different from that of Platonism. The body, according to the New Testament, is neither evil nor irrelevant; it is not a useless appendage to an essentially soulish person. The New Testament teaches a much more unified view of humans.

Plato's Dualism and Human Knowledge of the Forms

One of the more difficult problems Plato creates for himself is explaining how humans come to know the world of the Forms. In the *Meno* and the *Phaedo,* Plato offers the following account, based on a theory of reincarnation he seems to have learned from the Pythagoreans. The human soul continues to exist during the time between the death of one body and our birth into a new body. Consider the following diagram:

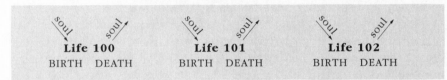

Figure 3.10

Plato suggests that the soul continues to exist between the end (death) of life 100 and the birth that marks the beginning of life 101. While the body that used to identify life 100 is decaying in the grave, the soul exists in the world of the Forms, where it beholds the Forms in all of their glory. When the soul returns to earthly existence via a new body (life 101), the soul forgets what it learned about the Forms during its disembodied state. But an implicit and unconscious knowledge of those Forms is present in the mind and rises to the level of consciousness when stimulated by various bodily experiences. To use our earlier example, every human possesses an unconscious and implicit knowledge of true Equality. When we sense two equal things, we achieve consciousness of the innate idea of the Equal itself and are able to form the judgment that the particular things we see are equal.

Few scholars believe that Plato meant this story literally. It is often explained as a myth, that is, a likely story. Often in Plato's writings, his inability to offer a satisfactory answer to a difficult question is followed by a likely story that he does not insist be taken literally. The theory of reincarnation appears to be such a story. The doctrine of reincarnation soon disappears from Plato's writings, but it served its purpose as a likely story of how humans attain a knowledge of the Forms.

Plato's Dualism, Human Evil, and the New Testament

Between 1920 and 1940, a number of American thinkers argued that such New Testament writers as St. Paul were influenced by elements of Plato's philosophy, notably his mind-body dualism and the evil of the body. Such writers typically focused on Paul's use of the word *flesh* in contexts associating it with evil. What could be more natural for any writer who approaches Paul's writings already convinced that Paul is a Platonist than to conclude that his view of the flesh is a reflection of the Platonic belief that matter and the body are evil?[23] To be sure, Paul repeatedly describes a moral conflict within humans. Dualists after Plato saw the moral struggle in terms of a conflict between body and spirit. Paul identifies the antagonists as flesh and spirit. But Paul's use of the word *flesh* is not a reference to a material body. It is instead his way of referring to our sinful human nature.

Paul's condemnation of flesh as evil has no reference to the human body. It does not refer to the physical stuff of body but rather to a psychological and spiritual defect that leads every human being to place self or the creature ahead of the Creator. The New International Version of the Bible makes this clear by translating the Greek word *sarx* (flesh) by the phrase "sinful nature." For instance, Romans 7:5, a verse often used as a proof text for the claim that Paul believed matter is evil, reads: "For when we were controlled by the sinful nature, the sinful passions aroused by the law were at work in our bodies, so that we bore fruit for death." Once it is clear that Paul did not use "flesh" as a reference for the human body, it is clear that he was not a Platonic dualist.

Paul never taught that his body was evil or the source of his sin or that the body is a prison house of the soul. Humans commit acts of sin because they are born with a sinful nature. Paul's use of "flesh" in this way has no parallel in pagan usage. Paul's teaching was undoubtedly derived from the Old Testament, though he develops the term beyond its Old Testament usage.

The claim that Paul believed that matter is evil is also refuted by his belief that the ultimate destiny of redeemed human beings is an endless life in a resurrected body, not the disembodied existence of an immortal soul as held by Plato. Paul's doctrine of the resurrection of the body (see 1 Corinthians 15:12–58) is clearly incompatible with a belief in the inher-

---

23. This strong statement becomes more attributable to Platonists in later centuries than to Plato himself. See Ronald H. Nash, *The Gospel and the Greeks* (Richardson, Tex.: Probe Books, 1992), chap. 3.

ent wickedness of matter. Attempts to attribute an evil matter–good spirit dualism to Paul also stumble over the fact that Paul believed in the existence of evil spirits (Ephesians 6:12), a belief that obviously implies that not all spirit is good. The additional fact that God pronounced his creation good (Genesis 1:31) also demonstrates how far Platonic dualism is from the teaching of the Old and New Testaments.

In the *Timaeus,* one of his most influential writings,[24] Plato presents a myth about the creation of the world. He has Socrates ask if the world is eternal or if it had a beginning. Socrates concludes that the world was created.[25] But how, then, did the world come to be, and who or what created it? Socrates explains that "the maker and father of the universe" is difficult to know and even more difficult to explain to others.[26] Plato goes on to describe the creation of the world as the work of a divine Craftsman, or Demiurge, who fashions the world out of a preexisting matter after the patterns he finds in the world of the Forms.

Many interpreters of Plato's thought have used the following example to explain his complex teaching. In order to set up a parallel with Plato's allegory of the cave, I call this approach the allegory of the kitchen.

According to Plato, the origin of the physical world depends upon four factors that we can compare to necessary conditions in the making of a cake. If we are going to bake a cake, we first need ingredients such as flour and sugar. Second, we need a recipe that tells how much of each ingredient to use. Third, we need an oven in which the cake will bake. And finally, we need a baker, the person who will use all of these components in the right way to produce the finished product. The following diagram will illustrate how the four elements of what I call the allegory of the kitchen relate to Plato's teaching in the *Timaeus.*

Plato's Conditions for Creation	The Allegory of the Kitchen
(1) Matter	(1) The Ingredients
(2) The Forms	(2) The Recipe
(3) The Space-Time Receptacle	(3) The Oven
(4) The Craftsman or Demiurge	(4) The Baker

(1) What Plato calls matter is difficult to explain. It is a kind of basic stuff from which the world will be made. But matter is unlike anything

---

Plato's View of Creation: The Allegory of the Kitchen

Figure 3.11

---

24. During much of the Middle Ages, Plato's *Timaeus* was one of the few Platonic writings known to scholars.

25. Plato *Timaeus* 28b.

26. Ibid., 28c. I use here the translation found in Francis Macdonald Cornford, *Plato's Cosmology* (New York: Library of Liberal Arts, 1957), 22.

we have ever experienced. Matter is unknowable, because it has no identifying features or properties. It has no color or shape or size or texture. Consider a rock, for example. In your imagination, begin taking away every property of the rock. Remove its hardness, color, shape, and every other distinguishing feature. What would you have left? Some people would answer that nothing would remain. But for Plato, what would still exist would be the unknowable, unperceivable stuff of which the physical world is made.

(2) We have already encountered Plato's Forms. They function in the *Timaeus* much as the recipe does in my allegory of the kitchen. They provide the models or patterns that the creator will use as its blueprint for the things it will make.

(3) If there is to be a creation, it must be created somewhere and at some time. Plato was like many philosophers and scientists who believe the world exists inside of something. That something is a very large box that includes both space and time. While the world of the Forms is independent of space and time, while the Forms are nonspatial and nontemporal, every physical object exists in a space-time continuum, Plato taught.

(4) Finally, we come to the analogue for the baker, the being responsible for making or creating the cake. Plato describes the creation of the world as the work of a divine Craftsman, or Demiurge, who fashions the world out of a preexisting matter after the patterns it finds in the world of the Forms. It should be obvious that this Craftsman bears no resemblance to the God of Judaism and Christianity. The Judeo-Christian God is personal and almighty. Even if Plato's Demiurge were divine in some sense, it is finite; its power is limited by the conditions within which it operates. It can do only so much with the matter that it must work with. In chapter 6 we will discover some modifications that Augustine attaches to this allegory of the kitchen.

The Craftsman, The Good, and Plato's God

What was Plato's view of God? Any attempt to answer this question is complicated by the fact that Plato's philosophy contains at least two candidates for deity. Plato never disavowed the gods of the Olympian religion, though this may have been due to concern about public opinion.[27] Even so, his attitude toward the Olympian gods was noncommittal, and it seems likely that he did not believe in them. What complicates our understanding of Plato's God is not the case of the Olympian deities; it is the presence of at least two other candidates for divinity that appear prominently in his writings. One of them is the Craftsman or Demiurge of the *Timaeus*. The other is the Form of the Good that plays such a cen-

---

27. One of the official charges for which Socrates was tried and executed was impiety toward the Olympian gods.

tral role in the allegory of the cave. Interpreters of Plato have puzzled over the relationship between the Craftsman of the *Timaeus* and the supreme Good of the *Republic*. No effort to combine these two figures into one being has succeeded. Does this mean that Plato leaves his readers with two candidates for God?

Speaking for Plato, Socrates makes three points about the Form of the Good.[28]

(1) The Good is the ultimate end of human life. The highest goal of which humans are capable is knowledge of the Good. Without knowledge of the Good, the knowledge of everything else would have no value. In comparison with the Good, all else pales in significance.[29]

(2) The Good is the necessary condition of human knowledge. Without the Good, the world could not be intelligible and the human mind could not be intelligent. Just as light from the sun is necessary to turn potential color into actual color, so the light from the Good is necessary in order to make knowledge of the other Forms possible.[30] If it were not for the Form of the Good, no human being could attain knowledge of any of the other Forms or of anything else that exists.[31]

(3) The Good is also the creative and sustaining cause of the intelligible world, the world outside the cave, the world of the Forms. Plato suggests that if the Form of the Good did not exist in some prior capacity, nothing else would exist, including the rest of the Forms.[32]

While all of this is interesting, it is impossible to say if Plato himself thought of this highest Form, the Good, as his God. We do know that this is how Xenocrates (396–315 B.C.), one of his early followers, understood the passage. Much later, the identification of God with the Good would become one of the more important innovations in Middle Platonism (approximately 100 B.C. to A.D. 100). Whatever Plato meant, his language sets out a curious parallel to several important elements of the Christian concept of God.

Christians regard God as the creative and sustaining cause of everything else that exists. Unless God exists, nothing else would exist. Christians also recognize that God is the necessary condition of human knowledge. Unless human beings possessed the image of God, they would be mere animals, incapable of knowledge. And finally, Christians view God as the supreme, absolute, and ultimate end of human life.

---

28. See Plato *Republic* 505a.

29. See ibid., 505a–b.

30. The language here is remarkably similar to things Aristotle says when talking about something he calls the active intellect. We will encounter this passage during our discussion of Aristotle's philosophy.

31. Plato *Republic* 508e–509a.

32. Ibid., 509b.

While it would be foolish to read too much into these apparent similarities between Plato's Good and the Judeo-Christian concept of God, the resemblances are striking. It has led some writers to suggest that Plato's discussion of the Good may be the closest any human came this early in history to a theistic concept of God outside the influence of Judeo-Christian revelation. Unfortunately, Plato was unable to appreciate what he had produced. This is apparent in the fact that Plato failed to build upon his suggestions; later in life he abandoned them. Further comments about the relationship, if any, between the Craftsman and the Form of the Good appear later in this chapter.

Plato's Ethics

We have already noted that Plato is an enemy of ethical relativism, the reason being his conviction that the world of the Forms includes absolute and unchanging standards of such moral concepts as goodness, justice, and virtue.

Ethics and God

In one of his earlier writings called the *Euthyphro,* Plato touches briefly on the relationship between moral goodness and God. Plato does this by asking what has become a well-known question: "Is something good because God commands it, or does God command it because it is good?"[33] The two options can be pictured as follows:

Figure 3.12

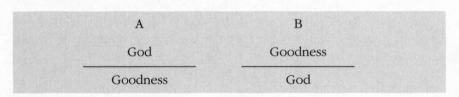

A	B
God	Goodness
Goodness	God

In the dialogue Plato recommends (B): if God wills x (some act), it must be because x is good prior to and independent of God's willing it. Plato's reason for rejecting A (that x is good solely because God wills it) is because it makes ethics arbitrary and capricious. If something is good only because God wills it, what would prevent God from willing something else? Or suppose God were to will one kind of behavior on even days of the month and the opposite kind of conduct on odd days? This would make possible days on which God commands murder, stealing, and adultery, instead of forbidding them as he does in the Ten Commandments. If morality is grounded on nothing more than an arbitrary command of God, it is possible that God could have commanded us to

---

33. Even though the *Euthyphro* approaches the issue in terms of the gods, the discussion has more relevance for contemporary readers if we change the plural to "God."

perform actions that we recognize as immoral. Option A makes ethics capricious and arbitrary.

But the other option (B) is equally unsatisfactory. If the only alternative to viewing ethics as capricious and arbitrary is believing that what God wills must be subordinate to a standard of goodness that is above or superior to God, then an important feature of Jewish and Christian belief must be abandoned, namely, the conviction that God is supreme and sovereign and that nothing is higher than God. Plato's two options seem to have trapped us on the horns of a dilemma:[34] If we accept A, ethics is arbitrary and capricious. If we choose B, God is neither supreme nor sovereign.

The two options presented in the *Euthyphro* are not exclusive. Both of Plato's options (A and B) are inconsistent with important Christian beliefs, namely, that God's moral commands are not capricious and that nothing is higher than God and stands in judgment over God's actions. Rather, in Christian theology, the Good or the moral law functions on the same level with God. (The precise sense in which this is true will become clear in chapter 6 on Augustine's worldview.) What God wills can never conflict with what God is. There is nothing higher than God, but neither is what God wills arbitrary. What God wills reflects and is consistent with his own eternal nature, which is immutably and necessarily good.

A third alternative holds that the Good is what God wills; this third position goes on to add, however, that God's willing is never arbitrary. The Good is defined not merely by God's will but also by God's eternal and unchanging nature.

This third alternative views the Good as identical in some way with God. The Good is identical with God's nature (what God is) and with what God wills (which is always consistent with God's nature). If there is no fundamental conflict between what God is and what God does, and if the Good is defined in terms of God's nature, it is impossible for God's moral commands to be arbitrary, since they have a ground; moreover, it is also impossible for God's moral commands to be grounded on anything higher than himself. God's moral law is not arbitrary; it does have a ground. God does have a reason for his commands, but that reason is not something higher than God himself. Plato himself moved toward a position similar to this when in his *Republic* he identified God with the Good.

Virtue Versus Commands

Plato's ethic has nothing to do with commandments, such as we find in Judaism and Christianity. Plato ignores commands and places all of his

---

34. The phrase "horns of the dilemma" refers to the two options that confront us in a dilemma. In the case before us they are that God is higher than the good or that the good is higher than God.

emphasis upon the importance of virtue or excellence, believing that if human beings possess a virtuous character, their conduct will be morally acceptable. A so-called virtue ethic has become popular in some contemporary circles.

Students of the New Testament cannot help but notice its emphasis upon character and virtue; it is important what kind of people we are (see Galatians 5:22–23). But talk about virtue is not sufficient, since not any trait of character will do. There are reasons why some human character is deemed a virtue rather than a vice. A properly virtuous person will behave in ways that obey God's commandments.

The Three Parts of the Human Soul

While there are two parts of a human being, body and soul, Plato thinks there are three parts of the human soul. Plato provides an illustration of this last point. He asks us to imagine a charioteer driving a chariot pulled by two winged horses, one white and the other black.[35] The relevant passage here is Plato's *Phaedrus* 254–256. As one commentator explains, the black horse

> is ill-bred and ignoble, inclined to pursue brutish pleasures: this one symbolizes the appetitive or concupiscent part of the soul.... The [white] horse is well-bred and noble, inclined to soar upward toward honor and glory: this is the spirited part ... of man's soul. Obviously, they represent two appetites in man, the desire for sensual satisfaction and the aspiration for success and fame. The driver of these two horses must know where he is going, love the better things, and assert his orderly control over his unruly steeds: reason ... is this highest part of man's soul. Philosophy is designed to train man's soul so that all three parts work together for happiness.[36]

Plato makes this threefold distinction because of the obvious conflicts humans sense within themselves. The rational part of the human soul (the charioteer) seeks the truth and acquires knowledge. The rational part of the soul is the seat of human immortality; no animals possess this faculty. The spirited and passionate parts of the soul are faculties of its irrational side. The spirited part of the soul (the white horse) exemplifies anger, resentment, and the desire to excel; the passionate part of the soul (the black horse) pursues the pleasures of food, sex, and the satisfaction of other bodily desires. It is easy to understand why Plato thought it necessary to make a distinction between the spirit and passions. When people yield to temptation, they can become angry with themselves.

---

35. The colors of the horses have no reference to racial or ethnic considerations.
36. Vernon J. Bourke, *History of Ethics* (Garden City, N.Y.: Image Books, 1970), 1:27.

The Four Cardinal Virtues

For Plato, there are four basic kinds of virtue, called the cardinal virtues: temperance, courage, wisdom, and justice. Temperance or self-control is the proper virtue of the passions. Courage means fortitude in the face of adversity, which is what the spirited part of the human soul requires. Wisdom means excellence in selecting the proper means to an end; its relation to the rational part of the soul should be obvious. The fourth virtue, what Plato calls justice, is the overarching virtue that is present when humans are temperate, courageous, and wise. Our picture of the four cardinal virtues and their relation to the parts of the soul looks like this:

Reason—Wisdom

Spirit—Courage

Passions—Temperance

and Justice, the virtue of the entire person
when the other virtues are present

Figure 3.13

Plato's account of the righteous or just human person takes us back to his example of the charioteer and the two horses. To assure that the chariot reaches its destination, the charioteer must know when to rein in one horse and give free rein to its partner. Plato's picture allows him to say that the just man or woman is one in whom reason rules the passions and the spirit.

Plato never completed his system, and this meant he never resolved a number of important questions that arise in his writings. Many later developments in Platonism were attempts to resolve those questions. Four of these unresolved questions have special relevance to developments within Platonism during the early Christian era.

The first question resulted from Plato's failure to remove the ambiguities in his view of God. We have already noted the two major candidates for Plato's God: the supreme principle, which in the *Republic* he calls the Form of the Good; and the Craftsman, or Demiurge, who brings the material world into existence, as described in the *Timaeus*. It is difficult to produce from Plato's writings any systematic and coherent theory of God, although several attempts to produce such a theory have been made. According to one of these, both the Good and the Craftsman may be considered to be God, because they are different ways of looking at the same being: the Good is God as he is in himself, whereas the Craftsman is God in relation to the world. A different interpretation sees the Craftsman, while still a divine being in some sense, as subordinate to the supreme being, the Good.

One of the more important features of the later thinkers known as Middle Platonists was their adoption of the view that there is only one

Unresolved Tensions in Plato's Philosophy

God who should be identified with Plato's Good. The identification of God with the Good became quite common in the period of time dated roughly from the death of Alexander the Great in 323 B.C. to A.D. 400–500.

A second unanswered question in Plato's system concerns the relation between God and Plato's world of the Forms. If the Craftsman of the *Timaeus* was Plato's God, then there is a sense in which the Forms are above God. At the least, they exist independent of the Craftsman, whose creative power is limited by them. If Plato's God is the Good, then the other Forms are subordinate in some sense to God. Plato teaches that the other Forms depend on the Good for their existence. The importance of this question becomes evident in the later systems of the Jewish thinker Philo (who died about A.D. 50) and the Middle Platonists. The Middle Platonists set forward the suggestion that the eternal Forms are ideas that subsist eternally in the mind of God. Centuries later Augustine made this concept a cornerstone of his theory of knowledge.

The third unresolved problem in Plato's system is his failure to bridge the great gap he established between his two worlds. How is the eternal, unchanging, immaterial, and ideal world of the Forms related to the temporal, changing, corporeal, and imperfect world of particular things? Given the extreme separation between them in Plato's system, how could any Platonist hope to bring them together?

Plato's system has a fourth unanswered question, namely, the lack of an adequate answer to the question of how human beings attain knowledge of the ideal world and of the good God who exists in that world. Plato's claim that humans apprehend the ideal world through reason does not answer the question; it only tells us where to look for an answer. Throughout his life, Plato sought an answer in several different myths and metaphors. One of these is his famous allegory of the cave, but, like most of his efforts, it ends up using unanalyzed metaphors. In some of his middle dialogues, such as the *Meno* and *Phaedo,* he suggested an answer based on the myth of reincarnation. If reincarnation were true, then presumably the immortal human soul would have to dwell somewhere between incarnations. If we assume that during these intervals the soul rises to the world of the Forms, it would be possible for the soul, unencumbered by its bodily prison, to see or view the Forms as they are. Of course, once the soul descended into another body, it would forget its vision of the Forms. But assorted experiences in life could bring some people to the point where a dim memory or recollection of the Forms could make knowledge possible. Many scholars doubt that the mature Plato meant this story to be understood literally. This doubt is supported by Plato's failure to utilize the doctrine of recollection in his later writings.

A clue to Plato's possible dissatisfaction with his earlier attempts to answer this problem may appear in the complicated argument of one of his dialogues, the *Parmenides*. In this, his most puzzling work, Plato describes an imaginary conversation between a very young Socrates and Parmenides, the greatest of the pre-Socratic philosophers. Parmenides challenges Socrates' belief in the theory of the Forms by using a series of arguments that Socrates apparently is unable to answer.[37] Our present question arises out of one of these arguments. Parmenides tries to get Socrates to see that once he admits a radical disparity between the world of the Forms and the world of bodies, he is faced with a whole series of problems. For one thing, Socrates admits that human beings are bound by their bodies to the lower world. But the only objects of true knowledge exist in the higher, nonmaterial world. If humans are stuck down here and the only possible objects of knowledge are up there, how can any human being ever know anything? Moreover, God is up there, in the world of the Forms. Consequently, Socrates' doctrine (which is really Plato's) also implies the impossibility of any human knowledge about God. As if this were not bad enough, God, who dwells in the world of the Forms and who has perfect knowledge of all the Forms, is precluded from knowing anything that exists in the physical world. And since human beings exist in the physical world, this means that God cannot have knowledge about any human being. While Socrates agrees that depriving God of any knowledge would be a monstrous thing, he offers no escape from the skeptical trap laid by Parmenides.[38]

In the work of later Platonists, this aspect of Plato's system evolved into a kind of general agnosticism with regard to the nature of God. As Philo, the Middle Platonists, and the Gnostics saw it, the good God is completely transcendent and is thus essentially unknowable. The earliest Christians, however, had a far different view. "In the past," they believed, "God spoke to our forefathers through the prophets at many times and in various ways, but in these last days he has spoken to us by his Son, whom he appointed heir of all things, and through whom he made the universe" (Hebrews 1:1–2).

Rationalism and Empiricism

Appendix

The debate between rationalists and empiricists is one of the perennial disputes in philosophy. Since the disagreement will be such a central issue in the worldview chapters of part 1, it seems wise to introduce the controversy now rather than later. Plato, Plotinus, and Augustine are rationalists, in spite of differences among their systems. Aristotle

---

37. It is clear that the historical Socrates did not hold to the theory of the Forms; the concept was Plato's.

38. See Plato *Parmenides* 134c–e. Gordon Clark provides an excellent introduction to the problems generated by this dialogue in *Thales to Dewey*, 85–90.

is an empiricist, as were the ancient atomists. The task of identifying where to place Aquinas in this debate is more difficult, as we will see.

I have found it helpful on occasion to borrow a teaching tool from Aristotle called the square of opposition. Aristotle used the device to illustrate logical relationships that exist among the four basic kinds of categorical propositions. A categorical proposition exhibits the form "*S* is *P*," where *S* is some subject and *P* is some predicate.[39] The four kinds of categorical propositions and their place in the square of opposition are as follows:

Figure 3.14

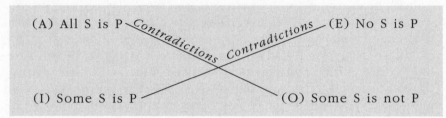

For convenience, the four kinds of propositions were named after the first four vowels; hence we get the A, E, I, and O propositions. Aristotle gave names to the various logical relationships among these four types of propositions. For our purposes the most important relationship is that of contradiction, the relation between the A and the O and between the E and the I propositions. When two propositions are contradictory, it follows that if one is true (A, let us say), then the other (in this case, O) is necessarily false; and if one is false, the other is necessarily true.

We can illustrate our four propositions further by substituting for the variables (*S, P*) so that we get the following:

Figure 3.15

(A) All elephants are mammals.	(E) No elephants are mammals.
(I) Some elephants are mammals.	(O) Some elephants are not mammals.

In the case of these examples, the A and I propositions are true, and the others are false.

A Definition of Rationalism and Empiricism

Applying the square of opposition to the four possible positions on the issue of rationalism and empiricism, we get the following:

---

39. Two other types of statements are worth noting. A hypothetical statement exhibits the form "If *S*, then *P*." A disjunctive statement exhibits the form "either *S* or *P*."

(A) All human knowledge arises from sense experience.	(E) No human knowledge arises from sense experience.
(I) Some human knowledge arises from sense experience.	(O) Some human knowledge does not arise from sense experience.[40]

Figure 3.16

Which of these four options should be viewed as statements of the positions we have called empiricism and rationalism? Empiricism, as I use the term, is identical with the A position, that all human knowledge arises from sense experience. When we examine the epistemologies of such empiricists as Aristotle and John Locke, this was their position. And what about rationalism? Here we encounter a problem. Except for those times when I am talking about Plato's brand of rationalism, my definition of rationalism is the O position, that humans possess some knowledge that does not arise from sense perception. For the rest of this discussion, however, and its continuation in chapter 4, we need to remember that Plato's rationalism is defined by the E position. That is, Plato did not allow any instance of genuine knowledge to arise from sense experience. I suspect we could find a few other thinkers in the history of philosophy who also thought this way. But Plato's extremism in this matter should not draw attention away from the fact that rationalism is best understood as the more modest assertion that some human knowledge arises from a source other than sense experience.

One reason why Plato took the more extreme position of holding that no human knowledge arises from sense experience is because he held the standards of knowledge so high that no human awareness to which sensation made any contribution could qualify as knowledge. Indeed, Plato thought that no awareness of any particular thing existing in this physical world could count as knowledge. It is worth noting that the

---

40. While the simplicity of my formulation presents several advantages, it can be faulted for being too simple. For one thing, it eliminates a major qualification of contemporary empiricism, namely, the admission that human knowledge of logical and mathematical truths is not derived from sense experience. Some twentieth-century empiricists called logical positivists maintained that the truths of mathematics and logic are tautologies. That is, they are redundant statements that convey no new information about reality. This factor could be plugged into our formulation by making the A proposition read "All nontautological human knowledge arises from sense experience" and making the O proposition read "Some nontautological human knowledge does not arise from sense experience." Since I am seeking the simplest possible way of stating my point, I have decided to omit these and other qualifications that a more technical discussion would require. Any reader who wishes may add the qualification throughout the subsequent discussion. It should be understood, however, that there are good reasons to believe that the logical positivist account of logical and mathematical truth as empty tautology is incorrect. This may help to explain why it is so difficult to find any living logical positivists.

Christian rationalist Augustine believed that human knowledge (*scientia*) could sometimes arise through the senses.[41]

Being a rationalist does not require one to believe that every item of human knowledge comes from a source other than the senses. That person is a rationalist (in my sense) who believes that only one item of human knowledge has a nonsensory source. But the empiricist must be prepared to show how every instance of human knowledge has sense experience as its necessary and sufficient condition. As the history of philosophy makes clear, that is a formidable task.

One more point must be made about empiricism. Not only is it the belief that all knowledge is derived from sense experience, but also it is the denial of the existence of any innate ideas, a term that we'll explore more fully in later chapters. For now, it is sufficient to know that an innate idea, if such there be, is an instance of human knowledge that is inborn (present implicitly in the human mind from birth). The word *implicitly* is crucial in this analysis. I am not saying that humans can be conscious or aware of such ideas from the moment of birth. Various things must happen along the way, as humans grow up and mature, that make it possible for those implicit items of knowledge to become explicit. All of this should be clear by the time we finish chapter 7.

41. See Augustine *On the Trinity* 15.12. 21, where he wrote, "Far be it from us to doubt the truth of what we have learned by the bodily senses."

OPTIONAL WRITING ASSIGNMENT

Without using either the text or your notes, write an essay to a friend or a family member who is unfamiliar with philosophy explaining the nature and importance of Plato's theory of the Forms.

FURTHER READING ABOUT PLATO

A. H. Armstrong, *An Introduction to Ancient Philosophy* (Boston: Beacon, 1963).

Frederick C. Copleston, *A History of Philosophy* (Westminster, Md.: Newman Press, 1962), vol. 1.

Francis Macdonald Cornford, *Plato's Cosmology* (New York: Library of Liberal Arts, 1957).

Francis Macdonald Cornford, *The Republic of Plato* (New York: Oxford University Press, 1945).

J. C. Gosling, *Plato* (New York: Routledge, 1984).

G. M. Grube, *Plato's Thought* (Indianapolis, Ind.: Hackett, 1980).

Terence Irwin, *Plato's Ethics* (New York: Oxford University Press, 1995).

Richard Kraut, ed., *The Cambridge Companion to Plato* (New York: Cambridge University Press, 1992).

Plato, *The Collected Dialogues,* trans. Edith Hamilton and Huntington Cairns (New York: Pantheon, 1961).

Plato, *The Dialogues of Plato,* trans. B. Jowett, 2 vols. (New York: Macmillan, 1892).

A. E. Taylor, *Plato: The Man and His Work,* 7th ed. (New York: Routledge, Chapman and Hall).

Chapter Four

Aristotle

IMPORTANT DATES IN ARISTOTLE'S LIFE

384 B.C.	Aristotle is born in Macedonia
367 B.C.	Aristotle comes to Athens to study at Plato's Academy
347 B.C.	Plato dies; Aristotle leaves Athens, travels in Asia Minor, marries
342 B.C.	Aristotle returns to Macedonia to tutor Alexander
336 B.C.	Aristotle leaves Macedonia
334 B.C.	Aristotle establishes his university, the Lyceum, in Athens
323 B.C.	Alexander the Great dies; Aristotle leaves Athens
322 B.C.	Aristotle dies

Aristotle was the first truly cosmopolitan thinker. He was interested in almost everything. He divided human knowledge into its basic categories and wrote systematically about most of them. In the words of British scholar G. E. R. Lloyd, "No Greek philosopher was gifted with greater originality than Aristotle. In logic, biology, chemistry, dynamics, psychology, ethics, sociology and literary criticism, he either founded the science or inquiry single-handed or else made a fundamental contribution to it. Yet he remained, of course, very much a product of his age and culture, as we can see when we consider some of the assumptions on which his philosophy is based and contrast them with our own ideas."[1]

---

1. G. E. R. Lloyd, *Aristotle: The Growth and Structure of His Thought* (Cambridge: Cambridge University Press, 1968), 302.

Aristotle was born in 384 B.C., fifteen years after the death of Socrates and three years after the founding of Plato's Academy. Aristotle's life began in the Greek colony of Stagira. His father was court physician to the king of Macedonia, who was the grandfather of the young man who would become known as the Alexander the Great. When Aristotle reached the age of seventeen, he moved to Athens and began studies at Plato's Academy. It was not unusual for the children of wealthy Greeks living in outlying colonies to return to Athens for their education. After Plato's death in 347 B.C., his will assigned the leadership of the Academy to his nephew, Speucippus. Aristotle decided this was a good time to leave Athens. He traveled to Asia Minor, where he married.

In 342 B.C. Aristotle received a call from Philip II, the king of Macedonia, to tutor Philip's thirteen-year-old son, Alexander. The relationship between the philosopher and the future conqueror lasted but three years. Philip was assassinated, and following a period of palace intrigue, Alexander succeeded his father as king of Macedonia.

Aristotle returned to Athens in 334 B.C. and founded his own school, the Lyceum, which functioned only during the last twelve years of his life. Aristotle's students were often called the peripatetics, due no doubt to his school's being located near a long covered walk called in Greek the *peripatos* (literally, the place to walk about). Much of the teaching occurred as the members of the school strolled in the pleasant surroundings and engaged in philosophical discussion.

Alexander the Great died in 323 B.C. Embittered by the sufferings they endured during Alexander's reign, many Athenians sought revenge against persons close to Alexander. Aristotle left Athens for the last time, justifying his sudden departure by saying that he wanted to spare Athenians the embarrassment of sinning twice against philosophy, namely, by killing two great philosophers, Socrates and himself.

After Aristotle's death, his library, including manuscripts of his own writings, passed to his successor, Theophrastus. When Theophrastus died, the library was hidden in a cave somewhere in present-day Turkey. The location of the buried library seems to have been forgotten, and about a hundred years later the library was finally recovered. During that time, the manuscripts suffered much damage. Incompetent handling did still more damage. Eventually Andronicus of Rhodes, working in Rome, undertook the task of putting the manuscripts in some kind of order. They were finally published in 70 B.C.

Much that Aristotle wrote has been lost, including most of his dialogues, popular writings that may have rivaled the dialogues of Plato. What survives besides small fragments of the dialogues are Aristotle's technical works that reflect what he taught in the Lyceum. They are thought to be based on the notes of both Aristotle and his students. They

Aristotle's Life

Aristotle

Antique sculpture
THE GRANGER COLLECTION, NEW YORK

were heavily edited by Andronicus and later redactors; material from a variety of sources and manuscripts was combined, edited, and synthesized. Whether or not the blame belongs totally to Andronicus, the product of his cutting and splicing did little to ease the task of understanding Aristotle's thought.

A General Overview of Aristotle's Philosophy

When a system is as complex and difficult as Aristotle's, it is good pedagogy to examine it from several different perspectives. In this section of the chapter, I will provide a brief overview that will be useful when later in the chapter I go into greater detail.

One way to approach Aristotle's philosophy is to see it as a development of what Plato began. In a sense, the essence of Aristotle's system is a rejection of Plato's more radical dualism. Aristotle rejected Plato's metaphysical dualism, namely, Plato's separation of the Forms from the material world. Aristotle objected to Plato's epistemological dualism, which had set reason in opposition to experience as an avenue to knowledge. And Aristotle replaced Plato's anthropological dualism with a holistic or unitary view of human beings.

Aristotle's Rejection of Plato's Metaphysical Dualism

As we saw, Plato's primary reality was the unchanging world of Forms that exists apart from the world of particular things. For Plato, the most important things that exist belong not to the earthly world of bodies but to the strange, spaceless, timeless world of the Forms. As Plato himself recognized in his *Parmenides,* the most serious problems with his theory result from the extreme separation between his two worlds. Aristotle repeated many arguments found in the *Parmenides* against the separate existence of the Forms. To these he added the new charge that the world of the Forms is a useless duplication of the physical world. Aristotle believed he could avoid introducing this unnecessary duplication of the one and only world that exists and still explain everything Plato tried to explain with his separate Forms.

The central issue in Aristotle's disagreement with Plato's theory of the Forms was Plato's insistence on their separate existence. Aristotle continued to believe that Forms or universals exist, and he believed that the Forms are the only proper objects of human knowledge. What Aristotle did—to describe his move in the rather crude way some professors adopt—was to bring Plato's Forms down to earth. Aristotle brought Plato's two worlds together. Although Forms exist, they exist in this earthly world as part of the particular things that constitute the world.

Whereas Plato's primary reality was the separate world of the Forms, the primary reality for Aristotle was this world of particular things. Plato's thinking was always directed upward toward the ideal world. Because

Aristotle's attention was directed toward this world, one benefit of his approach is the extent to which it encourages the development of scientific thinking. Within this world, the primary reality is what Aristotle called a substance. By *substance,* Aristotle meant any given thing that exists or has being. Hence the chair I am sitting on, my computer, and the paper on which these words are printed are all substances.

Aristotle believed that every being, with the exception of God and some other godlike beings, is a composite of two factors that he called form and matter. To put this distinction in its simplest possible terms, the matter of any given substance is whatever it happens to be made of. The matter of the chair on which I am seated happens to be wood, but it could as easily have been metal or plastic. The form of any given substance is the set of essential properties that makes it the kind of thing it is. Like Plato's Form, Aristotle's form is an unchanging essence. But unlike Plato's, Aristotle's form is an essential part of the substance it composes. For Aristotle, there are not two separate worlds; there is only one world, namely, the physical universe that we inhabit through our bodies. Although Forms exist, they exist in this earthly world as part of the particular things we encounter in this world.

Aristotle's Rejection of Plato's Epistemological Dualism

Aristotle recognized the difference between reason and sense experience. But whereas Plato denigrated the human senses and argued that they could never supply human beings with knowledge, Aristotle's account of human knowledge is more complex. Once Aristotle rejected Plato's doctrine of two separate worlds, he was released from Plato's major reason for grounding human knowledge on reason alone. According to Plato, the bodily senses bring humans into contact only with the things that exist in this world of particulars, and no particular can ever be a sufficient object of true knowledge; thus it is obvious why Plato was the kind of rationalist he was. But in Aristotle's system, the Forms (which for Aristotle continue to be the only proper objects of knowledge) are not in some other world where they can be apprehended only by reason. The Forms exist as essential parts of the particular things that we apprehend through our senses. Thus Aristotle rejected Plato's extreme disjunction between reason and sensation, regarding them instead as integral parts of the knowing process.

Aristotle's Rejection of Plato's Anthropological Dualism

Aristotle also rejected Plato's radical separation between soul and body. Aristotle's understanding of human nature (which includes his view of the relationship between body and soul) is one of the more complex parts of his system. But this much is clear: Aristotle stressed a unified view of

Aristotle and Ultimate Reality

human beings. Humans are not a composite of two radically different substances, body and soul. Humans are instead a holistic unit; both body and soul are essential aspects of a human being.

Substance, Essence, and Accident

I have already explained that Aristotle uses "substance" to refer to any given thing that exists or has being. Substances possess two kinds of properties: essential or accidental properties. An *accidental property* is a nonessential characteristic, such as size or color. A nonessential property of something is a characteristic that can be lost or changed without altering the essence or nature of the thing in question.

Everything also has essential properties; an *essential property* is one that, if it is lost, means the thing ceases to exist as that kind of thing. If a knife loses its ability to cut, it is no longer a knife; it has lost its essence. Essence is one of the more difficult notions in Aristotle's philosophy. For Aristotle, essence and form are different ways of referring to the same thing.

Form and Matter

Aristotle believed that every being, with the exception of God,[2] is a composite of two factors that he called form and matter. To put this distinction in its simplest possible terms, the *matter* of any given substance is whatever it happens to be made of. The *form* of any given substance is the set of essential properties that makes it the kind of thing it is. Like Plato's Form, Aristotle's form is an unchanging essence. But contrary to Plato, Aristotle's form is an essential part of the substance to which it belongs.

For Plato, grouping things into classes is possible because things share a fundamental similarity (notice the reappearance of Plato's Form of the Equal itself) to a separately existing universal. For Aristotle, each desk is a member of the same class because the essence or form of deskness is present as a part of the being of each particular desk. Is there a form of a desk? Yes. Where does it exist? In each particular desk. The form of the desk is not in some separate world; it is present in each particular thing as a part of that thing. If we could somehow remove the form of the desk, we would no longer have a desk. The thing would be changed so completely that it would cease to exist as a desk. The wood (matter) that originally made up the desk might continue to exist as pieces

---

2. Aristotle seems to have believed there was an unmoved Mover for every sphere of the universe. Each of them was an instance of Pure Form. Whether each member of this collection of Pure Forms was something Aristotle would regard as a god is a source of some dispute. But this issue need not concern us in this introductory study.

of wood or a pile of lumber or something else. But it would no longer be part of a desk.

Human beings are substances. We too are composed of form and matter. The matter is our body. Our form, that essential property that makes us a human being, is our soul. Naturally, we also have accidental properties. Hair is a nonessential property, as is the color of one's skin or eyes.

Aristotle's Four Causes

Aristotle used "cause" more broadly than we do. His search for the causes of a thing is a quest for its reasons or explanations. Whenever someone asks why, there are four different kinds of answers.

(1) The *material cause* is the stuff of which a thing is made. In the case of a baseball bat, the material cause is the wood that composes the bat.[3]

(2) The *formal cause* is the set of essential properties without which a thing could not be the kind of thing it is. In the case of our baseball bat, the formal cause is the essence of the bat.

(3) The *efficient cause* is the activity that brought a thing into existence. In the case of our bat, the efficient cause is the work of the bat maker.

(4) The *final cause* is the purpose for which a thing exists. In the case of our wooden bat, the final cause is its use in hitting a baseball.

Aristotle's four causes made a brief appearance in Plato's philosophy. Plato's material cause was the chaotic matter used by the Demiurge to make the world. Plato's formal cause included all of the Forms. Plato's efficient cause was the activity of the Demiurge in bringing the world into existence. And Plato's final cause was the Form of the Good.

The notion of final cause has puzzled people, especially in the case of nonliving substances. We can understand final cause in the case of a manufactured object such as a house because it was made for a specific purpose. But what shall we say about the final cause of a substance like a rock? While human activity and the products of human activity do make sense when they are described in terms of purpose, what about things like sunlight, rocks, and air? Henry B. Veatch offers some helpful comments about this difficult issue:

> Aristotelian final causes are no more than this: the regular and characteristic consequences or results that are correlated with the characteristic actions of the various agents and efficient causes that operate in the natural world.... There is no reason at all why the final cause of an efficient action should necessarily be an end in the sense of a conscious purpose.[4]

---

3. Amateur athletes these days use bats made of aluminum. I am interested only in professionals, such as the gentlemen who play for the Cleveland Indians.

4. Henry B. Veatch, *Aristotle: A Contemporary Appreciation* (Bloomington, Ind.: Indiana University Press, 1974), 48, 49.

For example, sunlight on a hard surface typically causes that surface to grow warmer. Operating as an efficient cause, sunlight brings about a change that represents "no more than the characteristic product or achievement that goes with that particular kind of efficient action."[5] A final cause produces a result we should expect from the kind of thing it is.

Aristotle's Doctrine of the Categories

We normally refer to the categories of things by means of predicates. In any categorical proposition of the form "S is P," we have a subject (S) and a predicate (P) linked by a verb. Take any subject and make a list of all the predicates applicable to the subject; they can be grouped into ten basic kinds of predicates (categories). These represent ten basic ways of thinking about anything.[6] Veatch explains that Aristotle's categories are "the ultimate headings under which anything and everything in the world can be classified—that is to say, the basic kinds of things, or the fundamental varieties of entities that may be said to comprise the ultimate furniture of the world."[7] A category is a fundamental way of thinking about anything that has being or exists.

Figure 4.1

A CHART OF ARISTOTLE'S CATEGORIES

Name of category	Type of change	Property type
substance	*generation/corruption*	*essential property*
quantity	augmentation/diminution	nonessential
quality	alteration	nonessential
place	locomotion	nonessential
relation		
time		
posture		
state		
action		
passion		

If we consider the extremely large number of words or phrases that we could possibly predicate of a subject like Socrates (as in a sentence: Socrates is _____), all of those predicates would fall into one of about ten basic kinds of predicates or categories. Consider these examples:

---

5. Ibid., 49.

6. Over his lifetime Aristotle offered different lists of categories, sometimes citing as few as eight.

7. Veatch, *Aristotle,* 23.

Socrates is a human being. (substance)

Socrates is short and rotund. (quantity)

Socrates is bald. (quality)

Socrates is in prison. (place)

Socrates is the husband of Xanthippe. (relation)

Socrates is alive in 400 B.C. (time)

Socrates is standing. (posture)

Socrates is dressed. (state)

Socrates is drinking hemlock. (action)

Socrates is being poisoned. (passion)

An important difference exists between the first category, substance, and the others. The reason is because the other nine categories are always dependent upon some existing substance. Adjectives always need a noun to modify. When we use adjectives like "red" and "tall," there must be some thing that is red and tall. The last nine categories must have some prior substance to qualify or modify. Unless the substance existed first, the other categories would not exist in this particular instance.

Potentiality, Actuality, and Change

Aristotle defines *change* as the passage from potentiality to actuality. Since the two terms can be difficult to define, it is perhaps best if we contrast them with each other.

Everything we're familiar with in our ordinary experience is potentially many other things. The oak tree is a potential table or door or bookcase. But while a thing possesses several, perhaps many potentialities, at any given time, it possesses only one actuality. Whenever we ask what something is, the answer identifies the actuality of a thing. A thing's *actuality* is determined by its form, while its *potentiality* is grounded in its matter. All change is the realization of one of a thing's potentialities.

Aristotle distinguished four kinds of change, each related to one of the first four categories (see the chart of the categories):

(1) Any change with regard to place is *locomotion,* such as moving a chair from one room to another.

(2) Any change with regard to quality is *alteration.* For example, something cold becomes hot, or something green becomes red.

(3) Change with regard to quantity is either *augmentation* or *diminution,* depending on whether the thing gets larger or smaller

(4) Change with regard to substance is *generation* or *corruption,* depending on whether an existing substance is destroyed or a new substance comes into existence.

A change with regard to anything other than substance is an accidental change. Even if a substance changes with respect to its place, size, or qualities, it remains the same kind of thing. But a chair can be changed in another way that is so radical and complete that Aristotle calls it a substantial change. Anything that undergoes a substantial change is modified so completely that it becomes a new kind of thing. Aristotle calls this kind of change generation or corruption, depending on whether we focus on the beginning of a new substance or the cessation of existence of an old thing. Consider an acorn. When it is planted in the ground, it changes into an oak tree. The acorn ceases to exist (corruption), but something new (an oak tree) comes into existence; this is what Aristotle calls generation.

In one of his more puzzling statements, Aristotle says that a thing's actuality comes before its potentiality. This seems to mean that everything has a purpose built into it. If things are permitted to develop naturally, they will develop in the direction of that built-in purpose. Nature is a purposeful (telic) process. What Aristotle calls *entelechy* is the final form of anything, that toward which the thing aims, that toward which it naturally develops, what it will naturally become if nothing interferes with its development.

Consider a developing human embryo. The embryo possesses potentiality. It is on the way to becoming a mature human being. What it is destined to become is already present within the embryo. Our current way of designating what Aristotle has in mind is the genetic code present in DNA, which we know determines a person's eye color, height, intelligence, race, and so on. If an acorn is allowed to develop naturally, it will grow into an oak tree. If the human embryo is allowed to develop naturally (if it is not aborted, for example), it will become a mature human being. The mature human being is the entelechy of the fertilized egg.

Substances and Properties

The distinction between substances and their properties plays a central role in the philosophy of Aristotle. In the following chart, I note four important differences between a substance and a property:[8]

Figure 4.2

Substance	Property
1. A particular thing	1. A universal
2. Can change	2. Cannot change
3. Cannot be in other things	3. Is in other things
4. Has causal power	4. Does not have causal power

Taking these four differences in order, we note first that a substance is a particular thing, like this apple, that table, this street sign, and that red

8. My discussion owes much to material written by J. P. Moreland in two books: J. P. Moreland, *Scaling the Secular City* (Grand Rapids: Baker, 1987), 79–80; and Gary R. Habermas and J. P. Moreland, *Immortality: The Other Side of Death* (Nashville: Thomas Nelson, 1992), 23–24.

light. To say that a property is a universal means at least two things: it is a characteristic of a particular thing, such as the color red of a sweater or the taste of sweetness of sugar or the diagonal shape of a street sign; a property can also belong to more than one thing at the same time. For example, the world is full of red things. Redness is a property of numerous substances. This is why we consider redness a universal; it belongs to many things at the same time.

Second, a property is immutable. The colors of red and green can never change. But the substances to which the colors sometimes belong can change. A red table can be painted green. And so the table can change with respect to its color, but a color cannot change. Redness will always be red. As J. P. Moreland explains, "a substance is a continuant—it can change by gaining new properties and losing old ones, yet it remains the same thing throughout the change. A leaf can go from green to red, yet the leaf itself is the same entity before, during, and after the change. In general, substances can change in some of their properties and yet remain the same substance. That very leaf that was green is the same leaf that is now red."[9]

Third, properties can never exist by themselves but only as properties of a particular substance. None of us has ever experienced yellowness or hotness or sweetness floating around a room. We experience such properties only as characteristics of particular things, such as a yellow ball, a cup of hot tea, or a sweet orange. Properties exist by virtue of their belonging to a substance. Substances exist by themselves; substances are never had by other things or exist in other things.

Fourth, substances have causal powers. Substances can function as efficient causes. A bat can hit a ball, a bulldozer can move a pile of rocks, a cat can meow, and so on. But properties cannot act in this way. As Moreland puts it, "properties do not have causal powers. They do not act as efficient causes. Properties are not agents which act on other agents in the world."[10]

Matter as the Basis of Individuation

We distinguish between kinds or classes of things. A dog is different from a cat, a horse, and a human being; see how easy philosophy can be? Things are grouped into such classes on the basis of their form (essential properties). But we also distinguish between particular members of a class. Consider five members of the class of human beings. What makes individual humans distinct members of their class? Matter is the basis of individuation, that which distinguishes you and me from the class of human beings. You and I are both members of the human species by

---

9. Habermas and Moreland, *Immortality*, 23.
10. Moreland, *Scaling the Secular City*, 79.

virtue of the form of humanness that we share. What makes us individual human beings is the matter that composes our respective bodies.

Is Pure Form Possible?

Can form exist alone, without matter? Aristotle's answer is yes, and his major example of Pure Form is his God. Aristotle understood God's perfection in a way that made it impossible for God to change. This meant that for Aristotle, God possesses no potentiality, only actuality. Since the possibility of change resides in matter, a God who possesses no matter cannot change. Such a God must be pure form or pure actuality.

Primary Matter

Aristotle's universe has three levels, as shown in the following diagram:

Figure 4.3

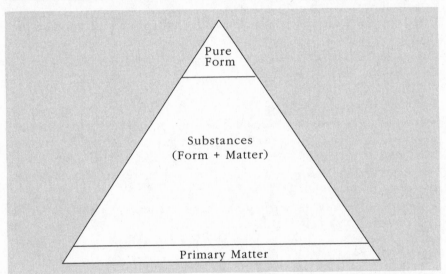

The middle layer, by far the most extensive, includes every particular substance in the physical world, that is, everything composed of form and matter. The peak of Aristotle's universe would include God and the few other beings who are pure form. The bottom layer of the universe is what Aristotle calls primary matter. Aristotle's doctrine of primary matter can be summarized in five propositions.

(1) Primary matter is a substratum common to all substances.

(2) It cannot exist by itself, that is, without some form. Therefore it is a theoretical abstraction.

(3) It has no distinguishable properties and is thus unknowable.

(4) It is eternal; it can never be created or destroyed.

(5) It is the ultimate basis of individuation; it is what ultimately sets apart different chairs, desks, and people.

A ristotle distinguished between soul (*psuche* in Greek) and mind (*nous*). He then drew a distinction between two aspects of the human mind, calling them the passive intellect and the active intellect. The relevant text here is one of the most perplexing and most frequently debated passages in all of Aristotle's writings.[11]

There is a part of the mind, Aristotle taught, that is *passive* in the sense that it receives information from the senses. Another part of the mind is *active* in the sense that it acts upon that which is received by the passive intellect. Aristotle explained our knowledge of the world as a product of the interaction of these aspects of *nous*. The physical world, as we have seen, is the only world that exists for Aristotle. Our knowledge of chairs and mountains and trees and humans is mediated by sensations that we have of those objects. The sensed object (a tree, for example) produces an image (phantasm) within the mind of the perceiver. This image of a sensed object is received by the passive intellect. But this sensible image of a particular thing is not yet knowledge; it is only potential knowledge. What is needed to turn this potential knowledge into actual knowledge is an additional process that is performed by the active intellect. The active intellect abstracts from the particular sensible image the form, or universal element, that alone can be the object of knowledge. Human knowledge, therefore, depends on two things: the passive intellect, which receives information from the senses, and the active intellect, which alone performs the crucial function of abstraction that isolates the form of the particular thing that has been sensed.

The complexity of Aristotle's system makes it necessary for us to postpone any further discussion of the active and passive intellects until we first examine some related features of his psychology.

W e have already noted the Greek word (*psuche*) that English translations call soul in Aristotle's writings. The Latin word for soul is *anima,* from which such English words as "animal" and "animated" are derived. Wise students will recognize that whatever soul means for Aristotle, it will have something important to do with life.

In the discussion that follows, I will focus on four basic issues: What does Aristotle mean by "soul"? What is his distinction among three levels of soul? What is the relationship between soul and body? What is the meaning of his distinction between the active and passive intellects?

What Does Aristotle Mean by "Soul"?

Aristotle's use of the word *soul* is quite different from Plato's. When Plato talked about the soul, he meant the essential and immaterial part of a human being: the seat of intelligence and the cause of motion. Plato thought of soul

Aristotle's Theory of Knowledge

Aristotle's View of the Soul

---

11. Aristotle *De Anima* 3.5.430a10–25.

and body as separate entities. Aristotle rejected Plato's notion of soul as a separate entity dwelling in a living body. Soul instead is the form that accounts for the creature's being alive. Body and soul are different dimensions of the same complex substance. For Aristotle, the human soul is the form of a composite substance; the matter of this substance is the human body. Just as one cannot separate sight from the organ that is a human eye or sharpness from the steel of an ax, it is impossible to separate the human soul from its living body. As Jonathan Lear explains, "Soul is not a special ingredient which breathes life into a lifeless body; it is a certain aspect of a living organism, and a living organism is a paradigm of a functioning unity."[12]

What Is Aristotle's Distinction Between Three Levels of Soul?

Aristotle believes there are varied levels of life: what distinguishes these levels is their respective function and the complexity of their structure. The simplest form of life is found in plants. A more complex level of life occurs in animals, and an even higher complexity of life occurs in humans. The functions of the nutritive or vegetative soul involve basic life processes, revolving around the acquisition of food, the digestion of food, excretion of wastes, and reproduction. Since animals can perform all of these functions, they possess a nutritive soul, which means that animals carry on basic life processes such as those already identified. But animals can perform functions that lie beyond the power of plants, such as perception and motion. These are functions of the sensitive soul.

Human beings also have a nutritive soul; we perform essential life functions: digestion, respiration, excretion of wastes. Some believe that Aristotle's comments about the human possession of a nutritive soul was his way of explaining processes supported by the involuntary nervous system, which keep the blood circulating, the heart beating, the lungs and kidneys functioning, and so on. Like animals, humans also possess a sensitive soul. We can perceive and move. We also possess a level of functioning not found on the animal and plant levels—reasoning. The following diagram helps to put all of this into perspective.

Figure 4.4

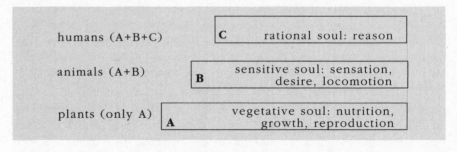

12. Jonathan Lear, *Aristotle: The Desire to Understand* (Cambridge: Cambridge University Press, 1988), 97. See Aristotle *On the Soul* 2.1.412b6–9.

And so we have learned the following: (1) Human beings possess all three levels of soul; animals lack the rational soul; and plants possess only the vegetative soul. (2) Each lower level of soul is a necessary condition for the higher levels. That is, a living being could not possess the sensitive soul without also possessing the vegetative soul. However, a plant possesses the vegetative soul without possessing the sensitive soul. (3) As one ascends the hierarchy of living forms, one encounters increasingly complex life forms.

Relation of Soul and Body

What is Aristotle's view of the relationship between the human soul and body? This is not an easy question to answer. Aristotle thought the relation was much closer than did Plato. But interpretations of precisely what Aristotle meant have ranged from positions that see him as a physicalist to views that present his position as similar to the New Testament's holistic view of a human being. It is clear that Aristotle believes the human soul and body are related in a much more integral way than they were in Plato's philosophy. The important question is whether human consciousness in Aristotle's system ends when the body dies.

Many contemporary philosophers believe that Aristotle's view of a human being entails that human consciousness and identity cease when the body dies. Most of Aristotle's *De Anima* seems incompatible with a belief in personal survival after death.

The issue of physicalism deserves a closer look. It includes the following set of beliefs: humans are only physical beings; they possess no soul or mind that exists or can exist independent of the body; and when the body dies, all consciousness ceases; there is no personal, conscious survival after death. While a physicalist reading of Aristotle holds obvious appeal for people who are inclined to this way of thinking, Aristotle gives such people reason to claim him as one of their own.

Putting the physicalist question aside for a moment, some believe that a properly formed Christian view of humanity would be closer to Aristotle's view of the soul than to Plato's. In this view, the New Testament emphasizes the wholeness of the human being. The New Testament does not picture the human body as a useless appendage that can be discarded. The New Testament does not teach that the body is an inferior and unnecessary part of a human. Humans after death are not disembodied souls but rather resurrected persons, body and soul.

What Did Aristotle Teach About the Active Intellect?

The subject of Aristotle's theory of the active intellect was introduced earlier and then shelved briefly. We are now in a position to return to this subject. Aristotle went on to say some mysterious things about the active intellect.[13] For instance, he declared that the active intellect is "separable and immortal." Coming from Plato, such words would not have raised so much as an eyebrow. But since so many scholars are convinced that the entire drift of Aristotle's psychology was away from a Platonic soul that could exist forever in separation from the body, this sudden turn in direction cannot be ignored. What could Aristotle have meant when he referred to an active intellect present in every human soul that is both separable and immortal?

Aristotle's argument in book 3 of *De Anima* can be summarized rather quickly; a little repetition in a matter of such importance will help rather than hurt. (1) Just as we find form and matter making up everything else that exists in the physical universe, we should not be surprised to find the form-matter, actuality-potentiality distinction within the human soul. Aristotle calls them the active intellect and the passive intellect.

(2) It then becomes clear that Aristotle is distinguishing between soul and two aspects of mind (*nous*) existing within the soul. A part of the mind is passive in the sense that it receives information from the senses. Another part of the mind is active in the sense that it acts upon that which is received in the passive intellect. The passive intellect fulfills the function of the mind's matter, while active intellect will be akin to form. Aristotle believes that our knowledge of the world is dependent upon our having sensations of the world. The sensed object produces an image (phantasm) within the mind of the perceiver. The passive intellect is that part of the human mind that receives this information from the senses.

(3) But the images in the passive intellect are not yet knowledge; they are only potential knowledge. What is needed to turn that sensible information into actual knowledge is some other process performed by the active intellect. The active intellect abstracts from the particular sensible image the form or universal element that alone can be the object of knowledge. In this way, potential knowledge is changed into actual knowledge. Aristotle then adds another point. Since that which acts is always superior to that which is acted upon, the active intellect is superior to the passive intellect.

At this point Aristotle introduces the analogy of light, an important feature of Plato's allegory of the cave. Without light we could perceive no color. In a totally dark room, the color of an object could only be potential color. Light is required to turn potential color into actual color. In a similar way, when the active intellect begins to work on the potential knowledge present in the passive intellect, it changes potential knowledge into actual knowledge.

---

13. Most of this material appears in Aristotle *De Anima* 3.5.

(4) This brings us to Aristotle's mysterious declaration that the active intellect is "immortal" and "separable." Does Aristotle mean to teach that the active intellect can exist apart from the body? That it is immortal? The challenge for Aristotle's interpreters is to understand how all of this can be reconciled with the rest of Aristotle's psychology. He seems to be saying that while the soul per se cannot exist separate from the body, one faculty of the soul (reason or the active intellect) can. While the passive intellect perishes when the body dies, the active intellect is different. There have been three major attempts to interpret Aristotle's doctrine of the active intellect in a way that would avoid any contradiction in his system. It is interesting to realize that these three interpretations played major roles in the three major systems of medieval philosophy. These three systems constructed by Plotinus, Augustine, and Thomas Aquinas are discussed in the remaining chapters of part 1.

Three Interpretations of the Active Intellect

(1) About A.D. 200, Alexander of Aphrodisias, greatest of the ancient interpreters of Aristotle, identified Aristotle's active intellect with God. According to this view, the active intellect, or light within the soul that makes knowledge possible, would not be a part of the individual human soul but a presence of God within the soul. As an interpretation of Aristotle, Alexander's view must be rejected because the immanent view of God it requires is incompatible with the transcendent, if not deistic, God of Aristotle's *Metaphysics*.[14] The God required to complete this interpretation is one present immanently in the world, a God actively and personally involved in every act of human knowledge. However, Alexander's work resonates with some ideas that showed up centuries later in the thinking of Augustine (354–430). We will examine this theory in more detail in chapter 6.

(2) During the third century the philosopher Plotinus (205–270) interpreted the active intellect as a cosmic principle of intelligence to which every human intellect is related. At death, the intellects of individual human beings are absorbed back into the cosmic mind (*nous*), which is eternal and impersonal. (This will make a great deal more sense after you have read chapter 5 on Plotinus.) Centuries after Plotinus, his theory appeared in the thought of such medieval Arabic Aristotelians as Averroës and the Christian Averroists whom Thomas Aquinas debated. According to this view, personal survival after death is denied in favor of an impersonal continuation of existence. As Aquinas would show, this doctrine is

---

14. Aristotle's notion of God can be difficult to understand. The point in this last paragraph is that Aristotle's account of God is so far removed from any direct contact with the physical universe that it cannot fit the demands of Alexander's interpretation.

incompatible with Christianity because it leads to a denial of personal survival after death.

(3) The third major interpretation of Aristotle's active intellect was proposed by Thomas Aquinas as an alternative to the heretical teachings of certain Christian disciples of Averroës at the University of Paris. Aquinas identified the active intellect as something individual and particular in each human being. If Aquinas was right and the active intellect is a separate part of each human mind, then Aristotle's claim that the active intellect is both separable and immortal could only mean that the great Aristotle believed there is something within human beings that is immortal.

Aquinas developed his interpretation as part of an attempt to make Aristotle's philosophy compatible with Christian thought of the time. When he wrote, the Christian church was suspicious of Aristotle's philosophy because it had entered the Christian world via certain Muslim interpretations. These Muslim influences made it appear that Aristotle's philosophy was incompatible with such Christian beliefs as creation and personal survival after death. Many leaders of the church in the thirteenth century thought Aristotle was an enemy of the church. Aquinas thought this philosophy could be made compatible with Christian belief. One of his clever moves was to argue that *De Anima* 3.5 taught human immortality. It was part of a brilliant public relations gambit to make Aristotle acceptable to the medieval church.

The major difficulty with Aquinas's interpretation—which should be kept distinct from its merit as an independent theory—is its obvious conflict with the picture of humankind presented in Aristotle's work *On the Soul*. Aquinas's interpretation is hard to reconcile with the rest of Aristotle's system. For this reason, even Roman Catholic interpreters of Thomas's position, among them Frederick C. Copleston, admit that as an interpretation of Aristotle, Aquinas's position is wrong and that the Averroist interpretation is probably the correct reading of Aristotle.[15] Unless a better reading of Aristotle turns up, it seems wise to concur with those who argue that the most plausible interpretation of Aristotle's puzzling words about the active intellect is the one proposed by Plotinus and modified by Averroës during the Middle Ages.

Aristotle's View of God

Aristotle was not an especially religious man. His God did not fulfill any particularly religious function; Aristotle did not worship or pray to his God. Aristotle believed in a supreme being because he thought certain things about the world could not be explained without the existence of a God. His God was a metaphysical necessity, a concept required lest

---

15. See Frederick C. Copleston, *A History of Philosophy* (Westminster, Md.: Newman Press, 1960), 1:330–31.

the rest of his system contain some huge holes. His system forced him to questions that he could not answer without postulating the existence of a perfect being who is the unmoved Mover of the universe, a being who is also Pure Actuality. Aristotle believed that there had to exist an uncaused and unchanging being who is the ultimate cause of everything else that exists. If this ultimate cause itself moved or changed in any way, it could not then be the ultimate cause, since we would be forced to ask why it changed and what changed it. Aristotle's God cannot act upon the world as an efficient cause because this would imply potentiality within God. Trapped by his own system, Aristotle is forced to say that his unmoved Mover can bring about change in the world only by being a final cause, that is to say, as an object of desire.

Because of Aristotle's earlier discussion of form and matter, he was forced to conclude that the ultimate cause of the universe had to be Pure Form unmixed with any matter. Matter, Aristotle thought, is synonymous with potentiality. But potentiality implies the possibility of change and hence imperfection. Therefore, Aristotle's God would have to be Pure Actuality, in other words, Form without Matter.

Aristotle's doctrine of God as Pure Form has raised all kinds of problems in the histories of philosophy and theology. For one thing, what can a God who is Pure Form, the unmoved Mover of the universe, do? He cannot do anything that entails change in his own being or knowledge, because he is perfect and incapable of change. To shorten and simplify a rather long and complex subject, the only thing Aristotle's perfect God can do is think. But since he is immutable perfection, it follows that he can only think about something that is itself perfect and unchanging. This means that he can think only about himself! We noticed how Plato's reflections about God led many of his followers to a concept of an unknowable, transcendent God. Aristotle's reflections have brought us to the same spot: the concept of a radically transcendent, wholly other God who, it appears, can have no direct, personal, and essential relationship with people or the world. The Christian God is transcendent. But in opposition to thinkers like Aristotle, the God of the Christian faith is also immanent in the sense that he is with his people and his creation.

Aristotle's view of God is an excellent example of how a philosopher can be trapped by his system. We have come a long way since we started talking rather innocently about form and matter, potentiality and actuality. Once Aristotle starts down this path, once he accepts certain presuppositions, he is stuck with the view of God that follows from these prior commitments. Moreover, we are stuck with an unknowable God who cannot know anything about us or the world in which we live. While Aristotle was not an atheist, he could hardly have moved to a spot more distant from the God of Judaism and Christianity.

Ethics

In the first book (chapter) of his ethical treatise, *The Nichomachean Ethics,* probably named after his son, Nichomachus, Aristotle begins by observing that all human action is directed at an end or a goal. When we act intentionally, we act with the aim of accomplishing a particular objective. Aristotle wonders if we can discover any single goal toward which all human beings aim. Is there any single goal so superior to every other goal that it is what every human being desires? Aristotle decides the answer is yes and identifies this supreme good as happiness. The Greek word usually translated as happiness (*eudaemonia*) means more than the word usually connotes for most people. It carries with it the idea of the truly good life.

Saying that the supreme good is happiness doesn't help us much, since people disagree over the nature of happiness; there are too many conflicting notions of what happiness is. Some confuse it with pleasure, money, fame, position, or power. None of these attempted identifications is correct, however. One problem with these identifications of happiness is that all of them are but means to an end. Whatever happiness is, it must be intrinsically good, good in itself instead of merely being good as a means to something else. The opposite of an intrinsic good is an instrumental good, something that is desired because it is a means to an end. True happiness must be good as an end in itself. For this reason, Aristotle rejects money as the ground of happiness. Money possesses only instrumental value; it is good only as a means to other things. Nothing can be the highest good if it is chosen for the sake of something else. Happiness is the supreme good because it is sought for itself; it is self-sufficient, and it is that toward which all humans aim.

Whatever the supreme good is, it must also be self-sufficient. This means that it must be so good that nothing can be added to it to make it any better. This criterion disqualifies virtue as the essence of happiness. It is possible for a person to be virtuous but still be miserable because of bad health or poverty. It is possible to add other things to virtue to improve the quality of life. But this cannot be true of the supreme good. *Eudaemonia* must also be connected with humankind's distinctive feature, reason. *Eudaemonia* is acting in accord with a human being's highest virtue, reason.

Aristotle never identifies what he believes happiness is until the end of his book. It is impossible to judge a life happy until that life is over. One swallow does not make a summer, Aristotle says; likewise, one happy moment or day does not make a happy life. Only after a life is over can one evaluate that life and judge whether the person was happy.

According to Aristotle, Lear writes, "man has a nature: there is something definite and worthwhile that it is to be a human being. Happiness consists in living this noble life: in satisfying the desires that are *necessary* for man to have in order to live a full, rich life."[16]

---

16. Lear, *Aristotle,* 155.

The Virtues

Aristotle's ethical theory has nothing to say about moral law, commandments, and their relationship to God. Aristotle focuses instead on human traits of character, upon dispositions to behave in certain ways, that he discusses under the heading of virtue. As Lear explains, "The virtues are stable states of the soul which enable a person to make the right decision about how to act in the circumstances and which motivate him so to act. It is these stable states of the soul that we think of as constituting a person's character."[17] Aristotle does not write about rules, which would tell virtuous people how to live.

In book 2 of the *Nichomachean Ethics,* Aristotle distinguishes two kinds of virtue: moral and intellectual. They are virtues or excellences of different parts of the soul. There are two distinct ways in which a person can be said to excel, with respect to morality and with regard to intellectual matters. A part of us is concerned primarily with thinking and the acquisition of knowledge. Another part of us is concerned with doing what our reason tells us to do, with choosing or willing. Moral and intellectual virtues are acquired in different ways. Moral virtue is acquired by habit, while intellectual virtue is acquired by teaching.

Truly virtuous persons in the moral sense have over time developed certain traits of character or dispositions. This is done by repeating certain kinds of behavior, thus establishing a habit. If we repeat certain kinds of conduct often enough, it becomes easier to do them. Only when a person's conduct flows from a fixed and constant disposition can we regard that person as morally virtuous.

The Golden Mean

Moral virtue normally relates to behavior that is a mean between two extremes. This is sometimes called Aristotle's doctrine of the Golden Mean. Moral virtue is a mean between two extremes, both of which are vices. Consider the matter of amusing other people. One extreme kind of behavior in such cases is buffoonery. This kind of person goes much too far in an attempt to make himself popular. The other extreme, also a vice, is boorishness. Somewhere between boorishness and buffoonery is the proper mean, something Aristotle calls wittiness, namely, knowing when to be entertaining and funny and when to be serious. Other examples of the Golden Mean include

too much	just right	too little
rashness	courage	cowardice
prodigality	liberality	illiberality
flattery	friendship	moroseness
bashfulness	modesty	shamelessness

Figure 4.5

---

17. Ibid., 164.

Aristotle seems involved in a contradiction. We must do virtuous acts in order to establish a virtuous disposition. But we cannot act in a virtuous way unless our action flows from a fixed and constant disposition. How then can we ever make progress toward attaining the virtuous disposition we seek? His answer: We should perform acts that resemble virtuous acts, that resemble what we would do if we had the disposition. In this way we build up the right habits. If the disposition I wish to acquire is liberality, the way to acquire it is to ask how I would behave if I possessed the habit and continue to behave that way.

Aristotle does qualify his doctrine of the Golden Mean in some cases. Some actions are always wrong. One example he gives is adultery. In such cases, there is no golden mean.

Pleasure and the Paradox of Hedonism

The single-minded pursuit of pleasure is self-defeating.[18] Imagine a person whose entire life is directed toward the attainment of pleasure. He is totally uninterested in books, sports, music, art, companionship; all the person wants is pleasure. Will such a person ever experience much pleasure? Pleasure accompanies other activities. The more a person seeks pleasure, the less pleasure he will experience. It is the person who forgets pleasure and loses himself in other activities who suddenly finds himself experiencing pleasure.

Pleasure is an ingredient of the good life; it is a part of the good life, but it doesn't make up the whole of the good life. One cannot bake a cake without putting baking soda in it. But few of us would enjoy eating cake composed entirely of baking soda.

Concluding Thoughts

Happiness is not money, success, or pleasure. Aristotle thinks happiness is contemplation, an activity in accordance with man's highest function (reason), that is intrinsically good, only intrinsically good, and self-sufficient. Contemplation is the only activity that satisfies all of these criteria. It is also a nice coincidence that contemplation, Aristotle's recommended way of attaining happiness, happens to be the one activity God engages in. When humans contemplate, they engage in the same kind of activity as does God. True happiness consists in thinking about God. It is also comforting to know that the person most likely to achieve happiness is a philosopher like Aristotle. That coincidence may be more than some people can tolerate.

---

18. I owe this way of phrasing Aristotle's point to Dr. Joel Feinberg.

Although Aristotle was an empiricist in the sense that he believed knowledge of universals arises by abstraction from observation of particular things, he nevertheless made an important contribution to rationalism.[19] He argued for a parallelism among thought, being, and language. One of rationalism's basic convictions is the belief that the world is rational. This means that a basic conformity exists between the structure of human reason and the structure of the world. The human mind, rationalists insist, is not involved in a struggle to understand a nonrational world. The laws that govern human thought are a reflection of the necessities that can be found in nature.

Aristotle, Human Rationality, and the World

Aristotle's philosophical system is an impressive piece of work. But we must not allow this imposing structure to blind us to its problems, some of them serious. Aristotle's view of God falls far short of being satisfactory. Not only is Aristotle's God a kind of afterthought, a *deus ex machina* slipped in to account for motion in the physical universe; it also falls short of being either philosophically, morally, or religiously satisfying. One cannot help thinking that if Aristotle had forgotten to add God to his worldview, nothing much would have been different. If one's worldview beliefs about God are the most fundamental part of a worldview, Aristotle's system has little or nothing to offer.

Conclusion

Aristotle's ethical observations are commendable in many respects. As I noted earlier, the notion of virtue (good character) appears prominently in the ethical passages of the Bible. Not only is it important what we do (commands), but also it is important what kind of people we are (virtue). But is Aristotle's advice about how we attain virtuous dispositions adequate? Can we attain virtue by repeating the same kinds of behavior until we realize that we possess the virtuous habit? The New Testament claims that at least nine important Christian virtues (love, joy, peace, patience, kindness, goodness, faithfulness, gentleness, and self-control) are fruit of the Holy Spirit. Many wise students of Scripture understand that to mean that we can attain those virtuous dispositions only through the aid of the Holy Spirit (see Galatians 5:22–23). Surely much more remains to be said about becoming a virtuous person. The Christian answer to this question is included in the central Christian doctrine called sanctification.

If I am correct that Plato refuted Aristotle's kind of position in his *Phaedo,* Aristotle didn't advance the cause of empiricism; his attempt to explain our knowledge of universals such as the Equal itself by abstracting the common idea from many particular examples of equal things is disappointing when compared with Plato's critique of this position in the *Phaedo.*

---

19. See chapter 8 for details about how Aristotle did this.

Aristotle's metaphysics (in the sense of the word introduced in chapter 1 of this book) appears impressive at first glance. The emphasis upon potentiality versus actuality can have important repercussions, as can his distinction between essential and nonessential properties (see the appendix to this chapter). Aristotle's theory of primary matter may be the Achilles' heel of his metaphysical system. The apparent inconsistencies and points of vagueness in his theory of human nature are also weaknesses within his system.

In chapter 7 we'll examine the attempt of the medieval Christian thinker Thomas Aquinas to eliminate some of Aristotle's difficulties and to move Aristotelianism closer to important Christian concerns.

Appendix

Essential Properties and the Incarnation

Aristotle's distinction between essential and nonessential properties is one of the more important elements of his philosophy. One way to demonstrate its value is to see its use in solving what many people regard as one of the more difficult problems in Christian theology, the frequently alleged inconsistency between the human and divine natures of Jesus Christ.

Christians believe that Jesus Christ is fully God and fully man. Many people respond by saying that these two claims look like a contradiction. Just as no object can be both round and square at the same time, they think, so no being can be both God and man without violating the law of noncontradiction. Such thinking is mistaken. Correct thinking about Jesus Christ diminishes neither his full and complete humanity nor his full and complete deity. Jesus Christ is God—let there be no mistake about this. But he is also human. Any wavering on either claim results in a defective understanding of Jesus Christ.

The general line of attack on the two natures of Christ goes something like this: The Christian God has attributes such as omnipotence, omniscience, incorporeality, and sinlessness. God also exists necessarily, which means, among other things, that there can be neither beginning nor end to his existence. Moreover, these properties belong to God essentially or necessarily, which is to say that if God were to lose any of these essential properties, he would cease to be God. A being cannot be God if he lacks omnipotence, omniscience, and the like.

But when we reflect on the nature (essence) of humanness, we encounter creatures without such properties. Human beings are not omnipotent, omniscient, incorporeal, or sinless. Nor do we exist necessarily. Our existence is contingent—that is, dependent on many things other than ourselves. Given these seemingly obvious incompatibilities between God and man, how could any being possibly be both God and man?

This is a serious difficulty. Developing an appropriate answer to this challenge will require hard thinking about complex issues. Thomas V. Morris, a former philosophy professor at Notre Dame, has sought a solution that leaves the two-natures doctrine intact.[20]

It is one thing for a doctrine about the eternal God to surpass human understanding (Romans 11:33–35; Job 11:7–8; Isaiah 55:8–9); it is another for that belief to lack logical coherence. Because something is above reason, it does not follow that it is against reason.

According to Morris, we can work our way out of the supposed logical inconsistency of the two natures of Christ if we first understand and then properly apply three philosophical distinctions, namely,

Aristotle's distinction between essential and nonessential properties;
the distinction between essential and common properties; and
the distinction between being fully human and being merely human.

Essential and Nonessential Properties

As we know, a property is a feature or a characteristic of something. Everything has properties, and one way we refer to those properties is by using them as predicates applied to a given subject. As we also know, properties come in two types, essential and nonessential. Consider a red ball. The color of the object is nonessential in the sense that if we changed the color to yellow or green, the object would still be a ball. But with a ball, the property of roundness is an essential property. We cannot have a ball that is not round.[21] If we change this feature of our object, it is no longer a ball.

Put in its simplest terms, an essential property is one that cannot be changed or lost without the object in question ceasing to be the kind of thing it is. Roundness is an essential property of being a ball. When an object that once was a member of the class of all balls loses its roundness, it also loses its membership in that class.

A number of properties are essential to the being of God, including at least the following: necessary existence, omnipotence, omniscience, and sinlessness. Any being lacking these and the other essential properties of deity could not be God. Obviously, then, when Christians affirm that Jesus is God, they are also affirming that Jesus Christ possesses eternally and

---

20. Morris's argument appears in both a book, *The Logic of God Incarnate* (Ithaca, N.Y.: Cornell University Press, 1986), and a more popular article, "Understanding God Incarnate," *Asbury Theological Journal* 43 (1988): 63–77.

21. Some people at this point wonder about an American football (as opposed to a ball used in soccer matches). While we Americans call a football a ball, it is not round. Perhaps we can evade this essentially irrelevant objection by calling an inflated ellipsoid made of pigskin a ball because it is close enough to a real ball to show us how analogies work.

necessarily all the essential properties of God. That much is easy and should be obvious.

Matters become more difficult when we try to identify the essential properties of a human being. Aristotle thought that rationality (thinking and reasoning) is an essential property of humans. Rationality seems to be one property among others that makes up the essence of a human being, that sets humans apart from other creatures on our planet.

The mistaken critic of the Incarnation assumes that such properties as lacking omnipotence, lacking omniscience, and lacking sinlessness are also essential in some way to humanness. But to proceed further with our argument we must first introduce the distinction between essential properties and common properties.

Essential Properties and Common Properties

What Morris calls common properties are often mistaken for essential properties. This error is the basis for believing that the doctrine of the Incarnation entails a contradiction. A common property is any property that human beings typically possess without also being essential. Morris gives the example of having ten fingers. Because almost every human has ten fingers, it is a common human property. But having ten fingers is not essential to being a human being. A person can lose one or more fingers and still be a human being. Therefore the common human property of having ten fingers is not an essential property.

Likewise, we could say that being born on planet earth is a common human property. But it is conceivable that at some time in the future, some people will be born and live their entire lives on other planets. So once again, a property that we have found common to all humans turns out not to be essential.

Now, we could say that all of us—each human being apart from Jesus—are characterized by properties that are the counterparts of such divine properties as omnipotence and omniscience. But on what basis can we say that these limitations are essential to our humanness? These limitations are possibly common human properties, not essential ones.

Being Fully Human and Being Merely Human

Morris explains that "an individual is fully human [in any case where] that individual has all essential human properties, all the properties composing basic human nature. An individual is *merely human* if he or she has all those properties *plus* some additional limitation properties as well, properties such as that of lacking omnipotence, that of lacking omniscience, and so on."[22]

---

22. Morris, "Understanding God Incarnate," 66.

Orthodox Christians, Morris adds, insist on the claim that "Jesus was fully human without being merely human."[23] This means two things: Jesus possesses all the properties that are essential to being a human being, and Jesus possesses all the properties that are essential to deity. Morris also suggests that the properties critics of the Incarnation make so much of and insist are essential to humanity (such as lacking omniscience) are being confused with common human properties.

Once Christians understand these distinctions about properties, they are equipped to counter challenges to the logical coherence of the doctrine of Christ's two natures. The historic understanding of the Incarnation expresses the beliefs that Jesus Christ is fully God—that is, he possesses all the essential properties of God; Jesus Christ is also fully human—that is, he possesses all the essential properties of a human being, none of which turn out to be limiting properties; and Jesus Christ was not merely human—that is, he did not possess any of the limiting properties that are complements of the divine attributes. In the face of these distinctions, the alleged contradiction in the Incarnation disappears.

---

23. Ibid.

OPTIONAL WRITING ASSIGNMENT

Without using your book or notes, write an essay to a friend who has asked you to provide one example of the usefulness of studying Aristotle's philosophy. Either select some aspect of Aristotle's philosophy yourself or use his distinction between essential and nonessential properties as it relates to the human and divine natures of Jesus Christ.

FOR FURTHER READING

Aristotle, *The Basic Works of Aristotle,* ed. W. D. Ross (New York: Random House, 1960).

Aristotle, *A New Aristotle Reader* (Princeton, N.J.: Princeton University Press, 1987).

Renford Bambrough, *Philosophy of Aristotle* (New York: New American Library, 1963).

Jonathan Barnes, ed., *The Cambridge Companion to Aristotle* (New York: Cambridge University Press, 1995).

Abraham Edel, *Aristotle and His Philosophy* (Princeton, N.J.: Transaction, 1995).

David Ross, *Aristotle,* 6th ed. (New York: Routledge, Kegan, Paul, 1995).

Henry B. Veatch, *Aristotle: A Contemporary Appreciation* (Bloomington, Ind.: Indiana University Press, 1974).

Chapter Five

Plotinus

IMPORTANT DATES IN PLOTINUS'S LIFE

205 Plotinus is born in Upper Egypt

233 Plotinus begins study in Alexandria, Egypt

244 Plotinus starts his own school of philosophy
in Rome

253 Plotinus begins writing what became
The Enneads

270 Plotinus dies in Rome

Without question, Plotinus was the third most important philosopher of the ancient world, surpassed only by Plato and Aristotle.[1] According to classical scholar A. H. Armstrong, Plotinus is "the most vital connecting link in the history of European philosophy. . . . [He is] the philosopher in whom the Hellenic tradition in full development and maturity was brought into touch with the beginnings of Christian philosophy."[2] An overview of Plotinus's system is an essential step in understanding the worldviews of Augustine and Aquinas. But Armstrong also warns that no Greek philosopher is more difficult to understand than Plotinus.[3] One reason for this is the complexity of his thought. Another is his majestic use of the Greek language, a fact that explains the difficulties translators have had rendering his ideas in other languages. "There are passages in the Enneads," Armstrong writes, "which rank with the greatest philosophical writing of any age and country and which in some ways go beyond the range of Plato himself."[4]

---

1. By the ancient world, I include the centuries before the birth of Augustine in 354.

2. A. H. Armstrong, *The Architecture of the Intelligible Universe in the Philosophy of Plotinus* (Cambridge: Cambridge University Press, 1940), 120.

3. A. H. Armstrong, *An Introduction to Ancient Philosophy* (Boston: Beacon, 1967), 176.

4. Armstrong, *Architecture of the Intelligible Universe*, 1.

For Plotinus, philosophy and religion are inseparable. Plotinus developed a system that contained both a speculative account of the world and a religious doctrine of salvation. As Samuel Stumpf explains, Plotinus "not only described the world, but also gave an account of its source, of man's place in it, and of how man overcomes his moral and spiritual difficulties in it. In short, Plotinus developed a doctrine about God as the source of all things and as that to which man must return."[5] Of course, one of the first lessons in philosophy is to learn that things are not always what they seem. In Plotinus's case, it would be wise for traditional Christian believers not to conclude that Plotinus is an ally.

Plotinus believed his system was faithful to the most important work of Plato and Aristotle. What might seem new in his system was only what Plotinus viewed as carrying Plato's and Aristotle's ideas to their logical conclusions. As Plotinus advanced in age, his thinking on some issues changed. There is no need to track these changes in detail. I will focus instead on what are usually described as the central beliefs of Plotinus.

The Life of Plotinus

Plotinus was born in Upper Egypt in 205, learned the Greek language and culture, and began to study philosophy in Alexandria, Egypt. He then traveled in Asia in the hope of encountering firsthand the ideas of Persian and Indian thinkers. By 244 his travels brought him to Rome, where he started a school of philosophy.

Plotinus didn't start to write until nearly his fiftieth birthday; even then his writings were intended primarily for his small circle of followers. After his death, possibly from leprosy, his student Porphyry organized Plotinus's writings into six books containing nine treatises each. For this reason, to emphasize the number nine, they were named *The Enneads*. Porphyry's organization created some problems because he arranged the writings by subject, which often meant that individual documents were broken apart and placed into different *Enneads*. Porphyry sometimes cut and spliced material written during different stages of Plotinus's life, often without attention to contradictions and changes in his thinking. This is another reason why Plotinus is so difficult to read.

The six *Enneads* deal with ethics (*Ennead* 1), the philosophy of nature and the material universe (2 and 3), Soul (4), Mind or Intelligence (5), and his First Principle, the One (6). Even philosophers appreciative of Plotinus's work admit that there are many serious difficulties in his writings, including a number of inconsistencies along with a fair amount of confusion.[6] It is possible, Armstrong says, to find in Plotinus's writings "several divergent and not completely reconcilable constructions of real-

5. Samuel Stumpf, *Socrates to Sartre: A History of Philosophy,* 4th ed. (New York: McGraw-Hill, 1988), 125.

6. See Armstrong, *Architecture of the Intelligible Universe,* 1.

ity. These are not of course clearly separable. They blend into each other and intermix in a most disconcerting way."[7]

The complexity of Plotinus's worldview is so daunting that I have decided to work through his system two times. The first approach will be a brief overview. The second will start at the beginning with Plotinus's God and provide enough details to make his system understandable, even if several readings of my account are necessary.

The Downward Path of Being

Plotinus pictures reality as a series of layers, each derived from the layers above it. One way to picture Plotinus's universe is to think of a multitiered fountain. Water flows out at the top of the fountain and fills the highest basin to overflowing. As water overflows the top of the highest basin, it drops into a second basin. When the second level fills up, the water overflows to still a third level, and so on.

Plotinus explains the world in terms of a downward movement from his supreme principle, the One (Plotinus's God). Everything that exists is tied in some way to Plotinus's ultimate principle, the One. But there is also an upward climb as the soul tries to free itself from the domination of the body and find its way back to its natural domain, the realm of God and eternal truth.

The Highest Level of Plotinus's Hierachy: God or the One

At the apex of Plotinus's universe is a supreme, transcendent, and unknowable God whom he calls the One or the Good. This God is so far above and different from anything we humans can know that human language is incapable of expressing any literal truth about it. The perfection of the One overflows and brings about the lower levels of being. As Plotinus says, "No beings would exist if The One remained shut up in itself."[8]

The Level of Mind or Intelligence *(Nous)*

The first level that emanates or flows out from the One is Mind or Intelligence. The Greek word used by Plotinus is *Nous.* One way to understand *Nous* is to think of it as the result of God's thinking. Several philosophers between Plato and Plotinus[9] had gone beyond Plato and

---

7. Ibid.

8. Plotinus *Ennead* 4.8.6 in *The Essential Plotinus,* ed. and trans. Elmer O'Brien, S.J. (New York: Mentor, 1964), 68. Unless otherwise indicated, translations of Plotinus are from this work, which is the most accessible and least expensive collection of Plotinian texts. Although it is incomplete, the book contains many of Plotinus's important passages.

9. Examples include various thinkers identified as Middle Platonists, as well as the Jewish thinker Philo (died about A.D. 50). For more information about Middle Platonism and

interpreted Plato's Forms as eternal ideas in the mind of God. Plotinus picks up this suggestion and carries it further than did his predecessors.

The Level of Soul

Just as the One gives rise to the level of Mind, Mind in turn gives rise to the level of Soul. The Greek and Latin words for soul are *psuche* and *anima*. Plotinus's separation of mind and soul is reminiscent of the similar distinction in Aristotle's system. While Plotinus thinks of Soul here in Aristotle's sense of life, Soul is linked essentially to Mind.

Bodies and (Primary) Matter

Far below the levels of God (the One), Mind (*Nous*), and Soul exist the large number of bodies or physical entities in the universe. And below them lurks the primary matter that we encountered in Aristotle's system. In a way that is difficult to understand, the level of Body flows from the level of Soul.

The Place of Human Beings

Explaining where and how human beings fit into all this takes some time. For now, let us be content with the statement that humans participate on the levels of Mind, Soul, and Body. While that statement may have a familiar ring to many readers and may seem simple, be forewarned that explaining the previous statement will prove to be an extremely complex task

Summary

With these fundamental levels of being before us, we are ready for what some call Plotinus's downward path of being. Reality is composed of various orders or levels that descend from the One, Plotinus's name for God. The One produces by emanation (a term we will explain later) first the level of Mind or Intelligence, which in turn produces the level of Soul, which gives rise to the particular bodies that have existed in the universe. According to the downward path of becoming, all of reality is a progressive emanation or movement away from the One.

The Upward Path of Salvation

According to the upward path of salvation, the human attainment of knowledge, virtue, and salvation requires that we find the way to gain deliverance from the domination of the body and achieve unity with the One. As long as humans are concerned with their bodies and sensation,

Philo, see Ronald H. Nash, *The Gospel and the Greeks* (Richardson, Tex.: Probe Books, 1992), chaps. 2, 5, 6. Additional information about Philo can be found in Ronald H. Nash, *The Meaning of History* (Nashville: Broadman and Holman, 1998).

their souls will remain enchained and entombed, like the prisoners in Plato's cave. The greatly simplified diagram that follows pictures the basic information contained in our first journey through Plotinus's system.

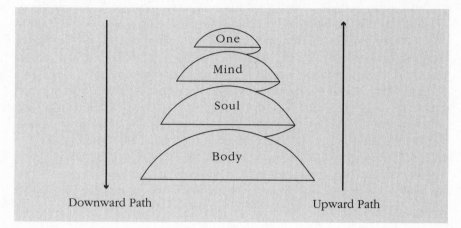

Figure 5.1

Additional Detail About Plotinus's System

The One

Plotinus's view of God is extremely difficult to grasp. What did Plotinus mean by referring to God as the One? It seems clear he meant to suggest that God is pure, undifferentiated unity, that is, contains no parts. Plotinus also taught that the One is "above being," that is, it lies beyond all of the levels of being noted in the previous section. This means at least two things: the One is transcendent, that is, wholly separate from and above everything else that exists, including even Plato's Forms; and since the One is above being, it cannot possess any qualities or properties, which amounts to saying that the One is unknowable.

As soon as we attribute any property or characteristic to the One, we effectively deny its unity. If we say "the One is _____," we introduce dualism into the One via the distinction between subject and predicate. And as soon as dualism is introduced into the nature of the One, it is no longer one. Examples of words that some (not Plotinus) would use to fill in the blank are "good," "all-knowing," "love," and "perfect." According to Plotinus, we must not attribute even existence to the One.

To say that God is One entails that God is transcendent and simple (without parts) and contains no potentialities or the limitations of body. God transcends all distinctions. God cannot even think in a way that implies a distinction between thoughts. The One possesses immediate self-awareness.[10]

---

10. See *Ennead* 5.4.2.

Many well-known thinkers have attempted to make God unknow-able.[11] However, this is a rather risky thing to try, since every one of these thinkers proceeded to produce a string of information about this sup-posedly unknowable deity. Plotinus himself knows quite a few things about his unknowable God. Consider the following quote from Plotinus: "As the One begets all things, it cannot be any of them—neither thing, nor quality, nor quantity, nor intelligence, nor soul."[12] How can a person know what God is not, without first knowing what God is?

First, Plotinus knew his unknowable God existed. That's an important piece of information. Second, he knew his unknowable God was unknowable. This statement has all the appearances of a logically self-defeating claim. Third, Plotinus knew there was one God, not two or twenty or thousands, as in the case of some religions that he knew about. The next thing Plotinus seems to know about his unknowable God is that he or it is immaterial and mental. Plotinus also knew that the One is not a Mind, though it gives rise to Mind (*Nous*).

An Explanation of Emanation

What gives rise to the various levels of being we have noticed? Plotinus would have rejected the Christian doctrine of *creation ex nihilo,* if he ever knew of it. He certainly rejected a literal interpretation of Plato's theory of creation as presented in the *Timaeus*. Plotinus explains the relationship of the levels of Mind and Soul to the One as a result of what he called *emanation*.

Stumpf explains the context for the theory of emanation:

> If God is One, He cannot create, for creation is an act, and activity, said Plotinus, implies change. Then how can we account for the many things of the world? Striving to maintain a consistent view of the Unity of God, Plotinus explained the origin of things by saying that they come from God, not through a free act of creation but through necessity. To express what he meant by "necessity," Plotinus used several metaphors, espe-cially the metaphor of *emanation*. Things emanate, they flow from God the way light emanates from the sun, the way water flows from a spring that has no source outside itself. The sun is never exhausted, it does not *do* anything, it just *is;* and being what it is, it necessarily emanates light. In this way, God is the source of everything, and everything manifests God. But nothing is equal to God, any more than the rays of light equal in any way the sun.[13]

---

11. For examples, see Ronald H. Nash, *The Word of God and the Mind of Man* (Phillips-burg, N.J.: Presbyterian and Reformed, 1992).

12. *Ennead* 6.9.9.

13. Stumpf, *Socrates to Sartre,* 126. See *Enneads* 1.7.1; 5.3.12.

I have already introduced the image of a multileveled fountain with each successive level overflowing to produce the lower levels. It is time to introduce a different illustration, namely, rays of light emanating from a source of light such as the sun or a candle.

Plotinus uses the imagery of emanation, of light radiating out from a primary source, to suggest that both God and the world (all of the levels of being that emanate from the One) are co-eternal. If we assume that the source of the light is eternal, the rays of light emanating from the source must also be eternal. And so the eternal One has always been producing the eternal level of *Nous* or Mind; the eternal *Nous* has always been giving rise to the eternal level of Soul and the other levels of being. The progression from the One to Mind occurs spontaneously without any choosing, willing, planning, or any activity by the One. Plotinus believes that if something is perfect, it necessarily gives rise to other things.

And so, the worlds of intellect, soul, and body emanate from God without diminishing God in any way. But the One does not do this willingly. It is necessary and unavoidable that if something is full, then it must overflow. The process of emanation means that what would have remained mere potentiality within the One is actualized in the world.

Nous (Mind)

As we have seen, the perfect nature of the One overflows and necessarily gives rise to the existence of lower levels of being. The first level that emanates from the One is *Nous* or Intelligence. In Plotinus's system, *Nous* is the residence of Plato's eternal ideas or Forms. The Forms are eternal thoughts of God. While no multiplicity or differentiation exists at the level of the One,[14] multiplicity does exist at the level of Mind or Intellect. This multiplicity is seen, for example, in Plato's Forms, which exist at this level.

We can now add a new wrinkle to Plotinus's doctrine of Intelligence. Plotinus came to distinguish at least two levels of Mind, the higher and the lower. We can simplify things if we view the upper level of Mind as the mind of God that contains Plato's Forms. Even though we may think of this upper level of *Nous* as the mind or thoughts of God, it is distinct from the One. As an example, focus for a while on some object of your own thinking, such as the proposition "the square root of twenty-five is five." While this

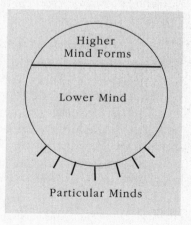

Figure 5.2

Higher Mind Forms

Lower Mind

Particular Minds

---

14. If such did exist at its level, the One would no longer be one.

proposition is not identical with your mind, it could not exist (in the sense that it is one of your thoughts) unless your mind exists.

Each particular intelligence in the world is an extension of the cosmic *Nous*. There is an ontological connection[15] between the mind of particular creatures and the mind of God (*Nous*). Every particular intelligence is an extension of the mind of God. This gave Plotinus an answer to Plato's question about how human minds know the eternal Forms. Humans know the Forms because their own minds are an extension of the cosmic *Nous* that is the natural home of the Forms.

One possible analogy would be that of a tornado that descends from a storm cloud and then ascends back to the cloud. When humans die, their *nous* or intellect is absorbed into the cosmic *Nous* from whence it came. You should now be in a position to understand the following quotations from Plotinus:

> The Intelligence dwells entire within that region of thought we call the intelligible realm, yet it comprises within itself a variety of intellective powers and particular intelligences. The Intelligence is not merely one: it is one and many. In the same way is there both Soul and many souls. From the one Soul proceeds a multiplicity of different souls . . . some of which are more rational and others (at least in their actual existence) less rational in form.[16]

> Again, in the intelligible realm there is The Intelligence [*Nous*] which like some huge organism contains potentially all other intelligences, and there are the individual intelligences, each of them an actuality. Think of a city as having a soul. The soul of the city would be the more perfect and more powerful. What would prevent the souls of the inhabitants from being of the same nature as the soul of the city? Or, again, take fire, the universal, from which proceed large and small particular fires; all of them have a common essence, that of universal fire. . . . [17]

Soul

The third level of Plotinus's universe is Soul, which Plotinus relates to Plato's World Soul, encountered earlier as the Demiurge in Plato's myth of creation. Like Aristotle, Plotinus separates mind and soul. Each particular soul (living thing) is an extension of the cosmic Soul. Just as Aristotle distinguished between vegetative, animal, and rational souls, so Plotinus believes that living plants possess a vegetative soul; living animals possess both a vegetative and a sensitive soul; and humans possess vegetative and sensitive souls plus a rational soul. All three levels of soul

---

15. An ontological connection is a link or tie in the realm of being and not just thought.
16. Plotinus *Ennead* 4.8. 6.
17. Ibid.

are extensions of the cosmic Soul. As one moves down the various levels of soul, there is increasing multiplicity. The world contains more bodies than souls, more souls than minds, and so on. Elmer O'Brien explains that "as The Intelligence has within it many intelligences, so The Soul has within itself many souls; from The Soul must come souls differing in the degree of their rationality for only thus can there be a traded hierarchy of animate beings."[18]

Plotinus thinks there are three levels of soul.

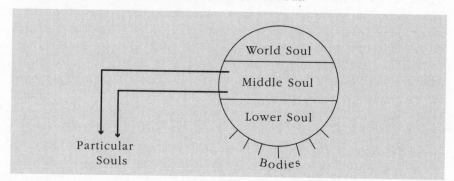

Figure 5.3

The upper level is a cosmic or World Soul, which helps explain motion and change in the world. The middle level is Plotinus's source for every particular instance of life in the universe. Each concrete instance of life or soul is an extension of or emanation from the cosmic or World Soul. When the living being dies, its soul is reabsorbed into the World Soul.

In ways that are anything but clear, the lowest level of Soul gives rise to body in general and to specific bodies. Only the lowest level of Soul is the source of matter that enters into direct contact with bodies.[19]

Human souls exist on the middle level of Soul, along with all the other particular souls existing in the universe. Plotinus rejects the materialistic theories of the soul advanced by the Stoics and the Epicureans. Even though he also rejects the kind of reincarnation Plato presented in his *Phaedo,* Plotinus does teach that human souls are immortal and exist prior to their embodiment in this world. For Plotinus, the soul is a substance that exists in its own right; that is, it can exist independently of the body. Sensation depends upon the immortal and immaterial soul working in harmony with the body.

The souls of particular human beings that emanate from the World Soul also contain a higher and lower element. The higher human soul has its home in the cosmic mind or *Nous.* The lower human soul is connected with its body. Human souls exist before their union with the body.

---

18. O'Brien, *The Essential Plotinus,* 60.
19. See *Enneads* 4.3.19; 4.8.2.

The linking of the preexisting soul and its body is described as a fall. Just as the soul preexists the body, it continues to exist after physical death; it seems that the soul has no memories of its incarnation.

Let me pause to draw your attention to the rapidly developing complexity of Plotinus's universe. Just a few minutes ago, or so it seemed, we were focusing on the pure, undifferentiated unity of the One. Before we could blink, a cosmic mind, millions of particular minds, a world soul, billions of particular souls, and added billions of bodies are bumping into each other, like so many atoms in a crowded subway train, all of them owing their being to a sublimely perfect being who gave rise to all of this without wanting to, without willing to, and without doing anything.

Plotinus did assert the existence of Forms of individual humans and other forms of life.[20] This ad hoc move had the result of giving each individual human soul its own niche in the realm of *Nous*. For Plotinus, it is not matter that grounds human individuality but this unique kind of Form possessed by immortal souls. The souls of individual persons are immortal.[21]

Plotinus's view of immortality encompasses more than just future existence. It also requires the eternal existence or divinity of the soul. According to Gordon H. Clark, "If the soul in eternity past lived in the celestial regions with the intelligible realities, how can it be explained that the soul has left its heavenly abode and has become incarcerated in the body as in a tomb? And if now incarcerated, an ethical theory must describe the way of escape."[22]

Plotinus is less concerned with explaining the joining of soul and body in the human person than with showing that the union of body and soul does not compromise the divinity of the soul during that union. Plotinus's way of defending the divinity of the soul depends on his arguing that in spite of the soul's union with the body, the human soul is never truly disjoined from the World Soul.

The human soul's unbroken union with the cosmic Soul allows Plotinus to believe that our eternal soul roams throughout the celestial regions and helps govern the universe. Consequently, the soul's entrance into union with a physical body is not an instance of evil. The soul is always superior to an inferior body. Humans must take care not to allow the inferior body to pull the soul down from its lofty position. But these previous comments represent only a part of Plotinus's thinking about the human soul. During the soul's incarnation in a body, it ceases to remain entirely in the heavenly realm. We are deeply immersed in an assortment of ambiguous opinions.

---

20. *Ennead* 5.7.

21. See *Enneads* 4.3.5; 6.4.4.

22. Gordon H. Clark, *Thales to Dewey,* 2d ed. (Unicoi, Tenn.: The Trinity Foundation, 1989), 173.

Soul, Body, and Matter

Below the level of Soul lies the material world of bodies. It is helpful to take Plotinus's imagery of light radiating from a central source another step or two. Plotinus explains the presence of matter in the universe in a similar way. Total darkness (the absence of light) is primary matter. While matter is an important factor in the existence of the physical world, at its most distant state from the One it ends up being the bottom stage of the universe. It is something like the extreme opposite of the One.

Only light exists; nonbeing is darkness. The light closest to the sun is always the brightest. The closer one gets to God, the more concentrated being (light) is. The further one moves away from God, the more diffused being (light) is.

The first emanation from the One (*Nous*) is much brighter than the level of Soul, which is far brighter than the level of body. The more distant some existing thing is from its source, the One, the closer it comes to nonbeing (darkness). At the most distant fringes of being—the point at which lies the indiscernible difference between being and nonbeing, between the dimmest light and darkness—we arrive at primary matter. At the lowest level of reality is primary matter, which trembles on the verge of nothingness. As being's journey away from the One reaches its outer limits, the darkness that is reached eventually becomes indistinguishable from nothingness.

This is as good a place as any to pause and examine a more detailed picture of Plotinus's universe:

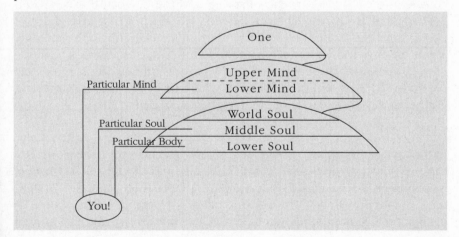

Figure 5.4

The Upward Path of Salvation

Neoplatonism is both a philosophy and a religion. Corresponding to the downward path of becoming is Plotinus's upward path of salvation. The ultimate goal for humans should be union with the One, but in order to attain this union the soul must rise upward; it must free itself from its bondage to the body, pleasure, and sensation. As the soul leaves behind the realm of sensation, it comes closer to its ultimate goal, the One. Plotinus's debt to Plato should be obvious. As long as humans are concerned with their bodies and sensation, their soul is enchained and entombed, like the prisoners in Plato's cave. Humans who truly yearn for union with the One can do only so much to bring themselves to the brink. Rarely, at unexpected times, this or that human being may suddenly experience a mystical vision of the One.

In the words of Plotinus, "Because what the soul seeks is The One and it would look upon the source of all reality, namely the Good and the One, it must not withdraw from the primal realm and sink down to the lowest realm. Rather must it withdraw from sense objects, of the lowest existence, and turn to those of the highest. It must free itself from all evil since it aspires to rise to the good."[23]

Other images from Plato's cave reappear in Plotinus's account of the soul's ascent. Like Plato, Plotinus holds that the objects of the mind can be seen only in an intelligible light from the One. Indeed, the mind can see both the light and its source.[24] However, unlike Plato, Plotinus puts the One above Goodness.[25] Speaking of what happens when the soul rises to the level of Mind, Plotinus writes: "So ascending, the soul will come first to The Intelligence and will survey all the beautiful Ideas therein and will avow their beauty, for it is by these ideas that there comes all beauty else, by the offspring and the essence of The Intelligence. What is beyond The Intelligence we affirm to be the nature of good, radiating beauty before it."[26] And to quote Plotinus one final time about the mystical encounter with the One: "There one, in the solitude of self, beholds simplicity and purity, the existence upon which all depends, towards which all look, by which reality is, life is, thought is. For the Good is the cause of life, of thought, of being."[27]

Evil

In the following chapter, we will learn how Plotinus's thinking about evil came to have a significant impact in the life and thought of Augustine. Nonetheless, serious tensions and apparent inconsistencies occur in Plotinus's treatment of evil. He carries certain implications of his theory of emanation through to their ultimate conclusion when he says that as light

---

23. *Ennead* 6.9.3.
24. *Ennead* 5.5.7.
25. See *Ennead* 6.9.4.
26. *Ennead* 1.6.9.
27. *Ennead* 1.6.7.

(which means the successive emanations from the One) gets progressively farther away from its source, it becomes increasingly diffused, thus giving rise to greater degrees of darkness. In this way he suggests we should think of evil as the absence of goodness, just as darkness is the absence of light.

But Plotinus also tells us that the kind of being that lies farthest from the One is primary matter, which "trembles on the verge of nothingness." Philip Merlan sets out the problem that Plotinus creates for himself. "To explain the origin of evil, Plotinus tries to reconcile the view that matter, though void of any quality and actually only deficiency, is still evil in some sense of the word and is the source of all evil.... In so doing, he sometimes comes dangerously close to the Gnostic theory that matter imprisons the soul ... and to a completely dualistic system."[28] In such a view, matter becomes the principle of evil. Is it necessary to point out how any move toward dualism would introduce serious incoherence into Plotinus's system, turn him into a Gnostic (a movement he explicitly opposed), and turn his talk about the One into empty rhetoric?

Philosophers representing the movement known as Middle Platonism had argued whether primary matter actively contributed to the existence of evil or whether it was an inactive entity without form that was neutral regarding evil. Plotinus inconsistently sides with both positions. He defended this view that goodness is linked to form; because primary matter is devoid of form, the absence of form in its case seems to link it to evil.[29] This seems to push Plotinus toward a form of dualism in which good and evil exist confrontationally as co-eternal and coequal principles. This appears to be a contradiction. Clearly wishing to avoid any appearance of dualism, Plotinus rejects the belief that matter exists on its own and argues instead that matter is the most distant point from the One, the point at which all emanations from the One disappear into the darkness of nonbeing.[30] The evil found in matter is not a positive force,[31] like the evil darkness of Manicheanism. It is an absence of being that passes its deficiencies on to the bodies that could not exist without it. In this way primary matter becomes the reason for all of the imperfections of the physical world. It also accounts for the moral failings of particular human souls.[32]

---

28. Philip Merlan, in *The Encyclopedia of Philosophy* (New York: Macmillan, 1967), 5:358.

29. See *Enneads* 1.8.10; 2.4.16.

30. See *Enneads* 1.8.7; 2.5.5; 3.4.1; 4.3.9.

31. See *Enneads* 1.8.3; 2.5.16; 3.16.14.

32. See *Ennead* 1.8.4.

Some Problems with Plotinus's Worldview

Our investigation of Plotinus's worldview has put us in touch with much that is impressive. Nonetheless, we must be faithful to our mission and not allow ourselves to be deterred from evaluating his worldview.

As much as he would like to avoid any suggestion that particular souls descend into evil, Plotinus cannot escape the fact that his own words imply that souls do. While in its bodily tomb, the soul becomes involved with evil, suffering, troubles, fears, and desires. Plotinus also uses language that implies that individual souls grow weary of being in the realm of the World Soul. Consequently, particular souls choose to break away from the World Soul and come under the control of the physical senses. While Plotinus's notion of the fall of the human soul involves human freedom in some obscure sense, it is also necessitated by God. One must continue to press by asking if Plotinus ever explains any of this. Does his position on the fall of the soul contain points that are inconsistent with other emphases of his teaching?

While the fall of the soul allows it to learn about evil, Plotinus believes no harm is involved if the soul refuses to linger in its union with body. For Plotinus, the fall of soul produces something of great value because it makes it possible for the potentialities of vegetative and sensitive souls to be realized; without this fall, the vegetative and sensitive souls would exist without any real purpose.

Obviously it would have been best for the soul to remain in the higher world. We must remember, however, that soul is by nature an intermediary between two worlds, the world of Intelligence above it and the world of body below. The soul must contact the physical world; it must contact the reality of the senses. While the descent of the soul brings it into contact with evil, this has the advantage of enhancing its understanding of the good. No soul is hopelessly lost in the realm of bodily sensation. The possibility of salvation is always there. But what does this mean, and is there anything that grounds such speculation? Taken together, Plotinus's assorted opinions about the fall of the soul appears to involve the fall of his system into incoherence.

Plotinus's propensity toward complexity and apparent contradictions surfaces when he teaches that particular human souls have some kind of union in the World Soul.[33] As much as this seems to entail a denial of personal immortality, Plotinus insists that each human soul is real and immortal. He refuses to believe that the historical Socrates ceases to exist as Socrates because his soul has left the body. But Plotinus is not content to claim that Socrates is as immortal as the World Soul. He also believes in the immortality of the souls of plants and animals.[34] It is easy to reach a

---

33. See *Ennead* 3.5.4.
34. Clark, *Thales to Dewey,* 173.

point at which one thinks that the best way to introduce rigor into Plotinus's mature position on immortality is to hold that all souls of plants and animals lose their identity and become part of the World Soul. And if this is the fate of cockroaches and tomato plants, consistency requires one to believe that this is also what becomes of Socrates, in spite of what Plotinus says about Socrates' immortality. Remember that the denial of personal immortality became an essential feature of the kind of Neoplatonism taught by medieval Muslim philosophers like Averroës.

In its final, ultimate form, salvation is not a matter of what one knows; it occurs instead in the form of a mystical trance. The mind of the human thinker is absorbed briefly, unconsciously, ineffably into the One. During this mystical trance, persons lose all awareness of the body. Indeed, there disappears any awareness that the thinker is human or real. This is hardly surprising during a state in which all distinctions disappear. After the trance is over, the person cannot report any information about the experience. But should we not be wary when we are invited to make a blind leap into the arms or lap of an unknowable deity? How do we know the entity that catches us will turn out to be the Good rather than some evil and sinister being?

The existence of the world requires movement beyond pure unity into the reality of multiplicity. Philosopher Gordon H. Clark finds much to criticize in Plotinus's erratic handling of the problem of the One and the Many. "If the first principle is a pure One," Clark asks, "how can the production of multiplicity be made intelligible? Illustrations of mirrors and shining lights do not suffice. If multiplicity and distinctions were in the One, even virtually, the One could not be pure Unity; but if there were no multiplicity in the One, how could it come out of the One?"[35] Plotinus simply and dogmatically asserts that it must. Plotinus's system, it seems clear, is a creation of his metaphors. Clark and others have pointed out that the Christian doctrine of the Trinity offers a distinctly different and far more promising approach to the problem of the One and the Many, to the relationship between unity and multiplicity. The triune God himself is both one and many, three eternal and divine centers of consciousness in one eternal divine nature.

Armstrong raises further objections to Plotinus's work. (1) Plotinus unnecessarily multiplies the number of entities in his system. (2) Plotinus attempts "to provide a comprehensible and coherent connection at points where the reason seems to show not a connection but a gulf, or at least a connection not comprehensible to the human intellect. Plotinus shares the common Hellenic fault of wishing to make reality too tidy, a fault which is after all only an exaggeration of a fundamental virtue, the desire

---

35. Ibid., 180.

to find a rational order in things that will make coherent thought about reality possible."[36] Armstrong is very critical of the theory of emanation. "The relation between the Absolute and relative and derived beings must always remain mysterious," he writes, "because one term of it is inaccessible to our knowledge and because it is necessarily a unique relation about which we can form no general concept. The wise philosopher will be content to note that there is at this point a gulf or cleft in being and leave it at that."[37]

It looks as though Plotinus's only reason for placing a cosmic Soul below the levels of the One and *Nous* to rule the physical world was his blind commitment to the legacy of Plato. The assorted functions that Plotinus assigns to the One, *Nous,* and Soul could have been attributed to one transcendent God. The simplification and coherence so needed in Plotinus will appear decades later in the philosophy of Augustine. As great as Plotinus's philosophical system building was in many respects, we can do better; and several philosophers have.

When we study Augustine, a man whose conversion to Christianity had much to do with his discovery of Neoplatonism, we will find ourselves in an entirely different religious arena. Augustine insists, quite properly, that the God of the Christian faith is a God who reveals himself, who makes himself known in revealed propositions but even more spectacularly in the person and work of his eternally divine Son.

---

36. Armstrong, *Architecture of the Intelligible Universe,* 114.
37. Ibid, 119.

OPTIONAL WRITING ASSIGNMENT

Without consulting your text or notes, write an essay comparing Plotinus's upward path of salvation with elements of Plato's allegory of the cave. As is true of all writing assignments, you should read the text material carefully and take notes. But once the writing begins, it must be done without consulting other material.

FOR FURTHER READING

A. H. Armstrong, *An Introduction to Ancient Philosophy* (Boston: Beacon, 1967).

A. H. Armstrong, *The Architecture of the Intelligible Universe in the Philosophy of Plotinus* (Cambridge: Cambridge University Press, 1940).

Emile Brehier, *Philosophy of Plotinus* (Chicago: University of Chicago Press, 1958).

Lloyd P. Gerson, *The Cambridge Companion to Plotinus* (New York: Cambridge University Press, 1996).

Plotinus, *The Essential Plotinus*, ed. and trans. Elmer O'Brien, S.J. (New York: Mentor, 1964).

J. M. Rist, *Plotinus: The Road to Reality* (Cambridge: Cambridge University Press, 1967).

R. T. Wallis, *Neo-Platonism* (New York: Charles Scribner's Sons, 1972)

Chapter Six

Augustine

IMPORTANT DATES IN AUGUSTINE'S LIFE

354 Augustine is born in North Africa

371 Augustine makes his first visit to Carthage

372 Augustine takes a mistress

373 Augustine's son, Adeodatus, is born; Augustine begins a nine-year attachment to Manicheanism

383 Augustine crosses the sea to Rome with his mistress and son

384 Augustine assumes the post of public orator at Milan; separates from his mistress

386 Augustine is converted and writes the first of his extant books, including *Against the Skeptics* and *Soliloquies*

387 Augustine is baptized in Milan

388 Augustine returns to North Africa

391 Augustine is ordained as a priest

395 Augustine is consecrated as bishop of Hippo Regius

400 Augustine completes his *Confessions*

410 Rome is sacked

413 Augustine begins writing *The City of God*

430 Augustine dies during the Vandals' siege of Hippo Regius

Augustine was the last major thinker of the ancient world and the first philosopher and theologian of the Middle Ages. His work is the bridge that links ancient philosophy and early Christian theology to the thought patterns of the Middle Ages. His work is still a model for those Christian thinkers who would use Platonism as a framework for their

Christian world-and-life view. Many ideas that received emphasis in the work of the Protestant Reformers were anticipated by Augustine. But his views of the church and the sacraments played a role in the development of doctrines that are distinctly Roman Catholic. Among the areas of Christian thought where Augustine's ideas are still much studied are the relationship between faith and reason, the problem of evil, divine grace and predestination, the doctrine of the Trinity, and the philosophy of history.

Augustine's life is a key to understanding his thought. He was born in 354 in what is now northeastern Algeria. Centuries before, Augustine's homeland had been a part of the great Carthaginian Empire that almost conquered Rome. After Rome defeated the Carthaginian army and its general, Hannibal, Carthage became romanized in culture and language, even though the everyday language of the common people remained Punic.

Augustine was born and reared in Thagaste, some distance from Carthage and the Mediterranean Sea. Augustine's father, Patricius, was not a Christian during his youth and had relatively little influence on him. But his mother, Monica, was a devout Christian and played an important role in his life, even during the years when he rejected her Christianity.

From the time of his first visit to Carthage, when he was about sixteen, Augustine exhibited a persistent weakness in matters of sexual sin. He took a mistress when he was seventeen or eighteen and fathered an illegitimate son before he was twenty. About that same time, he began a relationship with a religious and philosophical system known as Manicheanism. This system postulated the existence of two eternal and equally powerful gods, one of them good (Light) and the other evil (Darkness). Manicheanism appealed to Augustine because it appeared to offer a superior answer to the problem of evil than he could find in his mother's Christianity. Augustine was also drawn to Manicheanism because it made fewer moral demands on his life than did Christianity. He could be a good Manichean and continue to live as he pleased. During his late twenties, Augustine could no longer ignore serious doubts he had had about Manicheanism. He eventually abandoned Manicheanism, even though he delayed making his rejection public so as not to alienate powerful Manichean friends whose influence could help his career. His turn away from Manichean dualism was a major worldview shift for the young man. Once his education in Carthage was completed, Augustine earned a living teaching rhetoric in Carthage. He grew restless because of the poor quality of his students and their rowdiness in his classes.

Planning to shift the location of his teaching to Rome, Augustine crossed the Mediterranean in 383 with his mistress and son. But because his students in Rome were often delinquent in paying fees, he left Rome

Augustine's Life

Saint Augustine

for Milan in 384. Milan was the summer residence of the emperor and his court and offered Augustine many opportunities for advancement in the government. Strongly recommended by Manichean friends in high places, Augustine was given the position of public orator, a possible stepping-stone to even greater things.

While he was in Milan, Augustine became friendly with Ambrose, the bishop of Milan, who was reputed to be the greatest orator in the empire. Ambrose helped Augustine to see that many of his objections to Christianity were based on misconceptions of the faith. For example, Augustine once complained to Ambrose that the God of the Bible had a body. When Ambrose asked where Augustine had read such a thing, Augustine referred to Genesis 3:8 and its claim that the Lord God "was walking in the garden in the cool of the day." Ambrose responded that he was amazed to be standing in the presence of a teacher of rhetoric who could not recognize nonliteral language. The simple recognition that the Bible sometimes uses figures of speech and nonliteral language eliminated many of Augustine's misconceptions about Scripture.

By then Augustine had replaced his Manichean worldview with the strange variety of skepticism that had taken control of Plato's Academy. His experiment with skepticism ended with his discovery of the writings of certain Platonists, a term that seems to encompass Plotinus and some of his followers. Ironically Augustine's study of Neoplatonism[1] helped to remove many of the remaining intellectual obstacles to his becoming a Christian. For one thing, the Neoplatonists taught him how evil could exist in a world that depended for its existence on one perfectly good God. Following this lead, Augustine came to think of evil as the privation of goodness, much as darkness is the absence of light.

Augustine found that his assorted intellectual objections to Christianity had been stripped away. The obstacles that remained concerned his reluctance to renounce his moral failings. In 386, in a villa outside of Rome, he underwent one of the more dramatic conversions in the history of the Christian church. After hearing a voice say, "Take up and read," Augustine recounts how he opened the Bible at random and his finger landed on Paul's words in Romans 13:13–14.

> I seized it [the New Testament] and opened it, and in silence I read the first passage on which my eyes fell. "No orgies or drunkenness, no fighting or jealousy. Take up the weapons of the Lord Jesus Christ; and stop giving attention to your sinful nature, to satisfy its desires." I had no wish to read more and no need to do so. For in an instant, as I came to the

---

1. The name *Neoplatonism* is a relatively modern invention, designed to distinguish the thought of Plotinus and his followers from the older views of Plato and the intermediate position of thinkers now called Middle Platonism.

end of the sentence, it was as though the light of faith flooded into my heart and all the darkness of doubt was dispelled.[2]

By this time Augustine had separated from his mistress, who had returned to North Africa leaving their son, Adeodatus, with him. After being baptized in 387, Augustine determined to return to North Africa with his son and Monica, who had joined him in Italy. Augustine and Monica shared a remarkable vision in Ostia, the seaport to Rome, shortly before Monica died at the age of fifty-six. Augustine and Adeodatus continued their journey back to North Africa, where Adeodatus died.

In the years that followed his conversion, Augustine studied philosophy, theology, and the Scriptures, and he wrote a number of short books, including *Against the Skeptics, On the Happy Life,* and *Soliloquies.* His growing commitment to a religious vocation led to his ordination in 391. Four years later, he was consecrated bishop of Hippo Regius.

Augustine completed what many regard as his greatest book, *The Confessions,* in 400. The work begins with a powerful prayer: "Oh God, Thou hast made us for thyself, and our hearts are restless till they rest in Thee." These words capture Augustine's inner turmoil and the deepest yearnings of his heart. During all of the years he was running from God, he was seeking something that he would not find until he surrendered his heart and life to the Christian God.

In spite of the details that the *Confessions* provides about his life prior to 387, it would be a mistake to view the book merely as an autobiography. Augustine was less interested in readers' knowing the specifics of his life than he was in their understanding of the moral, intellectual, and spiritual struggles he went through in his search for the truth about God and himself. Augustine used the word *confession* in two senses: penitence and piety. First, he wanted to acknowledge his many sins, but more importantly he sought to glorify the God who had delivered him from those sins. After many years of writing and service to his church, Augustine died in Hippo in 430, during the city's siege by Germanic tribes.

Why did Augustine write his *Confessions?* One plausible theory is that he wrote it to persuade Christians in North Africa that the worldly, carnal, Manichean enemy of the Christian faith that they had known before his departure for Rome had experienced a genuine Christian conversion and had returned to his homeland as a committed Christian.

Many affinities exist between Augustine and Plotinus on such matters as illumination, the relationship between soul and body, the arguments for the immortality of the soul, sensation, and an approach to the problem of evil. Augustine's faithfulness to the Christian Scriptures and his

Augustine and Plotinus

---

2. Augustine *Confessions* 8.

own genius produced major alterations in the Plotinian doctrine, but Plotinus's influence cannot be ignored. In fact, many elements of Augustine's thought can be understood properly only when seen in the light of the Platonic tradition in philosophy. His reading of the Neoplatonists helped answer the problems and remove the obstacles that Manicheanism had placed in the way of his becoming a Christian. Many elements of Augustine's philosophy were formulated under the influence of Plotinus, but as Augustine's understanding of Christian belief matured, he came to recognize errors in Plotinus's system. On any issue where Plotinus's thought and Scripture were irreconcilable, Augustine parted company with Plotinus and sided with the Bible. This is seen, for example, in Augustine's renunciation of the preexistence of the soul.

Augustine's Christian Worldview

Augustine was not a systematic writer. It is necessary therefore to pull together his thoughts on the major elements of his Christian worldview from many works written over a period of forty years. It is important at times to take note of the larger context within which his views developed. For example, many of his convictions about God were shaped by his ongoing controversy with the Manichean religion that he had followed for so many years.

Augustine's View of God

Augustine had earnestly pursued two non-Christian views of God before his Christian conversion. The first was the two-god theory of Manicheanism; the second was the unknowable One of Plotinus. Taking note of the many ways in which Augustine's thinking about God contrasted with these other theories is a necessary step in grasping the development of his beliefs.

God, Manichean Dualism, and Evil

Augustine's acquaintance with Manicheanism led him to reflect on two problems: the problem of evil and the relationship between faith and reason. Christianity teaches that all reality is created by one true God. If this is so, and God is both good and all-powerful, as Christians claim, why does evil exist? Manicheanism explained the existence of good and evil as the unavoidable product of a never-ending struggle between two coequal and co-eternal deities, one good and the other evil. Evil exists because the good God (Light) is powerless to defeat the evil God (Darkness). Eventually Augustine came to see that this kind of dualism was unnecessary to explain the existence of evil. There is only one God, and he is both good and all-powerful. Everything God created was good. But the creation contained degrees of goodness. One feature of God's good creation was his endowment of certain creatures (the angels and humans) with free will.[3] Evil came into being when these creatures misused their free will to turn from a higher good to a lower good.

Evil is dependent upon a prior good in the sense that it is a kind of parasite or corruption of a prior good. Good and evil are not equal forces or powers in the universe. Evil is always subordinate to goodness. A parasite can never survive unless there is a separate and healthy organism upon which it can prey, from which it can draw sustenance.

Is light or darkness the more fundamental reality? It is a mistake to think that darkness is a power or a force that coexists with light. Darkness is the privation of light. Light is a positive force or power; darkness is nothing, it is nonbeing. In order for evil to exist, there must be an original goodness to corrupt. Could goodness have existed without evil? Certainly. In theism, God existed first, God is good, and then evil entered the universe as a corruption of created goodness. According to Augustine, God chose to include within creation free will. But free will carries the possibility either to choose or reject the Creator. The will of the creature can turn toward God and away from God, the good and the light. The origin of evil is located in a created will that turns away from its Creator, God. Creatures choose a lower good ahead of a higher good; they choose themselves rather than God.

Augustine's God Versus the God of Plotinus

Augustine's God was not the finite Demiurge of Plato or the unknowable One of Plotinus. He is the triune God of the Christian Scriptures who created *ex nihilo* all of reality (*Confessions* 11.4–5). God, who is immutable in both time and space, created the world of souls and bodies.

Augustine's view of God is distinctly Christian and remained so in spite of his early flirtation with some aspects of Plotinus's worldview. Plotinus's God was unknowable; Augustine's God was eminently knowable through both special revelation (the Bible) and general revelation, both in the physical universe (nature) and through the human soul. Plotinus's God was not the sovereign, free creator of the universe.

The Trinity

Historic Christian theism is unapologetically trinitarian. To quote the Apostles' Creed: "I believe in God the Father Almighty ... and in Jesus Christ his only Son our Lord ... [and] in the Holy Spirit." The doctrine of the Trinity reflects the Christian conviction that the Father, the Son, and the Holy Spirit are three distinct centers of consciousness that share fully in the one divine nature and in the activities of the other persons of the

---

3. Augustine's notion of free will had limits.

Trinity. The doctrine is a natural outgrowth of the church's efforts to reconcile those biblical passages that teach that there is but one God (Deuteronomy 6:4) with other texts that identify three distinct persons as God (Matthew 3:16; John 14:16–17; 2 Corinthians 13:14; Ephesians 4:4–6). The triune nature of God is illustrated in Jesus' Great Commission, in which he commanded his disciples to go and make disciples from all nations and then baptize them in the *one* name of the Father, Son, and Holy Spirit (Matthew 28:19). One of Augustine's greatest books is devoted to the subject of the Trinity. As A. H. Armstrong explains, "For Augustine and his followers all true thinking begins and ends with the Trinity. It is indeed for them only as Trinity that God creates us and only as Trinity that we can approach Him."[4]

Near the end of my chapter on Plotinus, I briefly noted his difficulties in explaining how a universe of enormous multiplicity (the many) could be derived from a source that was devoid of multiplicity (the One). This problem did not exist for Augustine. The fact that God is both three and one, plurality and unity, explains how thoughtful Christians like Augustine can explain the coming into being of a pluralistic universe, something Plotinus could only dream of. The problem of the one and the many receives its answer in a God who is both One and Many.

Metaphysics

Augustine's Rejection of Plato's Theory of Creation

The Bible begins with the words, "In the beginning God created the heavens and the earth." Many early Christian thinkers found it important to draw out certain implications of the biblical view of God and stipulate that God created the world *ex nihilo,* which is an important metaphysical tenet of the Christian worldview. This was necessary, they believed, to contrast the Christian understanding of Creation and Plato's speculation about the origin of the world.

My chapter about Plato included a discussion of Plato's theory of creation. In an attempt to set up a parallel to Plato's allegory of the cave, I invented Plato's allegory of the kitchen. As I noted, Plato explained the origin of the physical universe in terms of four factors: matter, or the stuff of which the world is made (the ingredients of the cake); the eternal Forms, or the pattern according to which the world was made (the recipe of the cake); the space-time receptacle or box within which the world comes to exist (the oven in which the cake is baked); and the Demiurge, Craftsman, or World Soul that made the particular things in the physical world by fashioning the formless matter after the pattern of the eternal Forms (the baker).

---

4. A. H. Armstrong, *An Introduction to Ancient Philosophy* (Boston: Beacon, 1967), 212.

Augustine's rejection of Plato's theory of creation provides helpful access into a better understanding of the Christian doctrine of creation *ex nihilo* and how it differs from Plato's.

(1) Augustine recognized that there was no room for Plato's eternal matter in a Christian worldview. If God's creative power is limited by a quantity of eternal and unknowable matter, then any deity operating in such a system cannot be all-powerful but must be finite. Augustine taught that when the Christian God created the world, he created it *ex nihilo*. This should not be understood to mean that "nothing" was "something" from which God made the world. It means that before God created, there was nothing else except God. God did not make the world out of any preexisting stuff. So the first thing we learn about the Christian view of creation *ex nihilo* is that Christians denied the existence of Plato's matter. Plato's creator could not be the God of the Christian faith, because of his finiteness and other limitations.

(2) What about the box or oven in our allegory? What about the space-time receptacle, the place within which Plato's creation took place? The Christian doctrine of creation *ex nihilo* rejects space and time as eternal givens. Augustine provides a good illustration of this Christian conviction in his *Confessions*. He notes that enemies of the Christian faith sometimes seek to embarrass Christians by asking what God was doing before he created the world. The embarrassment is supposed to arise for the following reason: Christians believe God is eternal; his existence has no beginning and no end. Therefore, regardless of when God created the world, it seems obvious that God waited for an infinitely long time before he created. What then was God doing during that eternal period of time?

Augustine offers two answers to the question. The first is a bit of Carthaginian humor, I suppose. In his reply to what God was doing before creation, Augustine's answer is that God was preparing hell for people who ask questions like that.[5] In a more serious answer, Augustine says that God was doing nothing before Creation. His point is that the creation was the first thing that God did. The reason is simple: before God created, there was no time. God created not only the world but also time. Therefore, since time began when the world began, there was no time before Creation. Hence, it makes no sense to ask what God was doing before there was time.

Augustine makes the same point with respect to space. If someone assumes the existence of empty space, he might seek to embarrass the Christian by asking, "Why didn't God create the world in this part of space rather than that?" Augustine's answer is that before God created, there was no space. If there were no space, it then makes no sense to ask why God

---

5. What I present is my paraphrase of Augustine's comment.

didn't place his creation in space A rather than space B. Since no space existed prior to Creation, there was no space-time receptacle. Both space and time began with the Creation. This means that the Christian doctrine of creation *ex nihilo* not only gets rid of Plato's first point (matter) but also eliminates the third point, the space-time receptacle (the oven).

(3) An informed Christian will also have to reject Plato's finite Craftsman or Demiurge. The Christian God is not Plato's finite Craftsman. He is the almighty, omnipotent Creator of heaven and earth. Belief in the Christian God eliminates any need for either Plato's matter or the space-time box.

(4) And finally, we must ask, what did Christians like Augustine do with Plato's eternal Forms? While Augustine affirmed the existence of Forms, he denied their existence apart from God. For Augustine, such eternal Forms as absolute Truth and Goodness exist, but they subsist in God's mind as his eternal thoughts, which explains his favorite Latin term for the Forms, *rationes aeternae*.

Hence we see that the Christian doctrine of creation *ex nihilo* found Plato's theory of creation to be a convenient set of errors against which Christians could more clearly contrast their understanding of God's creation of the world.

The doctrine of creation implies that the world God created is real. This differs with some Asian worldviews that regard all of reality as an illusion. The reality of the world means not merely that there is something there for us to investigate and know. The doctrine also implies that the world is intelligible, that it can be known. Finally, the doctrine of creation implies that God's creation is good. Hence, proponents of the Christian worldview object to other systems that view the world as illusory, unintelligible, or evil. In the words of philosopher Michael Peterson, the Christian worldview "gives truth an appropriate residence. Christian theism affirms that the world is real and that there can be a genuine knowledge of it. Since there is such a thing as truth, one of the deepest longings of our being can be satisfied."[6]

Augustine on the Link Between Being and Knowing

Augustine links ontology (being) and epistemology (knowing). There is a similarity between the structure of being and the structure of knowing, as figure 6.1 reveals.

In Augustine's philosophy, being and knowing are structured in a hierarchical series that is reminiscent of the levels described in Plato's figure of the divided line and alluded to in his allegory of the cave. The ontological levels[7] in Augustine's thought descend from God, the Creator, to the human mind, and finally to the world of bodies.

---

6. Michael L. Peterson, *Philosophy of Education* (Downers Grove, Ill.: InterVarsity Press, 1986), 83–84.

7. *Ontology* is a technical word for the study of being.

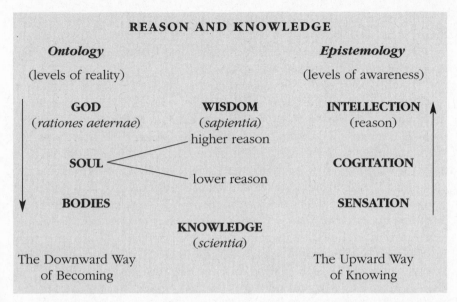

REASON AND KNOWLEDGE

Figure 6.1

Ontology
(levels of reality)

Epistemology
(levels of awareness)

GOD
(*rationes aeternae*)

WISDOM
(*sapientia*)
higher reason

INTELLECTION
(reason)

SOUL

COGITATION

lower reason

BODIES

SENSATION

KNOWLEDGE
(*scientia*)

The Downward Way
of Becoming

The Upward Way
of Knowing

On the highest level of reality, the level of God, Augustine finds Plato's Forms. Since Augustine regards the Forms as eternal ideas subsisting in the mind of God, he calls them the *rationes aeternae*. The Forms are eternal and immutable; they are the patterns of particular things; and they are grounded in the mind of God. The Forms are archetypal patterns of created reality. Because the Forms are the exemplary cause of everything that exists, they are the foundation of all created reality. Moreover, because the judgments humans make must accord with the eternal Forms, they are an indispensable element in human knowledge.

The second or middle level of Augustine's universe is the rational human soul. He distinguishes two functions of human reason. Humans can look up toward eternal reality by means of the higher reason, or they can look down upon the physical and visible reality by means of the lower reason.[8] Augustine understands the higher and lower reasons to be not two separate faculties but two different functions of the same mind.[9]

The two functions of reason differ not only in their object but also in their result, a fact that led Augustine to distinguish two kinds of knowledge. The knowledge acquired through the higher reason he called wisdom (*sapientia*), and that acquired through the lower reason was called knowledge (*scientia*). While *scientia* is a knowledge of true things, that is, a rational cognizance of the temporal, wisdom is a knowledge of Truth, that is, an intellectual cognizance of the eternal.[10] Wisdom is superior to

8. See Augustine *On the Trinity* 12.15.24–25; 13.1.1–2; 14.1.3.
9. Ibid., 12.3.3.
10. Ibid., 12.15.25.

scientia because it is concerned with the acquisition of happiness and the ultimate goal of human existence.

The lowest of the three levels of reality is the world of bodies. Obviously, the human body belongs to this level.

The three descending levels of being parallel three ascending levels of awareness. The lowest, sensation, is common to both humans and animals and has as its object sensible things existing in the world of particulars. The next level, cogitation,[11]is a judging of sensible objects by the rational standards of the eternal Forms; it too is peculiar to humans. It is akin to *scientia,* the judgment of sense objects by rational and eternal standards. Plato's account of how humans can know that two particular things are equal or similar because of their prior knowledge of the Equal itself is a good illustration of what Augustine has in view on this middle level. Because cogitation is a knowledge of sensible things and thus involves a use of the various senses, it is a lower level of awareness than is intellection.[12] The highest level, intellection, is unique to humans. This level is related to wisdom, since it is the contemplation of eternal truths.

Like the theories of Plato and Plotinus, then, Augustine's theory of knowledge is based upon an ascent of the soul that begins with humans tied by their bodies to the world of sensible particulars (compare the prisoners at the bottom of Plato's cave). After achieving freedom from the domination of the senses, humans turn to the realm of the Forms and there find knowledge. Augustine's ascent can be seen in the several levels of perception or vision already described. It is also illustrated by passages where Augustine traces the process by which he discovered unchanging and eternal truth above his mutable or changing mind.[13] First, he passed from the outer to the inner world, from the realm of bodies to the world of the soul. Then he passed from the lower to the higher capacities of the soul; that is, he moved from the lower reason, which judges sensible things, to the higher reason, which knows unchanging truth. And suddenly, "with the flash of a trembling glance," he arrives at a knowledge of that which is, of the God who told Moses, "I AM WHO I AM." As Augustine writes in *The City of God,*

> It is a great and very rare thing for a man, after he has contemplated the whole creation, physical and nonphysical, and has discerned its mutability, to pass beyond it, and, by the continued soaring of his mind, to

---

11. Cogitation is the function of the human mind by which we arrange, collect, and reassemble sense knowledge stored in the memory. Cogitation is related to the ability of the human mind to act upon sense images by relating them to the eternal Forms.

12. For more on this, see Ronald H. Nash, *The Light of the Mind: St. Augustine's Theory of Knowledge* (Lexington, Ky.: University of Kentucky Press, 1969), chap. 1.

13. Augustine *Confessions* 7.17.

attain to the unchangeable substance of God, and, in that height of contemplation, to learn from God Himself that none but He has made all that is not of the divine essence.[14]

Faith and Reason

The Manicheans had ridiculed faith as an activity unworthy of any cultured and educated person. Never take anything on faith, they taught; trust only what you know by reason. Augustine defended faith against this kind of attack. For him, faith is not inferior to reason; true faith never conflicts with reason. In fact, faith is an indispensable step in any act of knowledge, a point Augustine expressed in the famous phrase *Credo ut intelligam:* I believe in order that I may understand. All knowledge begins in faith. Faith is not unique to religion. Rather, it is an indispensable element in every act of knowing.

Augustine defined faith as indirect knowledge, that is, any belief that is dependent upon the testimony of another person or document. Faith is indispensable; it is the beginning of knowledge.[15] Faith is a precondition of knowledge. "Unless ye believe, ye shall not understand," he wrote.[16] Consider our knowledge of the data of history. Unless we first had faith in the reliability of our sources, we would never know anything about the past. Unless we had faith in the testimony of relatives and documents like birth certificates, we would never be able to know our own identity. While faith is mediated knowledge, reason is immediate knowledge; we know it for ourselves.

But if faith comes first in time, reason comes first in importance. According to Augustine, the sources for our information must be tested. The relationship between faith and reason is analogous to the two blades of a pair of scissors. It makes no sense to ask which blade does the cutting; the cutting occurs only when the two blades work together. Similarly, it makes no sense to ask whether faith or reason is the most important element in human knowledge. Humans know only when faith and reason are working together.

Skepticism

Augustine's arguments against skepticism still constitute the proper starting point for any refutation of this error. Skeptics claim that no one can know anything; no proposition is true. In chapter 1, we noted the logically

---

14. Augustine *The City of God* 11.2, in *Basic Writings of Saint Augustine II,* trans. M. Dods (New York: Random House, 1948). See also Augustine *On the Truth of Religion* 39.72 and Augustine *On the Freedom of the Will* 2.3.7 to 2.15.39.
15. Augustine *On the Trinity* 9.1.1.
16. Augustine *On the Freedom of the Will* 1.2.4.

self-defeating nature of such claims. Augustine does not mention this objection, focusing instead on a different line of attack. Even the most radical skeptics know that they exist. *Si fallor sum,* Augustine wrote. If I am mistaken, then I must exist. Existing is a necessary condition for making mistakes. Nonexistent people cannot be wrong. But if I know that I exist, then skepticism (the view that no one can know anything) must be false. If we know even one truth, then skepticism is refuted.[17]

This particular refutation of skepticism is interesting for several reasons. First, as Armstrong explains, "it means that man has direct and immediate cognisance, not through the senses, of at least one spiritual reality, himself as a thinking subject."[18] While Augustine admits that some human knowledge is attainable through the senses, "the highest and most important knowledge for him is that immediate contact of the mind with spiritual, intelligible reality to which the first step is our consciousness of our self as a living, thinking reality."[19] Moreover, Armstrong continues, "In knowing our own existence we know a truth and, having once refuted the [sceptics] and delivered ourselves from hopeless scepticism by arriving at this absolute certainty, we shall be able to go on and find that we know other truths."[20] Careful reflection about truths we are capable of knowing reveals them to be eternal and unchangeable. Where can such truth come from? For Augustine, it can come only from an eternal and unchangeable Mind.

Augustine's Defense of Sense Experience

Earlier I defined Plato's rationalism as the belief that no human knowledge arises from sense experience. Augustine, however, writes that the Christian "believes also the evidence of the senses which the mind uses by aid of the body; for if one who trusts his senses is sometimes deceived, he is more wretchedly deceived who fancies he should never trust them."[21]

One reason for Augustine's defense of sense experience may reflect the fact that important content of the Bible depends upon human experience and testimony. If the senses are completely unreliable, then we cannot trust the reports of witnesses who say, for example, that they heard Jesus teach or saw him die or saw him alive three days after his crucifixion. If there is no sensory testimony to the resurrection of Jesus, then the truth of the Christian faith is open to serious challenge.

---

17. See Augustine *The City of God* 11.26.
18. Armstrong, *Introduction to Ancient Philosophy,* 217.
19. Ibid.
20. Ibid.
21. Augustine *The City of God* 19.18.

Augustine on Human Knowledge of the Forms

It should be obvious that the key to human knowledge about the physical world for Augustine lies in human knowledge of what Plato called the Forms. As Plato explained in his famous discussion of Equality in the *Phaedo,* knowledge of particular things presupposes a prior knowledge of universals. The priority that Augustine gives to intellection reveals his commitment to the same kind of approach.

Augustine's account of intellection, human knowledge of the Forms, is linked to one of his more famous doctrines, the theory of divine illumination. Augustine believes that human knowledge of the *rationes aeternae* is impossible without assistance from God, help that assumes the form of God's enlightening the human mind. Augustine's theory of illumination includes at least three major points: God is light and illumines all humans to different degrees; there are intelligible truths, the *rationes aeternae,* which God illumines; and human minds can know the divine truths only as God illumines them. In his many references to the function of the divine light in making knowledge possible Augustine depends a great deal upon the analogy between physical and mental sight.[22] God is to the soul what the sun is to the eye. God is not only the truth in, by, and through whom all truths are true. And he is not only the wisdom in, by, and through whom all humans are made wise. He is also the light in, by, and through whom all intelligible things are illumined.[23]

The importance of this doctrine to Augustine's theory of knowledge is indicated in an often-overlooked passage in section 10 of *Epistle* 120, where Augustine writes that illumination plays a role in believing, knowing, remembering, imagining, sensing, and every area of knowledge. He also uses his doctrine of the divine light to make the point that no soul is self-sufficient; no soul can be a light unto itself. Instead our minds must be illumined by participation in God's light. Whatever we do—thinking, speaking, or acting—we need the help of God.

The Meaning of Augustine's Theory

There has been a long and unresolved controversy over the meaning of Augustine's theory of divine illumination. The divine light is Augustine's answer to how humans know the eternal ideas that subsist in the mind of God. Since Augustine believed that a knowledge of the Forms is a necessary condition for any knowledge of temporal reality, all human knowledge must be explained ultimately in terms of the divine light. Unfortunately, there is no generally accepted interpretation of Augustine's theory.

---

22. Augustine *On the Trinity* 12.15.24.

23. This is another way of saying that if it were not for the illuminating power of God, humans could never attain knowledge of such eternal ideas as Truth, Goodness, and Beauty. See Augustine *Soliloquies* 1.1.3.

Some of the most commonly accepted interpretations of Augustine's theory must be rejected. This includes the attempt to revive Thomas Aquinas's interpretation of Augustine's theory, a failed attempt that has the effect of turning the rationalist Augustine into an empiricist. Attempting to force Aristotle's theory of abstraction into Augustine's theory of knowledge, interpreters who followed Aquinas tended to deny Augustine's Platonism and turn him into an Aristotelian.[24]

It is also necessary to reject the famous interpretation of Etienne Gilson.[25] As Gilson saw it, the function of illumination is not to give the human mind some definite content (knowledge of the Forms) but to convey the quality of certainty and necessity to certain judgments. Gilson was correct in what he affirmed but wrong in what he denied. Divine illumination does account for our recognition of necessary truth, but, contra Gilson, it also provides an innate awareness of the content of universals and necessary truths. Many texts in Augustine's writings relate divine illumination not only to the quality of necessary judgments but also the content of necessary truths.[26] Gilson's unacceptable view leaves Augustine without any answer to the crucial question of how humans come to know the Forms.

Any adequate understanding of Augustine's theory of illumination must take account of the fact that two lights are involved in any act of human knowledge. Augustine is careful to distinguish between the uncreated light of God and a different, created light, namely, the human mind, which plays a necessary role in knowledge.[27] Just as the moon derives the light it reflects from the sun, so the rational human mind derives a created ability to know from God. Human knowledge can be regarded as a reflection of the truth originating in the mind of God. To be more specific, God has endowed humans with a structure of rationality patterned after the divine ideas in his own mind; we can know truth because God has made us like himself. This helps explain how we can know not only the eternal Forms but also the creation that is patterned after these Forms. We can know the corporeal world because we first know the intelligible world.

As an inherent part of our rational nature, we possess forms of thought by which we know and judge sensible things. Because God has created humankind after his own image and continually sustains and aids the soul in its quest for knowledge, human knowledge is possible. God is the original source of the light that makes knowledge possible because he is the

---

24. See C. Boyer, *L'Idee de verite dans la philosophie de sant Augustin* (Paris: N.p., 1921).

25. Etienne Gilson, *The Christian Philosophy of Saint Augustine* (New York: Random House, 1960), 79, 86, 91.

26. See Nash, *The Light of the Mind,* 109–11.

27. Augustine *Against Faustus the Manichaean* 20.7.

reason or logos of the universe.[28] All the truths of reason have their ground in his being; they subsist in his mind. Because humankind was created in the image of God, the human mind is a secondary and derivative source of light that reflects in a creaturely way the rationality of the Creator. A harmony or correlation exists therefore among the mind of God, the human mind, and the rational structure of the world. In part 2 of this book, the theory just described will reappear under a different name (the preformation theory) in a discussion of the epistemology of the German philosopher Immanuel Kant (chap. 11); Kant opposed this theory for weak reasons.

As we have noted, Augustine's theory of divine illumination was his answer to the question of how the human mind comes to know the eternal Forms that subsist in the mind of God. As a first step toward understanding Augustine's theory, it is important to recognize three possible answers that he rejected: a human being does not acquire knowledge of the Forms by sense experience, by Platonic recollection, or by teaching.

Augustine's Rejection of Three Theories

We Do Not Know the Forms via Sense Experience

Augustine's rejection of sense experience as the source of human knowledge of universal truth is similar to Plato's position in the *Phaedo*, material covered in chapter 3 of this book. Just as Plato taught that every judgment about equal things presupposes a prior knowledge of equality, Augustine argues that all judgments about number presuppose a prior knowledge of unity, the concept of oneness. But the notion of unity cannot be derived from sense experience. As Augustine states, "Whoever thinks with exactitude of unity will discover that it cannot be perceived by the senses. Whatever comes into contact with a bodily sense is proved to be not one but many, for it is corporeal and therefore has innumerable parts."[29] Our bodily senses can only bring us into contact with physical things, and such things, no matter how small, still have multiple parts. No physical object can be a true unity. If nothing else, one can distinguish one side from another or the top from the bottom. Knowledge of unity or oneness is logically prior to sense experience. For Augustine, knowledge of the Forms is independent of sense experience.

We Do Not Know the Forms via Preexistence of the Soul

While Augustine followed Plato in rejecting sense experience as a ground for human knowledge of the Forms, his mature position rejected Plato's appeal to the preexistence of the soul and recollection. During the first

---

28. For an extended analysis of this claim, see Ronald H. Nash, *The Word of God and the Mind of Man* (Phillipsburg, N.J.: Presbyterian and Reformed, 1992).

29. Augustine *On the Freedom of the Will* 2.8.22.

few years after his conversion (387–389), Augustine believed in the preexistence of the soul and accepted Plato's explanation of human knowledge in terms of recollection.[30] Even Augustine could clutter his Christian worldview with beliefs that contradicted important Christian tenets. But he knew that a worldview must be logically coherent. As Augustine's thought matured and he came to see the unbiblical implications of the doctrine of preexistence, he sought a different answer for the problem of how one comes to know the Forms.[31] He continued to believe that all human knowledge presupposes a prior knowledge of the forms and that these Forms cannot be known through the senses.[32] But he came to hold that God has implanted a knowledge of the Forms in the human mind contemporaneous with birth. In other words, Augustine's account of human knowledge replaced Plato's appeal to reincarnation and recollection with a theory of innate ideas that belong to humankind by virtue of our creation in the image of God.

We Do Not Know the Forms via Teaching

Finally, Augustine rejects the view that human knowledge of the eternal Forms might be acquired through teaching. The writing in which Augustine states this argument, *On the Teacher,* is complex and easy to misunderstand. But his conclusion is clear: Knowledge of *a priori* truth[33] cannot be passed from one person to another as through teaching. It must always arise within the soul. "Concerning universals of which we can have knowledge, we do not listen to anyone speaking and making sounds outside ourselves. We listen to Truth which presides over our minds within us, though of course we may be bidden to listen by someone using words. Our real Teacher is he who is so listened to, who is said to dwell in the inner man, namely, Christ, that is, the unchangeable power and eternal wisdom of God."[34]

For Augustine, the mind can have ideas even though it is not consciously aware of those ideas. Human knowledge of the Forms is not the result of our remembering truths learned in a previous existence. We remember or actualize latent knowledge of necessary truth stored in what

---

30. For a discussion of Augustine's early commitment to preexistence and the theory of recollection, see Gilson, *The Christian Philosophy of Saint Augustine,* 71–72. Compare also the following texts in Augustine: *Against the Skeptics* 2.9.22 with *Retractions* 1.1.3; *Soliloquies* 2.20.35 with *Retractions* 1.4.4; and *On the Measure of the Soul* 20.34 with *Retractions* 1.8.

31. Augustine leaves no doubt concerning his final rejection of Platonic recollection; see *On the Trinity* 12.15.24.

32. The claims in this sentence relate to the two premises of Plato's argument for the immortality of the soul, presented in chapter 3 of this book.

33. The reader must not ignore the adjective. Augustine makes this point exclusively with respect to universal, necessary, *a priori* truth, such as the truths of mathematics and logic.

34. Augustine *On the Teacher* 11. This work provides a marvelous picture of the intelligence of Augustine's son, Adeodatus.

Augustine calls the memory. To know *a priori* truth is to remember now as a result of the continuous presence of God's light within us. In *On the Teacher,* Augustine concludes that *a priori* knowledge cannot be taught— it cannot be passed from one person to another. *A priori* truth always arises from within the soul. The student learns by consulting the Truth present within his own mind.[35]

While Augustine's language sounds mystical, his point is philosophical. Every human knows the Forms because God endows him or her with this knowledge and continually sustains the intellect in the knowing process. The true teacher is Christ, who himself is the truth and who, in the words of the fourth gospel, "gives light to every man" (John 1:9).

Consider your knowledge that four plus four equals eight.[36] Words you may have heard from a parent or a teacher played a role in your forming the belief. But the judgment is not true simply because a teacher taught it to you. The teacher introduced you to the concepts; but it was always necessary that the content of the teaching faithfully represent the eternally and necessarily true content of the judgment. Had a teacher told a youngster that the sum of four plus four was some number other than eight, the child might have at that time lacked the ability to refute the teacher's claim. But as we mature and our grasp of *a priori* truth increases, we would one day attain the ability to reject the teacher's claim as false.

Summation

To know truth, the human mind is necessary but not sufficient.[37] According to Augustine, the created light of the human intellect needs a light from without.[38] Even the created intelligible light would be unable to account for human knowledge without the constant, immanent, and active presence of God.[39] We must not think of the Forms as having been given to humans once and for all. Though the Forms are part of the rational

---

35. See Augustine *On the Teacher* 11.

36. To forestall appeal to an especially egregious error, do not be deceived by an appeal to mathematical systems that have a base other than ten. In a base five system, for example, there is no number higher than five. But that does not falsify "four plus four equals eight." Movement to a different base system only requires us to use different symbols to say the same thing.

37. The term *necessary condition* is a technical term in philosophy that every student should be able to define. To say that *A* is a necessary condition for *B* means that if *A* did not exist, then *B* would not exist. An example: oxygen is a necessary condition for human life. Take away oxygen, and humans will die. The term *necessary condition* contrasts with *sufficient condition.* To say that *A* is a sufficient condition for *B* means that if *A* does exist, then *B* will also exist. Oxygen is not a sufficient condition for human life because you can have lots of oxygen but not have living humans if the temperature is too high, there is no water, or many other conditions are askew.

38. Augustine *On the Position of the Pelagians* 3.7.

39. Augustine *On Genesis* 7.31.59.

structure of the human mind and belong there by virtue of our having been created in God's image, the soul never ceases to be dependent upon God for its knowledge. B. B. Warfield, commenting on Augustine, says: "God, having so made man, has not left him deistically, to himself, but continually reflects into his soul the contents of His truths which constitute the intelligible world. The soul is therefore in unbroken communion with God, and in the body of intelligible truths reflected into it from God, sees God."[40] Thus, knowledge is possible because God has created each person after his own image as a rational soul and because God continually sustains and aids the soul in its quest for knowledge.

The Forms or eternal ideas exist in the mind of God independently of particular things, but in a secondary sense they also exist in the created mind of human beings. God created us with a structure of rationality patterned after the divine Forms in his mind. This innate knowledge is part of what it means to be created in the image of God. In addition to knowledge of Forms, knowledge of the world is possible because God has also patterned the world after the divine ideas. We can know the corporeal world because God has given us a knowledge of these ideas by which we can judge sensations and gain knowledge.

The Forms and laws of mathematics are present in the memory as latent or virtual truth. They are present not necessarily as objects of thought but as predispositions of the mind to think in certain ways.[41] Humans do not remember truths learned in a previous existence, as Plato taught, but actualize latent or virtual knowledge of necessary truths stored in the memory. Augustine's view of memory is an important link between his earlier commitment to Platonic reminiscence (where he took the word *remember* literally) and his later view of illumination where the word is used metaphorically.

Augustine believed that the laws that govern human thought reflect necessities that exist in the created universe: "The true nature of logical conclusions," he wrote, "has not been arranged by men; rather they studied and took notice of it so that they might be able to learn or to teach it. It is perpetual in the order of things and divinely ordained."[42] For Augustine, the truth of propositions like "two plus two equals four" does not consist simply in the mental act of making this judgment. Rather, its truth lies in the eternal reality that makes the judgment true. The truths of logic are not tautologies devoid of any reference to being.[43]

---

40. B. B. Warfield, *Calvin and Augustine* (Philadelphia: Presbyterian and Reformed, 1956), 397.

41. Suggestion: underline this last sentence and remember it when, in part 2 of the book, we begin discussing Reformed epistemology (chap. 12).

42. Augustine *On Christian Doctrine* 2.32.50.

43. A tautology is a true but vacuous statement. That is, it fails to say anything new. One example of a tautology would be "All red roses are red." This is true, isn't it? But it is a truth

Conclusion

Augustine's illumination theory answers certain questions raised previously by Plato in the *Phaedo*. At first Augustine accepted the full range of Plato's argument from recollection, but gradually he was led away from a belief in the preexistence of the soul to an alternative explanation of how humans come to know the Forms. Even though Augustine abandoned Plato's use of remembering, it was natural for Augustine to continue to use the notion of memory in his mature account of how humans know universals or the Forms.

In concluding this discussion of Plato's influence on Augustine's illumination theory, I wish to stress what Augustine learned from Plato through Plotinus. (1) Knowledge about sensible, physical particulars depends upon a prior knowledge of Forms or universals such as the Equal itself. (2) The ultimate objects of knowledge must be immutable and eternal and grasped by reason; these are the eternal essences Plato called Forms and Augustine calls *rationes aeternae*. (3) Without an external source of assistance, illustrated under the figure of light, the human mind could never attain this knowledge. But as I have hinted several times, Augustine did not believe that human knowledge could be explained solely in terms of an external light. He went on to argue that there is also an internal light, the human mind, which reflects the light from God and is also a necessary condition of knowledge.

A synthesis of all the passages in Augustine's writings that have a bearing on the soul's relation to the forms leads to the view that these ideas in the mind are *a priori,* virtual, preconditions of *scientia*. They are *a priori* because they cannot be derived from experience. They are virtual because they are in the mind even when they are not objects of thought.[44] And finally, the forms are preconditions of knowledge (*scientia*) because knowledge becomes possible only when these universals are applied to the images from sensation.[45]

Augustine on Plato's Three Kinds of Dualism

As we learned in chapter 3, Plato worked with three kinds of dualism. What did Augustine do with them? While Augustine accepted Plato's metaphysical dualism, he also modified it so as to make it more consistent with Christian truth. While Plato knew the ideal world existed, he never could figure out how, why, or where it existed. Augustine repudiated any possibility that the forms might exist above God or independent of God. The Forms subsist rather as eternal thoughts (*rationes aeternae*)

---

that does not advance your understanding of anything. It is devoid of significant information. Another tautology would be the statement "All bachelors are unmarried men."

44. See Augustine *On the Immortality of the Soul* 4.
45. See Nash, *The Light of the Mind,* chap. 8.

in the mind of God. Hence, in Augustine's worldview, the physical world of bodies exists because it was created by the unchanging, eternal, triune God of the Christian faith who is the ontological ground for the eternal forms. So Plato's distinction between the eternal, nonmaterial world of the forms versus the temporal, material world of bodies is transformed by Augustine into the distinction between God and his creation.

Augustine accepted Plato's anthropological dualism and its distinction between the human soul and body. Indeed, for a year or so following his conversion, Augustine even toyed with Plato's theory of reincarnation until he came to recognize its logical incompatibility with Christian truth.

Augustine defines a human being as a "rational substance consisting of mind and body."[46] Augustine's understanding of this point is in the Platonic tradition, but, as usual, what he learns from others is modified in the light of the Scriptures. He refuses to follow Plato and the Manicheans in holding the body to be evil. If the body were intrinsically evil, he asks, why would God resurrect the body?[47] Another modification of Platonism is Augustine's greater emphasis upon the unity of the human being. While a human's body and soul are both substances, human beings themselves are substances.[48] While Augustine may never have succeeded in harmonizing Platonic dualism with the scriptural emphasis on the unity of a human being, he tried. In the *Phaedo,* immortality is pictured as a property of the soul alone. Survival after death is portrayed as a disembodied existence, as separation from the body. No informed Christian such as Augustine could possibly accept this line of thinking for long; and he didn't.

As for Plato's epistemological dualism (reason versus sense experience), Augustine again modified Plato's position. While Plato's rationalism amounted to the belief that no knowledge arises from sense experience (the E position introduced in the appendix to chapter 3), Augustine recognized that the bodily senses are an important source of information. This seems to mark, in Augustine's case, a shift to the view that "some knowledge does not arise from sense perception."

Ethics

The fact that all human beings carry the image of God (another of Christianity's basic beliefs about human nature) explains why we are capable of reasoning, love, and God-consciousness; it also explains why we are moral creatures. Of course, sin (yet another of Christianity's important presuppositions about human beings) has distorted the image of God and explains why humans turn away from God and the moral law; why

---

46. Augustine *On the Trinity* 15.7.11.
47. See Augustine *The City of God* 13.16.
48. See Augustine *On the Trinity* 15.7.11.

we sometimes go wrong with regard to our emotions, conduct, and thinking. Because of the image of God, we should expect to find that the ethical principles of the Christian worldview reflect what all of us at the deepest level of our moral being know to be true.

Augustine believed that God is the ground of the laws that govern the physical universe and that make possible the order of the cosmos. God is also the ground of the moral laws that ought to govern human behavior and that make possible order between humans. Christian theism insists on the existence of universal moral laws; the laws of morality must apply to all humans, regardless of when or where they have lived. Such laws must also be objective in the sense that their truth is independent of human preference and desire.

People attracted by the ethical relativism of our day will have great difficulty understanding and appreciating Augustine's view of the moral life. Augustine argues for the importance of seeing that ethics has its ground in the perfect, unchanging character of God. The moral principles revealed in the Bible reflect the eternal character of God. Because he is holy and without moral blemish, God commands us to obey commandments that reflect his character. In such a context, there is no room for ethical relativism.

Four concepts provide the foundation of Augustine's ethical theory: law, love, character (virtue), and well-being.

Four Concepts in Augustine's Ethical Theory

Law and Love

Augustine rejects any suggestion that law and love can be antithetic. No Christian should ignore the place of law in the moral order. The Ten Commandments found in Exodus 20 are divine commands that provide indispensable guidance for human life. Another essential ethical passage in the Bible includes Jesus' words in Matthew 22, words that summarize the first four commandments, our duties to God, under the single commandment "Love the Lord your God with all your heart and with all your soul and with all your mind." The last six commandments, our duties to other humans, are summarized under the commandment "Love your neighbor as yourself."

The apostle Paul then throws additional light on the relationship between law and love when he teaches in Romans 13 that love is the fulfillment of the law. God's law identifies sinful actions and tells humans how love ought to be manifested.

Thomas Bigham and Albert Mollegen summarize a central dimension of Augustine's understanding of the relationship between love and the good life: "A man is not happy if he does not have what he loves; or if he has what he loves and it is hurtful; or if he does not love what he has, even though it is perfectly good. The happy life is 'when that which is man's chief good is both loved and possessed.'"[49]

Character and Virtue

A major function of the Christian ethic is the development of character and virtue. An evil person could on occasion appear to obey God's moral law while inwardly surrendering to evil motives. It is important that believers attain the appropriate virtues, that is, a disposition to behave in a moral way, a loving way. The New Testament emphasis upon character and virtue shows up in Paul's words in Galatians 5:22–23.

Why does God issue the commands that he does? Those commands reflect his eternal and holy nature. They also point to the kind of conduct that people with the proper Christian virtues or dispositions will exhibit in their lives. And finally, as we develop in a fixed way the appropriate Christian virtues, we place ourselves in a position to experience the greatest joys of life. According to Augustine, the best and quickest way to miss out on the best that God and his world have to offer is to abuse God's law.

Augustine on Four Cardinal Virtues

While Augustine is well aware of the prominence of the four cardinal virtues in Greek ethical thinking, he offers a corrective from his perspective as a Christian thinker. Unless the cardinal virtues of unbelievers result from their desire to love and honor God, the best of pagan virtues will be reduced to "splendid vices."[50] Augustine's reason for saying this is his belief that unbelievers' search for such virtues will be motivated by their selfish pride.

Augustine offers an insight on the relationship between the four cardinal virtues and Christian love: "temperance is love keeping itself entire and uncorrupt for God; fortitude is love bearing everything readily for the sake of God; justice is love serving God only, and therefore ruling well all else, as subject to man; prudence is love making a right distinction between what helps it toward God and what might hinder it."[51] As Bigham and Mollegen explain, "The four pagan virtues are transformed into Christian virtues only when faith (that by which we love God not yet seen) and hope (that by which we love what we have not yet reached)

---

49. Thomas G. Bigham and Albert T. Mollegen, "The Christian Ethic," in *A Companion to the Study of St. Augustine*, ed. Roy W. Battenhouse (New York: Oxford University Press, 1955), 373. The quotations come from Augustine's *On the Morals of the Catholic Church* 3–6, in *Basic Writings of Saint Augustine*, ed. W. Oates (New York: Random House, 1948).

50. Augustine *The City of God* 19.25, in *The Nicene and Post-Nicene Fathers* (henceforth NPNF). This multivolume nineteenth-century work was reprinted in 1956 by the Wm. B. Eerdmans Publishing Co., Grand Rapids.

51. Augustine *On the Morals of the Catholic Church* 15.19–25.

and love (which remains when faith has become sight, and hope has been realized) undergird them."[52]

Augustine's commitment to the transcendent and objective moral law revealed in Scripture appears in his conviction that acts such as lying are always wrong.[53] Clearly, then, other acts prohibited in the Ten Commandments, such as murder, stealing, and sexual immorality, are also wrong always and everywhere.

My brief discussion of Augustine's ethical theory must close with an observation about another of his famous statements: "Love [God] and do as what thou wilt ... let the root of love be within, of this root can nothing spring but what is good."[54] Some might say, think how rapidly churches might grow if they would announce that if Christians act in love, they can do anything they please. Augustine meant that if we truly love God, what we will then desire to do and choose to do will be what will please the just and holy God.

History

Augustine is one of the earliest thinkers to give history the kind of reflection necessary to make it an acceptable part of a worldview. Augustine's philosophy of history is spelled out in his monumental work *The City of God* (written between 413 and 426). The immediate occasion for Augustine's writing the book was the sack of Rome in 410. Non-Christians throughout the Roman Empire charged that Rome's catastrophe was a result of the city's turning from its pagan deities to Christianity. Augustine began his book for the express purpose of answering these charges. Before he finished, however, he found himself involved in discussions of numerous other topics, including what turned into a Christian philosophy of history. The first ten books of *The City of God* contain Augustine's answers to the pagan accusations as well as much important information about the late Roman Empire. The most interesting passages occur in the last half of the work (books 11–22), where he turns to the major theme of his study, the existence within the world of two cities or societies—the City of God and the City of Man. The two cities will coexist throughout human history. Only at the final judgment and the end of human history will the two cities finally be separated so that they may share their appropriate destinies—heaven and hell.

Almost all of the great civilizations existing before the beginning of the Christian era ascribed a cyclical pattern to history. This was certainly true of Greece and Rome. History was viewed either as one big circle or an endless succession of many cycles, each one identical to those that went before and that are yet to come.

---

52. Bigham and Mollegen, "The Christian Ethic," 377.
53. See Augustine *On Lying*.
54. *Epistle of St. John,* Homily 7.8; *On Nature and Grace* 70 (84), and *On Christian Doctrine* 1.28.(42).

The cyclical theory of history found among the Greeks and Romans denigrated history. If history goes round and round, there can be no goal either for individual humans or for the species. Whatever happens to humans will happen again; whatever humans accomplish, they must accomplish again and again—forever. There may be no better way for a professor to illustrate the despair created by a cyclical approach to history than to remind students that such a theory means they will have to take this course and read this book and hear this lecture an infinite number of times. Without a purpose or a goal, neither history nor individual lives can have significance.

Augustine eagerly assumes the task of challenging this pagan view of history. God forbid, Augustine says, that any true believer is foolish enough to believe that "the same periods and events of time are repeated; as if, for example, the philosopher Plato, having taught in the school at Athens which is called the Academy, so, numberless ages before, at long but certain intervals, this same Plato and the same school, and the same disciples existed, and so also are to be repeated during the countless cycles that are yet to be,—far be it, I say, from us to believe this."[55] Augustine's first reason for rejecting pagan cyclicism is an argument he borrows from the New Testament epistle to the Hebrews: "For once Christ died for our sins; and, rising from the dead, He dieth no more."[56] Christians cannot accept the cyclical view of history because it contradicts the clear teaching of the New Testament.

Augustine also attacks the moral implications of the cyclical view. If life is to have meaning, there must be at least the possibility of hope and progress. But there can be progress only when one is going somewhere, is moving toward a goal. Therefore, in order for life to have any value, history must have a goal, and the cyclical view of history must be false. History is linear; it has a beginning (God's creation of the world) and a definite end (God's judgment at the end of history). Only a linear view of history allows individual human lives and the specific events in those lives to have value and significance.[57]

Sin and Salvation

Augustine's worldview is the first covered in this book that discusses human sin. Augustine coins three Latin expressions to indicate the place and role of sin in human lives.

(1) *Posse non peccare* describes humans before the Fall as described in the book of Genesis. Adam was able not to sin. One consequence of Adam's sin was to end humankind's ability to refrain from sinning.

---

55. Augustine *The City of God,* 14.28 (Dods translation).

56. Ibid.

57. For more information about the philosophy of history in general and the Christian view of history in particular, see Ronald H. Nash, *The Meaning of History* (Nashville: Broadman and Holman, 1998)

(2) *Non posse non peccare* describes all humans after the Fall. We are unable not to sin. Following the Fall, all humans are born with a sinful nature that makes the avoidance of some sins impossible.

(3) *Non posse peccare* describes the state of redeemed humans in heaven. They will be not able to sin.

Augustine offered a brilliant answer to the question of why created beings such as Lucifer and Adam would sin if they possessed no prior tendency to do so. Rejecting Manichean dualism, Augustine taught that everything God created was good; nothing God created was evil. However, he added, it was necessary for God's creation to contain degrees of goodness. Because a plant possesses life while a rock does not, the plant possesses more goodness than does a rock. Because an animal possesses powers that a plant does not, it possesses more goodness than does a plant. Because humans can reason, their kind of existence possesses more goodness than does an animal. Obviously, the eternal God possesses the greatest goodness. When the angel Lucifer committed the first sin, he chose a lesser good (himself) over a higher good (God). This explained for Augustine how sin could enter a creation in which no evil existed.

Augustine went on to note that this approach also explains the sin of Adam. Adam chose a lower good (himself and his desires) over a higher good (God). Indeed, Augustine went on to say, every human sin emulates the sin of Adam. The sin of Adam is what we all do when we sin, putting ourselves in the place of God. In this way all sin amounts to sinful pride and subsequent rebellion against God and his will. When humans sin, they usurp the rightful place of God in their lives. God's answer to human sin lies in the death and the resurrection of Christ that provides the basis of the salvation described in the New Testament.

Conclusion

No worldview avoids every problem and offers a fully satisfactory answer to every question. Given all that Augustine learned from the Platonic tradition in philosophy (as mediated by Plotinus and his followers), it is important to note how Augustine filled some of the major gaps in the thinking of his predecessors and how he modified their thinking in light of the Christian Scriptures and the developing system of Christian belief grounded on those Scriptures. In part 2 of this book, we will encounter some ways in which the Augustinian position on several issues continues to influence modern thinkers.

OPTIONAL WRITING ASSIGNMENT

As we have seen, Plato, Aristotle, and Plotinus attempted to explain a human being's knowledge of Forms or universals. In no more than one paragraph, summarize their theories and then contrast Augustine's answer. Identify the theory that you believe is best and explain why.

FOR FURTHER READING

The writings of Augustine are available in many translations and editions, only a few of which are noted here. Check *Books in Print* for other sources.

Augustine, *The City of God* (New York: Doubleday, 1958).

Augustine, *The Confessions,* trans. Henry Chadwick (New York: Oxford University Press, 1992).

Richard Ackworth, "God and Human Knowledge," *The Downside Review* 75 (1957): 207–14.

Gerald Bonner, *St. Augustine of Hippo: Life and Controversies* (Norwich, Great Britain: Canterbury Press, 1986).

Vernon J. Bourke, *Augustine's Quest of Wisdom* (Milwaukee: Bruce, 1945).

Peter Brown, *Augustine of Hippo: A Biography* (Berkeley: University of California Press, 1967).

Mary T. Clark, *Augustine* (Georgetown: Georgetown University Press, 1994).

Frederick C. Copleston, *A History of Philosophy,* vol. 2, *Augustine to Scotus* (Westminster, Md.: Newman Press, 1962).

Etienne Gilson, *The Christian Philosophy of Saint Augustine* (New York: Random House, 1960).

Ronald H. Nash, *The Light of the Mind: St. Augustine's Theory of Knowledge* (Lexington, Ky.: University Press of Kentucky, 1969). This book is presently available from Books on Demand, Ann Arbor, Michigan.

Ronald H. Nash, *The Word of God and the Mind of Man* (Phillipsburg, N.J.: Presbyterian and Reformed, 1992).

E. Portalié, *A Guide to the Thought of St. Augustine,* translated by Ralph Bastian (Chicago: Regnery, 1960).

C. E. Scheutzinger, *The German Controversy on Saint Augustine's Illumination Theory* (New York: Pageant Press, 1960).

Chapter Seven

Aquinas

The system of Christian belief and philosophy constructed by Thomas Aquinas in little more than twenty years is one of the major intellectual achievements in human history. Even those who occasionally disagree with Thomas cannot help but stand in awe at what he accomplished before his death at the age of forty-nine. While Aquinas is not easy to read, every serious student of the history of ideas should be familiar with his more important writings.

The Life of Aquinas

Saint Thomas Aquinas

Italian steel engraving, 1812

THE GRANGER COLLECTION, NEW YORK

Aquinas was born near Naples, Italy, in 1225. His father was the count of Aquino. Between the ages of five and fourteen, Thomas lived and studied in the Abbey of Monte Cassino. From ages fourteen to nineteen, Aquinas studied at the University of Naples. Then, in 1244, against the wishes of his family, he entered the Dominican order. Unlike many of his peers who sometimes took religious orders to advance somewhat worldly objectives, Aquinas was moved by sincere motives and genuine piety. Thomas's father opposed his selection of the Dominican order, believing that Aquinas would advance more quickly by remaining in the Abbey at Monte Cassino. Thomas was kidnapped by his family and kept from his Dominican vows for about a year.

In 1245, at the age of twenty, Thomas began studying at the University of Paris with Albert the Great, perhaps the most renowned Christian teacher of the time. These studies strengthened his interest in the philosophy of Aristotle. Between 1252 and 1259, Thomas taught at the University of Paris, where he became an opponent of the so-called Latin Averroists, nominally Catholic thinkers who were influenced by the heretical ideas of the Muslim philosopher Averroës. Between 1259 and 1272, he taught in Italy and Paris.

Aquinas wrote approximately ninety works, the most famous of which are the *De Veritate, Summa Contra Gentiles,* and the massive *Summa Theologiae.* Aquinas died on March 7, 1274, at the age of forty-nine, while traveling from Naples to the Council of Lyons.

The Background to Aquinas's Work

For centuries a correct understanding of Aristotle was lost to the medieval world. One reason for this was lack of access to Aristotle's writings, which for the most part were located in territories conquered by Islam. This situation began to change in the twelfth century, when Muslim scholars translated a number of ancient writings into Arabic from the original Greek. When these writings in Greek and Arabic were translated into Latin between 1150 and 1250, efforts to understand Aristotle's philosophy underwent a dramatic change. The new Latin translations allowed access to such areas of Aristotle's philosophy as his logic and physics.

Much that was thought to be Aristotle's teaching at that time was derived from writings by Plotinus or his followers. Averroës (1126–1198), confident that he was only interpreting Aristotle, imported several elements of Plotinus's system into his exposition of Aristotle's thought. (1) As we've seen, Plotinus taught that the world is an eternal emanation of the One. Adopting this view meant that Averroës was in conflict with the Muslim doctrine that God created the world. (2) Averroës interpreted Plotinus to say that when human beings die, their *nous* or mind is reabsorbed into the cosmic *Nous.* This denied personal immortality after death; once again Averroës was in conflict with Islamic theology. Within medieval Islam, such disagreement with official thinking was not likely to produce a long and happy life. The threats issued against Averroës presented him with an obvious problem. If he continued to deny creation and personal immortality, he would be in serious trouble and his life might be in jeopardy. This led then to the third distinctive element of Averroës's position. (3) He taught a double theory of truth, suggesting that a belief in the eternity of the world could be true in philosophy and false in theology at the same time. This clever escape from potential theological risk seems to have worked in Averroës's case.

The thirteenth century also saw the founding of such universities as Oxford, Cambridge, and Paris. Especially at Paris, deviation from official church teaching became more common. The Roman church sought to counteract the influx of these new and dangerous ideas by banning the teaching of certain elements of Aristotle's thought. These warnings were especially directed to teachers at the universities of Paris and Oxford. The ban was unsuccessful at the University of Paris, where a group of Latin Averroists (that is, followers of Averroës who claimed to be Christians) accepted Aristotle's philosophy as true, even when they recognized its incompatibility with Christian doctrine. The leader of the Averroists at the University of Paris, Siger of Brabant (1235–1282), was widely believed to question God's creation of the world and personal survival after death. Many thought he and the other Latin Averroists then attempted to hide under the canopy of the double theory of truth.

Regarding the Latin Averroists as enemies of the church, Aquinas set out to challenge their influence and their interpretation of Aristotle. Only a different interpretation of Aristotle, Thomas believed, one that offered an alternative to the heretical views of the Averroists, could rescue Aristotle's philosophy for use in building a Christian worldview structured along the lines of his system.

Averroës (ibn-Rushd)

French lithograph, 19th century

THE GRANGER COLLECTION, NEW YORK

A starting point for a grasp of Aquinas's work is the sharp distinction he drew between philosophy and theology. To his credit, Thomas would have no part of a double theory of truth. Two contradictory propositions, even if they are found in different areas like science and theology, cannot both be true at the same time and in the same sense. Aquinas contends that if a proposition is true in theology, then it must also be true in philosophy, science, and other branches of knowledge. If a proposition is true in philosophy, history, and science, then it must also be true within the sphere of faith. Faith and reason, properly understood, can never conflict. God's word is true, Thomas asserts, and what God teaches will always be consistent with whatever truth humans discover outside the sphere of special revelation.

Everything Aquinas said up to this point had been taught by Augustine. Aquinas insists that there are two different types of knowledge.

Philosophy and Theology

There is the natural knowledge we find in philosophy, and there is super-natural knowledge, revealed by God and discussed by theology. While faith and reason are not logically incompatible, they are psychologically different activities of the soul, each operating within its own domain. The domain of reason includes all truths that humans can acquire unaided by divine revelation. Reason (philosophy) includes all the scientific, ethical, psychological, and philosophical knowledge that humans can gain apart from divine revelation.

For Aquinas, the sphere of philosophy includes any item of knowledge that humans can acquire apart from special revelation. The word *philosophy* therefore encompassed the science of his day and includes any item of human knowledge based upon human experience and reasoning. Theology, by contrast, is a function of faith grounded upon the content of divine revelation. The first principles or premises of special revelation come through revelation, whereas the first principles of philosophy (such as mathematics) are known by the unaided light of the intellect.

One item of knowledge, however, can be known by either reason (philosophy) or faith (theology), namely, the knowledge that God exists. If one has the interest to study them and the ability to understand them, there are sound philosophical arguments for God's existence. But those unable to grasp the philosophical proofs can know the existence of God by resting in the truth of divine revelation. Aquinas believes that with one exception—the knowledge of God's existence—it is impossible for the same person to know and believe the same thing at the same time. The reason for this is simple: the content of philosophy and theology belong to different spheres.

One way to illustrate Aquinas's view of faith and reason is to picture two ladders.

Figure 7.1

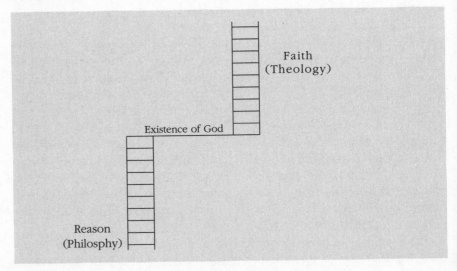

Faith
(Theology)

Existence of God

Reason
(Philosphy)

It is important to remember that Augustine defined faith and reason differently than Aquinas did. For Augustine, reason is whatever humans can come to know on their own, without any dependence on the testimony of others. Faith includes whatever we come to know on the basis of authority, that is, the testimony of a person or a document. On Augustine's analysis of faith, historical knowledge is impossible without trust in or assent to the testimony of written accounts and other sources of information about the past. Augustine's point is that any item of knowledge achieved via Thomas's lower ladder itself requires faith. According to Augustine, people cannot know anything unless they first believe something. The scientist and historian necessarily begin by believing things not provable via their empirical methods. A scientist must assume, for example, that scientists must tell the truth, that they should be honest, that the universe is orderly, and so on. For Augustine, the division between reason and faith is not nearly as neat and clean as Thomas's followers would have us believe. Everything known by Thomas's reason (the lower ladder) is dependent upon one or many acts of Augustinian faith.

At the same time, Augustine would agree with Aquinas's point that there are differences between what humans can come to know only via special revelation (such as the Bible) and what we can come to know by means of our mind and senses. Divine special revelation is needed because the human mind is incapable of grasping certain truths without the aid of special revelation.

Aquinas and the Averroist Denial of Creation

Aquinas's bifurcation of faith and reason provides him with one way of resolving the challenge raised by Aristotle's alleged teaching about the eternality of the world, a view clearly in conflict with the Christian doctrine of creation. Aquinas argues that human reason (philosophy) is incapable of discovering whether or not the world had a beginning in time. The doctrine of creation is a truth of faith, not a truth of reason. It can be known only by divine revelation. If Aristotle was wrong on this point (and, Aquinas suggests, Aristotle may only have been reporting the opinions of his predecessors), it was largely an error of overestimating the bounds of human reason.

Aquinas's Worldview

Aquinas does not stop with his attempt to show that Aristotelianism could be made compatible with Christianity, nor is he content to relate the Christian view of God and the world to the perspective of the classical world. He proceeds to build a remarkable system of thought in which answers are proposed to a wide variety of important problems in psychology, physics, metaphysics, ethics, and other areas of human knowledge. He is also concerned to relate his Christian worldview to the problems of his own time and meet the challenges of competing theories.

However much Christians may disagree about the supposed success of Aquinas's endeavor, most can endorse his objective of developing a coherent system of Christian thought.

God

Aquinas intends the God of his system to be the deity of historic Christian theism—a personal, eternal, omnipotent, omniscient, omnipresent triune God. As we will see, however, there is a lot of Aristotelianism in his system. One question we will have to examine concerns the extent to which the Christian view of deity to which Aquinas aspires is compromised by the elements of Aristotle's philosophy he incorporates into his own system. One such element is Thomas's belief that God is pure actuality.

The medieval doctrine of pure actuality was the scholastic[1] equivalent of Aristotle's teaching that God is Pure Form. Aquinas teaches that everything that exists (with the exception of God, the human soul, and angels) is a combination of form and matter. Everything possesses both actuality and potentiality. This is the whole point to his claim that God is pure form or actuality. The form or essence of a thing determines its actuality; its matter is the ground for the thing's several potentialities. While every existing thing can possess only one actuality at any given time, every existing thing possesses a number of different potentialities.

Like Aristotle, Thomas regards potentiality as a kind of imperfection. This conviction led both thinkers to believe that any potentiality in God would detract from his perfection.[2] This led to the conviction that God must possess no potentiality; God must be pure actuality. While God can act, he cannot be acted upon. Because potentiality cannot belong to God, God can possess no matter; he must be pure form.

In my chapter on Aristotle, I noted how Aristotle's doctrine of Pure Form seems difficult to reconcile with the Christian doctrine of God. For one thing, Aristotle taught that God cannot think about anything in the changing and imperfect world. The only perfect thing worthy of God's attention is God himself. For Aristotle's God to think about anything else would detract from his perfection. Can Aquinas evade problems like this?

Proofs for God's Existence

Aquinas is famous for advancing five arguments, the Five Ways, for God's existence. Many Christians have relied on Thomas's statement of these arguments or on later modifications of them. Critics of theism have often

---

1. The adjective *scholastic* and the noun *scholasticism* are often used as terms to describe philosophers in the thirteenth century. These terms, along with the word *schoolman,* are used with reference to the university professors and their method of teaching: a technical vocabulary, an impersonal style, logical rigor, and abstract thinking.

2. See Aquinas *Summa Contra Gentiles* 1.16.1.

used Aquinas's arguments as their foil in an effort to discredit the rationality of belief in God.

Many discussions of the arguments have misunderstood Aquinas's position, a mistake that it is easy to understand given their greatly condensed form. For example, Aquinas is thought to have argued that there must be a First Cause or a Prime Mover because it is impossible that there should be an infinitely long series of causes or motions. But Thomas specifically states that philosophy is incapable of showing the impossibility of an infinite series.[3] For this reason Aquinas concludes that philosophy can establish neither the truth nor the falsity of the doctrine of creation in time. It is highly unlikely that Thomas would have ignored this point that he had taken such pains to establish in arguing for something as important as God's existence.

(1) The Argument from Motion (Change). Things move or change. If something changes, it must possess the potential for change. No potentiality can actualize itself. Therefore, any change requires something prior to the event that brings about the movement from potentiality to actuality. An infinitely long series of actualizers is impossible. Therefore, there must be a Prime Mover. The most serious problem with this argument is its obvious dependence upon the impossibility of an infinitely long series. Aquinas clearly states that philosophy cannot prove the impossibility of an infinite series. Hence, this could not be Aquinas's meaning.

(2) The Argument from Cause and Effect to a First Cause. Aquinas is usually understood to have taught that every effect must be the result of an efficient cause. Nothing can cause its own existence. No series of efficient causes can be the cause of the series. Hence, there must be a First (efficient) Cause. The key step in this second argument appears again to be the impossibility of an infinitely long series of causes and effects. The central problem is that Aquinas disavows the ability to prove such a claim.

(3) The Argument from Contingent Beings to a Necessary Being. A contingent being is something whose nonexistence is possible. A necessary being is a being that is not dependent upon anything else for its existence and whose nonexistence is impossible. In other words, a necessary being is eternal and self-sufficient.

The world contains a very large number of contingent beings. In fact, it appears as though everything in the world that humans know about is contingent in the sense that its nonexistence is possible and it depends upon something else for its existence. If everything that makes up the

---

3. See the discussion in Frederick C. Copleston, *A History of Philosophy*, vol. 2 , *Medieval Philosophy: Augustine to Scotus* (Westminster, Md.: Newman Press, 1962), 366.

world is contingent, then the world is contingent. Hence, there must be a necessary being that is the ground of the sum total of contingent beings.

If only contingent beings exist, there would be no explanation for a world containing only contingent beings. The only explanation for the existence of a contingent world is in terms of a necessary being.

Following a brief summary of the last two ways, I will return to this particular argument and discuss how it functions as Thomas's primary argument for God's existence.

(4) The Argument from Degrees of Perfection to a Perfect Being. Things in our world differ in degrees of goodness, truth, beauty, and so on. But it seems before we can judge that *a* is better than *b,* that *c* is more perfect than *d,* that *e* is more beautiful than *f,* we must first know the standard of truth, goodness, and beauty. Things are more or less good only to the extent that they resemble something possessing the highest degree of goodness. The highest of all beings, that which contains the highest degree of perfection, is God. Any knowledge that one thing is more perfect than another (that there are degrees of perfection) involves comparing the two things to something that is unqualifiedly perfect. It should be obvious that we could never know that *x* falls short of some standard unless we know the standard. All of this entails the existence of something that is the cause of every perfection, namely, God.

(5) The Argument from Design in the World to a Designer of the World. Given our observation of many instances of design and purpose in the world, our minds drive us to the existence of God, the cause of this order and purpose. Arguments that resemble Thomas's fifth argument are often called teleological arguments for God's existence. According to William Paley (1743–1805), author of *Natural Theology,* an influential statement of the teleological argument,

> There cannot be a design without a designer; contrivance without a contriver; order without choice; arrangement without anything capable of arranging; subserviency and relation to a purpose without that which could intend a purpose; means suitable to an end, and executing their office in accomplishing that end, without the end ever having been contemplated or the means accommodated to it. Arrangement, disposition of parts, subserviency of means to an end, relation of instruments to a use imply the presence of intelligence and mind.[4]

We will have occasion to examine some contemporary versions of the teleological argument in part 2 of this book.

---

4. William Paley, *Natural Theology,* ed. Frederick Ferré (Indianapolis: Bobbs-Merrill, 1963), 8–9.

The Essence of Thomas's Arguments

In all five of Thomas's arguments, the notion of dependence is basic, noted in connection with the facts of motion, causation, coming into being and ceasing to exist, degrees of perfection, and purpose. A few paragraphs back, I drew attention to the fact that any interpretation of Thomas's arguments that makes any of them depend upon the supposed impossibility of an infinite series must be mistaken, since Thomas himself denies that claim. The challenge then is to find an interpretation of the first three ways that does not depend on an appeal to the impossibility of an infinite series.

Frederick C. Copleston, author of an acclaimed multivolume history of philosophy, notes that Aquinas's First Mover or First Cause could not have been first in any temporal sense of the word.[5] The First Cause Aquinas seeks is first in a logical sense, in the sense of importance or ultimacy. To quote Copleston, Thomas's "point is that the series, whether finite or infinite, itself requires an ultimate explanation. Therefore, when he speaks about the impossibility of an 'infinite regress' in, for example, the series of efficient causes, he is referring to an infinite regress not in the temporal order but in the order of ontological dependence."[6]

It may help if I use a picture to explain Thomas's third argument. Imagine a circle big enough to encompass the entire universe, that is, the sum total of contingent beings. Every individual thing that exists within the circle—within the world—is a contingent being; there is no contingent being that exists outside the circle. All of this is proper, given the fact that the world or universe or cosmos is the sum total of all contingent beings.

With respect to any individual thing existing within the circle, it is proper to ask what its sufficient reason is.[7] The *sufficient reason* for something is the reason it exists and why it is in the state that it is in. We would hardly be surprised if we discovered that the sufficient reason for everything existing within the circle was something else inside the circle. This is another way of saying that the sufficient reason for every contingent being is some other contingent being or beings. Take yourself as an example. You are a contingent being. Therefore, it is proper to ask why you exist. One sufficient reason for your existence is the prior existence of your parents, and beyond them their parents, and so on.

We have agreed that every individual thing within the world is contingent. But what shall we say about the world itself? Is *it* (the world, the sum total of all contingent beings, the big circle that includes everything else) contingent? The point here goes beyond the claim that all parts of

---

5. See Frederick C. Copleston, *Medieval Philosophy* (New York: Harper and Brothers, 1961), 91.

6. Ibid.

7. After all, a contingent being is one that has its sufficient reason or explanation in some other being.

the world are contingent. We have reached the point where many people think it makes sense to believe that the whole cosmos is contingent. After all, if every part of the world (past, present, and future) is contingent, it makes sense to regard the entire world as contingent.

Suppose we allow this last step for the sake of argument. If the world is contingent, then it is proper to ask for the sufficient reason for the world. Notice that we are not asking why this or that part of the world exists; we are asking why the whole thing exists. Notice also that we are not asking what first brought the world into existence. We are looking for the sufficient reason, the ultimate ground, without which the world would not exist. Why does the world exist? What is the sufficient reason for the entire total of contingent beings?

Only two answers to this question are possible. First, we might try to find the explanation for the existence of the world in some contingent being or set of contingent beings. But this will not work because we have already agreed that the world—what we are trying to explain—is the sum total of all contingent beings. By definition, there are no contingent beings outside the circle. We cannot explain the sum total of contingent beings by postulating another contingent being and acting as though this new contingent being were outside the circle and thus a possible explanation for the world. If any being is a contingent being, it is inside the circle and thus part of what we are trying to explain.

There seems, then, to be only one other possibility. The world exists because it, like all contingent beings, depends upon a being other than itself. But in this case, the existence of the world must depend on the existence of a being that is not contingent. And if the only possible explanation for the existence of the world is a noncontingent being, the explanation must be a *necessary* being.

Can we not continue to push our search for sufficient reasons further and ask what is the sufficient reason for the necessary being? After all, this is the sort of thing children do when they ask why God exists. The sufficient reason for any necessary being is *itself,* not something else. By definition a necessary being is *uncaused;* it is a being that must exist because its nonexistence is impossible. If all this were not the case, the being in question would not be necessary. Should anyone begin looking for the sufficient reason of a necessary being, he would reveal one important bit of information about himself: he does not know the meaning of the expression "necessary being."

The debate over this line of argument continues to the present day. It would take us too far afield to explore the dispute at this time.[8] What does seem clear to almost all of Thomas's contemporary interpreters is

---

8. Readers interested in pursuing that debate further can track it in Ronald H. Nash, *Faith and Reason* (Grand Rapids: Zondervan, 1992), chap. 9.

that something like the argument I have just explained must be the major point behind his famous Five Ways, or at least for the first three ways. Thomas's God is the eternal and necessary ground for everything that has being, for every causal relation, for every change that takes place.

If there is one thing we have a right to expect from the worldview of a Christian philosopher, it is an answer to the question of how humans attain knowledge about God. Thomas's reply to this question leaves much to be desired. Indeed, he appears trapped in this matter by some of his prior commitments to elements of Aristotle's philosophy.

In chapter 3, I defined an empiricist as someone who believes that all human knowledge rises from sense experience. Implicit in this definition is the denial of any and all innate ideas. When empiricism is understood in this way, Thomas is clearly an empiricist. Thomas's theory of knowledge shows a heavy reliance upon Aristotle's account of the passive and active intellects. Sense experience produces awareness only of particular things. The active intellect produces the universal by abstracting the idea of the universal from the sense image (phantasm). There is nothing in the active intellect that is not first in the passive intellect, and whatever reaches the passive intellect gets there through the senses. So in this respect, Thomas is an empiricist. Human knowledge requires sense perception, which in turn requires the soul's relation to a body.

Therefore, if humans are to know God, this knowledge must be built up from a patient analysis of sense data. But clearly humans do not perceive God in the same way that we perceive a tree or a house. Responding to this matter, Aquinas teaches that humans attain knowledge of God in two ways, the way of negation and the way of analogy.

The Way of Negation

In order to teach direct or positive knowledge of God's existence, one would have to be some kind of rationalist, such as Augustine. According to Augustine, we can recognize God in his creation because we come into life equipped with an innate idea of God, given us in the image of God. Thomas's empiricism makes this kind of appeal impossible.

As an empiricist, Aquinas claims that we have to approach God negatively. While we cannot have direct or positive knowledge of what God is, we can know what God is not. We can know that God is incapable of sin, ignorance, or weakness. But consider any proposition about God that asserts something that God is not. For example, let us suppose someone says that God is not a Chevrolet. This is true. However, before I can know that God is not a Chevrolet, I must have at least some positive knowledge about God. It is impossible for anyone whose mind is blank on the subject of God to know that God is not *A* or not *B* or not *C*. The only way we could know what God is not is if we first had some positive knowledge about God. Augustine and other rationalists can explain how such positive knowledge about God is possible. But Aquinas cannot. I believe we must judge Thomas's way of negation a failure.

The Way of Analogy

I begin with a warning. No serious discussion of Aquinas can omit this topic. However, many people find this issue very difficult to understand. If you get lost, do your best and don't get discouraged.

My next task is to define three terms: *univocal, equivocal,* and *analogical.* (1) Two words are used univocally if they are used in an identical sense. In the propositions "Socrates is a man" and "Plato is a man," the word *man* is used in the same sense, that is, univocally. (2) Two words are used equivocally if they are used in two entirely different senses. In the propositions "Bill Brown's car is a lemon" and "Charley Brown's mother is making a lemon pie" the word *lemon* is used in two different senses, that is, equivocally. (3) Two words are used analogically if their respective meanings are somewhat similar and somewhat different. In the propositions "A hornet's nest is its home" and "Bill's home is on Main Street," the words *home* are used in respects that are partly alike and partly different, that is, analogically.

According to Thomas, no words that humans apply to God can be used in a univocal sense. While God is transcendent and infinite, the categories by means of which humans attempt to describe him are drawn from our human experience of the imperfect world. For example, the word *wise* cannot mean the same thing when applied to Solomon and to God because God's wisdom is inseparable from his essence while Solomon's wisdom is not. This is so because Solomon on occasion could act in unwise ways. For this reason, no predicate can be applied univocally to God. Not even the term *existence* can be used univocally since God exists necessarily while everything else exists contingently.

But if univocal predication about God is impossible, as Thomas insists, does this mean that all predication about God is equivocal? If this were so, it would mean the end of natural theology since all of Thomas's proofs would commit the fallacy of equivocation. This well-known logical fallacy is committed whenever one argument uses the same key term in two different ways. If all human predicates applied to God are equivocal, any attempt to argue for God's existence on the basis of sense experience would be fallacious, and all meaningful predication about God would be impossible.

If the language we use to talk about God is univocal, we appear trapped in anthropomorphism, where we simply describe God in human terms. If our language is equivocal, we seem trapped in agnosticism. It is at this point where Thomas proposes the way of analogy. However, the way of analogy seems forever condemned to run back and forth between the two unacceptable extremes of univocity and equivocation. Even Copleston, one of Roman Catholicism's leading philosophers and interpreters of Aquinas, admits to some discomfort in the presence of the middle way, the way of analogy.

> It would appear . . . that the theistic philosopher is faced with a dilemma. If he pursues exclusively the negative way, he ends in sheer agnosticism, for he whittles away the positive meaning which a term originally had for him until nothing is left. If, however, he pursues exclusively the affirmative way, he lands in anthropomorphism [the supposed consequence of univocity]. But if he attempts to combine the two ways, as indeed he must if he is to avoid both extremes, his mind appears to oscillate between anthropomorphism and agnosticism.[9]

Fortunately, the Christian does not have to choose between the way of analogy and agnosticism. It ought to be obvious that there must be a univocal element present in any predication about God, and it need not follow that this univocal element leads to anthropomorphism. The very thing that keeps an analogy from being equivocation is the presence of some univocal element. As one critic of Thomas's position explains,

> All the analogies of common speech have a univocal basis. . . . No matter how complicated, or what type of analogy, an examination must discover some univocal element. The two terms [in an analogy] must be like each other in some respect. If there were no likeness or similarity of any sort, there could be no analogy. And the point of likeness can be designated by a simple univocal term or phrase.[10]

Even Aquinas admitted that without some point of similarity, the analogy could not be an analogy but would instead be an equivocation. Unless the two terms have some meaning in common, they would be not an analogy but an equivocation. If someone says that a bird's nest is analogous to a beehive, there must be something that the nest and the hive have in common. In this case, both are places where living creatures raise their young, or something like this. Without some common meaning (that is, a univocal element), we would have not an analogy but an equivocation.

But how can the position expressed in the previous paragraphs avoid Thomas's charge of anthropomorphism? The answer is simple: Anthropomorphism is avoided when the person explaining our knowledge of God is not an empiricist. Thomas's explanation founders because of his insistence that human concepts are derived from sensory experience. But if empiricism is rejected, if one holds instead that humans possess *a priori*

---

9. Frederick C. Copleston, *Contemporary Philosophy* (London: Burns and Oates, 1956), 96.
10. Gordon H. Clark, *Christian View of Men and Things* (Grand Rapids: Eerdmans, 1952), 311.

knowledge given to them by God, we have an explanation of how the univocal knowledge about God that grounds analogical knowledge is possible.

Consider the simple claim that God is love. An empiricist like Aquinas is forced to say that our first contact with love comes through our experiences with other human beings. But human love falls miles short of divine love, thus forcing us to treat our fundamental understanding of love as an analogy. But suppose instead that our contact of such predicates as "love" and "perfection" are ours as part of our innate idea of God present within us as part of the image of God. In this second case, we recognize instances of human love (the real analogy) because we have an implicit understanding of God's love. We are drawing a theological application from Plato's treatment of equality and Augustine's explanation of our knowledge of unity. The reason we can recognize two equal particulars is because we first know Equality itself. We can recognize imperfection in the creation because we first have an innate idea of perfection.

While analogy may be a useful device in literature, its value to theology is debatable. It is not enough to compare God and humans; a definite positive identification is needed. "A statement comparing a known with an unknown object gives us no knowledge of the unknown at all. Hence dependence on analogical knowledge, paradox, or symbols, with its denial of literal and positive knowledge of God, destroys both revelation and theology and leaves us in complete ignorance."[11] In the case of Aquinas, it seems, bad philosophy gives rise to bad theology. Avoid empiricism, and Thomas's defective doctrines of analogy and the negative way are not necessary.

Primary Matter and Individuation

According to Aquinas, individuation (that which grounds the individuality of each particular member of some class) has its basis in matter (primary matter). It is important, I believe, to note briefly how two of Thomas's contemporaries disagreed with him. Alexander of Hales (1180–1245) rejected matter as the ground of individuality and insisted instead that individuality is inherent in every substance. Bonaventure (1221–1274) also rejected matter as the ground of individuation. He denied that anything like primary matter, which is barely distinguishable from nothingness, can be the principle of individuality. As Hans Meyer notes, "If individuation can be traced neither to matter alone nor to the form alone, it must be derived from the actual union of matter and form."[12] Serious consideration should be given to searching for some ground of individuation other than primary matter.

---

11. Gordon H. Clark, "Wheaton Lectures," in *The Philosophy of Gordon H. Clark,* ed. Ronald H. Nash (Philadelphia: Presbyterian and Reformed, 1968), 78.

12. Hans Meyer, *The Philosophy of St. Thomas Aquinas,* trans. Frederick Eckhoff (St. Louis: B. Herder, 1944), 478.

Human Nature

According to Thomas, human beings are composed of matter and form, namely, body and soul. In spite of the resulting unity of the composition, soul and body are not identical. The soul continues to exist after death and is eventually reunited with a physical body at the final resurrection.[13]

Thomas rejected the kind of body-soul dualism we have already encountered in the worldviews of Plato and Augustine.[14] Aquinas was much more comfortable with Aristotle's teaching that the soul is the form of the body, a position that stresses the union of body and soul in the human person. Aquinas follows Aristotle's view of three types of soul, vegetative, sensitive, and rational. Plants possess only the vegetative soul; its functions include life, growth, and reproduction. Animals possess only a sensitive soul, which performs the functions of the vegetative soul plus sensation. However, Thomas insists that there is only one substantial form in a human person, namely, the rational soul. This constitutes a major modification of Aristotle's position. The human rational soul informs the matter of a human and is the ground of all human activities dealing with the processes of life, sensation, and reason. But there is only one soul in a human, not three.

If one accepts Plato's view of the soul as a separate, immaterial substance, it appears much easier to defend a belief in immortality. But if we begin with Aristotle's teaching of the soul, as Thomas did, the close linkage between soul and body would appear to rule out the possibility of survival after death, or at least make the attempt more difficult. Whereas Augustine described sensation as the act of a soul using a body, Thomas understands sensation as an act of the whole person who is a union of soul and body. Since no human possesses innate ideas, Thomas says, the human mind can attain no knowledge without sense experience. Given the union of soul and body in the thinking of Aristotle and Aquinas, how can Christians who support such a view ground their belief in personal survival after death? Unless Thomas can find a way to link his soul-body union to personal survival after death, Christians have a major problem with his worldview.

Aquinas taught that when human beings die, their soul separates from the body and the dead body decays. The death of the body brings a halt to the vegetative and sensitive functions. That which used to be the form of the human being is no longer informing the matter, and thus there is no longer a unified human substance. There are lots of new substances, such as fingernails, eyebrows, rib cage, and so on, until they also decay and undergo substantial changes into still newer substances.

A human being comes into existence when a rational soul informs a particular body. A human being dies when the rational soul separates

---

13. For Thomas's discussions on the issues covered in this section, see *Summa Theologiae* 1a.75–76.

14. I noted different emphases in Augustine and Plato.

from the body. Since a human cannot sense anything without bodily senses and hence without a body, both the body and the soul must be parts of the human person. One reason, therefore, why a soul and body are united is because the soul needs the body. The union is good for the soul; it makes it possible for the soul to act in accord with its nature.[15]

Since a human being is one substance, it should be obvious that the individual person has only one substantial form; for Aquinas, this is the human's rational soul. A human being's nature is composite, soul and body. But the human soul is itself a spiritual substance. As such it is incapable of corruption; it is immortal. The immortality of the soul Aquinas refers to is personal immortality. It is not possible to explain adequately the enormous diversity of human ideas and cognitive functions in the mass of human beings while believing that all humans share in one cosmic intellect. Aquinas acknowledged that human souls continue to exist following death at the good pleasure of God.

Thomas's Interpretation of Aristotle's Active Intellect

In spite of Thomas's assertion of personal survival after death, he still has to deal with Aristotle's comments about the active intellect in book 3 of his *De Anima*. As we learned in chapter 4, Aristotle taught there is an active intellect that alone makes knowledge possible and that is immortal, everlasting, and separable. The Averroists followed Plotinus and denied the particularity of the active intellect in favor of a cosmic intelligence (*Nous*). But Aquinas insisted that Aristotle believed that each human being has a separate, immortal, active intellect. Aquinas hoped his restructuring of Aristotle's doctrine would prove a philosopher like Aquinas can be an Aristotelian and still believe in the Christian doctrine of personal survival after death.[16]

Some Roman Catholic philosophers, such as Copleston, have raised doubts about the accuracy of Thomas's interpretation of Aristotle's active intellect.[17] But Aquinas was not just trying to demonstrate the compatibility of Aristotle's system with Christian thought; he was also attempting to show non-Aristotelian Christians that they had nothing to fear from the new philosophy. And in a situation like the one faced by Thomas, good public relations can easily outweigh bad exegesis.

Ethics

Both Augustine and Aquinas believed humans live in a universe governed both by physical and moral laws. One necessary condition for human well-being is the adjustment of our conduct to the physical and moral order of the universe. If someone exits a tenth-story window with-

---

15. See Aquinas *Summa Theologiae* 1a.6.5; 1a.89.1.

16. This would be a good time to return to chapter 4 and to my analysis of the three interpretations of Aristotle's active intellect.

17. See Copleston, *A History of Philosophy*, vol. 2, *Medieval Philosophy*, chap. 37.

out a parachute, his well-being will be in jeopardy. Whenever we ignore the physical order of the universe, we place ourselves at risk.

But our universe also exhibits a moral order. Though human disregard for the moral laws of the universe may appear at times inconsequential, the dire consequences will become apparent eventually. Human behavior that violates the moral order of the world will negatively affect our well-being. The consequences of sin include afflictions of the human spirit, heart, and soul.

Thomas's *Eudaemonism*

One common approach to the ethics of Aquinas is to see it as a form of eudaemonism.[18] Thomas agrees with Aristotle that all humans act with the aim of achieving happiness (*eudaemonia*). Nonetheless, Aquinas makes some significant modifications in Aristotle's *eudaemonism,* one of which is the claim that true happiness is not attainable in this life but only in heaven. The best that is available to us in this life is an imperfect version of happiness. What makes a human action good or bad is the extent to which it advances that person toward the good. All intentional acts may be judged good or bad to the degree to which they perfect us as rational beings.

Cardinal Virtue

Thomas teaches that God has given humans two guides to morally good acts. Virtues guide us from within, and laws guide us externally. Thomas follows Aristotle in defining virtue as a disposition that results from our performing good acts. When we practice the proper moral virtues, both our works and our character are perfected. Virtue has a positive effect on our mind and will. Thomas also agrees that moral virtue is a mean between vices. Furthermore, Thomas draws a distinction between the four cardinal virtues, borrowed this time from Plato, and the three theological virtues, drawn from the New Testament.

As we learned in chapter 3, the cardinal virtues are prudence, courage, temperance, and justice.[19] Thomas says cardinal virtues are natural in the sense that they are known not by special revelation, such as Scripture, but from general revelation in the created nature of things. The cardinal virtues are relevant to all humans, not just Christians.

Temperance means moderation. Temperate people keep their sensual desires under control by means of reason. Intemperate people are childish. Courage is steadfastness in the presence of danger. Prudence is wisdom applied to behavior. Prudence seeks the best means to a chosen

---

18. See Aquinas *Summa Theologiae* 1a2ae.1.6.

19. Thomas's comments about the virtues are scattered throughout several sections of his *Summa,* including 2a2ae.57, 58, 141, and 142.

end. However, Thomas adds, prudence does not give us a moral end; rather it presupposes it. Justice means giving other people their due.

Theological Virtues

The three theological virtues, faith, hope, and love, are known by special revelation and are attainable only by believers. The theological virtues are supernatural in the sense that they are attainable only by divine grace. The theological virtues prepare us for the most perfect kind of happiness, that which results from our knowledge of God. Faith, hope, and love are theological virtues for three reasons: God is their object, and their proper orientation is toward God; only God can infuse them in us; the only way we come to know these virtues is through the divine revelation God has given us in Scripture.

Faith leads our minds to see truth and guides our wills to assent to truth. Hope is the disposition that leads us to seek God's assistance in the attainment of eternal happiness. It inclines us toward our final end. Love is a gift of the Holy Spirit that inclines us toward friendship with God. In turn, our love of God is the ground for our love of neighbor. As Jesus taught in Matthew 22, all of the Ten Commandments are related to our loving God and loving our neighbor. Love is the foundation of the virtues; it is also what moves us toward the other virtues.

Thomas's Four Kinds of Law

Thomas is famous for his distinction among four kinds of law: eternal law, natural law, human law, and the divine law.[20]

Eternal Law

Eternal law is the law of God that applies to all of creation. The eternal law includes both moral laws and the physical laws that govern all of nature. Eternal law is God's mind conceiving and determining everything that exists. Every other form of law flows from the eternal law.

Natural Law

Natural law is the part of eternal law that applies exclusively to humans. Natural law is one of the ways by which humans participate in the eternal law. The natural law is written on the human heart. It is grounded in human nature. The content of the natural law corresponds to humankind's basic inclinations when they are not corrupted or impeded by sin. Since Thomas believed our natural human tendency inclines toward the good, the most general statement of the natural law is to do good and avoid evil.

---

20. Once again, Thomas's teachings about law are scattered through numerous sections of his *Summa,* including 1a2ae.57, 71, 91, 92, and 93.

The central message of natural law is that humans should do good and avoid evil. While evil acts are incompatible with human reason, good acts accord with our rational nature. Obviously, human reason can be wrong. Our human reason functions only as the basis for natural law as it participates in God's eternal reason. Obeying the natural law consists of following freely our natural human striving for Good. The natural law expresses what human beings would naturally strive for, provided they are not impeded by sin.

Human (Positive) Law

Human or positive law is the result of human efforts to govern themselves; it is the attempt of human reason to formulate practical laws based on natural law.

Divine Law

Aquinas taught that God's moral law has two sides. On the one side, we find the supernatural law revealed in Scripture. On the other side, we find the natural law as it is sometimes discovered by human reason. Since both laws have their source in God, they can never conflict. Divine law is God's eternal law communicated to humans through special revelation. It is the revelation of God's moral law through the Bible to believers.[21] While Aquinas suggests that natural law is for unbelievers and God's divine law is for believers, this is too simple. Life is full of circumstances when believers for one reason or another can be aided by their knowledge of the natural law and when unbelievers can be instructed in the content of revealed morality.

The following diagram illustrates the relationships among eternal, natural, human, and divine law:

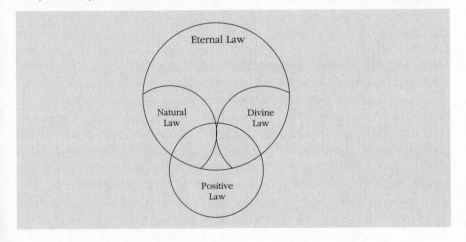

Figure 7.2

---

21. See Aquinas *Summa Theologiae* 1a2ae.91.

The Significance of Natural Law

One of Aquinas's more important contributions was his linking ancient non-Christian theories of natural law to the biblical understanding of the moral life. One way to approach the subject of natural law is to consider how often humans criticize human laws as wrong. Examples that come easily to mind are the policies of Nazi Germany that led to the Holocaust or the barbarous acts perpetrated by leaders of the Soviet Union against millions of their own people.

Whenever people resist a human law because of its perceived wrongness, those condemning the law appeal, whether they know it or not, to a higher moral law. Most law schools choose to remain silent or hostile toward the notion of natural law. Advocates of a position known as legal positivism insist that no such higher laws exist. Legal positivism leaves us with little recourse in the face of immoral or unjust laws. Aquinas rejected the move to reduce all law to positive or human law. He believed that human law ought to be dependent on natural law, which provides legitimacy to human positive law. The protection of human rights is impossible unless those rights are protected by positive laws that reflect the content of natural law. Natural law applies to all human beings, not only Christians. This makes it possible for natural law to function as the ground for positive law in societies composed of people representing diverse religions and religious convictions.

Because natural law is transcendent, it can function as a set of rules governing not only individual behavior but also relations between nations. Unless there is a natural law common to all humans regardless of their location in history or geography, there is no objective ground for judging the immoral behavior of evil tyrants.

Because natural law applies to all human persons and societies and nations, it provides a basis to distinguish between our duty as human beings as opposed to our Christian duties. The message of the natural law is *practice justice;* the message of the divine law is *practice justice, love, and personal righteousness.*

Humans access the natural law immediately via reason. The reason natural law is the same for all human beings is because human nature is similar. "Therefore neither the ultimate transcendent foundation of the natural moral law nor its promulgation by the practical reason means that the natural law is arbitrary or could be otherwise than it is. Human reason promulgates the law through reflection on human nature."[22]

Human reason imposes the obligations of the natural law. But these duties are grounded on our human nature. The moral law is both natural

---

22. Copleston, *Medieval Philosophy,* 96.

and rational. It is impossible for natural law to change since its foundation is unchanging human nature. The source of the natural law is the eternal law that exists in God. The eternal law is not an arbitrary law resting only in a changeable divine will; it is grounded instead in the reason of God.

Some Christians object to the concept of natural law on the grounds that it compromises the purity of Scripture by synthesizing it with ideas of pagans like Plato, Aristotle, and the Stoics. While these ancient philosophers acknowledged natural laws, that hardly involves Christians in any compromise of their faith. Plato and Aristotle also believed that two times two equals four. I don't know many Christians rushing to abandon the multiplication tables because that knowledge is shared with unbelievers. Moreover, natural law ethics would hardly appear plausible if no unbelievers had ever taught it. Such thinking in important philosophers outside of the sphere of biblical influence is what we should expect to find if the theory of natural law is true.

Conclusion

At least three accomplishments of Aquinas are worthy of note. (1) Aquinas provided wisdom and inspiration to numerous philosophers, theologians, and representatives of other disciplines who applied what they learned from him to the new problems and challenges of their own time. Many of these contributions can be useful to many people who study and use them with discernment.

(2) Thomas sought to develop a comprehensive world-and-life view. While some may disagree with features of his system, no one before him and few since him have developed a worldview as complete as his.

(3) Aquinas met the major intellectual challenges to the Christianity of his age on their own ground. Differences will arise over the exact way in which he answered that challenge, but contemporary Christians can applaud his refusal to take refuge in pietism, fideism, or irrationalism.

But Thomas's worldview has its weaknesses, many of which carry over from Aristotelianism. One collection of difficulties can be tied to attempts to utilize Aristotle's primary matter in a Christian worldview. As I noted earlier, many of Aristotle's contemporaries and others who followed in later centuries sought an account of individuation in something other than primary matter. While Thomas's treatment of the body-soul relationship offers distinct advantages over Platonism, it still leaves us wanting more in the way of an account of human survival after death, if philosophy can provide such an account.

Thomas's attempts to prove God's existence have led many admirers to expand them in new ways. His account of the Five Ways in *Summa Theologiae* needs amplification. Many critics find Thomas's empiricism to be a source of other difficulties. For one thing, can empiricism really account for our understanding of God's nature? Compare Thomas's troubled theories of analogy and the negative way. Can empiricism successfully ground a knowledge of God's existence? Aquinas denied the presence of any innate ideas in the human mind. Thus, if humans are to know God, this knowledge must be built up from a patient analysis of sense data. Many who reject Thomas's position doubt that God's existence can be demonstrated from sense experience alone. One can no sooner know God from nature without some *a priori* idea of God than one can know anything apart from some innate categorical structure of rationality.

Nonetheless, it would be churlish to leave the impression that Thomas's system is anything short of impressive. Perhaps a mysterious event in Thomas's life is a good point on which to end our examination of our six worldviews. Aquinas, near the end of his life, suddenly stopped writing. Some accounts suggest that he had a special experience with God that helped him realize the most important thing in life was not his books. We are told that he not only stopped writing but also refused to look at the intellectual accomplishments of his life. He told one friend that all of his books seemed to him as but straw. My mention of this fact should not be interpreted as denigrating philosophy. As interesting as the questions of philosophy can be (and they are), as exciting as philosophical debate can be (and it is), it would be a shame if any of us miss life's greatest happiness. If you do not know what that happiness is, then perhaps you should spend more time looking for it.[23]

---

23. One place to look for Thomas's answer might be Nash, *Faith and Reason,* chap. 20.

OPTIONAL WRITING ASSIGNMENT

Identify a contemporary philosophical or scientific challenge to religious faith, against which Thomas's distinction between faith and reason may be helpful. Explain Thomas's distinction and then discuss how his theory helps defuse the challenge. Conclude your discussion with comments about why you do or do not accept the double theory of truth with reference to this challenge.

FOR FURTHER READING

Thomas Aquinas, *Basic Writings of Saint Thomas Aquinas,* ed. Anton C. Pegis, 2 vols. (New York: Random House, 1945).

Thomas Aquinas, *Summae Theologiae: A Concise Translation* (Allen, Tex.: Christian Classics, 1997).

Vernon J. Bourke, *Aquinas's Search for Wisdom* (Milwaukee: Bruce, 1965).

Frederick C. Copleston, *A History of Philosophy* (Westminster, Md.: Newman Press, 1962), vol. 3.

Frederick C. Copleston, *Aquinas* (New York: Penguin, 1956).

Frederick C. Copleston, *Medieval Philosophy* (New York: Harper and Brothers, 1961).

Brian Davies, *The Thought of Thomas Aquinas* (New York: Oxford University Press, 1993).

Norman L. Geisler, *Thomas Aquinas* (Grand Rapids: Baker, 1991).

Etienne Gilson, *The Christian Philosophy of St. Thomas Aquinas* (Notre Dame, Ind.: University of Notre Dame Press, 1994).

Peter Kreeft, *Summa of the Summa* (San Francisco: Ignatius Press, 1990).

Norman Kretzman and Eleonore Stump, eds. *The Cambridge Companion to Aquinas* (New York: Cambridge University Press, 1993).

Ralph McInerny, *St. Thomas Aquinas* (Notre Dame, Ind.: University of Notre Dame Press, 1982).

Joseph Pieper, *Guide to Thomas Aquinas* (New York: Pantheon, 1962).

Conclusion to Part One

At the beginning of part 1, I noted two reasons for studying these six conceptual systems. (1) The possession of this kind of knowledge, specifically being conversant with the systems of Plato, Aristotle, Augustine, and Aquinas, used to be considered a requirement for being considered an educated person. The widespread indifference to this kind of knowledge in contemporary educational circles does not speak well for what higher education in America has become. (2) Our study of these six worldviews has introduced us to many of life's ultimate questions at different stages of their early development. We now have a better idea of what advocates of our six systems believed about God, ultimate reality, knowledge, ethics, and human nature. We have touched on such issues as the nature and existence of God, God's relationship to the world, how the world developed and what its ultimate nature is like, the issue of whether truth and ethics is relative, the nature of the human soul and its relationship to the body, along with the questions of human freedom and human survival after death and the relationship between reason and experience and between reason and faith. In case you care to look back, I never promised that our journey in part 1 would be easy.

During 1998 I flew to Colorado Springs, Colorado, ten times. During most of those trips, I drove a few miles west of Colorado Springs to a little town called Manitou Springs, at the foot of Pike's Peak, the fourteen-thousand-foot mountain that dominates that segment of the Rocky Mountains. Seeing Manitou and Colorado Springs from the ground so many times makes it easy to visualize all of that terrain from the perspective of an observer at ground level. But that terrain looks quite different from the top of Pike's Peak. It is much easier to grasp the relationships between the airport and the downtown and the Garden of the Gods and the Flying W ranch and the Air Force Academy from fourteen thousand feet than it is from ground level.

We are ready to begin another journey, this one in part 2 of the book. Our new journey will include more detailed examinations of a number of important philosophical questions. I believe the price we've paid in mastering the conceptual systems in part 1 will enable us to get much more from our study in part 2. The best way to see if this claim is true is to get started.

PART TWO

Important Problems
in Philosophy

Chapter Eight

The Law of
Noncontradiction

One characteristic of many allegedly educated Americans is their rejection of such laws of logic as the law of noncontradiction. Not too long ago, enemies of the historic Christian faith attempted to ridicule that faith and its adherents by describing them as irrationalists who separate faith from reason, from science, and from evidence, as well as from sound principles of logical thinking. Today some representatives of Christianity attack other Christians as being too rational. Something much like this happened to me after I had delivered the first of many lectures in the old Soviet Union in 1991. After my presentation, a Soviet philosophy professor complimented me on much that I had said but complained that I and my message suffered from one fundamental fault: I was too rational. Whatever the Soviet professor's intentions, I took her complaint as a compliment. After all, when did being an irrationalist constitute grounds for a compliment?

In chapter 1, I noted the important role the law of noncontradiction plays in evaluating conflicting worldviews. Any worldview that fails the test of reason, that is logically incoherent, must be false. In the same chapter, I noted Kimberly Manning's description of the gender feminist ideology to which she had become captive as a haven for irrationalists. Anyone critical of their rejection of logic and objective truth was ridiculed as anal-retentive.

In this chapter, I want to explain what the law of noncontradiction is and why accepting it is a matter of necessity, not of choice. Striving for logical consistency is not an option. The law of noncontradiction is not a principle we may or may not observe. It is an unavoidable principle of thinking, communicating, and speaking. Several of the points I make in chapter 9 offer additional support for the indispensability and unavoidability of the law of noncontradiction. Much of the material in the current chapter lays groundwork for my critical analysis and evaluation of the increasingly widespread repudiation of objective truth (chap. 10).

Aristotle and the Law of Non-contradiction

According to Aristotle, the laws of logic are not simply principles of human thinking. Because they are also laws of being, we may use them to grasp the logical structure of the world. The law of noncontradiction is a necessary principle of thought because it is first a necessary principle of being.

Perhaps the simplest definition of the law of noncontradiction is this: "A cannot be both B and non-B at the same time and in the same sense."[1] In this formulation, the letters A and B are variables in the same way that x and y are variables in algebra. All we have to do to use the variables properly is to substitute for them consistently. When we do this properly, we end up with propositions like "An object (A) cannot be both round (B) and square (non-B) at the same time in the same sense" or "A proposition (A) cannot be both true (B) and false (non-B) at the same time in the same sense."

The Inescapable Distinction Between *B* and Non-*B*

Figure 8.1

One reason why so many people fail to see the necessity of the law of noncontradiction is their failure to grasp the inescapable distinction between B and non-B. One helpful way to see this distinction is the following box in which I have located the terms B and non-B.

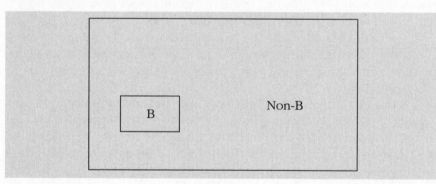

Let us suppose that the larger box (non-B) represents the entire universe in the sense that if anything (call it A) exists, it exists inside the box. Our larger box contains a smaller box that I have called B. This smaller box represents some class or group or set of things that have something essential in common. Hence, B could represent the class of all dogs or all horses or all humans.

---

1. Aristotle's way of saying this is worth noting. He writes that "the same attribute cannot at the same time belong and not belong to the same subject in the same respect." In another passage, he put it this way: "It is impossible that contrary attributes should belong at the same time to the same subject." Aristotle *Metaphysics* 1005b 18 and 1005b 26, trans. W. D. Ross (Oxford: Oxford University Press, 1908), 18, 26. I use the standard pagination for Aristotle's writings.

Non-*B* (the bigger box) is what we call the complementary class of *B*. This means that if, for example, the box we have called *B* represents the class of all dogs, then non-*B* stands for everything else in the universe that is not a dog. The complementary class of non-*B* includes cats, fish, Socrates, Pontius Pilate, the Ohio River, Mount Everest, the moon— in short, anything in the universe that is something other than a dog. If *B* represented the class of all human beings, then non-*B* would include everything in the universe that is not a human.

All that the law of noncontradiction says is this: If anything (call it *A*) is a member of the class we have called *B*, then *A* cannot under any condition also (at the same time and in the same sense) be a member of the complementary class of non-*B*.

Consider an example: It is impossible for Socrates to be both man and nonman. Since the class of nonman is the complement of the class of man, the claim that Socrates is also a member of the class of non-*B* (nonman) is tantamount to saying that Socrates is not only a human but also everything else in the universe. Thus, anyone who claims that Socrates can be both man and nonman is saying that Socrates can be a dog, a star, and indeed everything else in the universe at the same time. Philosopher Gordon H. Clark outlines the implications of this:

> If contradictory statements are true of the same subject at the same time, evidently all things will be the same thing. Socrates will be a ship, a house, as well as a man. But if precisely the same attributes attach to Crito that attach to Socrates it follows that Socrates is Crito. Not only so, but the ship in the harbor, since it has the same list of attributes too, will be identified with this Socrates-Crito person. In fact, everything will be the same thing. All differences among things will vanish and all will be one.[2]

There is no quicker way to become swallowed up in nonsense than to deny the distinction between *B* and non-*B*. I once heard of a young man who was called into his local office of the Internal Revenue Service for an audit. The reason for his trouble was his failure over several years to file a tax return. When asked by the IRS agent why he had failed to file, the youth replied that in college he had learned that the law of noncontradiction is an optional, nonnecessary principle. Once he had learned that there is no difference between *B* and non-*B*, it was only a matter of time before he realized that no difference exists between filing a tax return and not filing a tax return. "That's very interesting," said the tax agent. "I've never heard that one before. Since you believe that no difference exists between *B* and non-*B*, I'm sure you also believe that there is no difference between being in jail and not being in jail!"

2. Gordon H. Clark, *Thales to Dewey*, 2d ed. (Unicoi, Tenn.: The Trinity Foundation, 1989), 103.

Can the Law of Noncontradiction Be Proven?

Strictly speaking, the law of noncontradiction cannot be proven. This should not surprise us. Every argument must start by taking some things for granted. There are always some things that must be accepted without proof. In order for an ultimate principle like the law of noncontradiction to be proved, it would have to be deduced either from other principles (in which case the logical principle would no longer be ultimate) or from itself (in which case the supposed argument for the logical principle would be circular and not really a proof). Any so-called proof for the law of noncontradiction would have to presuppose the truth of the law and would thus beg the question and fail as a proof.

While no direct demonstration of the principle of noncontradiction exists, there is a persuasive negative or indirect argument that assumes three forms, all pointing to logical consequences that follow a denial of the principle. The three forms of the argument look like this.

(1) If the law of noncontradiction is denied, then significant thinking is impossible.
(2) If the law of noncontradiction is denied, then significant human conduct is impossible.
(3) If the law of noncontradiction is denied, then significant communication is impossible.

Each of the above carries with it several absurd consequences. Suppose we concentrate on one of them:

(3*) If significant human communication is impossible, then it is impossible to use language to refute the law of noncontradiction.

The type of reasoning being used here illustrates a simple and indisputable form of reasoning, known as *modus tollens*. According to *modus tollens*, if one proposition (p) implies another proposition (q) and q is false, then p must be false. As an example, consider the following:

(4) If (p) Ron Nash is a former winner of the Master's Golf Tournament, then (q) Ron Nash has played golf on the Augusta National Golf Course.
(5) But it is false that Ron Nash has played golf on the Augusta National Golf Course (not-q).
(6) Therefore, it is false that Ron Nash is a former winner of the Master's Golf Tournament (not-p).

As stated, if p implies q and q is false, then p is false. The denial of the law of noncontradiction necessarily implies all kinds of absurd or false consequences, one of which is indicated in proposition (3*). The falsity of the second proposition in the implication entails the falsity of the first proposition, which in turn provides the indirect proof for the law of non-contradiction that we are seeking.

Logic and Significant Human Communication

People who attack the law of noncontradiction are engaged in a self-defeating task since they must use the principle in every attempt to deny it. Underlying this argument is the inescapable distinction between *B* and non-*B*, both in language, thought, and being. Contrary meanings may not (if one is to speak or write intelligibly) be attributed to the same word at the same time and in the same sense. Since any refutation of the law of noncontradiction would have to be expressed in intelligible language and since significant speech presupposes the law, it is in principle impossible to use language to deny the law of noncontradiction. In order for a word to mean something (*B*), it must not mean something else (non-*B*). Obviously, any given word can have more than one meaning. As long as the possible meanings of a word are limited in number, we can always avoid the ambiguity by assigning a different set of symbols to each meaning.

Consider, for example, the proposition "Julius Caesar is a man." If "man" is ambiguous and has (let us say) five possible meanings, we may further specify by adding a number to each different sense of "man" such as "man–1," "man–2," and so on. But suppose the law of noncontradiction is denied. There would then be no difference in meaning between "man" and any substitutes for "nonman." Therefore, "man" and every other word in the dictionary would have thousands of meanings. And, if words have so many senses, intelligible speech becomes impossible. This is why the person who attempts to argue against the law of noncontradiction must use the very law he is trying to deny. If the law of noncontradiction is denied, nothing has meaning, including the sentences of people who think they are denying the law. If the laws of logic do not first mean what they say, nothing else can have meaning, including sentences that purport to deny the law.

This last point has considerable importance. If logic is indispensable to all human thought, speech, and action, it follows that the law of noncontradiction is not merely an arbitrary convention useful for constructing symbolic systems. "Three times three equals nine" is not true because humans say it is or stipulate it. That nine is the product of three times three is necessarily and objectively true.[3] The law of noncontradiction is

---

3. One must not get confused at this point by specious reasoning about mathematical propositions not developed on a base ten system. In a base seven system, for example, there is no numeral for nine. So what happens to sums or products in a base seven system is that we use different symbols, but the meaning is the same. Some reportedly intelligent people have said some foolish things about the supposed relativity of mathematical truth on such specious grounds.

not stipulative or conventional; rather it is a necessary and indispensable law of being and of thought.

Logic and Significant Human Action

I have already provided several examples of how a denial of the law of noncontradiction makes significant human action impossible. If there is no difference between *B* and non-*B,* there is no difference between drinking milk and drinking poison or between driving on the right side of the median of an interstate highway or driving on the left side. People who behave as though there is no difference between *B* and non-*B* may quickly find themselves in embarrassing or dangerous situations. Consider a politician who denies the distinction between *B* and non-*B.* Such a person could, I suppose, use his rejection of the necessary difference between *B* and non-*B* as an excuse for an act of adultery. If there is no difference between *B* and non-*B,* our politician would then be unable to distinguish between his wife and a car, a building, a river, or a stop sign. And since this is so, he would also have difficulty distinguishing between his wife and a person who is not his wife. The regrettable implications of this kind of irrationalism are just as risky in religion as in marriage and politics. Supposedly religious people who think in this illogical way would lack any rational ground for distinguishing between God and the Devil.

Logic and Significant Human Thinking

It should be obvious how the previous comments lead to another conclusion: If the denial of the law of noncontradiction precludes significant speech and behavior, significant human thinking also becomes impossible. When students find themselves taking a course, any course, taught by a professor who thinks in this illogical way, a consistent professor (note the implicit logical presence here) would have to admit there is no difference between a good exam and a bad one, between a good grade and a bad one. Unless such a professor cheats, it seems difficult to see how he could avoid giving all students the same grade.

Logic and God

Surprisingly, many religious people believe that God is above this stuff about logic because he created the law of noncontradiction and thus operates according to a different or higher logic than do created beings like us. On such a view, humans are stuck with the law of noncontradiction, but God is not. When such individuals are asked to explain how significant thinking, communication, and action are possible for a God for whom no distinction between *B* and non-*B* obtains, these people take refuge in mystery. While I do not deny that some features of the Christian faith are above reason in the sense that we cannot presently understand them, it does not follow that religious claims that we find difficult to comprehend are against reason in the sense of violating the law of noncontradiction.

It is helpful at this point to take note of several biblical accounts of things that God cannot do. For example, we are told that God cannot swear by a being greater than himself (Hebrews 6:13). This is true because there is no being greater than God. The reasoning clearly presupposes the application of the law of noncontradiction to God. The Bible also says that God cannot lie (Titus 1:2; Hebrews 6:18). Behind this claim is the clear distinction between a true statement (*B*) and a lie (non-*B*). If God does operate according to a different logic, a higher logic in which *B* and non-*B* are indistinguishable, nothing would prevent God at the final judgment from announcing that there is no difference between believers and nonbelievers and between God's keeping and breaking his promises. But there is no need to get upset, because on such grounds there can also be no difference between heaven and hell. People who attempt to separate God from the laws of logic should consider the possibility that they are enemies of the faith they profess.

An Example of Religious Irrationalism

In a 1955 article titled "Mysticism and Human Reason," former Princeton University philosopher W. T. Stace wrote, "God is utterly and forever beyond the reach of the logical intellect or of any intellectual comprehension, and that in consequence when we try to comprehend his nature intellectually, contradictions appear in our thinking."[4] As Stace saw things, "any attempt to reach God through logic, through the conceptual, logical intellect, is doomed."[5] Then Stace moves to the more extreme position that religious believers should reject logic when dealing with God.

Stace, himself a mystic, ridicules other mystics for yielding to their rational impulses and seeking ways to eliminate contradictions in their thinking about God. The proper course, for Stace, is to glory in the contradictions. As Stace puts it,

> My own belief is that all attempts to rationalize the paradox, to make it logically acceptable, are futile because the paradoxes of religion and of mysticism are irresoluble by the human intellect. My view is that they never have been, they never can be, and they never will be resolved, or made logical.[6]

One wonders where Stace's confidence comes from on these difficult points. He seems certain that the human mind can never have logically coherent knowledge about God. Does he arrive at this conclusion as a

---

4. W. T. Stace, "Mysticism and Human Reason," *University of Arizona Bulletin Series* 26 (1955): 19.

5. Ibid., 20.

6. Ibid.

result of rational thinking, or does some kind of irrational gut feeling produce this confidence? Given the depths of his own irrationalism, the first option hardly seems possible. If his pious irrationalism is itself the result of irrationalism, why should anyone give it credence? But Stace continues, "When you say that God is incomprehensible, one thing you mean is just that these contradictions break out in our intellect and cannot be resolved, no matter how clever or how good a logician you may be."[7]

Stace is especially critical of certain Buddhist monks who attempt to remove contradictions in their system by postulating two Brahmans, a higher and lower. "One may be quite sure," Stace advises, "that this is the wrong solution because the religious intuition is preemptory that God is one and not two."[8] Notice the oddness of Stace's thesis. He is convinced that God is unknowable. But then he dogmatically informs us that his irrational intuitions give him at least one piece of knowledge about this unknowable God, namely, that God is one and not two. Is Stace contradicting himself? Of course he is.

For Stace, logic does not apply in religion. Stace is not merely saying that religion could be unreasonable in the sense that it discusses things that are above human reason. For Stace, religion is against logic. "Should we say that there is contradiction in the nature of God himself, in the ultimate being? Well, if we were to say that, I think that we shouldn't be saying anything very unusual or very shocking."[9] Stace is much too cautious. I find his claims not only unusual and shocking but also nonsense.

At first Stace sounds like someone who thinks that God is above the laws of reason. But let us observe the problems that his irrationalism creates for him. If Stace were correct and logic has no relevance to the kind of mysticism he represented, it is difficult to understand most of what he wrote. For example, why, given his repudiation of logic, did he criticize Buddhists who rejected the unity of God in favor of two Brahmans? Once logic is disavowed, God can be both one and two (or two thousand) at the same time and in the same sense. If a distinction can be drawn between a monistic God and a dualistic or a pluralistic deity, then logic must have some relevance. Once logic is denied, inconsistency becomes a virtue.

Irrationalism in the Academic World

Irrationalism has also found a home in nonreligious areas of contemporary university life. Several years ago, a graduate student at a well-known university in New England told me the following story. One day her professor issued a lengthy diatribe against logic. This professor urged all of her graduate students to join her in a crusade against logic. In her world, logic was too confining; things were either black or white, valid

---

7. Ibid., 17.
8. Ibid.
9. Ibid., 18–19.

or invalid, true or false, either *B* or non-*B*. She preferred things that were cuddly, soft, and fuzzy, such as feelings and intuitions. She believed that people interested in logical and analytical thinking are anal-retentive. This professorial enemy of reason and logic was also quite critical of the historic Christian faith.

After class, the student asked the professor if she could pose three questions. "Since you reject all use of logic," the student began, "don't you realize this means you can never prove that any of your anti-Christian beliefs are true?" After all, proving something does seem to include an appeal to laws of rational inference. The student reported her shock that her professor had never realized this fact before hearing the question.

"What's your second question?" the professor asked. "Well," the student continued, "don't you realize that when you repudiate logic, you cannot prove that any of my Christian beliefs are false?" This point had also escaped the attention of the professor.

"And your third question?" "Since you've admitted that you cannot prove that your anti-Christian beliefs are true and that you cannot prove that my Christian beliefs are false, why don't you become a Christian?" This put the professor in a difficult position. She could not justify her rejection of the Christian faith with an argument; when she rejected logic, that became impossible. After several painful moments, the only reason she gave for her rejection of Christianity was the fact that she did not like the student's religion, effectively equating her atheism with someone's dislike of broccoli. At the end of the twentieth century, it appears that the real irrationalists in the world include many enemies of religion.

The Notion of Self-Referential Absurdity

An important application of the principle of noncontradiction is the discovery of positions that suffer from self-referential absurdity. This condition exists whenever the application of a theory to itself involves one in a necessary falsehood or logical nonsense.

Skepticism as an Example

One of the better examples of a logically self-defeating position is skepticism. Skepticism can be defined in two ways. To make my point clearer, I will isolate each of these two theses of skepticism in the center of the line. Here is the first.

(1) No one can know anything.

Look carefully at this claim. Then imagine yourself asking the proponent of (1) a simple question: "Do you know that no one can know anything?"

Consider the two and only two possible answers. If the skeptic answers yes, thereby asserting that he knows that no one can know anything, the self-defeating nature of his position becomes obvious. But our skeptic has another possible answer to our question. If his reply is no, the skeptic is admitting that he doesn't know what he's talking about.

Consider now the other way of formulating skepticism:

(2) No proposition is true.

Once again the strategy is to ask a simple question: "Is your proposition (2) true?" Suppose I allow you to do the rest. What is our skeptic's problem if he answers yes and then if he answers no?

Not too long ago, someone sent me via e-mail the following story that he had taken off the Internet. A philosophy professor was attacking the existence of God in a class full of timid and compliant students. The professor began with the following question: "Is there anyone in the room who has seen God?" No student responded. "All right," he continued, "have any of you touched God?" Again, there was no response. "Has anyone here heard God?" After another round of silence, the professor smiled triumphantly and said, "Therefore, there is no God."

At that point, one of the students rose and asked if he might speak. The professor nodded his approval. The student looked at the other students and asked, "Has anyone in this room seen our professor's brain?" No reply. "Has anyone touched our professor's brain?" Again, silence. "Has anyone heard our professor's brain?" After another bout of silence, the student smiled and said, "Then using our professor's logic, our professor has no brain."

While the story ended by stating that the student received an A for the course, attempting this maneuver with some professors might result in a different outcome. Of course, I would like to think that the professor's horrible logic was an attempt to provoke someone in the class, anyone in the class, to say something.

Logical Positivism

Strangers to philosophy are often surprised to discover how many self-referentially absurd positions one can find in the history of philosophy. One example of such a system is the logical positivism that was popular in Great Britain and the United States during the 1930s and 1940s. The book that came to be regarded as the most influential statement of logical positivism was A. J. Ayer's *Language, Truth, and Logic*.[10] For the record, Ayer abandoned logical positivism during his later years.

The touchstone proposition of logical positivism was something called the verification principle. Logical positivists thought they had discovered a criterion of meaningfulness that would exclude all kinds of claims they found distasteful. Only two kinds of propositions can have

---

10. (London: Gollancz, 1936).

meaning, the positivists argued: those that are true because of the meaning of their constituent terms (called analytic statements)[11] and those that are verifiable by sense experience (called synthetic statements). Positivists delighted in showing, or so they thought, that theological, metaphysical, and ethical statements failed to meet either criterion of meaningfulness. And because such statements were neither analytic (true or false by virtue of the meanings of their words) nor synthetic (true or false because they were verifiable by experience), they were discarded as meaningless. This meant that statements like "God exists" were neither true nor false; they were meaningless. What a clean and convenient way to eliminate theology, metaphysics, and ethics from the arena of responsible discourse and thought, or so the logical positivists thought.

The positivists used their verification principle like a sledgehammer, smashing a great many of the traditional positions in philosophy, including beliefs about God, the soul, and morality. At least they did so until people began to ask about the cognitive status of the positivists' verification principle. What kind of statement is it? The positivists' criterion of meaning showed itself to be meaningless because it could be classified as neither an analytic nor a synthetic statement. Efforts to rescue the verification principle failed.[12] So it is difficult to find any philosopher who is willing to admit adherence to logical positivism. The movement is dead, a result fitting for any logically self-defeating theory.

Scientific Positivism

Even though logical positivism has been put to rest, a different version of positivism continues to appeal to students and professors. The touchstone proposition of scientific positivism goes like this: "It is wrong to believe any proposition not verified by the scientific method." Please note that I have no quarrel with either science or the scientific method. The relevant issue is the assumption that science and its methodology are competent to bring us into the presence of all that is true. This is the point at which any thinking person must object. For example, at least one important proposition cannot be verified by the scientific method, namely, the touchstone proposition of the positivist position. What scientific experiment could possibly verify the claim that it is wrong to believe any proposition

---

11. Examples of analytic statements include tautologies like "Some bachelors are unmarried men" (which are necessarily true) and contradictions like "Some bachelors are married men" (which are necessarily false). An example of a synthetic statement would be "Some bachelors drive American-made cars."

12. One could spend years reading nothing but criticisms of logical positivism. Two critiques of the verification principle from different perspectives are Alvin Plantinga, *God and Other Minds* (Ithaca, N.Y.: Cornell University Press, 1967) and Brand Blanshard, *Reason and Analysis* (La Salle, Ill.: Open Court, 1962).

not verified by the scientific method? The answer is that there is none. Therefore, if it is wrong to believe any proposition so described and the touchstone proposition of scientific positivism fails its own test, it follows that it is wrong to believe in that touchstone proposition. Scientific positivism is a logically self-defeating position.

Evidentialism

The list of self-referentially absurd positions keeps growing. The touchstone proposition of what I here call *evidentialism* was expressed by a nineteenth-century thinker named W. K. Clifford, who wrote: "It is wrong always, everywhere, and for anyone, to believe anything upon insufficient evidence."[13] As Clifford saw it, people have duties and responsibilities with respect to their acts of believing. This is especially so, Clifford thought, in the case of religious beliefs. According to Clifford, there is never sufficient evidence or proof to support religious belief. Consequently, anyone who accepts a religious belief (such as the belief that God exists) is guilty of acting immorally, irresponsibly, and irrationally.

There is a rather hefty body of literature that takes this kind of evidentialism apart.[14] To save time, I will look at only one counterargument: evidentialism is a logically self-defeating position. As we have seen, the evidentialist believes that it is immoral to believe anything without sufficient proof. But where is the proof for his own claim? The fact is that he provides no evidence; nor could he. Therefore, the real immorality in these matters is believing the touchstone proposition of evidentialism.

Deconstructionism

The touchstone proposition of deconstructionism is this: "It is impossible ever to know the meaning of any written text." This happens to be a popular view in certain academic circles, especially in English departments that used to introduce students to literary classics. The prevailing view among many contemporary scholars is that all meaning is subjective; a text means whatever it means to the reader.

I must admit to being a little jealous when I encounter college students who studied literature under a deconstructionist professor. When I studied literature, it was a tough course. Today, writing an exam for such a professor is a snap. Without reading the book, without studying any critical essays, all one has to do is dream up an interpretation, any inter-

---

13. W. K. Clifford, "The Ethics of Belief," in *Readings in the Philosophy of Religion,* ed. Baruch A. Brody (Englewood Cliffs, N.J.: Prentice-Hall, 1974), 246. Clifford's essay was published in his *Lectures and Essays* (London: Macmillan, 1879) and has been reprinted in countless anthologies.

14. See Ronald H. Nash, *Faith and Reason* (Grand Rapids: Zondervan, 1992), chaps. 5 and 6.

pretation, explain it without messing up syntax and spelling, and get an A. A student of such a professor told me that her professor announced the final exam would require an essay about Moby Dick. All of my readers remember that Moby was the white elephant that swam around the Pacific ... or was it the white whale that swam around the Atlantic? If there's no difference between *B* and non-*B,* it doesn't matter, does it? This young woman began her final exam by writing this sentence: "Moby Dick is the Republic of Ireland." For the next ninety minutes, she pursued this preposterous thesis to its end. When she got back her exam, her grade was an A, followed by the professor's words, "What a creative essay." Of course it was creative—it had nothing to do with the novel.

One advantage of such a theory is that it must be hard to get a bad grade in such a course. One disadvantage of such a theory is that it is difficult to learn anything in such a course.

If it is impossible to know the meaning of any written text, how can one know what the teacher or his textbooks mean?[15] Things get interesting when deconstructionists teach their paradigm in educational institutions that are supported by conservative church members who take the Bible seriously. If it is impossible to know the meaning of any written text, then it follows that it is impossible to know the meaning of the Bible. Public disclosure of the fact an allegedly religious college engages in this kind of teaching might make student recruitment and retention more difficult, at least among members of the college's religious constituency.

I will return to this subject in chapter 10. For now, all that is necessary is to remember that deconstructionism is the paradigm of a logically self-defeating theory.

The Charge of Oversimplification

How might some critic respond to my objections to positivism, evidentialism, misology (the hatred of logic), deconstructionism, and the rest? Once or twice in my life, I have heard the allegation that the arguments in this section are oversimplified. There are two possible ways to respond to this charge of oversimplification. (1) I could frolic in deconstructionism and interpret the criticisms as endorsements of my position. And why not? Since all meaning is subjective, what prevents me from interpreting them any way I please? (2) Or I could assume the critic means that each of my arguments represents the position being criticized as a universal claim, a statement that allows no exceptions. The critic may believe that the apparent defeat of such positions as positivism, evidentialism, and deconstructionism is a cheap victory won unfairly by oversimplifying the positions being criticized. While it is true that I present

---

15. I have met students who press their deconstructionist professors to write their claims on the blackboard, thus turning their oral statements into written texts.

the positions as universal claims, it is not true that I am guilty of misrepresenting or oversimplifying the theories. Consider the following pairs of propositions:

(1a) All propositions not verified by the scientific method are false.

(1b) Some propositions not verified by the scientific method are false.

(2a) All statements that are neither analytic nor synthetic are meaningless.

(2b) Some statements that are neither analytic nor synthetic are meaningless.

(3a) All acts of believing propositions not supported by sufficient evidence are immoral.

(3b) Some acts of believing propositions unsupported by sufficient evidence are immoral.

(4a) All texts are meaningless.

(4b) Some texts are meaningless.

I can only assume that the critic wants everyone to believe that the (b) propositions represent more fairly the views of the positivist, evidentialist, and deconstructionist. And since the (b) propositions are obviously true, any attempt to reject positions stated in the (b) or qualified versions is unfair and simplistic.

The attempt to defeat my arguments in this way fails for two reasons. First, even though the (b) propositions are true, they are trivial in the sense that no informed person doubts them. It is difficult to interpret *some* texts. But the ambiguity of two or two thousand texts has nothing to do with deconstructionism. If all deconstructionists want to limit their position to proposition (4b), no one will object. But neither would anyone care. It would be like someone saying that during a 162-game season, every major-league baseball team is going to lose at least one game; to which one appropriate response is "So what?" Any attempt to defend evidentialism, positivism, and the other self-defeating positions by watering them down in the way I have indicated has the strongly negative effect of trivializing those positions.

My second reply is that proponents of these views do assert the universal claim. I have no problem admitting there are lots of texts in libraries around the world that are difficult to interpret. But believing that *some* texts are difficult to interpret does not make me a deconstructionist. Consider someone who introduces himself as a skeptic and then defines his position by saying that some propositions are not true (as opposed to saying no propositions are true). As far as skepticism is concerned, this person is a fraud.

And so the critic who charges me of oversimplification either is not thinking clearly or is playing a game. I have formulated these positions in the way their proponents advance them and in the only significant (that is, nontrivial) form they can have. The charge of oversimplification is a canard. There is no oversimplification, and the positions that have been critiqued truly are self-referentially absurd.

The law of noncontradiction cannot be ignored, avoided, or dismissed as mere convention. It is a true, universal, and necessary principle of human thinking, acting, and communicating. It is also a principle that functions in the mind of God. It is nonsense to suggest that God operates according to a different or higher logic than the law of noncontradiction. If God does not or might not recognize the difference between B and non-B, there is no difference between good and evil; there is no difference between God and the Devil. Such is the nonsense to which pious irrationalism would drive us.

For all of its importance, however, logical consistency can never be the only criterion by which we evaluate worldviews. While the presence of a contradiction will alert us to the presence of error, the absence of contradiction does not guarantee the presence of truth. For that, we need other criteria.

Conclusion

OPTIONAL WRITING EXERCISE

Assume that you have joined the company of those who claim that the law of noncontradiction is merely an optional way of thinking. Assume also that you decide to write an essay proving the dispensability of the law. Under no circumstances may you cheat and assume the difference between *B* and non-*B*. This will mean, however, that every word in your essay may have thousands of different meanings. Write your essay using this new approach to language. After you have finished, ask yourself the following questions. Did you have to work hard to write this essay? Can anyone else in the world understand your essay? Has your failure affected your opinion of people who contend that the law of noncontradiction is merely an option?

FOR FURTHER READING

Gordon H. Clark, *A Christian View of Men and Things,* 2d ed. (Unicoi, Tenn.: The Trinity Foundation, 1991).

Gordon H. Clark, *Thales to Dewey,* 2d ed. (Unicoi, Tenn.: The Trinity Foundation, 1989).

Ronald H. Nash, *The Word of God and the Mind of Man* (Phillipsburg, N.J.: Presbyterian and Reformed, 1992).

Ronald H. Nash, ed., *The Philosophy of Gordon H. Clark* (Philadelphia: Presbyterian and Reformed, 1968).

Chapter Nine

Possible Worlds

When I began my study of philosophy, books with chapters on the subject of possible worlds did not exist. Interest in the subject goes back several centuries, at least to the German philosopher Gottfried Leibniz in the eighteenth century. But the specific content in this chapter is relatively new, at least in this format.

During many of our school days, good teachers introduced heuristic devices or teaching tools to assist our understanding of rather complex ideas. It might have been a model of the solar system or a stick with two red balls on one end and one blue ball on the other to help us understand a molecule of water.

The doctrine of possible worlds can help improve our understanding of dozens of important philosophical issues. For example, philosophers distinguish between contingent and necessary truths. The proposition "Cosmo Kramer has red roses in his garden" is a contingent proposition. The proposition might be true or it might be false, depending on whether or not Cosmo Kramer has a garden containing some red roses. By contrast, the proposition "Five times five equals twenty-five" is a necessarily true proposition. It must be true; it cannot be false. The propositions "Five times five equals twenty-one" and "Cosmo Kramer is a married bachelor" are necessarily false. They cannot be true; they are contradictions and thus logically false. As we'll see, the doctrine of possible worlds can help us grasp this distinction.

A warning: some students find this material quite difficult. It really isn't, but any new way of talking or thinking about things can seem difficult at first. Master the definitions, think about what I say, and remember that much of this material is common sense. Once you understand what is going on and what the terms mean, the language of possible worlds will be a new way of talking about things that we're familiar with.

Some Preliminary Definitions

What Is a Proposition?

Many philosophers distinguish between sentences and propositions. A sentence is some combination of words in a particular language. If a sentence has meaning, its meaning is said to be the proposition expressed by the sentence. Consider, for example, the following sentences: (1) John is the husband of Mary, and (2) Mary is the wife of John. It is clear that (1) and (2) are different sentences that nonetheless refer to the same state of affairs. The different sentences have the same meaning and thus express the same proposition.[1] The same result can follow when one reflects on the sentence "John is the husband of Mary" and a sentence in French or German that refers to the same state of affairs and thus expresses the same proposition.

What Is a State of Affairs?

While it may not be possible to define the term *state of affairs,* it is possible to give examples. For every proposition (a meaningful sentence that is either true or false), there is a corresponding state of affairs. In the following list of examples, the proposition is in the left-hand column, and the corresponding state of affairs is on the right.

Figure 9.1

Proposition	State of Affairs
1) Bill Clinton is president of the U.S. in 1998.	1) Bill Clinton's being president of the U.S. in 1998.
2) The Florida Marlins won the 1997 World Series.	2) The Florida Marlins' winning the 1997 World Series.
3) The U.S.S.R. ceased to exist in 1991.	3) The U.S.S.R.'s ceasing to exist in 1991.

When a proposition is true, we say that the corresponding state of affairs obtains. When a proposition is false, we say that the corresponding state of affairs does not obtain. Therefore, if we consider the false proposition "The Cleveland Indians won the 1997 World Series," the corresponding state of affairs, "The Cleveland Indians' winning the 1997 World Series," does not obtain. There is a simple way to turn any properly formulated proposition into a state of affairs. First, using (2) as an example, take the subject of the proposition (the Florida Marlins) and make it possessive (the Florida Marlins') and then turn the verb into a gerund. When the verb in a proposition is "win," the corresponding gerund is "winning."

---

1. For more on the relationship between propositions and states of affairs, see Alvin Plantinga, *God, Freedom, and Evil* (New York: Harper and Row, 1974), 34–44.

Propositions and States of Affairs as Eternal Entities

Many philosophers believe that propositions and states of affairs are eternal and unchanging entities. Before you throw the book at someone, stop and reflect for a moment about the systems of Plato and Augustine, who believed in the existence of unchanging and eternal universals. According to Plato and Augustine, the properties of truth and goodness have always existed and can never change. Did you find Platonism that difficult to understand? All that's required here is that you add a few more "things" to the earlier list of eternal entities, in this case, propositions and states of affairs. If p is a proposition, then p has always existed; moreover, if p is true, then it has always been true.

The claim that propositions, as distinct from sentences, are eternally true or false entities seems contradicted by propositions that contain references to time and place. Consider the sentence "Nash is now typing." At the moment, the sentence is true. But it obviously ceases to be true the moment I lift my fingers from the keyboard and turn off the computer. Since the statement under consideration is sometimes true and usually false, how can one seriously maintain that propositions are eternally true? The answer lies in the fact that the example, "Nash is now typing," is too poorly framed to serve as the real proposition in question. The doctrine that propositions are eternally true requires any sentence that is in effect open because of some reference to time or place to be closed. This can be done by eliminating tensed verbs and making explicit any relevant information that may only be implied in the original.

Because my original sentence, "Nash is now typing," contains a reference to time (the word *now*), it is an open statement. In order to approximate the proposition we need, it is necessary to remove any reference to time or place in the verb and then close the sentence by making explicit a reference to the precise time and place. And so we get something like "Nash is [tenselessly] typing at 2:53 P.M. on May 16, 1998, in his home study in Longwood, Florida." If this proposition is true on May 16, 1998 (and it is), then the proposition is eternally true, has always been true. How can that be so, some might ask? Consider true propositions like "Two plus three equals five" and "The square of the hypotenuse of a right-angle triangle is equal to the sum of the squares of the two sides." These two propositions have always been true, I contend. When I am asked how the last two propositions can be eternally true, all I need do is point out that in the worldview I hold and defend in this book, all true propositions subsist in the mind of God. Hearken back to Augustine's conviction that all of Plato's Forms are eternal ideas in the mind of God. If that is a respectable claim, then why should there be any greater problem in believing that properly framed propositions are eternal truths in the mind of God? Furthermore, corresponding to the properly formulated proposition about Nash's typing is the following state of affairs: "Nash's typing at 2:53 P.M. on May 16, 1998, in his home study in Longwood, Florida." If the corresponding proposition is eternally true, why is there any further problem in believing the corresponding state of affairs is also an eternal entity?

Another warning: I understand how strange this can seem the first time one encounters it. Since a solid grasp of everything said thus far is essential to understanding what comes next, let me suggest that the reader return to the beginning of this chapter and read to this point. If you do this, place a check on this spot _____ and reward yourself with your favorite snack, possibly a doughnut and a cup of coffee. When you have finished, write on a piece of paper a properly formulated proposition that tenselessly describes what you just did and then write the corresponding state of affairs. Don't allow the fact that the proposition and state of affairs you have just recorded are eternally true to shock you. Of course, this will be the case only if you did this brief assignment correctly. All this will mean is that God has always known that you would do what you just did at this time and place.

What Is a Possible World?

Defining a Possible World

A possible world is a way the real world could have been. The language of possible worlds is a handy way of referring to the possibility that things in the actual world might have been different. It is possible that George Bush won the presidential election of 1992. This possible but nonactual state of affairs can be referred to in terms of a possible world in which the proposition "George Bush wins [tenselessly] the 1992 U.S. presidential election" is true and in which the state of affairs "George Bush's winning the 1992 U.S. presidential election" obtains.

To take examples from a far more distant point in history, all manner of things are known about the Socrates who lived in the actual or real world: he was snub-nosed, he was married to Xanthippe, he was the teacher of Plato, he was a sculptor, and he was executed in 399 B.C. These propositions about Socrates would have to be included in any complete list of true propositions about the real world. But what if Socrates had not been snub-nosed or had not taught Plato or had not been executed? All these possibilities can be considered by suggesting possible worlds in which Socrates had a Roman nose or ran in the Olympic marathon or kicked Plato out of his class for cheating or died of old age. In other words, it is possible to imagine innumerable possible worlds in which Socrates exists that differ in some way from the real world.

All that is required to have a possible world that is different from the real world is for one state of affairs that obtains in the real world to be altered in one respect. Was it possible for Socrates to have different colored eyes or not be bald? Then imagine a possible world in which a blue-eyed Socrates with a full head of curly hair plays third base for the Cleveland Indians. How many possible worlds are there? Obviously, the answer is a very large number.

Possible Worlds and Logical Possibility

The indispensable condition any state of affairs must meet in order to exist in some possible world is logical possibility. Something is logically possible if its description does not include a logical contradiction. "Two plus two equals three" is a necessarily false proposition. "Two plus two's equaling three" is a logically impossible state of affairs. Hence, there is no possible world in which the state of affairs expressed in the last sentence can obtain. There is no possible world in which two plus two can equal anything other than four. Likewise there is no possible world in which the state of affairs "two plus two's equaling three" can obtain.

Possible Worlds and Physical Possibility

Something is physically possible if someone can do it. Physical possibility can vary from world to world. Once upon a time, it was physically impossible for a human being to run a mile in less than four minutes. But then a man named Roger Bannister did, and suddenly running a mile that fast was physically possible. But long before Roger Bannister performed his feat, there were many possible worlds in which running a mile that fast was a common occurrence. So long as a description of some state of affairs is logically possible, there are possible worlds in which those states of affairs exist, even if in the real world they are physically impossible.

But consider an act that is logically impossible, such as squaring the circle. Since squaring the circle is logically impossible, then it cannot occur in any possible world. And if something is logically impossible, then it cannot be physically possible in any possible world, including the real world.

Hence, there are possible worlds in which Ron Nash is the world's greatest pianist, and/or golfer, and/or basketball player, and so on. If a state of affairs is logically possible, there are possible worlds in which it can obtain. The fact that none of these states of affairs are physically possible for the author of this book is irrelevant. All that matters is that they be logically possible.

A Possible World Is a Complete State of Affairs

With this point, we advance our understanding of a possible world a bit further. It is a mistake to think of one or a hundred states of affairs as a possible world. A possible world is and must be so complete that any attempt to squeeze even one more state of affairs into that world is impossible. The reason is because that extra state of affairs would prove to be logically incompatible with the complete state of affairs that makes up that possible world.

For Each Possible World, There Is a Book About That World

The word *book* in this context is a technical term. As we have seen, every possible world is a complete state of affairs, such that not even one more state of affairs can be added to it without introducing a logical contradiction. As we have also seen, corresponding to every state of affairs in a possible world there is a true proposition. The sum total of all true propositions about a possible world makes up what some philosophers call the book about that world. The book about the real or actual world is the sum total of all true propositions about our world from the beginning of its existence. Consider the sum of all true propositions about your life from its beginning. That would constitute a rather hefty body of propositions. Obviously, then, the book about the real world is even more intimidating in size and detail.

Should this new point about books about possible worlds seem daunting, stop and think about the points you accepted earlier in this chapter. If all true and properly formulated propositions are eternal entities and are eternally true, then no great leap is required to conceive of the sum total of those propositions as composing the book on our world. Earlier I suggested the mind of God as a proper locus for all of these propositions. When one conceives of God as an omniscient being, that is, as an eternally divine Person who believes all true propositions and who holds no false beliefs, accepting the book on the real world requires no great leap of faith. If all true propositions subsist eternally in the eternal mind of God, whence comes any difficulty in calling the sum total of these propositions the book about the real world?

This is a good time to explain my earlier point that a possible world is a complete state of logically possible affairs. Consider the totality of propositions corresponding to each logically possible state of affairs in some possible world. This complete set of propositions about possible world A is such that any attempt to add another proposition to the book about world A would introduce a logical contradiction into that book. The book on world A is so complete that any other proposition one might attempt to add to the book would be logically incompatible with one of the other propositions in the book on world A.

And so a possible world cannot be reduced to such limited states of affairs as the reign of King Henry VIII of England or the baseball career of Babe Ruth or the presidency of Ronald Reagan. All of these examples are what some have called a "slice of a possible world." The heaven that Christians believe will follow physical death, the final judgment, and the end of the world should also be viewed as a slice of a possible world. The actual world does not end with the death of any or all human beings or with the destruction of the earth.

In the figure below, I allow five circles to stand for five possible worlds. The first circle on the line will represent the real or actual world.

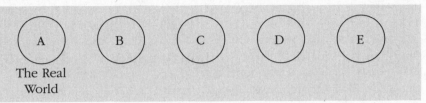

Figure 9.2

Many truths we encounter are contingent truths. For example, the proposition "The United States entered World War I in the year 1917" is true in the real world. But this is a contingent truth in the sense that things could have gone differently. It is logically possible that we might have entered the war in 1918 or might never have entered it; it is also logically possible that World War I might never have occurred. All of these possible states of affairs obtain in some possible worlds.

In addition to contingent truths, there are also contingent beings. Indeed, there are so many contingent beings that everything that we know about on this planet or in the universe is a contingent being. Of course, God is an exception to this claim. The definition of a contingent being contains two points: (1) a contingent being is one whose nonexistence is possible. It might never have existed, and the day will come when it will cease to exist. (2) A contingent being is one that depends upon some other being or beings for its existence.[2]

Every human being is a contingent being, a fact made obvious by the role our parents played in our existence. We are contingent also in the sense that our continuing to live is dependent upon access to oxygen, water, the right temperature, and hundreds of other necessary conditions. Every part of the earth is contingent, including Mount Everest, the Ohio River, the Atlantic Ocean, the continent of North America, and so on. There was a time when such things did not exist, and there will come a time when they cease to exist.

We are now ready to relate contingent beings and truths to possible worlds. A contingent truth is true in some possible worlds and not others. The contingent truth "George Washington is the first president of the United States" is true in many possible worlds, including the actual world. But it is not true in every possible world. A contingent being exists in some possible worlds but not all. You and I exist in the real world; we

Possible Worlds, Contingency, and Necessity

---

2. Readers with good memories will recall a similar discussion in chapter 7.

also exist in many other possible worlds. But there are numerous possible worlds in which we never have and never will exist. Thinking about that long enough can greatly increase one's humility.

A necessary truth is one that is true in every possible world. The proposition "An object cannot be both round and square at the same time in the same sense" is true in every possible world. The truths of mathematics are true in every possible world. While contingent beings exist in some but not all possible worlds, a necessary being exists in every possible world. Since God is a necessary being, God exists in every possible world. I will say more about this later in the chapter.

Essential and Nonessential Properties

The distinction between essential and nonessential properties first appears clearly in the writings of Aristotle (see chap. 4). Aristotle pointed out that many properties of a thing are nonessential (or accidental) in the sense that they could be changed or lost without affecting the essence of the thing. A table, for example, could be painted a different color or moved to a different location or made shorter or taller, but it would still be a table. Its essence would be unchanged. All the changes cited would affect only nonessential characteristics of the table. But it would also be possible to change the table in ways that would alter it so drastically that it would no longer be a table. One might, for example, take a sledgehammer and smash it into kindling. Essential properties belong to the nature of a thing and cannot be changed or lost without altering the kind of thing it is. However, any change of a thing's nonessential properties would not change the kind of thing it is. And so the property or set of properties that make up the essence of something are definable in this way: E is an essential property of S (some substance or existing thing) means that if S loses E, then S ceases to be the kind of thing it is. If Socrates, for example, loses the essential property of humanness, he is no longer a human being.

The definition of an essential property in the language of possible worlds is this. If E is an essential property of Socrates, then Socrates possesses E in every possible world in which he exists. Because Socrates is a contingent being, he does not exist in every possible world, nor could he. But in every possible world where Socrates does exist, he possesses the essential property of humanness.

A nonessential property is one that can be lost without a thing's ceasing to be the kind of being it is. A human being may lose one, two, three, or four limbs and still be a human being. Humans may lose their hair, their sight, and their appendix and still be humans, that is, still possess the essential property of humanness. A nonessential property of Socrates such as baldness is one that Socrates possesses in some of the possible worlds in which he exists but not all.

Possible Worlds and the Attributes of God

Some of the predicates applied to God denote not attributes or essential properties of God but nonessential properties that relate God to his creatures. Relational predicates like "Creator," "Ruler," and "Preserver" do not denote divine attributes. A property like "being Lord of Israel" is likewise a nonessential property. It is logically possible that God might not have had this property. He might never have created Israel, or Israel might never have accepted Yahweh as its God. Being Lord of Israel or Creator of the world are not essential to the being of God. Utilizing the analysis earlier in this chapter, there are possible worlds in which God did not create the world or was not Lord of Israel.

Once the essential properties (or attributes) of God are identified, one can be certain that any being lacking even one essential divine property could not be God. A being who lacks the essential property of omnipotence or omniscience or immutability would no longer qualify as a bearer of the title *God*. If the being called God lost just one of his essential properties, he would no longer be God. A divine attribute then is a property that God could not lose and continue to be God; it is an essential property of God. A divine attribute must be necessary to our idea of God.

Earlier I explained how the doctrine of essential predication should be expressed in the semantics of possible worlds. One might state that the essence of an individual person is that set of properties he or she possesses in every possible world in which he or she exists. If there is any property that Socrates might not have in some possible world and still be Socrates, that property could not be part of his essence. If it is possible that Socrates might not have been snub-nosed, snub-nosedness is a nonessential property of Socrates. Any property that Socrates might have lacked in any possible world in which he exists could not be part of his essence.

The terminology of possible worlds can now be used to define an attribute of God. A divine attribute is a property of God in every possible world in which God exists. Just as some being in a possible world who lacked Socrates' essence could not be Socrates, so a possible being who lacked one of the divine attributes could not be God, would not qualify as bearer of the title *God*. This means that God is omnipotent, omniscient, and so on in every possible world in which he exists. And since, I contend, God is a logically necessary being, it follows that God's essential properties are his in every possible world.

Possible Worlds and the Kenosis Theory of the Incarnation

The kenosis theory is an attempt to explain the incarnation of Jesus Christ. The theory is based upon a bad interpretation of Philippians 2:5–8, which reads as follows:

Your attitude should be the same as that of Christ Jesus:

Who, being in very nature God,
    did not consider equality with God something to be grasped,

but made himself nothing,
> taking the very nature of a servant,
> being made in human likeness.

And being found in appearance as a man,
> he humbled himself
> and became obedient to death—
> even death on a cross!

Proponents of the kenosis theory believe this passage teaches that during his sojourn on earth, Jesus Christ set aside certain divine attributes, such as omnipotence and omniscience. To quote from a fairly recent defense of the kenosis theory, the theory holds "that in becoming human God the Son emptied himself or voluntarily relinquished such properties as omnipotence and omniscience."[3]

The implications of these remarks are troubling. Divine attributes such as omnipotence and omniscience are essential properties of God. If Jesus Christ divested himself of even one divine attribute, he would have ceased to be God. Omnipotence and omniscience are, we suggested, properties of God in every possible world in which God exists. Therefore, any loss of even one essentially divine property would have the result that God, or in this case, the Son of God, would cease to be God. We appear to be left with one of two choices: either proponents of the kenosis theory have a faulty understanding of God's essential properties, or they are willing to embrace a seriously mistaken view of the Incarnation, such that Jesus Christ could not have been fully God and fully man.[4]

In Philippians 2:6, the passage stating that Jesus "did not consider equality with God something to be grasped" is explained in the notes of *The New Geneva Study Bible* as follows: "This figure of speech means that something desirable was already possessed. Jesus was not trying to become God, that is, He already was God and did not cling to the privileges that were always His."[5] In other words, the verse does not refer to Jesus' abandonment of any divine attribute, only certain privileges that as God he already possessed.

Philippians 2:8 continues this theme by stating that "he [Jesus] humbled himself." About these words *The New Geneva Study Bible* correctly observes that "Christ is not said to have removed from Himself His identity as God. The phrase means that He humbled Himself, relinquishing His heavenly status, not His divine being."[6] The nature of his self-emptying is

---

3. C. Stephen Evans, *The Historical Christ and the Jesus of Faith* (Oxford: Clarendon, 1996), 132.

4. For a defense of the logical coherence of the Incarnation without any movement in the direction of a kenosis theory, see the appendix to chapter 4 of this book.

5. *The New Geneva Study Bible,* ed. Luder Whitlock Jr. (Nashville: Thomas Nelson, 1995), 1877.

6. Ibid.

explained in terms of his "taking the very nature of a servant," "being found in appearance as a man," and becoming "obedient to death." Nowhere in this magnificent passage is there a suggestion that Jesus Christ gave up or could give up any divine attribute.

In chapter 2, I summarized what many people regard as a powerful objection against naturalism. As a reminder, the naturalist claims that if anything exists, it exists as part of the box that we call the natural order. Naturalists don't have any options here; the box must be the sum total of reality. If even one thing should turn out to exist outside of the box that is the natural order, then naturalism would have been disproven. The argument then noted that even the naturalist must assent to the existence of one thing existing beyond the limits of the box, namely, the laws of logic. Without access to such laws, the naturalist would be unable to prove that naturalism is true or reasonable. But the laws of logical inference are different from the usual components of the box; the laws of logic are necessary and must therefore transcend the boundaries of the box. Since therefore even the naturalist must acknowledge the existence of one thing that exists outside the box, naturalism turns out to be a self-defeating theory.

Naturalism Revisited

Often when I explain this argument, I look into a sea of blank faces, a sure indication that most students have no idea what's going on. When I ask such students to tell me what they don't understand, it becomes clear that they see no difference between the necessary laws of logic and the nonnecessary laws of physics. Since the laws of physics don't transcend the box, why should the laws of logic? And since they cannot see the point to the argument, they find this refutation of naturalism unpersuasive.

Let us now relate the doctrine of possible worlds to our argument against naturalism. Students who feel as though the laws of nature (for example, physics) are not transcendent are correct. Physical laws like the law of gravity are contingent laws; this means they exist in the real world and may exist in lots of other possible worlds. But they do not exist in every possible world. In other words, there are possible worlds in which the law of universal gravitation does not obtain.

What makes the laws of rational inference different is the fact that they are logically necessary, not contingent. This means that the laws of logical inference exist in every possible world. Just as some simple truth of arithmetic cannot be confined within the box of the natural order, so the law of noncontradiction and other laws of rational inference cannot be confined within the bounds of the natural order. The laws of logic and arithmetic exist inside the box since humans who also exist inside the box can think about them. But they must also extend outside of the box. And it is this feature of the laws of logical inference that the naturalist is helpless to explain, on his naturalistic principles.

Possible Worlds and Anselm's Ontological Argument

Saint Anselm of Canterbury

One of the most important and original thinkers in the history of Christianity was the twelfth-century archbishop of Canterbury, Anselm (1033–1109). Anselm is best known for developing a famous argument for God's existence known as the ontological argument. Philosophy professors who find Anselm's argument as fascinating as I do can easily fill several class meetings looking at the various interpretations of Anselm's argument and the number of failed attempts to refute it. Philosophers who believe the argument is faulty can spend lots of class time presenting alleged refutations of Anselm's reasoning. Because I do not have the space to go into that much detail, I will limit my remarks to an interpretation of Anselm's argument that builds upon the expertise concerning possible worlds that is now shared by every reader of this book.

The key to Anselm's argument is his definition of God. According to Anselm, God is that Being than which a greater being cannot be conceived. Part of Anselm's point is that if more people had a clearer understanding of the nature of God, they would have fewer reservations about his existence. Anyone who seriously doubts the existence of God, Anselm believed, suffers from an inadequate grasp of God's nature.

What does it mean to say that God is that Being than which a greater cannot be conceived? Anselm is not endorsing a relativistic view of God, such that Mr. Jones could identify God with the greatest being he's capable of conceiving and Miss Smith can end up with a different concept of God. Nor is Anselm suggesting that any human being can attain a complete and perfect concept of this greatest conceivable being. His definition functions as a kind of boundary or standard that any adequate concept of God must approach.

Imagine that Mr. Jones has a concept of God such that his God lacks such properties as omnipotence with respect to power and omniscience with respect to knowledge. One of the ways in which Jones's God is lacking in power is the fact that his God did not and could not create the world. In Mr. Jones's thinking, God and the world are co-eternal. For Jones, God's knowledge is also severely limited, because among other things, he cannot know the future. In the terms of contemporary theology, Mr. Jones might well be a follower of process theology. His God lacks perfect knowledge about many future events and also lacks the power, let us say, to create the world, to control history, and to bring about his will in history. In short, Mr. Jones's God is limited and finite. Let us assume that Mr. Jones, who picked up his attachment to process theology from a college or seminary course, is content with his finite god. Among other things, it gives him some explanation for the existence of evil: evil exists because Jones's finite God cannot do anything about it.[7]

---

7. For more detail about process theology, see Ronald H. Nash, *The Concept of God* (Grand Rapids: Zondervan, 1983).

Now let us suppose that a friend introduces Mr. Jones to Anselm's thinking about God and that Mr. Jones is interested in exploring Anselm's theory in more detail. One day, Jones asks himself if his finite god is that being than which a greater cannot be conceived. Surely, it seems, Mr. Jones can conceive of a being greater than his finite god, namely, a God who has perfect knowledge about the future along with the kind of power usually in view when traditional Christians think about omnipotence.

Anselm believes that if anyone thinks about a being who is not the greatest conceivable being, the way Mr. Jones does, he or she is not thinking about *God!* Mr. Jones's finite god isn't God. In other words, Anselm's definition sets up a standard that any proposed candidate for God must satisfy in order to qualify. If the being someone conceptualizes as God is surpassable in greatness by some other candidate for God, the first candidate is disqualified.

Suppose then that Mr. Jones upgrades his concept of God to include the following attributes: omnipotence, omniscience, omnipresence, love, holiness, and any other properties present in Christian thinking about God. Mr. Jones believes he is thinking about a Being than which a greater being cannot be conceived. Let us also suppose that Mr. Jones holds back in just one respect. He believes that this being he conceives of and that he calls God exists only as an idea in his mind.

Miss Smith comes along and advises him politely that he still doesn't have it right. While her concept of God includes all of the same essential properties that Jones attributes to God, she and Jones differ in one major respect. Jones believes that the God he is thinking about exists in some possible worlds but happens not to exist in the real world. In the real world, Jones's God exists only as an idea in Jones's mind. Miss Smith, however, points out that Jones's God cannot be that Being than which a greater being cannot be conceived. And this is so because, as Miss Smith points out, the God she is conceiving does not just exist in some possible worlds other than the real world. The God she is thinking about is a logically necessary being who necessarily exists in every possible world, including the real world.

Consider the choice between two candidates for God who are alike in every respect but one. While Jones's God exists only in some possible worlds but does not exist in the real world, Miss Smith's candidate exists in every possible world, which means that he also and necessarily exists in the real world. Which of these two candidates is the only one that satisfies Anselm's definition of God, namely, that Being than which a greater cannot be conceived? The answer is obvious. But notice what we've learned. Since the only being who satisfies the standard of being God exists necessarily, he therefore exists in every possible world. But if God exists in every possible world, it follows that he also exists in the real world. Therefore God exists in the real world. Any candidate for God that does not exist necessarily cannot be God. It is impossible then for Jones's God to be the greatest conceivable being.

The debate over this argument has gone on for centuries. In a brief appendix to this chapter, I will offer a brief answer to one kind of objection. I place that material in the appendix so as not to interrupt the organization of this chapter.

Possible Worlds and Perfect Being Theology

Many contemporary religious thinkers believe there is another profitable line of thinking made possible by Anselm's definition of God. This second line of thinking explores ways in which Anselm's understanding of God as the most perfect being opens up possibilities for thinking about God's nature. While the Bible has much to say about God's nature, many have been skeptical about how successful people can be in reaching conclusions about God's nature via reasoning that is independent of special revelation. However, Anselm's approach seems promising.

Imagine a candidate for God that lacks such specific attributes of God as omnipotence, omniscience, omnipresence, love, holiness, justice, or any other property of God known through special revelation. Could any being lacking any one of these properties possibly qualify as that Being than which a greater cannot be conceived? If we have two candidates for the title of God, and one is morally perfect while the other is lacking in holiness, can the second candidate qualify as that being than which a greater cannot be conceived? Ask the same question with respect to love, perfect knowledge, and justice.

Think now of someone with little or no prior contact with special revelation. Is it possible that such a person, armed with Anselm's approach to God's nature, could arrive at a fairly complete listing of the properties of the biblical God? Explore this with respect to the contrast between a personal God and a pantheistic deity. Which of these two is more perfect, greater than the other? I'm not sure how far I wish to push this. It does strike me as an interesting way to think about God's nature.

Possible Worlds and Middle Knowledge

Many have thought that if God has perfect knowledge of the future, such knowledge would pose a serious threat to human freedom. After all, they say, if God knows that Mr. Brown is going to choose a hamburger for his lunch, can Brown really be free to choose something else? If Brown did have that power, it would seem that he could turn God's foreknowledge into ignorance.

During the sixteenth century, a Jesuit theologian named Louis de Molina advanced an ingenious but dubious attempt to reconcile God's perfect knowledge of the future and human freedom. Molina began by accepting three claims. (1) Propositions about future human actions have truth value; for example, the proposition "A priest named Martin Luther will start the Protestant Reformation in October of 1517" has always been true in the sense that I explained earlier. (2) God knows all true propositions about the future; and (3) human beings are free in the sense that they can either perform some particular act or not. But if God knows that Miss Smith will choose to attend her philosophy course on a given day in the future, then she will attend that class. But since it is certain that the student will attend class, how could she possibly do otherwise; and does this not negate her freedom?

One of the easiest ways to see how Molina defends human freedom is to use the language of possible worlds. As we know, there is a very large number of possible worlds (complete states of affairs), only one of which is the actual or real world. In order for one possible world to differ from another, at least one state of affairs must be different. Let us imagine a possible world in which Judas Iscariot is offered thirty pieces of silver to betray Jesus. We know at least two things about this possible state of affairs: (1) we know that it is also part of the actual world; and (2) we know that the hypothetical proposition "If Judas is offered thirty pieces of silver, then he will betray Jesus" is true.

Now imagine a second possible world that is the same as the real world with but one difference; in this second possible world, Judas is offered only twenty pieces of silver. This possible state of affairs is referred to by the following sentence: "If Judas had been offered twenty pieces of silver, he would have betrayed Jesus." Is this second hypothetical statement true or false? We can only guess. One way to view this second hypothetical situation is to imagine two more possible worlds. In one of them Judas is offered twenty pieces of silver and betrays Jesus; in the other, Judas is offered the twenty pieces and refuses to betray Jesus.

I doubt that any human being could ever know which of these two possible worlds would have been actual if Judas had been offered only twenty pieces of silver. But it is basic to Molina's theory that God knows the content of every possible world. God knows what Judas would have done if he had been offered twenty pieces of silver, or only one, or none. God knows what Judas would have freely done in every possible world.

Molina called this strange kind of knowledge *middle knowledge* because it supposedly comes between two other kinds of knowledge that God can have. The Roman Catholic philosopher Reginald Garrigou-Lagrange explains:

> This knowledge is called middle by reason of its proper object, which is the conditional future or the conditionally free act of the future. It is intermediate between the purely possible which is the object of God's knowledge of simple intelligence, and the contingent future which is the object of God's knowledge of vision. By this middle knowledge, according to

Molina, God knows, previous to any predetermining decree, how a free will would act if placed in certain circumstances, and how in certain other cases it would decide otherwise. After that God decides, according to His benevolent designs, to render this free will effective by placing it in those circumstances more or less favorable or unfavorable to it.[8]

In other words, by means of his *natural knowledge* God knows everything that can be; by means of his *simple vision,* God knows what will be, that is, what will occur in the real world; and by means of his *middle knowledge,* God knows what would be if the world were different in some way. By means of his middle knowledge God knows all possible worlds and what each possible individual would do in them. God then decrees certain antecedent conditions with full knowledge of how the human agent will act in that situation. But God's decree does not violate the freedom of the agent. In the case of Judas, God knows that if Judas is offered thirty pieces of silver, Judas will of his own free will choose to betray Jesus. God actualizes the set of circumstances in which his will is accomplished. But God's decree in no way interferes with the free choice of his creatures.

It is important to distinguish between a presentation of middle knowledge as an account of God's knowledge versus its use as an explanation of how human free will fits into a universe in which God has perfect knowledge of the future and exercises sovereign control over all things. It is this second role for middle knowledge that appears most problematic. Many believe there is merit in recognizing that God's knowledge includes middle knowledge. If God only knows what will happen, instead of knowing what would happen under every conceivable set of circumstances, it is difficult to see how God could control the world.

Molina's success in offering a way to understand a middle-knowledge approach to God's approach to bringing about his will in human affairs without infringing on human freedom seems much more problematic. Nevertheless, it makes an interesting subject for a class discussion.

Conclusion

I began this chapter by summarizing several major points stressed by many philosophers when they utilize the language of possible worlds. It is important to remember that I avoid any verdict on the existence of possible worlds other than the actual world. My purpose has been to help the reader understand the theory behind possible-world thinking and recognize its value as a heuristic device or teaching tool with respect to such important concepts as necessity, possibility, essential and nonessential properties, the existence and nature of God, middle knowledge, and so on.

---

8. Reginald Garrigou-Lagrange, *God: His Existence and His Nature* (St. Louis: B. Herder, 1936), 2:82.

Appendix: God, Logical Necessity, and Factual Necessity

This appendix deals with some unfinished business from my brief treatment of one interpretation of Anselm's ontological argument. Necessary existence is one fundamental difference between God and his creatures. Creatures exist contingently. That is, their existence might not have been; their existence is dependent on something other than themselves. They do not exist in all possible worlds. God's nonexistence, however, is impossible. God's existence does not depend upon anything else; it is entirely uncaused. A being who is less than a necessary being would be unfit to bear the title *God*.

God's necessary existence has been interpreted in two quite different ways. Some have understood the notion in the sense of *logical necessity;* others have attempted to delineate a sense of *factual necessity.*

If God's existence is understood as logically necessary, the proposition "God exists" is logically true. A logically necessary being is one that exists in every possible world. If all this is the case with respect to God, then the proposition "God exists" is true in every possible world. Just as it is impossible for a triangle to have four sides,[9] so it is logically impossible for God not to exist. It follows then that any denial of God's existence is as self-contradictory as statements like "Some triangles have four sides." However, it is important to note in this connection that some propositions can be self-contradictory without being self-evidently so. People can contradict themselves without realizing it.[10] Therefore, the claim that "God does not exist" is self-contradictory cannot be countered by arguing that it does not look like a contradiction.

In recent years, many religious thinkers have given up on the notion of a logically necessary being. For reasons that never held water,[11] they decided the concept was not only indefensible but even damaging to theism. Consequently, in order to retain a sense of necessity with respect to God, these thinkers explained God's existence as necessary in a nonlogical sense: God's existence, they said, is a factual necessity.[12]

A being who is necessary in the factual sense is one about whom four claims can be made. (1) The being is eternal; that is, it had no beginning, and its existence will never end. (2) The being is uncaused, which is to say that it does not depend upon anything else for its existence. It is, in a sense already explained, *a se.* (3) Everything else that exists

---

9. That is, there is no possible world in which a triangle has four sides.

10. Just because I find a state of affairs conceivable, it does not follow that it is logically possible. I might, for example, find it conceivable that the square root of 60,616 is 244. While it might be conceivable, it turns out to be logically impossible. There is no possible world in which 244 is the square root of 60,616.

11. See Nash, *The Concept of God,* chap. 9.

12. For example, see John Hick's "God as Necessary Being," *Journal of Philosophy* 57 (1960): 725–34.

depends upon the necessary being for its existence. This brings us to the key difference between the notions of logical and factual necessity: (4) a factually necessary being does not exist in all possible worlds. In the sense of factual necessity, the proposition "God does not exist" is not logically false. A factually necessary being is, in a sense, accidental.

While the notion of God as a logically necessary being is once again becoming respectable, new doubts are being raised about the cogency of the notion of a factually necessary being. By definition, a factually necessary being does not exist in all possible worlds. Only a logically necessary being could satisfy this condition. Once one recognizes that there are possible worlds in which a factually necessary God does not exist, it makes sense to ask why God exists in the real world. But the point to talking about a necessary being is supposedly to defuse questions like this. Advocates of factual necessity fall into a trap of their own making. The question as to why God exists in any particular world cannot arise in the case of a logically necessary God. He exists in world A or world B (and so on) because he exists in every possible world. But once a theist acknowledges that there are possible worlds in which God does not exist, the question as to why God exists in the real world gains force. Moreover, what prevents this factually necessary being from existing by chance, that is, without reason?

It appears then that the notion of factual necessity appeals implicitly to key features of the concept of logical necessity. Either a necessary being exists in every possible world or it does not. A logically necessary being does exist in every possible world. In this sense, it is like the number two or the concept of a square. To question why a logically necessary being exists in the real world makes no sense.

OPTIONAL WRITING EXERCISE

Imagine that a friend asks you to explain why learning the language of possible worlds is worthwhile. Write a *short* essay answering his request.

FOR FURTHER READING

Several of these books are very technical.

William Lane Craig, *The Only Wise God* (Grand Rapids: Baker, 1987).

David Lewis, *Counterfactuals* (Cambridge, Mass.: Harvard University Press, 1973).

Thomas V. Morris, *The Logic of God Incarnate* (Ithaca, N.Y.: Cornell University Press, 1986).

Ronald H. Nash, *The Concept of God* (Grand Rapids: Zondervan, 1983).

Stephen Parrish, *God and Necessity* (Lanham, Md.: University Press of America, 1997).

Alvin Plantinga, *God, Freedom, and Evil* (New York: Harper & Row, 1974).

Alvin Plantinga, *The Nature of Necessity* (Oxford: Clarendon, 1974).

Alvin Plantinga, ed., *The Ontological Argument* (New York: Anchor, 1965).

James E. Tomberlin and Peter Van Inwagen, *Alvin Plantinga* (Boston: D. Reidel, 1985).

Chapter Ten

Epistemology I: Whatever Happened to Truth?

The major thinkers of the past believed one of life's crucial tasks was the discovery of truth about humans, the world in which they live, and the God whose existence makes everything else possible. While attitudes toward God's existence varied greatly from 1800 through the middle of the twentieth century, the pursuit of truth remained at the center of such disciplines as theology, history, and philosophy. In the last half of the twentieth century, however, people used new paradigms in an attempt to put an end to the human consensus about the importance, nature of, and accessibility to truth.

What Is Truth?

Truth is a property of propositions that correspond to the way things are. If I state, for example, that on August 22, 1998, the New York Yankees are in first place in the eastern division of the American League, we can easily check to see whether the claim is true. It is true if the team occupied that position in its league; otherwise it is false. Truth in this sense is objective, that is, is independent of human preference and desire. Our feelings cannot alter or change the truth.

Tests of Truth

It is important to distinguish between the nature of truth (correspondence) and various tests that might be necessary to help us recognize truth. Many contemporary discussions of truth confuse the nature of truth with tests of truth. Three tests have tended to dominate discussions of this subject: correspondence, coherence, and pragmatism.

The Test of Correspondence

Consider the proposition "There are 893 steps to the top of the Washington Monument." What would be the most obvious way to test the truth of this claim? Right, we climb up those steps and count every one of them. If there are 893 steps, the proposition is true.

While the test of correspondence is usually available, there are times when it is not. Imagine a wife who is told that a small plane her husband was flying crashed in the part of the Atlantic Ocean known as the Bermuda Triangle. After days of searching, the Coast Guard tells the woman it believes her husband is dead. But without a body, the test of correspondence is difficult to apply.[1]

The Test of Coherence

One test people might turn to in the case of the missing husband is coherence. Does the information contained in the proposition "John Smith is dead" fit with everything else that we know? Suppose the insurance company holding a two-million-dollar accidental life insurance policy on the husband thinks something suspicious is going on. Suppose someone looking very much like the husband has been seen on various islands in the Caribbean. Suppose phone records show that the wife has received several collect phone calls from these islands. Suppose Western Union records reveal that she has cabled large amounts of money to these islands.

In cases where it is impossible to demonstrate correspondence between a proposition and the reality it describes, we can test a proposition's truth in terms of how well it coheres with all other relevant information available to us. In the example cited above, the insurance company would seem to have good reason to believe that the proposition about John Smith being dead is false. As useful as coherence may sometimes be as a test of truth, it too has its failings. When coherence is used as the exclusive test for truth, it seems to equate falsity with incomplete knowledge. It also seems unable to provide adequate verification of specific empirical claims.

The Test of Pragmatism

The third theory of truth, pragmatism (or practice), holds that the test of truth is whether a belief works. One of several problems with pragmatism is the fact that false propositions sometimes work while true propositions do not, a point illustrated during the sixteenth-century debate between proponents of the older Ptolemaic model of the solar system that often produced more accurate predictions of the movement of the planets than did the new Copernican system.[2]

---

1. Correspondence as a test of truth suffers from other problems. For example, it stumbles over the great deal of human knowledge dealing with objects of thought, such as mathematics.

2. One reason this happened was because followers of Copernicus thought of the orbits of planets as perfect circles. Once this mistaken belief was corrected by the work of Kepler, the superiority of the predictive powers of the Copernican system was established.

So while most people agree that correspondence between a proposition and reality constitutes the nature of truth, problems arise when we attempt to identify one and only one test for truth.

Epistemological Relativism

In 1987, University of Chicago philosopher Allan Bloom stated that "there is one thing a professor can be absolutely certain of: Almost every student entering the university believes, or says he believes, that truth is relative."[3] According to a poll published in the early 1990s, almost three out of four Americans between the ages of eighteen and twenty-five doubt the existence of objective truth.[4] While this relativism is seldom, if ever, supported with arguments, it nonetheless travels in the company of other theories and beliefs—equally untenable—that help provide psychological support for students and professors who want to believe that there are no objective standards of truth or morality or, indeed, of anything.

Relativists love to draw attention to disagreements among people, as though the mere existence of these disagreements proves the relativity of what it is that people quarrel over. Nothing follows from the fact that two individuals or two cultures disagree over the truth of a particular proposition. When person A says the world is flat and person B claims the world is round, it hardly follows that there is no objective truth about the matter.

We have all heard people say, "That may be true for you, but it isn't true for me." As Mortimer Adler explains, talk like this rests on a serious confusion "between the truth or falsity that inheres in a proposition or statement and the judgment that a person makes with regard to the truth or falsity of the statement in question. We may differ in our judgment about what is true, but that does not affect the truth of the matter itself."[5]

As an example, Adler considers

> a difference of opinion about the number of peaks in the Colorado Rockies that exceed 14,000 feet. One person sets the number at fifty; the other says, "Not so." The number of peaks in Colorado exceeding 14,000 feet is some definite integer, and so the statement that sets it as fifty is either true or false, regardless of what the persons who dispute this matter of fact may think about it.... We do not make statements true or false by affirming or denying them. They have truth or falsity regardless of what we think, what opinions we hold, what judgments we make.[6]

When two people hold directly opposing beliefs, we are entitled to conclude that one of them is right and the other is wrong.

---

3. Allan Bloom, *The Closing of the American Mind* (New York: Simon and Schuster, 1987), 25.

4. See George Barna, *The Barna Report: What Americans Believe* (Ventura, Calif.: Regal Books, 1991), 83–85.

5. Mortimer Adler, *Six Great Ideas* (New York: Collier Books, 1981), 41.

6. Ibid.

There are several versions of epistemological relativism, and Plato refuted one of them. During the lifetime of Socrates, a thinker named Protagoras (c. 490–c. 421 B.C.) uttered what has become a rather famous statement: "Man is the measure of all things." Plato understood the statement to mean that each person is the ultimate judge of truth and goodness. Whatever a person thinks is true *is* true. Every person's opinion is correct.[7]

Plato developed several arguments against Protagoras's relativism, placing them as he often did in the mouth of Socrates. What follows is a paraphrase of part of Socrates' discussion with Protagoras as it appears in Plato's *Theaetetus.*

> Socrates: "So you believe that each man's opinion is as good as anyone else's."
>
> Protagoras: "That's correct."
>
> Socrates: "How do you make a living?
>
> Protagoras: "I am a teacher."
>
> Socrates: "I find this very puzzling. You admit you earn money teaching, but I cannot imagine what you could possibly teach anyone. After all, you admit that each person's opinion is as good as anyone else's. This means that what your students believe is as good as anything you could possibly teach them. Once they learn that each person is the measure of all things, what possible reason would they have to pay you for any further lessons? How can you possibly teach them anything once they learn that their opinions are as true as yours?"

In another objection, Socrates states that the man-measure doctrine might appear plausible until one applies it to the test of future experience. So long as people limit themselves to what appears to be the case in the present, they will never find out what is wrong with the opinion. All that is necessary is to wait long enough, and the test of future experience will make clear that some beliefs are false. For example, consider a follower of Protagoras who needs medical advice but assumes that when it comes to illness, each man is the measure of all things. So he selects as his physician someone who flunked out of kindergarten but charges lower fees than do his competitors. At the moment the advice is

---

7. There is a long story here that I do not have time to explore. As Plato explained Protagoras's position in his *Theaetetus,* Protagoras assumes that sense experience is identical with knowledge. The reason why everything is relative is because knowledge is identical with the way we perceive the world through our senses. Two people might be aware of the same breeze. One of them, suffering from a fever, might experience the wind as cold and suffer a chill. The other person might find the breeze quite pleasant. Both would be right in Protagoras's view of things. There is no higher principle to which we could ever appeal. Each person is the measure or ultimate judge of all things.

given, there may be no basis on which to reject the opinion. But wait long enough, and the bad medical advice will be proven false. It may also mean that the Protagorean's family is seeking the services of an undertaker.

In another argument Socrates points out the logically self-defeating nature of Protagoras's position. Since Protagoras believes that every person's belief is true, it follows then that every citizen of Athens who believes Protagoras's theory is false must be correct.

I conclude this section with a story containing one sentence that some people find offensive. If it offends you, that was not my intention. I relate the story because it's true and because it's relevant to Plato's critique of relativism.

Twenty years ago or so, I was teaching introduction to philosophy at a large state university in the mid-South. One of my freshmen students was unable to go home for the weekend, so he stayed in town and attended a city church on Sunday morning. As the student reported the event, the pastor's sermon thesis was that "All religious beliefs are true." Not wishing to provoke a confrontation with the pastor, the student attempted to slip out of the church; he failed. The pastor insisted that the student share one of his religious beliefs so the pastor could demonstrate his open-minded tolerance. Finally the student sighed, surrendered to the pastor's demands, and said: "Since you won't let me leave until I tell you what I believe, here it is. Sir, with all due respect, one of my religious beliefs is that you are going to hell."

Angered by the student's remark, the ministerial defender of religious relativism replied, "Well, I guess I made a mistake. All religious beliefs are true except yours." Of course, this response was logically inconsistent with his sermon's thesis. When someone says that all religious beliefs are true and then asserts that there is at least one false religious belief, he is contradicting himself. The conjunction of these two statements is a logical contradiction. The preacher's statements were a classic example of a logically self-defeating position. This was the same point that Socrates (Plato) made with respect to Protagoras's relativism.

Postmodernism: The New Face of Relativism

What appears to be a new variety of epistemological relativism has popped up in the last decades of the twentieth century. It is associated with names like postmodernism and deconstructionism. Because of its popularity in certain academic circles, it demands our attention.

The word *postmodernism* represents a variety of positions along a continuum. There are more and less radical versions of the position. Some scholars talk of constructive versions of postmodernism, those that try to make the best of a bad situation (modernism) without succumbing to the excesses of the destructive versions of postmodernism. Most of my remarks will deal with more radical types of postmodernism. The name *postmodernism* refers to a contemporary movement that rejects beliefs supposedly taught by thinkers during the Enlightenment and by followers of those ideas who helped produce the movement we now know as modernism.

Postmodernism and Language

I am about to do something that is either impossible or a miracle. I am going to use language to explain how postmodernists use language to destroy language as a vehicle of communication. What I say must be brief.

Language, postmodernists believe, cannot refer beyond itself. Words can refer only to other words; they can never refer to things or objects. Texts can never convey objective truth about an objective reality because the only thing texts can do is point to other texts, never to an objective reality. It would take a great deal of time to present or pretend to present an argument for such claims. Even if I had the time and space to attempt this task, postmodernists have little use for logic. To make things even worse, it would be necessary to present such an argument in human language. So, for the sake of argument, let us concede the truth of the early claims made in this paragraph. Whether these claims are objectively true or not is something we will ignore for now.

As a next step, postmodernists want us to believe that language is an arbitrary, social construct, that is, a creation of our culture. If we still had any respect for logic, we could then draw such inferences as the following: (1) the meaning of language is an arbitrary social construct. Meaning cannot be grounded either in "reality" or in texts. (2) The relation between words and meaning is arbitrary. (3) No meaning or interpretation is better than any other.

It is interesting to see what self-described Christian postmodernists infer from everything noted so far.[8] Two such writers, J. Richard Middleton and Brian Walsh, authors of a book titled *Truth Is Stranger Than It Used to Be*,[9] reject the status of divine revelation for the words and propositions of Scripture. Their position amounts to a repudiation of the objective truth of the Bible.[10] Commenting on what he regards as their aberrant theology, Carl F. H. Henry observes that Middleton and Walsh "reject any identification of Scripture as revelation; what comprises divine revelation is for them amorphous and nebulous, since they deny revealed truths."[11]

---

8. But since postmodernists don't respect logic, why should we allow them to draw any inferences? Fair is fair, as we used to say.

9. (Downers Grove, Ill.: InterVarsity Press, 1994).

10. See their comments in a promotional article for their book, "How Pomo Can You Go?" in *Academic Alert,* September 1995. This is a promotional newsletter for InterVarsity Press books.

11. Carl F. H. Henry, "Truth: Dead on Arrival," *World* (May 20–27, 1995): 25.

Even the truth of the Christian gospel, Henry complains, "is a human construction" for Middleton and Walsh.[12] Postmodernists like Middleton and Walsh fail to see that their repudiation of the possibility of revealed propositional truth in Scripture conflicts with their confidence in their own ability to communicate propositional truths in their own writings. They act as though they can do something that God cannot do.

The Hermeneutics of Suspicion[13]

Postmodernists regard texts as attempts by powerful people to impose their will upon the weak and powerless. A text represents a hidden agenda. Not only must we look beyond the apparent meaning of a text, but also we must dig deeper and uncover the relationships of power that make up the culture. Postmodernists do this by means of what they call "subversive readings." Reading a text does not mean seeking out its objective meaning, which is something that cannot be done anyway. Rather, the postmodernist seeks to uncover what the text is hiding. Deconstructionsts break down the text; they deconstruct it in order to uncover the relationships of power hidden beneath the text. I will have a bit more to say about the hermeneutics of suspicion later in this chapter.

Metanarratives

Postmodernists are also fond of the term *metanarrative,* a word that their communities have socially constructed to refer to a story about a story. Postmodernists assert that there are no legitimate metanarratives. But worldviews are metanarratives, which leads Gene Edward Veith Jr. to describe postmodernism as "a worldview that denies all worldviews."[14] This reminds me of the mythical search for the universal solvent. The catch was, the searchers would never be able to find anything to store it in.

Rodney Clapp, an editor at the company that published the Middleton-Walsh book, admits that enemies of Christianity can claim "that the Bible presents a metanarrative—a truth for everyone, everywhere."[15] This leads Clapp to ask Middleton and Walsh: Since the biblical narrative claims to be objectively and universally true, should we reject it? Middleton and Walsh acknowledge the potential problem but attempt to evade it by using passages in the Bible to show that the Bible is on the side of the weak and the powerless. Perhaps this is supposed to free the Bible from any threat from the hermeneutics of suspicion. It appears to be an attempt to keep the Bible in the game by suggesting that even though it

---

12. Ibid.

13. Until recently, hermeneutics was the science of interpretation. Postmodernists took the science out of interpretation.

14. Gene Edward Veith Jr., *Postmodern Times* (Wheaton, Ill.: Crossway), 49.

15. "How Pomo Can You Go?"

is a metanarrative, it's a nice one, as though this has any relevance to the subject before us. If all metanarratives are impossible or bad, the biblical metanarrative is in deep trouble and the supposed friends of the Bible are a part of the team digging the grave. It certainly looks as though consistent postmodern Christians are obliged to dispense with the biblical metanarrative.

Realism Versus Antirealism

In the previous section, we noted how postmodernists argue that knowledge about the real world is impossible. This position is sometimes known as *antirealism*. For postmodernists, the word *reality,* D. A. Carson says, "is always *some group's* construction of reality that invariably ends up being the dominant construction that guides social life."[16] In Middleton and Walsh's account of antirealism, they contrast their position with modernism's assumption "that the knowing autonomous subject arrived at truth by establishing a correspondence between objectively given 'reality' and the thoughts or assertions of the knower. To the postmodern mind, such correspondence is impossible, since we have no access to something called 'reality' apart from that which we 'represent' as reality in our concepts, language and discourse. . . . We can never get outside of our knowledge to check its accuracy against 'objective' reality. Our access is always mediated by our own linguistic and conceptual constructions."[17]

One of the better accounts of this dispute between realists and antirealists has been written by philosopher Keith Yandell of the University of Wisconsin at Madison. Acknowledging the difficulty of defining the word *realism,* Yandell instead opts for an example. He writes: "Realism concerning smurfs is the view that independent of our experience, thought and language, there are little blue persons who look like Snow White's dwarves dipped in cups of blue Easter egg dye and left out to dry."[18] For the record, let me say that with regard to smurfs, I am an antirealist. As Yandell explains, "Anti-realism about smurfs is the view that insofar as there are smurfs, they are dependent on our experience, thought and language. Anti-realism about persons and physical objects is the view that, insofar as there are persons and physical objects, they are dependent on our experience, thought and language."[19]

---

16. D. A. Carson, *The Gagging of God* (Grand Rapids: Zondervan, 1996), 135.

17. J. Richard Middleton and Brian J. Walsh, "Facing the Postmodern Scalpel," in *Christian Apologetics in the Postmodern World,* ed. Timothy R. Phillips and Dennis L. Okholm (Downers Grove, Ill.: InterVarsity Press, 1995), 134.

18. Keith Yandell, "Modernism, Post-Modernism, and the Minimalist Canons of Common Grace," *Christian Scholar's Review* 27 (fall 1997): 15–26; the quote is on page 18. I have taken the liberty of correcting typographical errors without noting them.

19. Ibid.

Anyone who has read the earlier chapters in this book knows that I am a realist with respect to universals, properties, states of affairs, numbers, mind, truth, and God. I am an antirealist with regard to mermaids, unicorns, golden mountains, square circles, and Tinker Bell. Postmodernists tend to be antirealists about everything. Everything, or so they claim, is a construct of language, which is itself a construct of communities. Let us call this unqualified position *universal antirealism.*

According to Yandell, this universal antirealism is an untenable position. He correctly notes that "one cannot without self-contradiction be an anti-realist about absolutely everything. A constructivist needs some principled distinction between what is real and what is not. A radical or universalist sort of constructionism or anti-realism can make no such distinction."[20]

If antirealism could be true (but it cannot),[21] we could eliminate death, poverty, and unhappiness from the world by thinking. This would be so because language about this trinity of bad things has no objective meaning; death, poverty, and unhappiness are arbitrary constructs. If antirealism is true, it is within our reach to wake up in the morning to a world without any unpleasant reality.[22]

Postmodernism and Reason

Postmodernists complain about modernism's attachment to reason, a word they use to mean (is this an act of discovering some kind of objective meaning?) "universal reason" or the laws of logic, the sort of thing we covered in chapter 8. Unfortunately, something is seriously wrong with the postmodernist's analysis of reason.

It is true that the Enlightenment was marked by an almost unbounded confidence in human reason. The natural sciences had just begun to push back the frontiers of human knowledge. But the growing confidence in the powers of the human mind helped to produce a growing skepticism toward religious claims to truth. Many who were affected by the Enlightenment's rationalism became skeptical toward traditional religion, hostile toward faith, and uncertain with respect to religious authority. Human reason, the enlightened believed, could be trusted when the Bible and the church could not.

It is important to distinguish two different senses of the word *reason.* (1) In its most important sense, reason refers to the objective and transcendent laws of logic that are indispensable to human thinking, acting,

---

20. Ibid.

21. This is so because on postmodernist grounds, no position can be objectively true.

22. See Howard Robinson, *Matter and Consciousness* (Cambridge: Cambridge University Press, 1982), 82.

and communicating. Sensible people would never reject this sense of reason. (2) In the sense used by most Enlightenment thinkers, however, reason referred to the process of human reasoning or thinking, which such thinkers believed had earned the right to be elevated above the Judeo-Christian Scriptures and the historic doctrines of the Christian faith. When the word is understood in this way, people whose unbelief made them unreceptive to the teachings of Scripture had a convenient way of dismissing historic Christian beliefs as unreasonable. All they meant was that the beliefs were unreasonable to them. In this way, what amounted to a display of self-importance was made to appear more significant than it deserved to be.

The antonym of reason for most scholars during the Enlightenment was not a collection of logical contradictions but rather divine special revelation, that is, revealed propositions from God. The target of Enlightenment-style reason was God-revealed truth superior to anything humans could come to know by their effort. The modernists opposed revelation and greatly exaggerated the supposed competence of unaided human thinking.

This view of reason during the Enlightenment led many to believe that the human mind could and indeed should function as a judge of the content of Scripture and the historic Christian faith. This understanding was also subjective to individual humans or groups of humans who elevated their own thinking above that of Scripture. The correct understanding of reason during the Enlightenment seems embarrassingly similar to the subjective view of reason advanced by many postmodernists. On this point, at least, many self-proclaimed postmodernists turn out to be ultramodernists.

By any standard, there was plenty wrong with the Enlightenment and its intellectual heritage. Many representatives of modernism exaggerated the powers of the human mind. As Veith points out, "The postmodernists are right to question the arrogance of the Enlightenment, the assumption that human reason can answer every question, and solve every problem. They are wrong, though, to deny reason altogether. They are right to question the certainty of modern truths; they are wrong to reject the very concept of truth in favor of intellectual relativism."[23] Obviously, human beings cannot reason their way to a solution to every problem in life, including the difficult questions about the nature of God. Wise religious people have always made a distinction between beliefs that are above reason and those that are against reason, that is, those that violate the law of noncontradiction. Modernism deserves criticism, but when postmodernism goes so far as to deny reason, it is wrong. Postmodernism

---

23. Veith, *Postmodern Times*, 68.

cannot nullify the laws of mathematics, the multiplication tables, and logic, even though some people act as though it has.

Both the radical rationalism of the Enlightenment and postmodern irrationalism are incompatible with the Christian worldview. When postmodernists denigrate truth and logic, they begin sliding down a slippery slope into what Veith calls "a Pandora's box of New Age religions, syncretism, and moral chaos."[24] The postmodernist attack against what they call universal reason is misdirected. The postmodernist acts as though his weapons are aimed at others, even as he is shooting himself in the foot.

A More Detailed Look at Deconstructionism

Deconstructionism is a new kind of relativism. According to the most radical version of deconstructionism, all meaning is dependent on the interpreter and not the text. One reason why texts cannot convey objective truth about an objective reality is because all they can do is point to other texts. Meaning becomes relative to the person doing the interpreting, and no interpretation has any advantage over any other. There is need to take a closer look at the deconstructionist component of postmodernism. My examination will proceed via four steps.

Step One: The Attack of Professor Rothbard

A 1989 treatment of deconstructionism written by American scholar Murray Rothbard is a place to begin. My inclusion of Rothbard's discussion does not necessarily imply my agreement with his views. Rothbard gets right to the point:

> Either there is no objective truth or, if there is, we can never discover it. With each person being bound to his own subjective views, feelings, history, and so on, there is no method of discovering objective truth. In literature, the most elemental procedure of literary criticism (that is, trying to figure out what a given author meant to say) becomes impossible. Communication between writer and reader similarly becomes hopeless; furthermore, not only can no reader ever figure out what an author meant to say, but even the author does not know or understand what he himself meant to say, so fragmented, confused, and driven to each particular individual. So, since it is impossible to figure out what Shakespeare, Conrad, Plato, Aristotle, or Machiavelli meant, what becomes the point of either reading or writing literary or philosophical criticism?[25]

According to Rothbard, deconstructionists believe the activity of the interpreter is more important than the text being interpreted. In effect, the text becomes nothing, and the interpretation becomes everything.

---

24. Ibid., 192–93.
25. Murray Rothbard, "The Hermeneutical Invasion of Philosophy and Economics," *The Review of Austrian Economics* 3 (1989): 45.

There is no correct interpretation. Since even authors do not know what they mean, how can any interpreter hope to do better? As Bloom says, "the one thing most necessary for us, the knowledge of what these texts have to tell us, is turned over to the subjective creative selves of these interpreters, who say that there is both no text and no reality to which the texts refer."[26]

Deconstructionism, Rothbard says, reduces to the claim that no one, not even deconstructionists, can understand literary texts—not even their *own* literary texts. This means that all writings of deconstructionists in which they analyze the writings of other authors are only "subjective musings."[27] But why should anyone care? And even if we did care about this or that author, the deconstructionists' own principles would prevent us from understanding those musings. If deconstructionists are right, we can never understand any text, including the texts in which deconstructionists describe the principles of their own position. Deconstructionism turns out to be a self-refuting theory.

Rothbard finds it significant that Karl Marx is regarded as a forerunner of this movement:

> This century has seen a series of devastating setbacks to Marxism, to its pretentions to "scientific truth," and to its theoretical propositions as well as to its empirical assertions and predictions. If Marxism has been riddled both in theory and in practice, then what can Marxian cultists fall back on? It seems to me that [deconstructionist hermeneutics] fits very well into an era that we might . . . call "late Marxism" or "Marxism-in-decline." Marxism is not true and is not science, but so what? The [deconstructionists] tell us that nothing is objectively true, and therefore that all views and propositions are subjective, relative to the whims and feelings of each individual. So why should Marxian yearnings not be equally as valid as anyone else's? . . . And since there is no objective reality, and since reality is created by every man's subjective interpretations, then all social problems reduce to personal and nonrational tastes.[28]

Rothbard warns it would be a serious error in judgment to think of deconstructionism as nothing more than a self-refuting exercise in interpretation or noninterpretation. What deconstructionists teach is intellectual permissiveness, to be sure. But it is much more than that. They also preach practical permissiveness. Those who insist the truth is relative say (when they are consistent) that ethics is relative too. Deconstructionism logically entails the end of human learning. The catch is that there is no reason to take deconstructionism seriously. Rothbard argues that advocates of such

---

26. Bloom, *Closing of the American Mind,* 379.

27. I borrow the phrase from Jonathan Barnes's review of two books by Hans-Georg Gadamer in the *London Review of Books,* November 6, 1986, 12–13.

28. Rothbard, "Hermeneutical Invasion of Philosophy and Economics," 49.

a nihilistic and self-refuting position are not worthy participants in any dialogue or conversation. Instead of a respective point-by-point analysis and refutation of their writings, which by their own principles can never be interpreted correctly, what they deserve instead, Rothbard contends, "is scorn and dismissal. Unfortunately, they do not often receive such treatment in a world in which all too many intellectuals seem to have lost their built-in ability to detect pretentious claptrap."[29]

According to Rothbard, one sure sign of rational human beings is their ability to recognize an intellectual charlatan when they see one. What better candidate for this title can there be than people who claim that truth and meaning are relative and presume to tell us this by means of statements they assume to be both true and meaningful? Finally, Rothbard asks, what must we think of a society and of academicians who regard this sort of thing as serious scholarship?

While Rothbard's attack upon deconstructionism is rather severe, what interests me is the kind of response his words provoke in typical deconstructionists. Should deconstructionists respond in a hostile and negative way, their reaction would strongly suggest that Rothbard's language conveyed precisely the meaning he intended. But deconstructionists insist that this kind of communication is impossible. Does not their hostility toward Rothbard seem to disprove their theory? If all meaning is subjective, how do the deconstructionists explain their anger over statements that they cannot possibly understand?

Step Two: The Hermeneutics of Suspicion

So far as I can tell, the people who utilize the hermeneutics of suspicion operate on the far left of the culture. Never once, so far as I know, has the hermeneutics of suspicion ever been applied to a liberal. If the tables were turned and the hermeneutics of suspicion were applied to the practitioners of the method, the result might go something like the following.

> Either deconstructionists are among the dumbest people ever to get university teaching positions, or there is something sinister going on. But deconstructionists are not dumb, though at times they can put on a convincing act. So what are they really up to? As we learn from the hermeneutics of suspicion, whatever a text is hiding has to do with power, never with truth. It hardly seems a coincidence that many deconstructionists are Marxists. Naturally, this does not mean they are Marxists in any sense that the historic Marx or even Lenin would approve. Marxian deconstructionists recognize that most nontrivial sentences in the writings of Marx and Lenin have been falsified. They know that Marxian economics is a fraud. After years of watching Russian and Chinese and Cuban leaders impoverish every citizen in their nations, except the rich

---

29. Ibid., 53.

and powerful people at the top, we know that no Marxist cares about poor and oppressed people. Their entire program is keeping the power they have and smuggling as many American dollars as they can to their Swiss bank accounts.

As for Marxian intellectuals in America, the name of their game is also power. They know that deconstructionism is bunk. The real purpose of the deconstructionist power brokers is to separate as many Americans as possible from their families and from their literature and traditions. If we cannot know the meaning of any text, then we cannot know the meaning of the Bible, including the Ten Commandments. Neither can we know the meaning of the United States Constitution or any other text that might sustain social order or provide meaning and direction to life. Once students become alienated from their families, their religion, their values, and their traditions, they will be like lambs prepared for the slaughter. And when that day comes, who do you suppose all the people with empty heads and empty chests will look to for their orders? They will look to their deconstructionist, Marxian, power-seeking professors who introduced them to the mysteries of a world without meaning. The real name of the deconstructionist game is not meaning or truth; it is power, raw political power.[30]

I thought Rothbard's attack was strong. I'm glad I'm incapable of writing words like these. How could I, since the hermeneutics of suspicion is exclusively a tool of the radical political and cultural left?

Step Three: Some Scenarios

Imagine that I am delivering a public lecture assessing the book of a deconstructionist author who happens to be in my audience. Suppose that I intentionally present an outrageous interpretation of the professor's book, all the while pretending admiration for his brilliance. Imagine that I present his book as an ingenious and original argument for the existence of God and the objective truth of the Christian faith. Suppose I play my game so successfully that the indignant author marches to the front of the lecture hall, clears his throat, and begins to denounce my stupidity to the audience. "Only a fool," he asserts, "only an idiot could twist my words to say the opposite of what I clearly meant to say." At which point, I rise from my seat in the audience and politely thank the author for doing a better job of refuting deconstructionism than I could ever have hoped to do.

A student listens to her deconstructionist professor declare the impossibility of her ever knowing the meaning of any written text. Shyly, she raises her hand and invites the professor to write those words on the blackboard. The professor obligingly turns his back to the class and writes the

---

30. The author of these words insists on remaining anonymous.

following text on the blackboard: "It is impossible ever to know the meaning of any written text." Is something wrong here? Is something absurd going on here?

Step Four: Communication Does Take Place

Look at the way deconstructionist writers confidently communicate with us and with others. Their actions make it clear that they believe communication is possible. Even when an audience is composed of people from different cultures, communication is possible, as is the attainment of knowledge.

Carson offers important insights regarding the alleged cultural vagueness of a theological utterance such as "Jesus is Lord."

> The semantic content of "Jesus is Lord" as expressed and understood by an English-speaking believer who has at least some rudimentary knowledge of the Bible and Christian theology must be grasped and believed by men and women everywhere in every culture, however it is expressed and articulated within each culture. Of course, there are all sorts of ambiguities about this way of wording things. But my point is that if linguistics has taught us anything, it has taught us that whatever can be said in one language can be said in another, *even if not in the same way and brevity.* What I as a Western believer mean by "Jesus is Lord" can be conveyed in Thai, to a Thai Buddhist. But it will not be conveyed, in the first instance, by a mere slogan. Christian understanding of the confession is dependent upon an entire worldview that takes in a personal/transcendent God, the revelation of the Scripture, understanding of who Jesus is, and so on. The initial Thai *mis*understanding turns on another entire worldview: an essentially pantheistic view of God, radically different understanding of revelation, relative or perhaps complete ignorance of Jesus and so forth. To explain to the Thai what I mean by "Jesus is Lord" can be done, but not easily, not quickly, and not with mere slogans. Once there is a confessional Thai church, of course, the cultural barriers inherent in all Christian witness can be crossed more quickly.[31]

Veith makes the same point: "Truth exists, though it often eludes us, and we may fail to grasp it perfectly. Christians have always known this. What God reveals in His Word is absolutely true."[32] We can think about these truths, fit them in with other truths, and apply them. Moreover, Veith adds, "the revelation that God created the universe gives us a basis for believing in other kinds of objective truths."[33]

I have repeatedly stated that any proposition that entails a false or absurd proposition must itself be false. If A implies B and B is false, then A must be false. In deconstructionism, A is any set of claims that sup-

---

31. Carson, *The Gagging of God,* 99–100.
32. Veith, *Postmodern Times,* 68–69.
33. Ibid., 69.

posedly implies the impossibility of communicating true information (*B*). As we have seen, *B* is false. What else can reasonable people conclude than that *A* is false?

In 1995 a modest book appeared containing a chapter with the unusual title, "There's No Such Thing as Objective Truth, and It's a Good Thing, Too."[34] Equally strange is the fact that the author of the chapter attacking objective truth, Philip Kenneson, is a professor at a small liberal arts college that serves a constituency of relatively conservative Christians who take the objective truth of their religious beliefs seriously. The fact that such a college serving such a constituency has a faculty member who repudiates objective truth is a stark symbol of how rapidly segments of contemporary Christendom are moving away from paradigms that have been in place for almost two thousand years. Need I point out that this takes us back almost eighteen centuries before the modern age? It is also worth noting that Professor Kenneson earned his doctorate at Duke University, a hotbed of deconstructionist ideology.

In the old days, when an author wrote sentences like "No proposition is objectively true," it was easy to infer that he was a relativist. But Kenneson does not want anyone to believe that he is an epistemological relativist. Whatever Kenneson's real reasons might be for denying his relativism, let us see his public reason. Kenneson says the reason he is not a relativist is

> because *I don't believe* in objective truth, a concept that is the flip side of relativism and that is necessary for the charge of relativism to be coherent. In other words, one can defend objective truth or relativism only by assuming that it is possible for human beings to take up a "view from nowhere"; since I don't believe in "views from nowhere" [what is this supposed to mean?], I don't believe in objective truth or relativism. Moreover, I don't want *you* to believe in objective truth or relativism either, because the first concept is corrupting the church and its witness to the world, while tilting at the second is wasting the precious time and energy of a lot of Christians.[35]

Kenneson is saying that because there is no such thing as objective truth, it is impossible for him to be a relativist with respect to truth. The term *relative* has meaning only when its antonym *objective* applies.

The first thing to notice about this maneuver is the absence of anything that might function as an argument. It is a clever attempt to distract

The Attack on Objective Truth

---

34. The chapter appears on pages 155–70 of *Christian Apologetics in the Postmodern World,* already cited in this chapter.

35. Kenneson, "There's No Such Thing as Objective Truth," 156.

people by means of an illicit analogy. To see the failings of this move, apply Kenneson's reasoning to a commonly held belief about God. All Christians believe that God is good. According to Kenneson's faulty thinking, however, no one is entitled to call God good before God created the universe, the reason being that before God created anything, there was no evil. And without a contrasting evil to compare God with, it would be improper to call God good. This is Kenneson's way of evading the charge of relativism. If there is no objective truth, then there is no such thing as relativism, and therefore Kenneson cannot be called a relativist.[36]

Many readers will continue to wonder, however, why Kenneson objects so strenuously to being called a relativist, especially when on his grounds the word has no objective meaning. Could it be because he is aware of the powerful arguments that can be leveled against epistemological relativism and subjectivism? Is it because he knows there is no way he could evade or answer these objections, leaving him with little more than the pretense that he is not a relativist or a subjectivist? Or, interjecting an opinion from a proponent of the hermeneutics of suspicion, could his denial of relativism have something to do with the fact that he teaches in a college supported by a largely conservative constituency that might be displeased by news that a college they support hires faculty that deny objective truth?

Symptoms of Kenneson's Postmodernism

Many signs identifying Kenneson as a postmodern ideologue appear in his chapter. He makes clear, for example, his acceptance of antirealism. Kenneson rejects any theory of knowledge that views it "as a kind of picture or mirror of the way the world *really* is."[37] Such thinking deceives us into believing we need a way to test the difference between our view of the world and the way the world is.

> Within such a view of knowledge, truth (or Truth) is not so much a concept as it is an entity "out there" in the world, waiting to be discovered; Truth is merely the word for the way the world really is, which we are trying to picture or mirror with our knowledge. When human beings discover this Truth, picture it faithfully in their minds and mirror it accurately in their language, we say that they have genuine knowledge. Moreover, such knowledge is "objectively true" when its status as true does not ultimately depend on the testimony of any person or group of persons. Indeed, the whole point of claiming that something is "objectively true" is to say that any person, unhindered by the clouds of unreason and the prejudices of self-interest, would come to the same conclusion.[38]

---

36. The major point in this paragraph was suggested to me by J. P. Moreland.
37. Kenneson, "There's No Such Thing as Objective Truth," 157.
38. Ibid.

This is full of distortions and oversimplifications that I have already dealt with. But it unmasks the ideological assumptions that control Kenneson's thinking.

Kenneson rejects the correspondence theory of truth.[39] He prefers a view in which all knowledge is "rooted in trust."[40] This is an especially odd statement since any view of truth must involve trust at some stage.[41] Is this a distinction without a difference? Kenneson seems uninterested in the obvious question of whom we should trust. Normal people understand that one of the conditions of trusting in people is knowing that they typically tell the truth, that is, objective, propositional truth. I doubt that Kenneson would ever trust a person with a reputation for lying. But lying cannot occur in a world in which there is no objective truth.

Kenneson does not talk about logic in his essay. There's a good reason for this. Postmodernists not only reject objective truth; they also have no use for objective laws of logic. It follows then that in Kenneson's world, no argument can be wrong, just as no proposition can be false. It also follows that no argument, including any Kenneson might attempt, can be valid. When relativists like Kenneson reject the law of noncontradiction, they are abandoning the very principles of logic that make all significant thought, action, and communication possible (see chapter 8 in this book). As Harold Netland argues, "The price one must pay for rejecting the principle of non-contradiction is simply too high." He explains,

> The price of rejecting the principle of noncontradiction is forfeiture of the possibility of meaningful affirmation or statement about anything at all—including statements about the religious ultimate. One who rejects the principle of noncontradiction is reduced to utter silence, for he or she has abandoned a necessary condition for any coherent or meaningful position whatsoever.[42]

This path leads to nothing less than intellectual suicide.

Kenneson is also silent about ethics. A package that denies objective truth and objective laws of logic will contain a denial of objective moral standards. As Veith observes, "When the objective realm is swallowed up by subjectivity, moral principles evaporate."[43]

Kenneson's chapter also says nothing about the Christian Scriptures. Can we think of a good reason for this silence? His commitment to postmodernism and deconstructionism entails a repudiation of the truth of Scripture, the truth of Christian creeds, and the truth of the Christian

---

39. See ibid.
40. Ibid., 157–58.
41. This was an especially important point in Augustine's theory of knowledge.
42. Harold Netland, "Exclusivism, Tolerance and Truth," *Missiology* 15 (1987): 84–85.
43. Veith, *Postmodern Times*, 58.

gospel. He says that typical Christian doctrine cannot be true.[44] As our hermeneutician of suspicion might say, "When you're teaching in a church-related college, you don't want news like this to leak out."

"Where's the Beef?"

During the 1984 campaign for the Democratic nomination for president, one of Walter Mondale's spin doctors suggested the Democratic candidate take an expression from a Wendy's television commercial of the time and use it against his Democratic rivals. And so the question "Where's the beef?" moved from a hamburger commercial to a political campaign. In its political context, I suppose the question is a way of saying, "Where's your argument?"

Now that we know that Kenneson denies the existence of objective truth and is a postmodern relativist, we have a right to expect him to support his relativism with an argument. In other words, "Mr. Kenneson, where's the beef?" At this point we learn that Kenneson has no intention of offering us an argument.

Let me suggest two reasons for the absence of an argument. The first is simple: Kenneson has no argument! The second reason is because producing an argument requires access to objective laws of logic, and Kenneson doesn't believe such principles exist. As we learned in chapter 8, when you reject logic, you cannot prove your beliefs are true or prove that your opponent's beliefs are false. So he begs us to allow him to frolic for a while with a different model or paradigm of truth. He asks us to abandon our rigid, old ways of thinking about truth and logic and see what kind of world this would be if everyone thought and behaved as though objective truth did not exist.

Kenneson claims that "Christians are not *obligated* to accept the old paradigm of [objective truth]." Whether we believe in objective truth is optional; it is up to us. This implies that we also are under no obligation to accept his new paradigm in which there is no objective truth. What's he going to do if we refuse to play his game according to his rules? What can he do when things are this person-relative?

Kenneson seems to think that individual Christians and Christian communities would be more faithful to God without objective truth than with it. "My point is that Christians need not continue to answer 'the truth question,' and the sooner we see that we needn't, the sooner we can get on with the business of being Christians, which in no way entails accepting a certain philosophical account of truth, justification and 'reality'."[45] Kenneson seems to believe that only Christians who reject objective truth live faithful Christian lives.

---

44. See Kenneson, "There's No Such Thing as Objective Truth," 168.
45. Ibid., 161.

Within such a model, the church has a word to speak to the world not because it has a message that is objectively true, a message which could be separated from the embodied message that the church always is. Rather, the church has a word to speak to the world because it embodies an alternative politics,[46] an alternative way of ordering human life made possible by Jesus Christ. The central practices and virtues of such a community, practices and virtues which embody—even if imperfectly—the character of the God it serves are such things as forgiveness, reconciliation, peacemaking, patience, truth-telling [if there is no objective truth, what does "truth telling" mean?], trust, vulnerability, faithfulness, constancy and simplicity of life.[47]

Please note that Kenneson says nothing about where such virtues might come from or how in his world without objective standards we might ever know the difference between truth telling and lying, between peacemaking and warmongering. May church people develop any list they prefer? Kenneson gets his list from the Bible but fails to recognize that his rejection of objective truth denies him the right to treat the teachings of Scripture as objective truth or revealed truth.

Kenneson asserts that Christians who reject objective truth will be Christians who live better lives that will lead the unevangelized to seek something from us. Under the old paradigm, that which the unevangelized would seek to hear from Christian beliefs is the truth of the gospel. But that is no longer possible in Kenneson's world. Once Christians convince themselves and their non-Christian friends that there is no objective truth which entails that nothing about Christianity is objectively true, our non-Christian friends will beat down the doors to accept such a religion. While I don't doubt that such a move will make the Christian faith vastly more popular in an irrational age, the claims about Kenneson's theories producing better Christians and stronger churches and more faithful living and witnessing is the counterintuitive stuff of which utopian dreams are made.

Near the end of his chapter, Kenneson states: "If we could unequivocally prove to people that the proposition 'God exists' is objectively true, the inhabitants of our culture would yawn and return to their pagan slumbers."[48] Maybe . . . maybe not. Apparently Kenneson wants Billy Graham to go on national television and tell the world that the proposition "God exists" is untrue. Were this to happen, should we also expect the inhabitants of our culture to yawn and return to their pagan slumbers?

---

46. What's an alternative politics got to do with this? For a possible account of what Kenneson has in mind, see Ronald H. Nash, *Why the Left Is Not Right: The Religious Left* (Grand Rapids: Zondervan, 1995).

47. Kenneson, "There's No Such Thing as Objective Truth," 162–63.

48. Ibid., 166.

Objective Truth in Scripture

Could the readers of this book find propositions in the Bible that the human authors of Scripture clearly regarded as objectively true? One example might be Paul's summary of the gospel in 1 Corinthians 15:3–8. The claims that Christ died for our sins and rose again the third day are so objectively true that Paul goes on to say that if they were not, Christians would be the most pitiable people on God's green earth (1 Corinthians 15:14, 19). The gospel writers believed their accounts of Jesus' deeds and teachings were objectively true. As John writes in John 21:25: "Jesus did many other things as well. If every one of them were written down, I suppose that even the whole world would not have room for the books that would be written."

Objective Truth in Everyday Life

While it may be easy to dismiss objective truths while imprisoned in a philosophical or theological ivory tower, it may be good to consider a few propositions that any sensible human would accept as objectively true.

(1) Place your name in the following blank and the date of your birth in the second blank.
     _____ was born on _____.

(2) "You are under arrest for driving through a red light." (spoken by police officer)

(3) "It's a girl." (spoken by a nurse in a maternity ward)

(4) "Your loved one has just died." (spoken by a doctor in an intensive care unit)

(5) "I'm sorry, but you have cancer. In three months, you'll be dead." (another physician)

(6) "I'm sorry, but your grade for this course is an F." (a nonpostmodernist professor)[49]

Earlier I indicated my admiration for Yandell's handling of antirealism. I want to end this chapter with some other points he makes that I could not include before. Yandell insists that postmodernism and deconstructionism are types of intellectual suicide. He offers three examples:

The claim *No one can know anything said in English* is self-defeating in that no one could know it were it true. The claim *nothing said in English can be true* is self-refuting in that its being true is incompatible with what it says is true. *Nothing can be said in English* is self-destroying, being an instance of what it says cannot exist. A more interesting exam-

---

49. Consistent postmodernists would give every student an A.

ple of self-destruction is the claim *All language is metaphorical;* as a non-metaphorical use of language, it is itself the very sort of thing it says there cannot be. Such claims, and views to which they are essential, commit intellectual suicide; there is no chance that they constitute knowledge.... We may legitimately add to our simple truths. *No view that commits intellectual suicide can be known to be true.* Unfortunately, suicidal views often have a zombie existence as they stalk the halls of the academy. Postmodernism seems largely to be a museum of such zombies.[50]

Viewed from the outside, Yandell continues, "postmodernism looks like a decent candidate for being a movement in which accepting one or another bundle of self-defeating views is a condition of membership."[51] Applying Yandell's arguments to Kenneson, Kenneson's denial of truth is like an "in-place bumper sticker that tells us there are no cars."[52]

As Veith states with great dismay,

> To disbelieve in truth is, of course, self-contradictory. The belief means to think something is true; to say, "It's true that nothing is true" is intrinsically meaningless nonsense. The very statement—"there is no absolute truth"—is an absolute truth. People have bandied about such concepts for centuries as a sort of philosophical parlor game, but have seldom taken these seriously. Today it is not just some esoteric and eccentric philosophers who hold this deeply problematic view of truth, but the average man on the street. It is not the lunatic fringe rejecting the very concept of truth, but two-thirds of the American people.[53]

Conclusion

Carson is a respected scholar and author of several dozen well-received books. He offers his picture of the practical consequences of postmodernism and deconstructionism for the Christian church.

> The rise of radical hermeneutics and of deconstructionism has sapped the faith of many undergraduates and introduced a raft of new challenges to those interested in evangelizing them. Thus, Miss Christian goes off to a local state university, full of zeal and the knowledge of a few fundamental truths. There she will not find lecturers who will devote much time to overturning her truths. Rather, she will find many lecturers convincing her that the meaning in her religion, as in all religion, is merely communal bias, and therefore relative, subjective. No religion can make valid claims of a transcendent nature. Truth, whatever it is, does not reside in an object or idea or statement or affirmation about reality, historical or otherwise, that can be known by finite human beings; rather it

---

50. Yandell, "Modernism, Post-Modernism, and the Minimalist Canons of Common Grace," 24.

51. Ibid., 24–25.

52. Ibid., 25.

53. Veith, *Postmodern Times,* 16.

consists of fallible, faulty opinions held by finite knowers who themselves look at things that certain way only because they belong to a certain section of society. Miss Christian is told, a trifle condescendingly, that if her religion helps her, she should be grateful, but that no intelligent person this side of Derrida, Foucault, and Fish [of Duke University], could possibly believe that her beliefs have a transcendent claim on everybody everywhere. Thus, without overtly denying her faith, Miss Christian discovers that its vitality has been sapped. It has been relativized, trivialized, marginalized. Without ever having had a single one of its major tenets overturned by historical or other argument, the whole edifice of Christian truth has been detached from the objective status it once held. Miss Christian drifts off, and it may take years before she thinks seriously about Jesus again—if she ever does.[54]

As powerful as I think Carson's warning is, he fails in one respect. The kind of disaster he describes is no longer confined to the campuses of secular and public universities. The scenario is repeated daily on the campuses of colleges and seminaries that still claim to be Christian.

I began this chapter by asking whatever happened to truth. I can now provide the answer. Nothing happened to truth. It's still there, and it's still the truth. But plenty of things have happened to humans who late in the twentieth century either lost or abandoned their critical faculties and became addicted to thought patterns that led them to say stupid things about truth. The real question is Whatever happened to the human species at the end of the twentieth century?

---

54. Carson, *The Gagging of God,* 36.

OPTIONAL WRITING ASSIGNMENT

This time you have a choice. (1) If you reject objective truth, write a short essay defending your position. Are the claims made in your essay objectively true? If not, why should anyone believe you or care what you believe? (2) If you do believe in objective truth, write an essay explaining how you would respond to someone who does not.

FOR FURTHER READING

In addition to sources identified only in footnotes throughout the chapter, the following are especially pertinent.

Francis J. Beckwith and Gregory Koukl, *Relativism* (Grand Rapids: Baker, 1998).

D. A. Carson, *The Gagging of God* (Grand Rapids: Zondervan, 1995).

Critical Review 3, 1 (winter 1989). Special issue.

John M. Ellis, *Against Deconstruction* (Princeton, N.J.: Princeton University Press, 1989).

Thomas Nagel, *The Last Word* (New York: Oxford University Press, 1998).

Ronald H. Nash, *The Word of God and the Mind of Man* (Phillipsburg, N.J.: Presbyterian and Reformed, 1992).

Nicholas Rescher, *Objectivity: The Obligations of Impersonal Reason* (Notre Dame, Ind.: University of Notre Dame Press, 1998).

George Steiner, *Real Presences* (Chicago: University of Chicago Press, 1989).

Gene Edward Veith Jr., *Postmodern Times* (Wheaton, Ill.: Crossway, 1994).

Chapter Eleven

Epistemology II:
A Tale of Two Systems

It is impossible to cover more than a small portion of the history of epistemology between the time of René Descartes (1596–1650) and the present. Descartes represented a version of the rationalism defined at the end of chapter 3: "Some human knowledge does not arise from sense experience." He was a French Roman Catholic of modest religious convictions, though the existence of God did play a central role in *The Meditations*. Two other rationalists are worthy of mention, even though their beliefs, like those of Descartes, cannot be explored. The parents of Baruch Spinoza (1632–1677) were Portuguese Jews who fled persecution in Spain and moved to Amsterdam, where their son was born. Spinoza was expelled from the synagogue of Amsterdam for heretical beliefs, including pantheism. The third famous Continental rationalist of the seventeenth century was Gottfried Leibniz (1646–1716), a German Protestant.

Historians of philosophy typically contrast these three European rationalists with three eighteenth-century British empiricists, namely, the Englishman John Locke (1632–1704),[1] the Irishman George Berkeley (1685–1753),[2] and the Scotsman David Hume (1711–1776). These six were then followed by the German thinker Immanuel Kant (1724–1804), whose work is sometimes misleadingly represented as a synthesis of rationalism and empiricism.

All of these systems are worthy of careful study, but not in this text. I have time only to take a brief look at some central ideas of Hume as preparation for a slightly more detailed examination of the epistemology of Kant. I will draw attention to several significant implications of Kant's work and raise several challenges. In chapter 12, I will jump ahead to our own time and examine the content of a system known as Reformed

---

1. With Locke's death in 1704, it is obvious that the label of eighteenth-century empiricism stretches things a bit, since all of Locke's major works were written in the seventeenth century.

2. George Berkeley was a bishop in the Anglican church. He was the only important philosopher to visit America before 1900. He came hoping to start a missionary training college for the evangelization of the Indian tribes of New England.

epistemology. This latter view has links to a Scottish thinker named Thomas Reid (1710–1796), the great Reformed theologian John Calvin (1509–1564), and before him, Augustine (354–430).

However, before the theories of Hume, Kant, Reid, and others begin zooming past your eyes, I must include an introductory section that will acquaint you with a few major topics and problems raised by thinkers before Hume and Kant.

Some Philosophical Background to Hume and Kant

The Theory of Ideas

During the seventeenth century, many philosophers accepted the basic premise of a position known as *the theory of ideas*. The first step into the theory of ideas involves assent to the claim that the immediate objects of human knowledge are ideas that exist in the mind. In other words, when I perceive a brown table on the other side of the room, what I am immediately conscious of is not the table but an idea of the table. While the table presumably exists outside my mind, exists in the external world, the idea of the table exists in my mind. Most people make this distinction and also believe that the idea of the table in the mind is caused somehow by the table itself.[3]

The Problem of the External World

In ways too complex to explore here, the existence of that real chair and all of the other furniture of the so-called external world (the world supposedly existing outside of our minds) became problematic, so much so that some philosophers felt obliged to produce arguments proving that the world outside our minds does exist when no human is perceiving it. This problem of the external world will occur in somewhat different forms in the positions of Hume, Kant, and Reformed epistemology.

The Problem of Other Minds

Philosophers became puzzled by the question of how we might ever know that persons other than ourselves have minds. Look at some other person now; if you're alone, you might have to turn on the television. What you perceive is a human body moving in familiar ways and uttering sounds and appearing to respond to other human bodies. But we never see the other

John Locke

Engraving from painting by Sir G. Kneller, 1830s

Corbis/Bettmann, New York

---

3. John Locke went on to distinguish between primary qualities that exist as a part of the table outside my mind (such as size and shape) and secondary qualities that are not a part of external objects but exist in the mind (such as color, taste, and smell). George Berkeley rejected the distinction between primary and secondary qualities and argued that everything humans regard as a physical and material object is a collection of ideas existing in human minds and primarily in the mind of God. These are fascinating subjects, but I do not have time to explore them. Check out a good history of philosophy book.

person's mind. Of course, our relationship with our own mind (thoughts, images, other items of which we are conscious) seems both immediate and undeniable. My awareness of the brown table is mediated by other things; I do not perceive the table itself immediately. But my awareness of my mind's idea of that table is direct and immediate. While I find it possible to doubt the existence of the table (I might be dreaming or hallucinating), it is impossible to doubt my awareness of my idea of the table.

So it is easy to believe that I have or I am a mind. But how do I know that you have a mind? Lots of philosophers offered lots of arguments in an attempt to prove that other people have minds. But their arguments failed.[4]

The Apparent Failure of Empiricism

Over a period of centuries, the failed efforts of many philosophers laid bare numerous weaknesses of empiricism. The belief that all human knowledge arises from sense experience proved inadequate to explain many important human ideas, including the concept of Equality itself (see Plato), the notion of oneness (see Augustine), the idea of infinite space (Locke), and causality (Hume). And finally, for now, empiricism cannot explain the many instances of necessary truth that humans can know. Once people commit themselves to the claim that all human knowledge arises from sense experience, the inability to carry this out with respect even to one idea is fatal. If humans can have as little as one idea that does not arise from sense experience, empiricism is proven false and the moderate type of rationalism explained in chapter 3 is true.

David Hume

The writings of David Hume (1711–1776) are a watershed in the history of philosophy. Born in Scotland, Hume was and still is perceived as an agnostic or atheist whose anti-Christian views led to his being denied a university professorship in Scotland. Hume's grave in Edinburgh is worth a visit by any traveler to this fascinating city.

Much of Hume's notoriety among Christians results from a less than careful reading of his works. Hume is commonly believed to have attacked the foundations of Christianity, such as the existence of God, personal survival after death, and miracles. It is true that Hume's personal beliefs did not mirror the orthodox Calvinism that surrounded him in his early youth. Nevertheless, what Hume intended in his writings is often quite removed from what his interpreters have thought.

There are three common misconceptions about Hume's philosophy. (1) Hume denied the reality of causal relations, that there is ever a necessary connection between that prior event we call a cause and the subsequent event we call its effect. (2) Hume rejected the existence of what

---

4. For an excellent review of such attempts, see Alvin Plantinga, *God and Other Minds* (Ithaca, N.Y.: Cornell University Press, 1967).

philosophers call the external world; that is, he doubted the existence of a real world outside of his mind. (3) Hume doubted the existence of what philosophers call the self, that is, the real I, the foundation of a person's identity through time.[5] These three erroneous claims make up what might be called the philosophical package. What led to their promulgation has a bearing on one of Hume's key teachings.

The philosophical package came to be attributed to Hume because of the writings of two of his fellow Scotsmen, Thomas Reid and James Beattie.[6] In later years, philosophers came to believe that Hume's enterprise was quite different from what Reid and Beattie envisaged. According to Hume, everyone holds to a number of beliefs around which most other beliefs, individual actions, and social institutions turn. These pivotal beliefs include the reality of causal relations (that some things can and do cause changes in other things), the reality of the external world (that the existence of the world does not depend upon its being perceived), and the continuing existence of the knowing self. Hume had no quarrel with these beliefs; it would be fundamentally foolish, he held, to doubt them. What most concerned Hume was how these beliefs come to be known. Hume showed that neither reason nor experience is sufficient to ground a knowledge of these matters. But there is no other way for them to be known. Therefore, if these pivotal beliefs cannot be known by reason and experience, they cannot be known at all.

It was at this point that Hume's critic Beattie presumably made a mistake. Beattie wrongly concluded that Hume denied these pivotal beliefs. Hume really denied that there is any sense in which we can be said to know these things. But this is a far cry from saying that we should doubt them. We must continue to believe them, since the consequences of not believing are too absurd to contemplate. And no one has to force or persuade us to believe them; believing them is the natural thing to do. With this last observation we begin to approach Hume's basic point: Hume tried to show that most of our pivotal beliefs about reality are matters that human reason is powerless to prove or support.

David Hume

Mezzotint, 1776, after a painting by Allan Ramsay, 1766

THE GRANGER COLLECTION, NEW YORK

---

5. This notion also goes by another name, that of a continuing self. If we consider the mind or self of a person at the time of birth and again at the time of death, it is easy to believe that individual is the same person at his death that he was at his birth. One argument for a continuing self is that the notion of reward or punishment after death makes no sense unless the person receiving the reward or punishment is the same individual who perfomed the original actions.

6. Beattie's major work in this area was his *Essay on the Nature and Immutability of Truth,* first published in Edinburgh in 1770. Thomas Reid is by far the more significant philosopher of the two. Worth consulting is his *Essays on the Intellectual Powers of Man,* first published in 1786 and reprinted several times. Some contemporary philosophers contend that Reid's handling of Hume's philosophy is misunderstood. And even if Reid's critique of Hume were flawed, it would not detract from Reid's own positive contribution to the theory of knowledge.

Hume's Gap

Hume was doing two things. First, he was attacking the supremacy of human reason, one of the cardinal tenets of the Enlightenment, by seeking to show that human reason has definite limits. (I leave it to the reader to decide if Hume, who died in 1776, was a postmodernist.) All who attempt to extend reason beyond its limits become involved in absurdities and contradictions and become prone to the disease of skepticism.[7] Philosophers have been too optimistic in assessing the claims of human reason, Hume believed. Most of the important things we think we know are not known at all. That is, they have not been arrived at on the basis of reasoning, and they are not supported by experience.

Hume's second point was that these pivotal beliefs rest on something other than reason and experience, namely, on instinct, habit, and custom. Some nonrational inner force compels us to accept these pivotal beliefs. In his writings on ethics also, Hume argued that moral judgments rest not on reason but on nonrational human nature. In ethics, as in metaphysics and religion, human reason is and ought to be the slave of human passions, that is, our nonrational nature.[8] This is tantamount to the claim that we cannot have knowledge about the transcendent. This axiom is the foundation of what I call Hume's gap.

If Hume was a skeptic, then he was not one in Beattie's sense of the word. Hume did not doubt the existence of the external world. As Hume saw it, this kind of skepticism is absurd because it contradicts common sense and violates our natural instinct to believe (against all reasoning) in certain propositions.[9] Nature, instinct, and common sense all lead us to believe in an external world. According to Hume, we should ignore the arguments of the rationalists and trust our instincts. He believed that investigation ought to be limited to areas such as mathematics where knowledge is possible. Speculative knowledge claims about certain topics in metaphysics, theology, and ethics should be avoided.[10] Such matters should be accepted on the basis of Hume's type of faith, not knowledge.

---

7. As I show later in this chapter, this conviction was also a fundamental thesis of Kant. The claim that there are more similarities between Hume and Kant than meet the eye is argued by Lewis White Beck in "A Prussian Hume and a Scottish Kant," in *McGill Hume Studies,* ed. David Fate Norton et al. (San Diego, Calif.: Austin Hill Press, 1979), 63–78.

8. Hume's well-known statement about reason being the slave of the passions appears in his *Treatise on Human Nature,* 2.3.

9. The possibility that Hume's position was essentially the same as that advanced by the Scottish Common Sense philosophers Reid and Beattie is examined by David Fate Norton in "Hume and His Scottish Critics," in *McGill Hume Studies,* ed. David Fate Norton et al. (San Diego, Calif.: Austin Hill Press, 1979), 309–24.

10. This is what Hume meant in the famous conclusion to his *Enquiry Concerning Human Understanding.* "When we run over libraries, persuaded of these principles, what havoc must we make? If we take in our hand any volume; of divinity or school [scholas-

Hume's Religious Beliefs

It is sometimes thought that Hume was an atheist, that he attempted to prove that God does not exist, and that he argued that miracles are impossible. To be sure, Hume was not a Christian in the New Testament sense of the word. He did not believe in miracles, which is, however, something different from trying to prove them impossible. He did not personally believe in special revelation, immortality, or religious duties like prayer. But he was not an atheist; he did not attempt to prove the nonexistence of God.[11] And he never argued that miracles are impossible. Hume's famous attack on miracles amounts to the assertion that no one could ever reasonably believe that a miracle had occurred.[12]

Hume believed in the existence of a divine mind that was in some unknown way responsible for the order of the universe.[13] Hume was both shocked and amused by the dogmatic atheism of the French *philosophes* whose views represented the French Enlightenment. What this means is that we have a leader of the Scottish Enlightenment attacking the leaders of the French Enlightenment for their unacceptable use of reason in denying the existence of God. Does this make Hume a postmodernist? This information supports my claim in chapter 10 that contemporary postmodernists have misrepresented the view of reason held during the Enlightenment. Hume's point was that we cannot have any knowledge about God. But it is natural to have faith that God exists. In fact, the same nature that compels us to hold the pivotal beliefs mentioned earlier leads us to believe in the existence of God. But nature does not compel us to go beyond this basic belief in God's existence and accept the theological claims added by conservative Christians. Those theological claims must be rejected because they go beyond the limits of human knowledge. To argue, as many Christians do, that reason can prove the existence of God is to exceed the bounds of human knowledge, Hume believed.

---

tic] metaphysics, for instance; let us ask, *Does it contain any abstract reasoning concerning quantity or number?* No. *Does it contain any experimental reasoning concerning matters of fact and existence?* No. Commit it then to the flames: for it can contain nothing but sophistry and illusion."

11. I am aware of Hume's arguments against traditional theistic proofs such as the cosmological and teleological arguments. But at the end of his *Dialogues Concerning Natural Religion,* in which Hume's objections to theistic proofs appear, Hume appears to affirm his belief in God's existence. See Ronald H. Nash, *Faith and Reason* (Grand Rapids: Zondervan, 1988), chaps. 9–10.

12. See Nash, *Faith and Reason,* chap. 16.

13. Consider the following quote from Hume's *Natural History of Religion* in *The Philosophical Works of David Hume* (London, 1874–1875), 4, 309: "The whole frame of nature bespeaks an intelligent author; and no rational enquirer can, after serious reflection, suspend his belief a moment with regard to the primary principles of genuine theism and Religion." In this connection, section 12 of Hume's *Dialogues* should be studied. Students of Hume's thought know how difficult it is to reconcile everything Hume says in this work.

Some Christians no doubt have overestimated the ability of human reason with respect to proofs about God's existence. I have no desire to attempt to defend that use of reason. (See this book's chapters 13 and 14 about the existence of God.) More serious, however, is Hume's denial of the possibility of any knowledge about God in general and the possibility of revealed knowledge. In these respects also, Hume can sound like a postmodernist or at least a forerunner of postmodernism.

To summarize, Hume's goal in his discussions of religion was the same as his objective in philosophy: he wished to show that reason is powerless to convert anyone to the claims of faith. "To be a philosophical sceptic," he wrote, "is the first and most essential step towards being a sound believing Christian."[14] German religious thinker J. G. Hamann (1730–1788) believed that Hume's skepticism could be a godsend for Christianity.[15] Living in the same German city as Immanuel Kant, Königsberg, he translated Hume's *Dialogues* into German, hoping it would lead rationalists[16] like Kant to see the light and move toward accepting a more traditional view of the Christian faith. It is unclear whether Hamann recognized that Hume's own preference seems to have been for a nonrational faith in a god unsupported by reason, revelation, miracles, or evidence of any kind.

Given this background, the nature of what I earlier called Hume's gap can now be identified. Hume's gap is the rejection of the possibility of a rational knowledge of God and objective religious truth. Hume grounded humankind's belief in God in our nonrational nature. Hume was a precursor of those philosophers and theologians who insist that religious faith must be divorced from knowledge and who believe that the impossibility of knowledge about God will in some way enhance faith. Like Kant, as we'll see, Hume was engaged in denying knowledge in order to make room for faith, a nonrational and unbiblical kind of faith. To both Hume and Kant, knowledge and faith have nothing in common. The arrogance of rational religion (the Enlightenment? modernity?) must be destroyed so that faith (a nonrational faith) can assume its proper place as the only legitimate ground of religion.

---

14. The quotation comes from the conclusion to section 12 of Hume's *Dialogues Concerning Natural Religion*.

15. Hamann is an interesting but little known person. Born in Königsberg, East Prussia, he came under the influence of the kind of Enlightenment rationalism we have noted earlier. At the age of twenty-eight, while working in London, he had a profound religious experience that led to his abandonment of Enlightenment theories. His life was not always a consistent testimony to Christian practice. The Christianity toward which he hoped to influence thinkers like Kant was at least closer to the historic faith than that found in the writings of Kant.

16. Keep in mind that "rationalist" has several meanings. I use it here in the sense of a person who elevates human reasoning above the Scriptures and teachings of the historic Christian faith.

Hume's gap appears prominently in the thought of many modern thinkers. The contemporary eclipse of God can be seen in Jean-Paul Sartre's "silence of God," in Martin Heidegger's "absence of God," in Paul Tillich's "non-being of god," and finally in radical theology's assertion of "the death of God." Paul's sermon to the philosophers on Mars Hill (Acts 17) concerning worship of the unknown god is all too relevant to the contemporary theological scene. Liberal Protestant theology for the past two centuries is a chronicle of futile attempts to retain respectability for religious faith while denying religion any right to revealed truth. Ironically, this is precisely where almost all of the postmodern religionists of the current generation also can be found. In radical theologian Tillich's version of Hume's thesis, all that is left of Christianity is a religion that is neither objective, rational, miraculous, supernatural, nor even personal. About the only thing that liberal, neoliberal and postconservative thinkers can agree about is that God has not spoken and, indeed, cannot speak.

One trademark of theological liberalism for the past seventy years is a reduction of faith to "courageous ignorance."[17] Many contemporary spokespeople for the historic Christian faith have shamefully ceased defending God's objective communication of truth. Hume's gap has affected their thinking to the extent that many now ignore or deemphasize the cognitive dimension of divine revelation.

The most obvious consequence of Hume's gap is a minimal theism. Once Hume's stance is adopted, New Testament Christianity, with its proclamation of a divine Christ whose death and resurrection secured redemption from sin and gave hope beyond the grave, must be replaced with a religion that talks about how good it feels to have an experience with a god about whom nothing definite can be known. The legacy of Hume's gap undermines the Christian faith not by denying it but by directing our attention away from the importance of its knowledge claims and its truth content. Postmodern Christians owe much to that legacy. With friends like that, the Christian faith has no need for any enemies.

Immanuel Kant

Immanuel Kant (1724–1804) is justly counted among the most important and influential thinkers in the history of philosophy. Early in his philosophical career, Kant had been trained in a kind of sterile German rationalism that denigrated the role of sense experience in human knowledge. All of this changed when Kant encountered the system of Hume. As Kant wrote, "I openly confess my recollection of David Hume was the very thing which many years ago first interrupted my dogmatic [rationalist]

---

17. See Carl F. H. Henry, "Justification by Ignorance: A Neo-Protestant Motif?" *Journal of the Evangelical Theological Society* 13 (1970): 13.

Immanuel Kant

German aquatint
engraving, early
19th century

The Granger Collection,
New York

slumber and gave my investigations in the field of speculative philosophy a quite new direction."[18] Kant thought that Hume's work contained a spark which, if fanned, could ignite a revolution in philosophy. Kant ventured to suggest that perhaps even Hume himself did not fully see the implications of his attack on metaphysics, understood here to mean the use of human reason to solve some of the deepest mysteries of the universe.

Kant's Copernican Revolution

Kant's theory of knowledge is often described as a Copernican revolution in philosophy. Just as Nicolaus Copernicus (1473–1543) had revolutionized the model of the solar system by placing the sun instead of the earth at its center, so Kant's theory of knowledge produced a similar upheaval in philosophy. Philosophers prior to Kant, or so Kant claimed, had assumed that human knowledge is possible only as the mind is adapted to the world. Kant reversed this order.[19] Instead of the mind adapting to the supposed objects of its knowledge, all objects are adapted to the knowing mind. The universal and necessary features of reality are known to be features of reality by virtue of their first being characteristics of the human mind that seeks to know. The rationality (that is, the universality and necessity) that human beings find in nature is there because the human mind puts it there.

Form and Content

Let us forget Kant and philosophy for a moment and imagine ourselves in the serene surroundings of an old American farmhouse in the 1940s or 1950s. Let us imagine ourselves browsing through the pantry off the kitchen. Our eyes are drawn to the scores of glass containers full of homemade fruit preserves: strawberry, grape, blueberry, and peach. There's not a store-bought jar of jelly in the house. The jars in which the preserves are contained come in all sizes and shapes; the jars differ in their form. And as we've seen, the glass jars contain different content. Hold those images briefly while we return to Kant's system.

---

18. Immanuel Kant, *Prolegomena to Any Future Metaphysics* (New York: Liberal Arts Press, 1950), 8. Kant's relation to Hume's thought is a subject of much controversy. A good overview of this debate can be found in Beck's "A Prussian Hume and a Scottish Kant," in *McGill Hume Studies*.

19. In Kant's words, "Hitherto it has been assumed that all our knowledge must conform to objects. But all attempts to extend our knowledge of objects by establishing something in regard to them *a priori,* by means of concepts, have, on this assumption, ended in failure. We must therefore make trial whether we may not have more success in the tasks of metaphysics, if we suppose that objects must conform to our knowledge." Kant, Introduction, *The Critique of Pure Reason,* trans. Norman Kemp Smith, 2d ed. (New York: St. Martin's Press, 1965).

Kant sought to go beyond both rationalism and empiricism by making human knowledge a composite of two factors, form and content. The content of human knowledge is given by sense experience. In fact, all human knowledge begins with sense experience. This is an important point, to which we will return. It is also a mistake, making it necessary, as we will see, to place Kant in the empiricist camp. Having made this point, however, Kant goes on to say the following: "Although all our knowledge begins with experience, it does not follow that it arises from experience."[20] What Kant means[21] is that while sense experience is necessary for human knowledge in that no one would have any knowledge without it, sense experience is not a sufficient condition for knowledge. Something else (a form or structure) must be added to the content supplied by the senses. Unless the content is given form or structure by the human mind, knowledge would be unattainable.

Let us return to that marvelous country pantry. It is easy to see the role that both the fruit preserves and their containers play. As attractive as the glass jars (our analogue for Kant's form) might be by themselves, their real value lies in their service as containers for those precious preserves (our analogue for Kant's content). As you stand before the shelves of preserves (in your imagination, of course), imagine that you have the power, by snapping your fingers, to make the glass jars disappear, leaving nothing but the preserves. If that were to happen, the preserves would suddenly become a massive inconvenience as they slowly oozed and dripped their way from shelf to shelf to the pantry floor.[22] I don't know many people who would rejoice at the sight of that mess. My point is this: Whether the subject is epistemology or preserves, both form and content are necessary.

Kant's Sausage Machine

Using our imagination, let's proceed with a different example. When I was ten years old, I remember visiting my grandmother's house on East 32nd Street in Cleveland, Ohio, on days when she attached a metal sausage grinder to her kitchen table, pressed cuts of fresh meat into the grinder, and turned the handle. Out of the nozzles of that meat grinder came ground beef or pork. A bit of reflection on this example can help us get a better grasp on important details of Kant's theory of knowledge. In the following

---

20. Ibid.

21. For any deconstructionists who happen to be eavesdropping, I'm interpreting and explaining the meaning of a text. Even though deconstructionists claim this task cannot be done, I'm doing it. This is textual analysis.

22. Were Plotinus to be in the pantry at the time, he might see this as an example of the downward path of oozing.

diagram, I use the rough analogy of something like a sausage machine to illustrate the operations of the human mind in Kant's system.

Figure 11.1

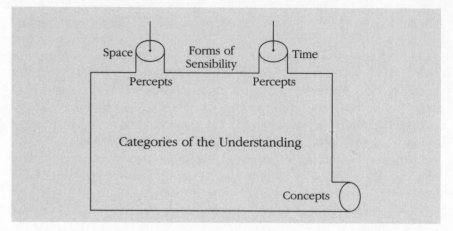

In the case of a sausage machine, the nozzle at the top is the device by which the cuts of meat enter the machine. In the case of Kant's picture of the human mind, there are two nozzles that he calls the forms of sensibility. The forms of sensibility were Kant's way of explaining two of the most puzzling problems of philosophy. For centuries prior to Kant, philosophers struggled to explain human knowledge of space and time. We need not concern ourselves with those earlier answers. By calling space and time the forms of sensibility, Kant was denying that space and time exist independently of the human mind and are somehow perceived or apprehended outside the mind. Instead, Kant argued, the notions of space and time are added to our perceptions by the mind. Everything that we perceive (sense experience) appears to us as though it were in space and time.

Most readers remember seeing the movie *Superman* starring Christopher Reeve. Dressed in his Superman costume, Mr. Reeve appeared to be flying when in reality[23] he was hanging from steel wires in front of a green background. The movie technicians superimposed the visions of clouds and sky on the green background in such a way to make it appear that he was flying. In a similar way, Kant maintained, the human mind superimposes the notions of space and time upon all of our sense perceptions, so that they appear to us as though they were in space and time when they are not. (This might be a good time to reread the brief section of this chapter titled "Kant's Copernican Revolution.") The center of the epistemological universe is not reality but the mind. The world appears

---

23. Keep in mind how antirealist postmodernists deny the difference between the action on the movie screen and the reality of an actor suspended by wires.

the way it does not because that's the way it is but because the world is a construct of our mind. For most postmodernists, Kant and his philosophy were an essential part of the modern world. But think a bit. When Kant teaches that the world as we believe it to be is a construct of the human mind, is he a modernist or a postmodernist? How much of what postmodernists tell us about modernity is accurate?

Moving down my diagram brings us to the parts of the machine that turn those cuts of beef into mincemeat. Entering the box of Kant's sausage machine brings us to what he called the categories of the understanding. We first encountered the word *category* in our chapter on Aristotle, who used the word to refer to basically different ways humans think about things. Kant talked about twelve categories by means of which the human mind shapes, influences, and affects the raw material of human knowledge that comes via sense experience. What enters the human mind through the forms of sensibility, what Kant calls percepts, is never an object of knowledge at that time. Human consciousness of the objects of knowledge only begins once the categories of the human understanding have added form or structure to the sensible content. (Remember the glass jars and the preserves?)

Kant's twelve categories were his way of dealing with twelve puzzling types of human knowledge. Consider several examples encountered earlier in this book. Think of Plato's account of how human beings know that two things are similar or equal, of Augustine's explanation of oneness, of Locke's failed attempt to explain the idea of infinite space, and of Hume's analysis of causation. For Kant, humans think in such terms because our minds force us to.

Percepts and Concepts

In one of his better-known statements, Kant says: "Concepts without percepts are empty; percepts without concepts are blind." For Kant, the word *concept* functions here as a name for what the categories of the understanding produce. *Percept* is another name for the raw material of human knowledge, the sense information that enters the mind through the forms of sensibility.

For one final time, let us return to our country pantry. Imagine that the fruit preserves represent sense information, the raw material of human knowledge. Suppose that the glass jars represent the categories of the understanding or what we are now calling concepts. Unless the content (the preserves or percepts) is given form or structure (the jars or the categories) by the human mind, knowledge is impossible. To amplify on Kant's famous statement, concepts (the form supplied by the categories) without percepts (the content supplied by the senses) are empty. Remove the preserves from the container and all you have is an empty jar. Percepts without concepts are blind. Take away the glass jars and you've nothing but a mess of oozing sugar syrup and pieces of fruit. Take away the categories and all you have is a collection of colors, sounds, and smells that add up to nothing. Human knowledge, then, has two necessary conditions: the form supplied by the mind (otherwise known as the categories) and the content supplied by the senses. But neither condition is sufficient by itself to produce knowledge.

One more analogy may wrap things up, at least to this point. Many years ago, I used to have a safety deposit box in a small bank in Kentucky. In the back, the bank had a coin-counting machine. One day I watched a bank employee pour a large bag of coins into the machine and turn on the electric motor. In no time at all, the machine sorted out the pennies, nickels, dimes, and quarters, deposited each in a different bag, and calculated the total value of the coins. Always the philosopher, I said to myself, *There's another example of Kant's picture of the human mind.* The unsorted coins represent the percepts, the raw material of knowledge. The gears inside of the machine represent the categories of the understanding. Just as that machine sorted out the different coins, so the mind functions as a manifold that places our percepts into appropriate categories and produces the class concepts that advance the knowing process.

Summary

Knowledge, for Kant, is a compound of the impressions received through the senses and that which our inborn faculty of knowledge supplies. Humans possess an *a priori*[24] rational structure of the mind (the categories) that organizes sense data or precepts. Kant sought to avoid the traditional difficulties of empiricism, especially as they came to light in the thought of Hume. For example, Hume showed that empiricism cannot justify any judgment of the form x causes y. Kant argued that our knowledge that x causes y is a result of our mind necessarily disposing us to think in terms of causation. Likewise our knowledge of space and time is not derived from numerous particular experiences. Rather, each and every sensory experience presupposes a knowledge of space and time.

Kant's Two Worlds

Since all human knowledge must be mediated by the categories of the human understanding, humans cannot know anything that is not so mediated. The unfortunate consequence of this claim, however, is a radical disjunction between the world as it appears to us (the world modified by the categories of our understanding) and the world as it is. According to Kant, human knowledge never brings us into contact with the real world, what he called the *noumenal world.* Since our knowledge is always per-

---

24. The term *a priori* refers to that which is independent of sense experience.

ceptually modified by the *a priori* categories of the mind, the real or noumenal world is not only unknown but also unknowable. Since Kant's categories operate only in the phenomenal world, one could not possibly know of a thing-in-itself in the noumenal world.

Hume had his gap; Kant had his wall. Kant's system had the effect of erecting a wall between the world as it appears to us and the world as it is. Human knowledge is restricted to the phenomenal world, the world of appearance, the world shaped by the structure of the knowing mind. Knowledge of any reality beyond the wall, which includes the world of things in themselves, is forever unattainable. Human reason can never penetrate the secrets of ultimate reality (noumenal world). Answers to the most basic questions of theology and metaphysics lie beyond the boundaries of human knowledge. Kant's epistemology creates the possibility that the real world (the world of things-in-themselves) may be quite different from the world that appears to us (the phenomenal world). Since God is not a subject of experience and since the human categories cannot be extended to transcendent reality, Kant's God is both unknown and unknowable. Whenever human reason attempts to penetrate beyond Kant's wall, either in a search for knowledge about God or in a quest for answers to ultimate questions, it becomes involved in antinomies or contradictions.

Ironically, Kant thought his agnosticism with respect to God was an aid to the Christian faith. He wrote that he had "found it necessary to deny *knowledge,* in order to make room for faith."[25] While they had come to their destination by different routes, Hume and Kant arrived at nearly the same point. For both Hume and Kant, faith and knowledge have nothing in common. Every time human reason attempts to leap across Hume's gap or tries to break through Kant's wall separating the phenomenal and noumenal worlds (as speculative metaphysics and theology seek to do), reason becomes bogged down in contradictions. Human reason cannot penetrate the secrets of ultimate reality. The most basic questions of metaphysics and theology are questions to which human reason can find no answers, not even from God. Hume's gap and Kant's wall represent the limits beyond which human reason cannot go;[26] they imply, among other things, that human knowledge about God is impossible.

In Kant's system of thought, God does have a role to play. Even though God was one of the unknowables, Kant managed to slip God through the back door as a necessary postulate required to salvage morality. For Kant, the existence of God was entirely a matter of faith, to which Kant gave a distinctively practical twist. The Christian should abandon any knowledge

---

25. Kant, *The Critique of Pure reason,* 29.

26. There is an important difference between Hume and Kant on this point. While Hume regarded faith as nonrational because it was based on custom or instinct, Kant believed that faith could be grounded in practical reason.

claims about the transcendent and take refuge in a faith grounded not in theoretical but on moral and practical considerations.

Comments, Criticisms, and Questions

(1) Many believe that Kant's epistemology was a synthesis of rationalism and empiricism. After all, they point out, Kant stresses the importance of both percepts and concepts. Is this not a way to merge the most important elements of reason and experience? I'm afraid not. Keep in mind that Kant clearly states that all human knowledge begins with sense experience. This claim identifies Kant as an empiricist. Kant's belief that percepts are a necessary condition for human knowledge is highly problematic and a telltale sign that Kant is an empiricist. A genuine rationalist insists there can be genuine and reliable intellectual intuitions, that is, intuitions not dependent on prior sense experience. One example of such an intellectual intuition would be our knowledge of our own existence. If one instance of intellectual intuition exists, the door is open to the possibility of others.

(2) Kant insisted that it is impossible for the categories of the understanding, including the category of causation, to be applied beyond his wall to the world of things-in-themselves. But he also believed that those pesky, unknowable things-in-themselves existing in the noumenal world are the ultimate cause of our percepts. This is a flagrant contradiction in which Kant does what he says cannot be done, namely, take one of the categories and extend beyond his wall into the world of things-in-themselves.

(3) Any theory of knowledge that tells us that the real world is unknown and unknowable is close enough to skepticism to make any thinking person shudder. Keep in mind my earlier warning that any belief that implies a false belief must be false. In chapter 8 I explained why skepticism is a logically self-defeating theory. Since skepticism is false, any theory that entails skepticism must also be false. This is enough to dash the hopes of any followers of Kant's epistemology.

(4) Reflect a bit on Kant's insistence that every human being possesses the same set of categories. What is his explanation for this astonishing piece of information? When we search through Kant's writings, we encounter an even more incredible situation. Kant never offers an answer to this question. In fact, Kant never raises the question. Is there some explanation for Kant's silence on this issue? There is. Assume, for the sake of argument, that every human as a matter of fact possesses the same structure of rationality. What hypothesis best explains this remarkable state of affairs? No theory of evolution yet known to humanity will do. If such a state of affairs were the effect of a nonpurposeful collocation of nonrational forces, we would have to stand in the presence of a truly astounding coincidence.

According to a different hypothesis, all humans are created by a rational God who made humans in his own image. This looks very much like the theory we discovered in the worldview of Augustine. Is there a good reason why Kant might have avoided such a suggestion? Of course there is. A theistic answer to the question of why all humans share in the same structure of rationality would constitute the kind of argument for God's existence and provide the kind of knowledge about God that Kant said was impossible. Kant had to ignore and avoid such a theory because it entails the falsity of his theory of knowledge.

An Alternative to Kant's Epistemology

Any adequate theory of knowledge ought to satisfy at least the following conditions. (1) It must affirm the existence of universal and necessary truths that transcend sense experience. (2) It ought to preserve Kant's recognition of the need for an *a priori* structure of human rationality. (3) It ought to avoid Kant's skepticism about the real world. That means it must eliminate the unknowable noumenal world, the thing-in-itself. Almost all of the major German philosophers who followed Kant recognized the need to eliminate Kant's distinction between the phenomenal and noumenal worlds. (4) It ought to contain an explanation for why all humans contain the same categories, the same structure of rationality. (5) It ought to offer an account of how the human mind can attain knowledge about the real world as well as about God. That would be quite an accomplishment. My own efforts in these directions can be found in two books.[27]

An alternative to Kant's position, somewhat similar to the description in the previous paragraph, existed in his own time. It is sometimes referred to as the *preformation theory*. According to this view, knowledge is possible only because God has endowed humans with certain innate ideas along with dispositions or aptitudes to think in certain ways. These forms of thought correspond to the real world, which is also a creation of God.

Kant mentioned this possibility in an often overlooked section in the second edition of *The Critique of Pure Reason*. "Some one might propose to adopt a middle way between the two, namely, that the categories are neither self-produced first principles *a priori* of our knowledge, nor derived from experience, but subjective dispositions of thought, implanted in us with our existence, and so arranged by our Creator that their employment should accurately agree with the laws of nature, which determine experience."[28] Kant's criticism of this preformation theory is so off-target as to

---

27. Ronald H. Nash, *The Word of God and the Mind of Man* (Phillipsburg, N.J.: Presbyterian and Reformed, 1992) and *The Light of the Mind: St. Augustine's Theory of Knowledge* (Lexington, Ky.: University Press of Kentucky, 1969), now available from Books on Demand, Ann Arbor, Michigan.

28. Kant, *Critique of Pure Reason*, #27 of Transcendental Analytic.

suggest that Kant misunderstood whatever source he had in view. For example, Kant denied that, on the preformation view, the aptitudes of thought could be innate and *a priori* first principles of knowledge. Gordon H. Clark replies: "If our Creator has implanted in us certain categories or aptitudes for thought contemporaneously with our existence, Kant is hardly justified in denying that they are *a priori*."[29] If such implanted aptitudes are not innate, then surely nothing is. Furthermore, how could Kant possibly describe the aptitudes of the preformationist as optional? Since humans are so made that they cannot think in any other way, their necessity appears undeniable. And since created human rationality reflects the rationality of the divine mind, no options exist. God cannot endow humans created in his image with thinking patterns that deny the law of noncontradiction.

Kant's chief objection to preformationism is his claim that the dispositions of the preformationist are not necessary conditions for knowledge. Kant wrote,

> By adopting it [the preformation theory], the categories would lose that necessity which is essential to them. Thus the concept of cause, which asserts, under a presupposed condition, the necessity of an effect, would become false, if it rested only on some subjective necessity implanted in us of connecting certain empirical representations according to the rule of causal relation. I should not be able to say that the effect is connected with the cause in the object (that is, by necessity), but only, I am so constituted that I cannot think these presentations in any other way.[30]

What Kant says here is that when humans judge there is a necessary connection between some cause x and some effect y, they may be mistaken in the sense that such a necessary connection may not exist in the noumenal world. Kant says this because the human's judgments are a result of his being so constituted that he cannot think in any other way. Thus, on Kant's view, the only necessity attending the categories is a psychological necessity. It is amazing that Kant failed to see how this argument vitiated his own theory of knowledge but not that of the preformationist. If any view reduces to skepticism on this ground, it is Kant's. The preformationist, however, can reply that for him there can be necessary connections between events in the real world.

The preformationist position avoids Kant's problems. First, it avoids skepticism. In Kant's view, we don't know the real world; it is an unknown and unknowable thing-in-itself. Our minds impose order on the chaotic sense data received from our senses. But it is in principle impossible for us ever to discover whether the order our minds impose

29. Gordon H. Clark, *Thales to Dewey*, 2d ed. (Unicoi, Tenn.: The Trinity Foundation, 1989), 410.

30. Kant, *Critique of Pure Reason*, #27 of Transcendental Analytic.

and the order of the noumenal world are the same. However, the laws governing reality are not simply the result of a subjective aptitude of the human mind to think in a certain way. Not only has God implanted dispositions for knowing, but also he has ordered things so that the human mind harmonizes with the structure of the world. The rational structure of the human mind is similar to the rational order of the world. For example, the law of noncontradiction holds for things as well as for thought. Even things-in-themselves cannot be non-things-in-themselves.

While Kant did not take notice of why all humans possess the same categories, the preformation theory has no such problem. According to preformationism, God is a rational deity who created a rational world. He also created humans with minds capable of attaining knowledge both of God and his created world. As Clark observes, "Kant wrote as if space, time and the categories were the same in all human minds and that these a priori forms could guarantee a sort of unitary human experience. But when he argues against all types of preformation systems that would unify experience by grounding the possibility of knowledge in the Creator's ordering of human minds, he ruins every hope of discovering unity and of making knowledge possible. Only theism can do this."[31] Clark's line of argument constitutes an interesting argument for God's existence.

Conclusion

Basic to the Christian worldview is the presupposition that the human being is a creature who carries the image of God. Essential to this image is rationality, a rationality that reflects the rationality of God's own mind. Human language is adequate as a vehicle for divine revelation and for human communication about God because it is a divinely given instrument. God can therefore reveal truth about himself through words. Thought exists behind language as its necessary condition. Communication is possible because the human creatures using language are enlightened by the divine Logos,[32] are in possession of certain innate ideas.

Throughout the epistemological sections of this book, I have argued that a blank mind (*tabula rasa*) cannot know anything: human knowledge of anything depends upon an *a priori* possession of innate categories of thought. These categories are ours by virtue of having been created in God's image, a fact that guarantees that the human structure of reasoning images the divine reason.[33] Reason subsists in the mind of God eternally.

---

31. Gordon H. Clark, *Philosophy of Education* (Grand Rapids: Eerdmans, 1946), 163.

32. For more on the notion of *Logos,* see Nash, *The Word of God and the Mind of Man.*

33. Surely it is obvious that this last sentence does not entail that the human mind can approach anything resembling a complete account of the divine mind. God's thoughts are not our thoughts, as the prophet Isaiah said. However, this hardly entails that God believes that two plus two equals anything other than four. Nor does my statement in the text deny the extent to which original sin affects human reasoning. But original sin does not negate the multiplication tables.

Reason also characterizes the human mind. And reason is objectified in the world because of its relation to the divine mind. Language is a divinely given gift to facilitate a communion between God and humans that is both personal and cognitive. Any flight from reason and logic is a flight from reality. All who repudiate logic automatically cut themselves off from any possible knowledge of God and his creation. Their failure to recognize this fact is one consequence of their failure to live out the logical and practical consequences of their position. The Word of God (that includes revealed information from God and about God) is not alien to the human mind. Neither the nature of God nor the nature of human knowledge and language precludes the possibility of the human mind attaining cognitive knowledge about God and his revelation.

OPTIONAL WRITING ASSIGNMENT

Kant believed his theory of knowledge made knowledge about God impossible. Discuss Kant's refusal to explain why all humans possess the same structure of rationality and show how his failure in this regard opens the door to an argument for God's existence. What is your opinion of this argument?

FOR FURTHER READING

C. D. Broad, *Kant: An Introduction* (London: Cambridge University Press, 1978).

Justus Harnack, *Kant's Theory of Knowledge* (New York: Harcourt Brace and World, 1967).

David Hume, *Dialogues Concerning Natural Religion,* available in many editions from many publishers.

David Hume, *Enquiry Concerning Human Understanding,* available in many editions from many publishers.

Immanuel Kant, *The Critique of Pure Reason,* available in many translations in many editions from many publishers.

Immanuel Kant, *Prolegomena to Any Future Metaphysics,* available in many translations in many editions from many publishers.

S. Körner, *Kant* (Baltimore: Penguin, 1955).

Ronald H. Nash, *The Word of God and the Mind of Man* (Phillipsburg, N.J.: Presbyterian and Reformed, 1992).

David Fate Norton, ed. *The Cambridge Companion to David Hume* (New York: Cambridge University Press, 1993).

David Fate Norton et al., eds., *McGill Hume Studies* (San Diego, Calif.: Austin Hill Press, 1979).

Norman Kemp Smith, *The Philosophy of David Hume* (London: Macmillan, 1949).

Chapter Twelve

Epistemology III: Reformed Epistemology

Every once in a while, a philosopher or group of philosophers makes what appears to be a new beginning in some branch of the discipline. Usually their early work goes unnoticed until one or two publications get attention, and then friends and critics begin to talk about the new movement. After more time passes, people begin to see that the new movement is a restatement of positions that got lost in the shuffle decades or centuries ago. It's as though someone finds an antique painting in an attic, dusts it off, and puts it in a new frame. Suddenly it becomes the talk of the town.

This new movement in epistemology now passes under the label of Reformed epistemology. One does not have to be a follower of Reformed epistemology to appreciate what it brings to the table or to welcome the fresh perspective it provides on a number of old philosophical problems such as the existence of God, the existence of the external world, and the existence of other minds.

The early leaders of this resurgence of Reformed epistemology are such well-known American philosophers as Alvin Plantinga (University of Notre Dame), Nicholas Wolterstorff (Yale University), and William Alston (retired after a distinguished career at such schools as the University of Michigan, the University of Illinois, and Syracuse University). Plantinga and Alston are former presidents of divisions of the American Philosophical Association.[1]

An Introduction to Reformed Epistemology

In recent publications about epistemology, philosophers apparently operating on different tracks have found agreement on several important points. In the case of my own track implied in earlier chapters of this book, it is a mistake to accept an extreme form of empiricism that claims that all human knowledge arises from sense experience. Older advocates of this empiricism used to illustrate their basic claim by arguing that the

---

1. Many journal articles related to developments in Reformed epistemology have appeared in *Faith and Philosophy,* the official journal of the Society of Christian Philosophers.

human mind at birth is like a *tabula rasa,* a blank tablet.[2] At birth, the human mind is like a clean blackboard devoid of any writing. In other words, human beings are born with no innate ideas or knowledge. As the human being grows and develops, the senses supply the mind with an ever-increasing stock of information. According to this empiricist model, all human knowledge results from what the mind does with ideas supplied through the senses. Such sensible ideas are the basic building blocks of knowledge.

As explained earlier in the book, my alternative to this kind of empiricism can be summarized in the claim that some human knowledge does not arise from sense experience. As many philosophers have noted, human knowledge of the sensible world is possible because human beings bring certain ideas, categories, and dispositions to their experience of the world. The impotence of empiricism is especially evident in the case of human knowledge of universal and necessary truth. Many things in the world could have been otherwise. The Buick that I drive these days is white, but it could have been red. Whether it is white or not is a purely contingent feature of reality. Whatever color the Buick happens to be, it could have had a different color. Indeed, there are many possible worlds (see chap. 9) in which that Buick is a different color. But it is necessarily the case that my Buick could not have been white all over and red (or any other color) all over at the same time and in the same sense. The necessary truth that my Buick is white all over and not at the same time red all over cannot be a function of sense experience. Sense experience may be able to report what is the case at a particular time. But sense experience is incapable of grasping what must be the case at all times. The notions of necessity and universality can never be derived from our experience. Rather, they are notions (among others) that we bring to sense experience and use in making judgments about reality.

How do we account for the human possession of these *a priori* (that is, independent of sense experience) categories of thought or innate ideas or dispositions that play such an indispensable role in human knowledge? According to a long and honored philosophical tradition that includes Augustine, Descartes, and Leibniz,[3] humans have these innate ideas, dispositions, and categories by virtue of their creation by God. In fact, such a claim may identify a major feature of what is meant by the phrase *the image of God*. After all, Christians believe, God created the world. It is reasonable to assume that he created humans such that they are capable

---

2. This suggestion appears explicitly or implicitly in the work of such thinkers as Thomas Aquinas and John Locke.

3. I trust it is apparent that an innocent piece of information such as this does not entail support for every single element of such thinker's philosophical systems. I am neither a Cartesian (follower of Descartes) nor a Leibnizian.

of attaining knowledge of his creation. To go even further, it is plausible to think that he endowed the human mind with the ability to attain knowledge of himself and to communicate information about him in human language.

Recently, a number of philosophers have approached a similar position from a different direction, namely, the epistemology of the eighteenth-century Scottish philosopher Thomas Reid (1710–1796). Nicholas Wolterstorff explains:

> At the very foundation of Reid's approach is his claim that at any point in our lives we have a variety of dispositions, inclinations, propensities, to believe things—*belief dispositions* we may call them. What accounts for our beliefs, in the vast majority of cases anyway, is the triggering of one and another such disposition. For example, we are all so constituted that upon having memory experiences in certain situations, we are disposed to have certain beliefs about the past. We are all disposed, upon having certain sensations in certain situations, to have certain beliefs about the external physical world. Upon having certain other sensations in certain situations, we are all disposed to have certain beliefs about other persons.[4]

Continuing to follow Reid's trail, Wolterstorff notes that Reid was also interested in how humans came to have these belief-producing dispositions or mechanisms. It was Reid's conviction, Wolterstorff explains,

> that somewhere in the history of each of us are to be found certain belief dispositions with which we were simply "endowed by our Creator." They belong to our human nature. We come with them. They are innate in us. Their existence in us is not the result of conditioning. It must not be supposed, however, that all such nonconditioned dispositions are present in us at birth. Some, possibly most, emerge as we mature. We have the disposition to acquire them upon reaching one and another level of maturation.[5]

It is also open to such classic rationalists as Augustine (or me) to concur with what Wolterstorff describes in this paragraph. Classic rationalists always distinguish between persons' having certain ideas innately (at birth) and becoming conscious of those ideas as they reach some level of maturation. Another important comment: Wolterstorff goes on to note that Reid also acknowledged the existence of belief dispositions that are "acquired by way of conditioning."[6] This is a sensible point to make.

---

4. Nicholas Wolterstorff, "Can Belief in God Be Rational?" in *Faith and Rationality,* ed. Alvin Plantinga and Nicholas Wolterstorff (Notre Dame, Ind.: University of Notre Dame Press, 1983), 149. The chapters in this book are commonly taken to be the first major statement of the elements of Reformed epistemology.

5. Ibid., 150.

6. Ibid.

This is a good time to introduce the distinction between inborn cognitive equipment such as Kant's categories and dispositions and innate cognitive content such as implicit inborn knowledge about God, goodness, equality, and unity. Two types of Reformed epistemologists exist: (1) those who are content to talk about innate cognitive equipment such as belief-forming dispositions that produce certain beliefs in the presence of certain experiences; and (2) those who accept everything included in (1) and also believe in the existence of innate cognitive content. This distinction might justify calling the members of (2) rationalists in the strong sense and the philosophers in group (1) rationalists in the weak sense.

Alvin Plantinga draws attention to an important similarity between what Reid said concerning the belief-forming mechanisms that make knowledge of the world possible and what Reformed thinkers like John Calvin said about belief in God.

Belief-Forming Dispositions and God

> Reformed theologians such as Calvin . . . have held that God has implanted in us a tendency or *nisus* to accept belief in God under certain conditions. Calvin speaks, in this connection, of a "sense of deity inscribed in the hearts of all." Just as we have a natural tendency to form perceptual beliefs under certain conditions, so says Calvin, we have a natural tendency to form such beliefs as *God is speaking to me* and *God has created all this* or *God disapproves of what I've done* under certain widely realized conditions.[7]

Plantinga shows no reluctance in describing the idea of God as "innate," a fact that justifies considering him as a rationalist in the strong sense (see the earlier paragraph in this chapter).

Foundationalism is a particular model or picture of human knowledge. It is one of several ways of looking at such related topics as belief, rationality, and justification. The central analogy in the foundationalist picture of knowledge is a structure such as a building where various upper levels or stories are supported by lower stories. The entire structure is supported by a set of beliefs that serves as the foundation. The entire building, the upper stories and the foundation, stand for what some contemporary philosophers now call a person's *noetic structure*. Without saying everything, a noetic structure is the sum total of a person's beliefs plus the relationships among those beliefs. No two people will ever share the same noetic structure. For one thing, each of us holds beliefs about our past experiences. Since my past differs from yours in at least some

Reformed Epistemology and Foundationalism

---

7. Alvin Plantinga, "Self-Profile," in *Alvin Plantinga,* ed. James E. Tomberlin and Peter Van Inwagen (Boston: D. Reidel, 1985), 63–64. Plantinga's quote comes from Calvin's *Institutes of the Christian Religion* 1.3.43–44.

respects, my beliefs about my past will differ from yours and hence my noetic structure will differ. Human beliefs about the future also differ.

Starting with this notion of a person's noetic structure, Plantinga explains that foundationalism is the view

> that some of our beliefs are based upon others. According to the foundationalist a rational noetic structure will *have a foundation*—a set of beliefs not accepted on the basis of others; in a rational noetic structure some beliefs will be basic. Nonbasic beliefs, of course, will be accepted on the basis of other beliefs, which may be accepted on the basis of still other beliefs, and so on until the foundations are reached. In a rational noetic structure, therefore, every nonbasic belief is ultimately accepted on the basis of basic beliefs.[8]

According to foundationalism, then, the total set of beliefs held by individual persons should be thought of as hierarchies in which every belief is either basic or derivative (nonbasic). *Nonbasic beliefs* are those that are grounded on or dependent in some way on more basic beliefs. *Basic beliefs* are those not derived from or dependent on other beliefs. In order for a belief to be rational, it must either be a basic belief or be justified by its relation to a basic belief. Every noetic structure contains such basic beliefs that are not derived from or dependent on other beliefs. These basic beliefs can be said to make up the *foundation* of that particular set of beliefs.

The foundationalist picture of human knowledge has dominated western philosophy for centuries. Any list of foundationalist philosophers would have to include Plato, Aristotle, Aquinas, and Descartes, along with the authors of many other philosophical systems. Thinking of epistemological activities in terms of the foundationalist model offers putative answers to some important questions. For example, *When should a belief be eliminated from a person's noetic structure?* Answer: When that belief is neither properly basic[9] nor properly grounded on a properly basic belief. *How should we judge the strength of a nonbasic belief?* Answer: In terms of the degree of support it receives from basic beliefs. *When does argument end?* Answer: When it arrives at properly basic beliefs.

Two Kinds of Foundationalism

Contemporary thinkers distinguish between classical and modern foundationalism. Classical foundationalism was the dominant model in ancient and medieval times. While I make a few passing comments about the classical variety, I will focus most of my attention on modern foundationalism.

---

8. Alvin Plantinga, "Reason and Belief in God," in *Faith and Rationality,* ed. Alvin Plantinga and Nicholas Wolterstorff (Notre Dame, Ind.: University of Notre Dame Press, 1983), 52.

9. A *properly basic* belief is one that rightly belongs in the foundation of a rational collection of beliefs.

Two quite different forms of modern foundationalism can be found in today's intellectual marketplace. *Narrow foundationalism* insists that only beliefs that satisfy two or three specific criteria are properly basic, that is, belong properly in the foundation of a rational noetic structure. *Broad foundationalism* agrees with the distinction between basic and nonbasic beliefs and with the claim that the rationality of nonbasic beliefs depends on the extent to which they are supported by properly basic beliefs. But broad foundationalism breaks with narrow foundationalism over the latter's attempt to limit properly basic beliefs to those that satisfy two or three criteria. A broad foundationalist is willing to allow many different kinds of beliefs to qualify as properly basic—to belong properly in the foundation of a rational noetic structure—even though they do not meet the strict criteria of the narrow foundationalist.

Narrow Foundationalism

What I call narrow foundationalism is characterized by two theses:

(1) Within any individual's set of beliefs, some beliefs are properly basic (do not require justification in terms of any more fundamental beliefs); basic beliefs serve to justify, ground, or otherwise support other nonbasic beliefs.

(2) Only beliefs that fall into one of two categories are properly basic. Those two and only two types of properly basic beliefs are those that are self-evident or incorrigible.[10]

Thesis (1) is held by anyone who is a foundationalist. What differentiates a narrow from a broad foundationalist is thesis (2), the narrow foundationalist's insistence that in order to be properly basic, a belief must be self-evident, or incorrigible. In a moment, I will explain the meaning of these two terms.[11]

I am now ready to address the question of what the terms *self-evident* and *incorrigible* mean.

Self-evident propositions are statements that people see are true or false simply by understanding them. Consider some mathematical truth.

---

10. While narrow foundationalism in our time recognizes only self-evident and incorrigible beliefs as properly basic, classical foundationalism replaced incorrigible beliefs with beliefs that are evident to the senses. The specific reasons for all this need not concern us in this book.

11. Modern foundationalism represents an important piece of what postmodernists oppose in modernism. As my discussion in this chapter proceeds, I too will repudiate modern foundationalism, that is, the belief that nonbasic beliefs are rational if and only if they can be grounded on basic beliefs that are either self-evident or incorrigible. Does that make me a critic of modernism? Perhaps. Does that make me a postmodernist? It does not. Is there any lesson to be learned here that is relevant to postmodernism? Yes, and one of them is that postmodernists are arrogant and uninformed when it comes to alternative critiques of modernity. If that's too strong, let us say that when it comes to oversimplifying things, postmodernists do it *in excelsius*. The arrogance I refer to appears when they represent themselves as the *only* opponents of modernity.

Once one understands the proposition, its truth is seen immediately. Propositions may also be self-evidently false, as in the case of "The square root of nine is two." Self-evident propositions are necessarily true or necessarily false. The following are self-evident propositions:

The sum of the angles of any triangle is 180 degrees.

Everything blue is colored.

All bachelors are married men.

Self-evident propositions are properly basic; they belong properly in the foundation of any noetic structure. They are propositions that people have a right to believe without basing them on any more basic belief.

Incorrigible propositions are statements that cannot be doubted, even though they fall short of logical necessity.[12] Incorrigible propositions are statements in which we report truthfully whatever is present in our consciousness. The way to turn any dubitable proposition about the world (such as "I am now in Monument Valley") into an incorrigible proposition is to preface the proposition with the words "it seems to me." It may be untrue that I am now in Monument Valley; perhaps I've seen too many John Wayne movies lately.[13] But whether I'm awake or sleeping, rational or not, if my report that "it seems to me that I'm in Monument Valley" faithfully describes what is present to my consciousness, it is an incorrigible proposition. And as an incorrigible proposition, it is properly basic for me; I have a right to believe it without support from any other belief.

To review, a foundationalist is someone who pictures noetic structures hierarchically. Every noetic structure is composed of two kinds of belief: (1) nonbasic beliefs that are believed, justified, and made rational by virtue of their relationship to other, more basic beliefs; and (2) basic beliefs, which do not require support from other beliefs. Basic beliefs make up the foundation of a person's noetic structure. Every foundationalist agrees that self-evident and incorrigible propositions point to beliefs that are properly basic. When a person utters a proposition that passes one of these tests, it makes no sense for someone to say, "Prove it!" Any person who demands a proof for a properly basic belief reveals that he or she is suffering from a cognitive malfunction.

What has this to do with anything? Suppose for the sake of argument that we can uncover a serious failing in narrow foundationalism. Keep in mind that in one of its two forms (classical or modern foundationalism),

---

12. This last sentence records a fundamental difference between self-evident and incorrigible propositions. The denial of a self-evident truth is a logical contradiction while the denial of an incorrigible proposition is not.

13. John Wayne fans will know that such westerns as *Stagecoach, The Searchers,* and *She Wore a Yellow Ribbon* were filmed in Monument Valley.

this has been the dominant model of human rationality throughout the history of philosophy. Remember also that most of the attempts philosophers have made throughout history to undermine belief in God have proceeded on narrow foundationalist grounds. That is, these antitheists have assumed the narrow foundationalist model and also assumed that belief in God is a nonbasic belief. What this means is simple: unless belief in God can somehow be traced back to one of narrow foundationalism's two kinds of basic belief, belief in God can be dismissed as irrational, as unworthy of acceptance by rational men and women. Keep in mind as well that precisely this feature of narrow foundationalism makes postmodernism so attractive to many contemporary Christians who have trouble thinking clearly. Just because narrow foundationalism has often been an essential feature of modernism and has often been used to attack the Christian faith, it hardly follows that postmodern relativism is the only alternative to narrow foundationalism. Nor does it follow that a repudiation of narrow foundationalism on postmodernist grounds will generate good news for people sympathetic to the Christian faith. As we showed in chapter 10, postmodernism may well turn out to be as antithetic to historic Christian belief as modernism was. So where do we go from here? Answer: We take two steps. First, we introduce the model of broad foundationalism, and then we relate it to Reformed epistemology.

Broad Foundationalism

There is nothing wrong with approaching human knowledge via a foundationalist model or picture. The problem comes when, as we have seen, foundationalists restrict properly basic beliefs to two or three types. In the rest of this chapter, we will see what happens when a foundationalist recognizes the limitations and problems of narrow foundationalism and opens up the foundation of his noetic structure to other kinds of properly basic beliefs. In particular we will see what happens when a broad foundationalist (someone who believes that the foundations of a noetic structure may properly include basic beliefs that are not self-evident or incorrigible) decides that belief in God is a properly basic belief.

Narrow foundationalism is subject to two objections. It is important to remember, however, that the failings of narrow foundationalism do not compromise the fact that self-evident and incorrigible beliefs remain properly basic. What the critics of narrow foundationalism are correct in pointing out is that there are other kinds of properly basic beliefs.

Objections to Narrow Foundationalism

Objection One

Narrow foundationalism is incompatible with a great deal of what everyone knows. As Plantinga argues, if narrow foundationalism is true, then enormous quantities of what we all in fact believe are irrational. . . . Relative to propositions that are self-evident and incorrigible, most of the beliefs that form the stock in trade of ordinary everyday life are not probable. . . . Consider all those propositions that entail, say, that there are enduring physical objects [this is the problem of the external world], or that there are persons distinct from myself [this is the problem of other minds], or that the world has existed for more than five minutes; none of these propositions, I think, is more probable than not with respect to what is self-evident or incorrigible for me.[14]

Hence, narrow foundationalism is much too restrictive; it results in many of our most important beliefs being irrational. As Plantinga goes on to say, many propositions that fail the narrow foundationalist's tests

are properly basic for me. I believe, for example, that I had lunch this noon. I do not believe this proposition on the basis of other propositions; I take it as basic; it is in the foundations of my noetic structure. Furthermore, I am entirely rational in so taking it, even though this proposition is neither self-evident nor evident to the senses nor incorrigible for me.[15]

According to narrow foundationalism, true memories fail the test of rationality since they are themselves neither basic beliefs nor based on properly basic beliefs. But surely any theory that casts doubt on the rationality of not only memory beliefs but also all kinds of other beliefs, such as our belief in the external world or other minds, is deficient. Our knowledge of true memories or other persons or the continuing existence of the external world is not inferential, that is, based on more basic beliefs. But it *is* knowledge. As Plantinga sees it, this means we have to admit such beliefs into the foundations of our noetic structure; even though such beliefs do not pass the restrictive tests of the narrow foundationalist, they too must be properly basic. One problem with narrow foundationalism, then, is its greatly restricted view of what qualifies as a properly basic belief.

Objection Two

Narrow foundationalism fails its own test of rationality; it is self-referentially absurd. As we all remember, narrow foundationalism contends that properly basic beliefs must be self-evident, or incorrigible. Observe what happens when one asks the narrow foundationalist whether this thesis is self-evident, or incorrigible, or is based on propositions that are. A little reflection will show that none of these conditions obtain. From this fact, several consequences follow.

---

14. Plantinga, "Reason and Belief in God," 59, 60.
15. Ibid., 60.

It is clear that the narrow foundationalist himself accepts a belief, namely, his theory, as properly basic even though it fails to satisfy his own criteria of proper basicality. Since the narrow foundationalist fails to provide any arguments, reasons, or evidence for his thesis and since it fails his own tests for proper basicality, it follows that his acceptance of his thesis violates epistemic duties. Since being rational for him means fulfilling one's epistemic duties, it follows that the narrow foundationalist is behaving irrationally when he advances his thesis.

It is also clear that the narrow foundationalist accepts as properly basic one proposition (again, his own thesis) that is an exception to his thesis. His own practice shows that there are other ways in which a belief may become part of the foundation of a noetic structure. Even the narrow foundationalist is forced to admit (in practice, at least) that a belief that is not self-evident or incorrigible may be properly basic.[16] And so we can thank the narrow foundationalist for opening this door. We can follow his lead and begin to consider the possibility that other propositions may be properly basic.

An Alternative to Narrow Foundationalism

Plantinga has provided a valuable service in drawing attention to the often unnoticed way that one particular model of human knowledge, narrow foundationalism, has influenced discussions of the rationality or irrationality of religious belief. He has also provided a clear account of the nature of foundationalism along with powerful criticisms of narrow foundationalism. What is wrong with narrow foundationalism is not its recognition that every noetic structure contains basic beliefs that provide justification for (and thus serve as the foundation for) that noetic structure's nonbasic beliefs. What is wrong is the exclusivism of the narrow foundationalist who claims that only two types of belief are properly basic, a claim that is used both to eliminate belief in God from the foundation and to undermine the rationality of belief in God.

Plantinga's challenge to narrow foundationalism includes two key moves. The first is the claim that narrow foundationalism is too restrictive with regard to the kinds of beliefs it recognizes as properly basic. While it is true that self-evident and incorrigible beliefs belong properly in the foundation of a person's noetic structure, it is also the case that many other kinds of beliefs may belong there. Narrow foundationalism is unable to do justice to the privileged status we accord to a great many beliefs that are not self-evident or incorrigible. Examples of beliefs that should be treated as properly basic include our belief in the existence of

---

16. In chapter 1, I pointed out that one mark of an adequate theory is its proponents' ability to live that theory without cheating and borrowing from some competing theory. The narrow foundationalist cannot live consistently within the constraints of his own system.

the external world, our belief in the existence of other selves, and our memory beliefs.

Plantinga's second key move against those narrow foundationalists who would seek to use their position to undermine the rationality of belief in God is to refute that position and then declare that "belief in God is properly basic." Belief in God belongs properly in the foundation of a person's noetic structure. Plantinga's move at this point is so bold that it requires time for the significance of his claim to sink in. In Plantinga's words, "Under widely realized conditions it is perfectly rational, reasonable, intellectually respectable and acceptable to believe that there is such a person as God without believing on the basis of [an argument or proof]."[17] It is reasonable to believe that God exists without arguments or reasons. Christians may be within their epistemic rights to believe in God,[18] even though they may not be able to prove God's existence to someone else; indeed, even though they may not be able to think up any argument for themselves. Belief in God, like any foundational belief, does not need support from any other belief; it is basic!

In one of its many facets, Plantinga's position is reminiscent of the view of faith and reason set forth by Augustine, a position that would centuries later reappear in the work of such Protestant Reformers as Calvin. As we saw in chapter 6, Augustine saw that in order for any person to know anything, he must begin by believing something. *Credo ut intelligam;* I believe in order that I may understand.

One legitimate way for faith to operate is for us to accept propositions as true on the testimony of some reliable authority. This is how we come to learn about history; it is also the way in which most people are introduced to religious truth.

I have already identified our belief in other minds as an example of a properly basic belief. Belief in God clearly belongs to the same family of beliefs. There is no argument, or so Plantinga has argued, or evidence that can prove that other people have minds. But, Plantinga insists, we have a right to hold this belief, even in the absence of proof or evidence. Belief in other minds is a properly basic belief. So too is belief in God. In both cases we have a right to hold the belief, even if we cannot come up with an argument that will prove the belief to ourselves or to someone else.[19]

---

17. This quote comes from public lectures that Plantinga has not yet published.

18. This means that when I believe in God under these conditions, I am not violating any relevant rule or principle of epistemology. I am justified in holding that belief.

19. Some additional details of Plantinga's claim that belief in God is properly basic arise in connection with Plantinga's answers to certain objections. As important as this material is, it lies outside the scope of this introductory text. Interested readers can pursue these matters by reading Plantinga's essay, "Reason and Belief in God," in *Faith and Rationality,* 74–78. For a brief summary, see Ronald H. Nash, *Faith and Reason* (Grand Rapids: Zondervan, 1988), 88–91.

Natural theology is an attempt to discover arguments that will prove or otherwise provide warrant for belief in God without appealing to special revelation, that is, the Bible. One major assumption of natural theology is that belief in God is not properly basic. When natural theologians set out to prove God's existence, they usually seek to base God's existence on more basic beliefs. Thomas Aquinas's Five Ways of arguing for God's existence are one of history's more famous examples of natural theology. Thomas, or so it would seem, did not regard belief in God as properly basic, thus making it necessary for him to offer philosophical arguments.

Reformed epistemologists do not regard such classic arguments for God's existence to be necessary. Such arguments, they think, often suffer from one or more logical defects. Moreover, they note, most religious believers come to faith by some route other than a philosophical argument. Nonetheless, even if arguments for God's existence are not necessary, this does not mean they are useless. It is one thing to need an argument; it is something else to have an argument to bolster or confirm a belief.

A Recapitulation

Early in this chapter, I explained how certain human dispositions or belief-forming mechanisms predispose us to believe certain things when we find ourselves in certain situations. When I am appeared to in the way I normally am when it seems that I'm sitting down to a breakfast of eggs and bacon, I am naturally disposed to believe that there really are eggs and bacon on the plate before me.

I also discussed how a number of philosophers, including Reid, explained this: the dispositions that noninferentially[20] produce beliefs like these results from God's having constituted the human mind in a certain way. As Arthur Holmes explains,

> According to Thomas Reid, God so constituted the mind that we believe without proof that external objects exist, we believe that memory tells of a past, we believe the causal principle[21] and the axioms of geometry, we believe there is a distinction between right and wrong; and that God exists. These beliefs which we know so surely to be true are, according to Reid, spontaneous interpretations of experience rather than logical inferences. The appearance of a sign is followed by belief in the thing signified; a sensation by belief in its present existence; a remembrance by belief in its past existence; and imagination is not accompanied by beliefs at all. This is all due to the human constitution, a matter of com-

Reformed
Epistemology
and Natural
Theology

---

20. In other words, my beliefs about the eggs and bacon on the table in front of me are not a result of some thinking process; I do not infer the existence of the food. My belief is immediate and noninferential.

21. The "causal principle" Holmes refers to concerns the readiness with which, under the conditions so familiar to us, we believe that one event is the cause of another.

mon sense, not reason, and it is common to all men. Our very nature evokes universal beliefs and bears witness to their truth.[22]

People who misunderstand all this complain that Reformed epistemology's insistence that belief in the existence of God is properly basic makes it impossible for humans to support such important beliefs with grounds. Plantinga counters this claim by explaining how basic beliefs like "I see a tree" can have grounds or warrant. In fact, if we were not in circumstances of a certain kind, we probably wouldn't be disposed to believe that we see a tree. Various circumstances (such as experiences of a certain kind) may trigger or serve as justifying grounds for a basic belief (like "I had eggs and bacon for breakfast") without being part of a formal argument with premises and a conclusion. Certain conditions then may, in conjunction with certain God-given dispositions, trigger beliefs that are properly basic. As Plantinga puts it,

> Our cognitive faculties [are] designed to enable us to achieve true beliefs with respect to a wide variety of propositions—about our immediate environment, about our own interior life, about the thoughts and experiences of other persons, about the past, about our universe at large, about right and wrong ... and about God. These faculties work in such a way that under the appropriate circumstances we form the appropriate belief. More exactly, the appropriate belief is *formed in us;* in the typical case we do not *decide* to hold or form the belief in question, but simply find ourselves with it ... Upon being appeared to in the familiar way, I find myself holding the belief that there is a large tree before me; upon being asked what I had for breakfast, I reflect for a moment and then find myself with the belief that what I had was eggs on toast. In these and other cases I do not *decide* what to believe; I don't total up the evidence ... and make a decision as to what seems best supported; I simply believe.[23]

The history of philosophy is full of failed attempts to justify basic beliefs such as our belief in the external world and our belief in other minds. It also tells the story of misguided efforts to certify the reliability of belief-forming mechanisms such as the senses and memory. But as Stephen Wykstra notes, "Our creaturely epistemic condition is that we must *trust* the basic belief-forming mechanisms with which we are endowed, presuming their reliability until we have reasons for revising them."[24]

---

22. The quote comes from an unpublished paper by Arthur Holmes, "The Justification of World View Beliefs."

23. This quotation comes from an as-yet unpublished paper by Plantinga.

24. This remark by Wykstra appears in his review of the Plantinga-Wolterstorff book *Faith and Rationality.* The review is in *Faith and Philosophy* 3 (1986): 207. It is not clear whether, in this and in other Wykstra comments quoted later, he is describing the views of Reformed epistemologists like Plantinga or also shares their position.

So we see that for contemporary Reformed epistemologists as for Reid before them, God has created humans in such a way that when we have experiences of a certain kind, such as seeming to see a red rose in the garden, there is a natural tendency for us to believe immediately and non-inferentially that there is a red rose in the garden. While Reid himself refuses to take this additional step, other thinkers taught that God has also created us with a similar tendency or disposition (the *sensus divinitatis*) to believe in God. Plantinga relates this position to views he thinks can be found in the work of Calvin.

> According to Calvin everyone, whether in the faith or not, has a tendency or *nisus,* in certain situations, to apprehend God's existence and to grasp something of his nature and actions. This natural knowledge can be and is suppressed by sin, but the fact remains that a capacity to apprehend God's existence is as much part of our natural noetic equipment as is the capacity to apprehend perceptual truths, truths about the past, and truth about other minds. Belief in the existence of God is in the same boat as belief in other minds, the past, and perceptual objects; in each case God has so constructed us that in the right circumstances we form the belief in question.[25]

As Wykstra explains, "Such experiences are not 'evidence' from which theism is *inferred;* rather, they 'actuate' an appropriate noninferential disposition, as hearing someone cry triggers belief that she feels pain. Such basic beliefs self-evidently entail that God exists, so if they are proper, so is theism."[26]

Reformed Epistemology and Arguments for God's Existence

This Reformed account of human knowledge provides us with a new way[27] of viewing the arguments for God's existence so beloved by natural theologians. Appeals to the sorts of evidence utilized in the cosmological and teleological arguments for God's existence carry so much weight with so many people because God has implanted in each human being a natural tendency to see his hand in the world. E. J. Carnell once approached this view in some comments about the apostle Paul's words in Romans 1:20: "Paul truly taught that God is known through sense perception but that does not involve us in empiricism [or natural theology]. May it not equally be that, *knowing* God (by innate knowledge, which Paul teaches) we are *reminded* of Him in His works?"[28] Carnell went on

---

25. Plantinga, "Reason and Belief in God," 89–90.
26. Wykstra, review of *Faith and Rationality,* 207.
27. It is a new way only for those unfamiliar with the long history of this approach.
28. E. J. Carnell, *An Introduction to Christian Apologetics* (Grand Rapids: Eerdmans, 1948), 149n.

to conclude that "rather than building up a knowledge of God through a patient examination of the content of sense experience, we proceed to such experience *equipped* with an awareness of God."[29] Whether we say with Plantinga that humans are born with a disposition to believe in God or say with Carnell that God has given us an innate knowledge of himself, this God-endowed disposition or knowledge makes it possible for humans to recognize God in the creation.[30]

But this brings us to a possible problem. If every human being is born with a disposition to believe in God, then why doesn't every human being come to recognize God's existence? If we knew a person who did not come to hold a particular belief (such as the belief that he is seeing a tree) while being appeared to in the typical and familiar way, we would conclude that his cognitive equipment was malfunctioning. Much the same thing occurs in cases when alcoholics suffering from delirium tremens are convinced they see pink rats crawling up their legs. The Christian worldview teaches that something has happened to the human race that affects not only our actions and dispositions but also our noetic structure. As Plantinga puts it,

> God has endowed us in such a way that we have a strong tendency or inclination toward belief in God. This tendency has been in part overlaid or suppressed by sin. Were it not for the existence of sin in the world, human beings would believe in God to the same degree and with the same natural spontaneity that we believe in the existence of other persons, an external world, or the past. This is the natural human condition; it is because of our presently unnatural sinful condition that many of us find belief in God difficult or absurd. The fact is, Calvin thinks, one who does not believe in God is in an epistemically substandard position—rather like a man who does not believe that his wife exists, or thinks she is like a cleverly constructed robot and has no thoughts, feelings, or consciousness.[31]

A number of thinkers like Karl Marx and Sigmund Freud argued that the reason some people believe in God is because their cognitive equipment is malfunctioning. If Plantinga is right, it is the cognitive equipment of atheists like Marx and Freud that is malfunctioning.

The introduction of sin and the Fall at this point is not an arbitrary or ad hoc measure. Everyone familiar with Christianity knows that the Fall plays a central role in the Christian view of man and the world. It would be strange to write about the Christian worldview and pretend that sin— or the set of Christian beliefs about sin—does not exist. We are fallen

---

29. Ibid., 151n.

30. I am less confident than other philosophers that there is a hard and fast distinction between innate dispositions and innate ideas. But that is a subject best left for another book. For a brief discussion, see Ronald H. Nash, *The Word of God and the Mind of Man* (Phillipsburg, N.J.: Presbyterian and Reformed, 1992), chap. 7.

31. Plantinga, "Reason and Belief in God," 66.

creatures. The Fall affects not only what we do but also how we think. There is a noetic dimension to sin. Sin has clouded the human mind so that often we cannot see the truth.

Stephen T. Davis, a philosopher at Claremont University in California, provides additional information about Plantinga's thinking. According to Plantinga, he writes, humans were created

> with a "design plan," a set of epistemic inclinations and dispositions which is designed to work in a certain way. It is also designed to work in a certain context, that is, the environment of our epistemic situation as human persons in this world. The plan is the way that God intended our epistemic faculties to function. Some people misuse their epistemic equipment; on some occasions that equipment malfunctions. That is when human beings formulate beliefs that have little or no warrant.

As Davis continues,

> But those who come to believe in God are following the divine design plan; their epistemic equipment is functioning properly. If *warrant* is that which when added to true belief produces knowledge, Plantinga argues that any true belief is warranted when it is produced by our epistemic faculties functioning properly in a proper context. Those who believe in God are not only rational in their belief that God exists—they can legitimately be said to *know* that God exists.[32]

This position set forth in this chapter holds several important implications for the so-called theistic arguments. Even if we should discover that some—or even all—theistic arguments fail as proofs for God's existence, they may still be useful insofar as they function as evidence or grounds or triggering conditions for belief. Any argument may provide reasons that support belief, even though it falls short of being a proof.[33] Even if various arguments for God's existence are not sound, they may still draw attention to things like order and purpose that can complement and support the believer's conviction that God exists. In other words, even if an argument fails as a proof, it may still function as a justifying ground that can help trigger belief. Since humans have the *sensus divinitatis,* consideration of a theistic argument may present them with information or lead them to experiences that, in conjunction with God-implanted dispositions, will trigger belief in God in ways similar to how nonreligious experiences or other justifying conditions trigger such beliefs as "I am now seeing a tree." In the next chapter, we'll take the matter of arguing for God's existence a step or two further.

---

32. Stephen T. Davis, *God, Reason, and Theistic Proofs* (Grand Rapids: Eerdmans, 1997), 85.

33. The word *proof* is a slippery and often misunderstood term. I offer an analysis of the term in *Faith and Reason,* chap. 8.

OPTIONAL WRITTEN ASSIGNMENT

Write an essay that compares the belief-forming mechanisms of Reformed epistemology with Kant's categories and with Augustine's eternal ideas.

FOR FURTHER READING

Kelly Clark, *Return to Reason* (Grand Rapids: Eerdmans, 1990).

Stephen T. Davis, *God, Reason, and Theistic Proofs* (Grand Rapids: Eerdmans, 1997).

Ronald H. Nash, *Faith and Reason* (Grand Rapids: Zondervan, 1988).

Alvin Plantinga and Nicholas Wolterstorff, eds., *Faith and Rationality* (Notre Dame, Ind.: University of Notre Dame Press, 1983).

Chapter Thirteen

God I:
The Existence of God

In the last chapter, I explained that proofs for God's existence are not necessary for belief in God to be rational. But I went on to say that this does not mean that arguments for God's existence are useless. It is one thing to need an argument and something quite different to have an argument. The case chapter 12 presents for the properly basicality of belief in God does not negate the usefulness of good arguments. After all, Reformed epistemology acknowledges that all kinds of things can function as triggering conditions that, in conjunction with our belief-forming dispositions, can produce immediately and noninferentially the belief that God exists. There is no reason to doubt that arguments can function as triggering conditions in this way, nor is there reason to question the fact that less than totally certain inductive arguments can work like this.

Earlier pages in this book have already introduced several philosophical arguments for God's existence ranging from Thomas Aquinas's Five Ways to a version of Anselm's ontological argument. As unpersuasive or unimpressive as these may have seemed to some, we are on speaking terms with the cosmological and teleological arguments.

Even though belief in God's existence does not require arguments or proofs, it would be wrong to assume that good arguments cannot be found or that they are useless. For one thing, many people fail to understand that belief in God is properly basic and therefore still feel compelled to seek proofs.

What standards must an argument satisfy before it qualifies as a proof? We must be careful not to set the standards of proof too high.[1] If our standards of proof are too rigorous for the material we're dealing with, we can make our search for the truth much more difficult than it has to be. In geometry, such things as probability, personal judgment, the weighing of evidence, and noncoercive arguments[2] are inappropriate. The

How High Should Our Standards Be?

---

1. We should also avoid setting the standards of proof too low.
2. A coercive proof is one that rational people seem compelled to accept. A noncoercive proof is one that may still be disputed by reasonable people.

standards of proof in geometry are as high as they can possibly be. Many people nonetheless act as though any adequate proof for a proposition like "God exists" must meet equally high standards. In fact, they might say, how can we be satisfied with anything less, given all that is at stake in our reflection about God? It is important to remember, however, that reasonable people do recognize how different kinds of inquiry can proceed properly with different but appropriate standards of proof.

Philosopher Rem B. Edwards wisely counsels that "in the final analysis we must settle for a more modest understanding of what constitutes a rationally justified philosophical belief."[3] He then applies his comments to arguments designed to prove the existence of God.

Occasionally, perhaps, even some of the traditional proofs for the existence of God have been interpreted as providing conclusive evidence for their theistic conclusions. From the outset, however, we must recognize that it is a mistake so to regard them, not because we know before we even begin that they do not prove anything, but rather because we know that there are *no* philosophical beliefs anywhere that are supported by conclusive evidence. To expect indubitable premises and rigorous deductive validity from the traditional proofs [for God's existence] is to expect too much. No philosophical proofs of anything rest on indubitable premises. Philosophical proof simply cannot meet such exacting requirements, but this is not to make lame excuses for sloppy thinking.[4]

Consider the standards applied in many courts of law. In criminal cases where the seriousness of the matter could result in imprisonment or execution, the law is correct in requiring proof beyond any reasonable doubt. But in many other kinds of legal cases less proof may be acceptable. C. Stephen Evans explains:

In a civil damage suit over an airplane crash, it is not necessary to prove beyond any reasonable doubt that the crash was due to the airline's negligence, but only that it seems highly likely or probable that was so "in the judgment of a prudent person." The task in this sort of case is to make a judgment which is in accordance with "the preponderance of the evidence." A "clear and convincing proof" in this context is defined in terms of "a high probability." This seems to me to be the kind of "reasonable case" we ought to strive for in religious matters as well. We ought to strive to make a judgment which is in accordance with "the preponderance of evidence" and which seems highly probable or plausible.[5]

---

3. Rem B. Edwards, *Reason and Religion* (New York: Harcourt Brace Jovanovich, 1972), 222.

4. Ibid. I take exception to Edwards's claim that no philosophical beliefs are supported by conclusive evidence.

5. C. Stephen Evans, *The Quest for Faith* (Downers Grove, Ill.: InterVarsity Press, 1986), 28–29.

If we accept the relevance of Evans's analogy between proofs in the kinds of court cases he describes and proofs for such religious claims as "God exists," several important points follow. For one thing, as Evans notes, "good evidence for religious faith will not be some kind of absolute proof that some philosophers seem to seek. Rather, it will be evidence which is sufficient to satisfy a reasonable person."[6] Though such proofs are appropriate for their subject matter, they will seldom result in universal acceptance. "Must an argument be universally accepted to be a proof? Accepted by all sane people who consider it? Frequently something like this standard seems to be presupposed in these discussions.... Such a concept of proof seems impossibly high. It also seems unfair, since this is not the standard of proof we require for nonreligious areas."[7] Juries in court cases are not required to seek proof beyond all possible doubt but only beyond a reasonable doubt.

The case for God's existence should be cumulative. There is nothing wrong with reaching a decision based on a cumulative argument. As Evans states, "One bit of evidence against a criminal may not be enough to convict him. The same may be said of a second or third bit, or any number of bits, when taken in isolation. If each bit does have some force, however, then all of the bits taken together may be more than enough to convict the accused and send him off to prison."[8] Our judgment in such matters, then, is seldom the result of one argument or piece of evidence.

And so, Evans notes, "the case for religious faith will not be based on a single argument functioning as a proof, but upon the total evidence available from every region of human experience."[9] Edwards makes a similar claim when he writes,

> Giving philosophical proof is very similar to what a lawyer does in a courtroom. The philosopher "builds up a case." He explains as best he can why he believes what he does and why he rejects the chief alternatives to his position, and he is always willing to reexamine the elements out of which his case is built. Many lines of converging evidence must be put together into a coherent case.... Many complex elements enter into the case for belief in God. Often the diverse "proofs" are compared, quite correctly, to strands or fibers in a rope, none of which does the work of the whole rope, yet some of which must do some work if the rope is to have any strength at all.[10]

Cumulative Arguments

---

6. Ibid., 29.
7. Ibid., 26.
8. Ibid., 25–26.
9. Ibid., 29.
10. Edwards, *Reason and Religion*, 223.

Probabilistic arguments such as those under consideration can bolster and confirm a belief; often they are strong enough to produce moral or psychological certainty.

Finally, the weighing of evidence in all such matters is something that must be done by human beings, not computers. As Edwards explains this point:

> Assessing the strength of [the case for God's existence], like giving a judgment in a courtroom, is not like running a mathematical proof through a computer. Many complex elements enter into the case for belief in God.... As in a courtroom verdict, the verdict for or against the existence of God cannot be rendered in some purely automatic fashion. Finally, when all is said and done, someone must simply pass judgment.[11]

Each of us must interpret and weigh the arguments; each of us is ultimately responsible for our own final decision.

Deduction or Induction?

Many people approach the theistic arguments believing that only deductive arguments will do. Many critics act as though there is something suspicious about any inductive argument purporting to support the conclusion that God exists.

This deductive-or-nothing attitude fails to appreciate that inductive or probabilistic arguments are appropriate in some contexts. According to thinkers like British philosopher Richard Swinburne, the proper way to argue for God's existence is to utilize inductive arguments. As Swinburne explains, an inductive argument is "an argument from premises to a conclusion in which the premises count in favour of, provide evidence for, the conclusion, without entailing it."[12] In other words, the truth of the premises does not necessarily imply the truth of the conclusion; they may only imply that the conclusion is probably true.

According to this inductive approach, the theistic arguments should not be viewed as deductive arguments that drive us inescapably to the conclusion that God exists. They should be approached rather as efforts to direct our attention to certain features of reality, the inner and outer worlds. The noted features of reality are exactly what we should expect to find if the theistic worldview is true. The case for theism is made even stronger when we find things in the world that we would not expect to find if naturalism were true or if theism were false.

Philosopher Antony Flew, whose commitment to atheism is well known, criticizes philosophers who admit that certain arguments fail as deductive proofs and who then attempt to utilize them as inductive proofs. He writes:

---

11. Ibid.
12. Richard Swinburne, *The Existence of God* (Oxford: Clarendon, 1979), 45.

It is occasionally suggested that some candidate proof, although admittedly failing as a proof, may sometimes do useful service as a pointer. This is a false exercise of the generosity so characteristic of examiners. A failed proof cannot serve as a pointer to anything, save perhaps to the weakness of those who have accepted it. Nor, for the same reason, can it be put to work along with other throw outs as part of the accumulation of evidences. If one leaky bucket will not hold water that is no reason to think that ten can.[13]

But Swinburne answers Flew by pointing out that arguments that may be deductively weak can be inductively strong:

But of course arguments which are not deductively valid are often inductively strong; and if you put three weak arguments together you may often get a strong one, perhaps even a deductively valid one. The analogy in Flew's last sentence is a particularly unhappy one for his purpose. For clearly if you jam ten leaky buckets together in such a way that holes in the bottom of each bucket are squashed close to solid parts of the bottoms of neighbouring buckets, you will get a container that holds water.[14]

Swinburne thinks it is clear that a number of inductive theistic arguments that may be weak when considered alone may, when taken together, make up a strong cumulative case. Sometimes, he admits, "philosophers consider the arguments for the existence of God in isolation from each other, reasoning as follows: the cosmological argument does not prove the conclusion, the teleological argument does not prove the conclusion, etc., etc., therefore the arguments do not prove the conclusion."[15] But treating these same arguments as parts of a cumulative case can lead to a different conclusion:

An argument from p to r may be invalid; another argument from q to r may be invalid. But if you run the arguments together, you could well get a valid deductive argument: the argument from p and q to r may be valid. The argument from "all students have long hair" to "Smith has long hair" is invalid, and so is the argument from "Smith is a student" to "Smith has long hair"; but the argument from "all students have long hair and Smith is a student" to "Smith has long hair" is valid.[16]

The fact that arguments that may be weak when considered separately may support each other becomes even clearer when we consider inductive arguments:

That Smith has blood on his hands hardly makes it probable that Smith murdered Mrs. Jones, nor (by itself) does the fact that Smith stood to gain from Mrs. Jones's death, nor (by itself) does the fact that Smith was near

13. Antony Flew, *God and Philosophy* (New York: Dell, 1966), 62–63.
14. Swinburne, *Existence of God,* 14.
15. Ibid.
16. Ibid.

the scene of the murder at the time of its being committed, but all these phenomena taken together (perhaps with other phenomena as well) may indeed make the conclusion probable.[17]

Although none of the theistic arguments by themselves prove that God exists or even that God's existence is probable, Louis Pojman argues,

Together they constitute a cumulative case for theism. There is something crying for an explanation: Why does this grand universe exist? Together the arguments for God's existence provide a plausible explanation of the existence of the universe, of why we are here, of why there is anything at all and not just nothing.[18]

The explanatory power of theism is based not on single, isolated arguments but on the cumulative case one gets by reflecting on the existence of the universe, the order of the universe, and the facts of human rationality, moral consciousness, and religious experience.

Scientific Explanations Versus Personal Explanations

Swinburne has one final contribution to make at this point. He suggests that we view the theistic arguments as explanations. He then sets up a contrast between two antithetic types of explanations: scientific explanations and personal explanations. In a scientific explanation, the effect is inferred from accompanying causes, conditions, and the relevant laws. The paradigm of a scientific explanation is the way various phenomena are explained in physics.[19]

A personal explanation, in contrast, is one where the phenomena are explained in terms of a rational agent's intentional action. Suppose one very cold winter morning, you walk out to your car and discover a crack in your car's radiator. Remembering your failure to install antifreeze and noting the current temperature of 10 degrees Fahrenheit, you discover a scientific explanation for the condition of your radiator. But suppose on some other morning, you notice that all four of your auto's tires are flat. Looking closer, you see that a sharp knife is buried deeply in each tire. Will a scientific explanation be sufficient in this case? Of course not. This time, you have to explain the damaged tires in terms of some human's intentional behavior; you need a personal explanation.

In a typical theistic argument, the theist draws attention to certain phenomena of either the outer world or the inner world[20] that need

---

17. Ibid.

18. Louis J. Pojman, *Philosophy of Religion: An Anthology* (Belmont, Calif.: Wadsworth, 1987), 28.

19. See Carl G. Hempel, "Explanation in Science and History," in *Ideas of History,* ed. Ronald H. Nash, 2 vols. (New York: Dutton, 1969), 2:79–106. Hempel's rather famous position failed to do justice to personal explanations. The shortcomings of his position are pointed out in later essays in this same volume.

20. See chapter 1 of this book.

explanation. Suppose we find that a scientific (that is, a nonpersonal) explanation fails to do justice to the phenomena. If we have only two choices—if an explanation must be either scientific or personal—and if we discover that phenomena like human rationality cannot adequately be explained in terms of impersonal causes and conditions, it is natural to conclude that we must then seek for an explanation in terms of the intentional action of some rational agent. Swinburne provides an example:

> When a detective argues from various bloodstains on the woodwork, fingerprints on the metal, Smith's corpse on the floor, money missing from the safe, Jones's having much extra money to—Jones's having intentionally killed Smith and stolen his money, he is arguing to an explanation of the various phenomena in terms of the intentional action of a rational agent. Since persons are paradigm cases of rational agents, I will term explanation in terms of the intentional action of a rational agent personal explanation.[21]

Given the kind of phenomena Swinburne describes in this paragraph, only an explanation in terms of some person's intentional action can possibly do justice to the evidence. Likewise, Swinburne continues,

> when the theist argues from phenomena such as the existence of the world or some feature of the world to the existence of God, he is arguing ... to an explanation of the phenomena in terms of the intentional action of a person [that is, God]. ... A theistic explanation is a personal explanation. It explains phenomena in terms of the action of a person.[22]

What's gone on in this section is an account of the distinction between natural and intelligent causes. In our everyday experience, we recognize this difference. Police detectives, for example, want to know if a person was murdered or died of natural causes. The difference holds profoundly different consequences for many people. The difference also holds significantly different consequences for attempts to understand and explain the world.

Swinburne's category of personal explanation is an important contribution to the debate over God's existence. When major features of the inner and outer worlds (see chapter 1 of this book) cannot be given an adequate scientific explanation, we will have to give added weight to any personal explanation that does explain them. Should we ever become convinced that important features of reality require explanation in terms of the intentional actions of a rational Being, we will have discovered significant support for belief in the existence of God.

---

21. Swinburne, *Existence of God,* 20.
22. Ibid., 22, 93.

How to Proceed?

The procedure adopted in this chapter is to draw attention to some phenomenon or state of affairs that requires an explanation. The second step is to ask what conditions or set of conditions best explains this feature of the inner or outer world. How might a naturalist account for this phenomenon? Is a naturalistic explanation adequate? Is a scientific (that is, nonpersonal) explanation adequate? Is a personal explanation better? Does an adequate personal explanation provide clues that point in the direction of God?

Another way of looking at these arguments is to see them as attempts to place people in situations where they see something and where the *sensus divinitatis* can take over in a way that produces conviction. When someone uses a version of the teleological argument in this way, he does not view it as a sound deductive argument in which the proposition "God exists" follows necessarily from claims about order and design in the world. Instead, he attempts to direct the attention of others to some of the impressive signs of this order and design. He then asks if such design and order make sense in a worldview without God.

The Argument from Truth

Since we are looking for features of the world that clearly require a personal explanation, it is important to remember that we encountered one such set of clues in our examination of Kant's theory of knowledge (chap. 11). If we grant Kant's claim that all humans possess the same rational categories, the next step is to ask what condition or set of conditions explains this remarkable state of affairs. As we learned, the preformation theory offers an explanation that is both personal and theistic.

I turn now to some questions about truth. Since we have already established that truth exists, can the existence of truth be explained scientifically? Hardly, since a scientific explanation would bypass any reference to mind or intelligence, while the subject at hand, truth, is preeminently a matter of mind or intelligence. The argument we'll examine in this section made its first appearance in book 2 of Augustine's *On the Freedom of the Will,* written in 395. Aquinas surely believed this line of thinking was sound.[23] One modern proponent of the argument is philosopher Gordon H. Clark, whose presentation utilizes six steps.[24]

> (1) Truth exists.
> (2) Truth is immutable.
> (3) Truth is eternal.
> (4) Truth is mental.
> (5) Truth is superior to the human mind.
> (6) Truth is God.

23. See Thomas Aquinas *On Truth* question 1, article 2, reply.
24. For Clark's argument, see Gordon H. Clark, *A Christian View of Men and Things* (Unicoi, Tenn.: Trinity Foundation, 1989), 318–23.

(1) "Truth exists." Clark establishes this point by reminding us of the self-defeating nature of any attempt to deny the existence of truth.[25] Since skepticism is false, there must be knowledge; and if there is knowledge, there must exist the object of knowledge, namely, truth.

(2) "Truth is immutable." It is impossible for truth to change. As Clark says, "Truth must be unchangeable. What is true today always has been and always will be true."[26] For Clark, all true propositions are eternal and immutable truths, a point I have supported earlier in this book. Clark has no use for pragmatic views of truth that imply that what is true today may be false tomorrow. If truth changes, then pragmatism will be false tomorrow—if it could ever be true.

(3) "Truth is eternal." It would be self-contradictory to deny the eternity of truth. If the world will never cease to exist, it is true that the world will never cease to exist. If the world will someday perish, then that is true. But truth itself will abide even though every created thing should perish. But suppose someone asks, "What if truth itself should perish?" Then it would still be true that truth had perished. Any denial of the eternity of truth turns out to be an affirmation of its eternity.

(4) "Truth is mental." The existence of truth presupposes the existence of minds. "Without a mind, truth could not exist. The object of knowledge is a proposition, a meaning, a significance; it is a thought."[27]

For Clark, the existence of truth is incompatible with any materialistic view of humans. If the materialist admits the existence of consciousness, he regards it as an effect and not a cause. For a materialist, thoughts are always the result of bodily changes. This materialism implies that all thinking, including logical reasoning, is merely the result of mechanical necessity. But bodily changes can be neither true nor false. One set of physical motions cannot be truer than another. Therefore, if there is no mind, there can be no truth; and if there is no truth, materialism cannot be true. Likewise, if there is no mind, there can be no such thing as logical reasoning, from which it follows that no materialist can possibly provide a valid argument for his position. No reason can possibly be given to justify an acceptance of materialism. Hence, for Clark, any denial of the mental nature of truth is self-stultifying. In Clark's words,

> If a truth, a proposition, or a thought were some physical motion in the brain, no two persons could have the same thought. A physical motion is a fleeting event numerically, distinct from every other. Two persons cannot have the same motion, nor can one person have it twice. If this

---

25. As we saw in chapter 8, the claim "Truth does not exist" can be countered by asking whether the claim itself is true or false. If it is false, then truth exists; and if the claim is true, then truth exists.

26. Clark, *Christian View*, 319.

27. Ibid.

is what thought were, memory and communication would be impossible.... It is a peculiarity of mind and not of body that the past can be made present. Accordingly, if one may think the same thought, twice, truth must be mental or spiritual. Not only does [truth] defy time; it defies space as well, for if communication is to be possible, the identical truth must be in two minds at once. If, in opposition, anyone wished to deny that an immaterial idea can exist in two minds at once, his denial must be conceived to exist in his own mind only; and since it has not registered in any other mind, it does not occur to us to refute it.[28]

To summarize Clark's argument thus far, truth exists and is both eternal and immutable. Further, truth can exist only in some mind.

(5) "Truth is superior to the human mind." By this Clark means that by its nature, truth cannot be subjective and individualistic. Humans know certain truths that are not only necessary but also universal. While these truths are immutable, the human mind is changeable. Even though beliefs vary from one person to another, truth itself cannot change. Moreover, the human mind does not stand in judgment of truth; rather truth judges our reason.[29] While we often judge other human minds (as when we say, for example, that someone's mind is not as keen as it should be), we do not judge truth. If truth and the human mind were equal, truth could not be eternal and immutable since the human mind is finite, mutable, and subject to error. Therefore, truth must transcend human reason; truth must be superior to any individual human mind as well as to the sum total of human minds. From this it follows that there must be a mind higher than the human mind in which truth resides.

(6) "Truth is God." There must be an ontological ground for truth. But the ground of truth cannot be anything perishable or contingent. Since truth is eternal and immutable, it must exist in an eternal and immutable Mind. And since only God possesses these attributes, God must be truth. Is all this any more than the assertion that there is an eternal, immutable Mind, a supreme Reason, a personal, living God? The truths or propositions that may be known are the thoughts of God, the eternal thoughts of God.[30]

Recent Advances in Science

I move now to a discussion of recent scientific discoveries that seem to offer support for belief in God. The two lines of argument that arise out of these discoveries end up as highly advanced and sophisticated ver-

---

28. Ibid., 319–20.

29. For the source of this view, see Augustine's *On the Teacher* as well as his *On True Religion.* For an exposition of the extremely important but tricky argument of Augustine's *On the Teacher,* see Ronald H. Nash, *The Light of the Mind: St. Augustine's Theory of Knowledge* (Lexington, Ky.: University Press of Kentucky, 1969), chap. 6. The book is available from Books on Demand in Ann Arbor, Michigan.

30. Clark, *Christian View,* 321.

sions of the design argument. The reason this information was not available until recently was the development of technology that provided information about living cells and information about DNA's genetic code. This technology includes the electron microscope, x-ray crystallography, and nuclear magnetic resonance. The first type of argument we'll examine explains how a living human being contains a number of molecular machines that are examples of irreducible complexity. According to the second type of argument, the genetic code of DNA contains an embedded language representing a specified complexity.

Two Kinds of Order

Earlier in the chapter, I discussed the important difference between scientific and personal explanations. It is now important to draw a distinction between two kinds of order in the universe. The first kind of order results from the nature of the material of which a thing is made. An example is a snowflake. The order represented by a snowflake does not entail the existence of intelligent Cause. The second kind of order does not arise from a natural set of causes. It entails the existence of an intelligent cause.

In Arches National Park in the state of Utah, there is a rock formation that resembles a sheep.[31] The resemblance is so uncanny that some might regard it as the work of a brilliant sculptor. But once we examine the rock, we see that it is a product of natural erosion. As Walter Bradley and Charles Thaxton explain, "The formation may look as though it was deliberately carved. But on closer inspection, say from a different angle, you notice that the resemblance is only superficial. The shape invariably accords with what erosion can do as it acts on the natural qualities of the rock (soft parts worn away, hard parts protruding). You therefore conclude that the rock formed naturally. Natural forces suffice to account for the shape you see."[32]

The second type of order, the kind that requires an intelligent cause, is represented by the faces on Mount Rushmore.[33] As the authors explain, "The angles of the four faces on the granite cliff do not follow the natural composition of the rock; the chip marks cut across both hard and soft sections. These shapes do not resemble anything you have seen resulting from erosion. In this case the shape of the rock is not the result of natural processes. Rather, you infer from uniform experience that an

---

31. For readers who have not been to Arches, you may view this rock formation at the beginning of the movie *Indiana Jones and the Last Crusade*.

32. Walter L. Bradley and Charles B. Thaxton, "Information and the Origin of Life," in *The Creation Hypothesis: Scientific Evidence for an Intelligent Designer*, ed. J. P. Moreland (Downers Grove, Ill.: InterVarsity Press, 1994), 204.

33. To conclude our trip through movie history, see the end to the Cary Grant film *North by Northwest*.

artisan has been at work. The four faces were intelligently imposed onto the rock material."[34]

Once the difference between these two kinds of order is understood, the distinction between natural and intelligently imposed order is obvious. If the only kind of order we discovered in the universe were natural order, we would be justified in saying that the sufficient reason for this order is natural causes; no intelligent cause is necessary. A scientific explanation is sufficient; there is no need for personal explanation.

But what do we do if and when we encounter the second kind of order, that which points to the existence of intelligence? When science provides us with evidence of this second kind of order, it in effect points to the need for a personal explanation, an intelligence beyond the physical world.

A Comment About Darwinism

An inverse relationship exists between these new types of scientific arguments and the fortunes of Darwinian evolution. As the fortunes of these arguments rise, the prospects of Darwinism decline.

The evolutionary changes so basic to Darwin's theory resulted from random genetic mutations. When such mutations increased an organism's ability to survive, the gene pool responsible for the sudden mutation was passed on to succeeding generations, which presumably enhanced their carriers' ability to survive. This feature of the theory is often discussed under the label of the survival of the fittest.[35] Under the terms of this theory, the changes appeared and took hold in the genetic makeup of subsequent representatives of the life form very gradually. In this connection, Darwin himself made a damaging admission: "If it could be demonstrated," he wrote, "that any complex organ existed which could not possibly have been formed by numerous, successive, slight modifications, my theory would absolutely break down."[36]

The Black Box of the Human Cell

In 1996, Michael J. Behe, a professor of biochemistry at Lehigh University, published a book titled *Darwin's Black Box: The Biochemical Challenge to Evolution.*[37] As Behe explains, his use of the whimsical expression "black box" means

> a device that does something, but whose inner workings are mysterious—sometimes because the workings can't be seen, and sometimes

---

34. Bradley and Thaxton, "Information and the Origin of Life," 204.

35. See Charles Darwin, *The Origin of Species,* 6th ed. (New York: New York University Press, 1988). The first edition of Darwin's work appeared in 1859.

36. Darwin, *Origin of Species,* quoted by Tom Woodward, "Meeting Darwin's Wager," *Christianity Today,* April 28, 1997, 15.

37. (New York: Free Press, 1996).

because they just aren't comprehensible. Computers are a good example of a black box. Most of us use these marvelous machines without the vaguest idea of how they work, processing words or plotting graphs or playing games in contended ignorance of what is going on underneath the outer case.... There is no simple, observable connection between the parts of the computer and the things that it does.[38]

In the case of Behe's book, the immediate referent of "black box" is the human cell, the basic building block of a human being. When Darwin developed his theory, scientists understood very little about the cell. It was a black box.[39] We now know how the cell functions at the level of molecules. Most importantly, the cell contains many irreducibly complex systems. When we look at the cell, all manner of evidence supports the conclusion that cellular systems were the result of intelligent design. Why are Darwin's contemporary disciples so stubbornly silent about these cellular systems?

The processes of life within a cell are made possible by machines composed of molecules. According to Behe, "Molecular machines haul cargo from one place to another in the cell along 'highways' made of other molecules, while still others act as cables, ropes, and pulleys to hold the cell in shape. Machines turn cellular switches on and off, sometimes killing the cell or causing it to grow.... Manufacturing machines build other molecular machines as well as themselves. Cells swim using machines, copy themselves with machinery, ingest food with machinery."[40] Every process occurring in a cell is controlled by complex and sophisticated molecular machines. In the words of Nancy Pearcey, "Such structures cannot have emerged gradually by any conceivable Darwinian process."[41]

Behe's Notion of Irreducible Complexity

The key to Behe's argument lies in his notion of what he calls an irreducibly complex system. He explains his point: "By irreducibly complex I mean a simple system composed of several well-matched, interacting parts that contribute to the basic function wherein the removal of any one of the parts causes the system to effectively cease functioning."[42] Behe offers a helpful example of an irreducible complexity, a mousetrap.

A mousetrap contains five essential parts: a wooden base, a holding bar, a spring, a hammer bar, and a catch. All of them must work together in

---

38. Ibid., 6.

39. Even today, the best light microscopes leave us without access to the specifics of cellular structure. It is easy to appreciate the handicaps under which Darwin did his theorizing.

40. Behe, *Darwin's Black Box,* 4–5.

41. Nancy R. Pearcey, "The Evolution Backlash," *World,* March 1, 1997, 14.

42. Behe, *Darwin's Black Box,* 39.

order to catch a mouse. If just one of these parts is missing, the mousetrap cannot do its job. In the case of an irreducibly complex machine, all parts must be present. Imagine a person who gathers the various parts of a mousetrap and first attempts to catch the mouse using only the wood base. When he fails, he then tries to catch a mouse by placing the spring on top of the base; and so on. Obviously, the mousetrap must be completely assembled before it can work. A mousetrap cannot come into existence over a long period of time as a result of tiny changes in a series of predecessors. It must be assembled with all of its components as part of the system.

Behe then takes his reader on a tour through the cell, noting various irreducibly complex systems. Behe utilizes five organic systems to illustrate his notion of irreducible complexity: the cilium that allows some cells to swim, blood coagulation, the transport system between cells, antibodies, and the immune system.[43] In no case would the gradual steps of Darwinian evolution be sufficient to produce one of these instances of irreducible complexity. Irreducibly complex molecular machines cannot be explained by random mutation and natural selection. They cannot evolve via small, gradual steps. As Behe explains, "For all the advances in modern science, no single discovery can give a detailed account of how the cilium, or vision, or blood clotting, or any complex biochemical process might have developed in a Darwinian fashion. . . . If something was not put together gradually, then it must have been put together quickly or even suddenly."[44] Living organisms clearly manifest signs of design that cannot be explained by Darwinism. The Achilles' heel of Darwinism lies in such details as metabolic pathways, function, and structure.

The example I will focus on is a cilium, a whiplike structure that allows cells to swim (as in the case of sperm) or to move something past a stationary cell (as in the case of respiratory cells). Without its motors, connectors, and microtubules, a cilium cannot move. A cilium is an irreducibly complex machine.[45]

A second example of irreducible complexity within a cell is vesicular transport. Without all components of this second irreducibly complex system, two bad things would happen: either the proteins would be moved to places where they are not needed, or they would get to the right place but could not enter the targeted destination. As noted earlier, Darwin admitted that his theories would be in trouble if they could not explain macrophenomena. Little did he realize that his theory would be devastated by its inability to explain microphenomena, such as those noted.

---

43. These five examples only scratch the surface.

44. Behe, *Darwin's Black Box,* 187.

45. For more information, see Behe, *Darwin's Black Box,* 65–66, or a standard biochemistry textbook.

It is impossible to get by a series of slight changes from a slightly different system thought to exist earlier in a presumed sequence to an irreducibly complex system. If some imagined precursor lacked even one part of the functioning system, it could not function. There is no gradual way to produce the parts of the irreducibly complex system. If there are no Darwinian pathways for systems like cilia or blood coagulation, they could not have come about as a result of mutations affected by subsequent natural selection. They must have been made as integrated units and this points to design. At the molecular level, Darwinism fails.

Information Systems and the Cell

Behe's information about the irreducibly complex machines in the cell counts as one example of intelligent order. Possibly an even more impressive example of a sign of intelligent order in the human cell is the information stored in DNA within the cell, without which life could not exist and development could not occur. The answer to the origin and development of life lies within the components of the cell. In the last two decades, a number of scientists have described DNA[46] as an information system that is part of a biological structure. In the words of Pearcey and Thaxton, "The DNA molecule functions as a code, and it is best explained using concepts borrowed from modern communications theory."[47]

The explanation of the structure of DNA and the discovery of the genetic code mark a great leap forward in our understanding of living systems. The DNA molecule guides human development from the single cell to adulthood. DNA determines all of our physical features. The DNA molecule is often pictured like a long ladder twisted into a spiral shape. The sides of the ladder are composed of sugar and phosphate molecules. The rungs of the ladder contain four bases[48] that function like the letters of a genetic alphabet. These bases join in different sequences to form the chemical equivalent of words, sentences, and paragraphs. Such sequences provide the instruction necessary to direct how the cell functions.[49]

According to Bradley and Thaxton,

Molecular biology has uncovered an analogy between DNA and language, giving rise to the *sequence hypothesis*. The sequence hypothesis assumes that an exact order of symbols records information. The base

---

46. DNA is shorthand for deoxyribonucleic acid.

47. Nancy R. Pearcey and Charles B. Thaxton, *The Soul of Science: Christian Faith and Natural Philosophy* (Wheaton, Ill.: Crossway, 1994), 221–22.

48. These bases are adenine, thymine, guanine, and cystosine.

49. See Bradley and Thaxton, "Information and the Origin of Life," 205. On the same page the authors state that "There exists a structural identity between the base sequences in a DNA message and the alphabetical letter sequences in a written message, and this assures us that the analogy is 'very close and striking'.... This structural identity is the basis for the application of information theory to biology."

sequences in DNA spell out in coded form the instructions for how a cell makes proteins, for example. It works just the way alphabetical letter sequences do in this article to give information about origins. The genetic code functions exactly like a language code—indeed it *is* a code. It is a molecular communications system: a sequence of chemical "letters" stores and transmits the communication in each living cell.[50]

Pearcey and Thaxton explain that "when you think that sophisticated modern computers operate on a two-symbol code (a binary code), it is obvious that the four-symbol code in DNA is quite adequate to carry any amount of complex information. In fact, the amount of information contained in a single human cell equals the entire thirty volumes of the *Encyclopedia Britannica* several times over."[51]

When any of us encounter written messages, we have no difficulty recognizing they result from an intelligent cause. It is understandable why we see how the information sequences in DNA also result from an intelligent cause. "Since DNA is an essential molecular component of every form of life we know, we likewise conclude that life on earth had an intelligent cause."[52]

So we have learned that DNA carries genetic messages, that life is a chemical message system, and that the answer to the mystery of the origin of life is tied necessarily to the origin of information. "If we want to speculate on how the first informational molecules came into being, the most reasonable speculation is there was some form of intelligence around at the time. We cannot identify that source any further from a scientific analysis alone. Science cannot supply a name for that intelligent cause."[53]

What we have been examining in this chapter are powerful updatings of the design argument. Just as it is impossible to believe the faces carved into Mount Rushmore are a result of natural causes only, DNA and the irreducibly complex machines necessary for the operation of the cell contain obvious signs of intelligent workmanship.

---

50. Ibid. Robert Pollack, a professor of biological science at Columbia University, compares the human genome to an encyclopedia. "Like any proper encyclopedia, a human genome is divided and subdivided into volumes, articles, sentences, and words. And, as in an encyclopedia written in English or Hebrew ... words are further divided into letters." Robert Pollack, *Signs of Life: The Language and Meanings of DNA* (Boston: Houghton Mifflin, 1994), 19.

51. Pearcey and Thaxton, *The Soul of Science*, 225, 227. "If the amount of information contained in one cell in your body were written out on a typewriter, it would fill as many books as are contained in a large library." Percival Davis and Dean H. Kenyon, *Pandas and People* (Dallas: Haughton Publishing Co., 1989), 7.

52. Bradley and Thaxton, "Information and the Origin of Life," 206.

53. Ibid., 209.

OPTIONAL WRITTEN ASSIGNMENT

Read Behe's book and write a short essay explaining his basic thesis to a friend unfamiliar with his book.

FOR FURTHER READING

Michael J. Behe, *Darwin's Black Box: The Biochemical Challenge to Evolution* (New York: Free Press, 1996).

William L. Bradley and Charles B. Thaxton, "Information and the Origin of Life," in *The Creation Hypothesis: Scientific Evidence for an Intelligent Designer,* ed. J. P. Moreland (Downers Grove, Ill.: InterVarsity Press, 1994), 173–210.

Werner Gitt, *In the Beginning Was Information,* trans. Jaap Kies (Bielefeld, Germany: Christliche Literatur—Verbeitung e.V., 1997).

F. Hoyle, *The Intelligent Universe* (London: Michael Joseph, 1983).

Phillip E. Johnson, *Defeating Darwinism by Opening Minds* (Downers Grove, Ill.: InterVarsity Press, 1997).

B. O. Kuppers, *Information and the Origin of Life* (Cambridge, Mass.: MIT Press, 1990).

J. P. Moreland, ed., *The Creation Hypothesis: Scientific Evidence for an Intelligent Designer* (Downers Grove, Ill.: InterVarsity Press, 1994).

Ronald H. Nash, *Faith and Reason* (Grand Rapids: Zondervan, 1988).

Nancy R. Pearcey and Charles B. Thaxton, *The Soul of Science: Christian Faith and Natural Philosophy* (Wheaton, Ill.: Crossway, 1994).

Robert Pollack, *Signs of Life: The Language and Meanings of DNA* (Boston: Houghton Mifflin, 1994).

Chapter Fourteen

God II:
The Nature of God

Even though I wish I had more time to discuss the existence and nature of God, it is not as though other chapters in the book have ignored the most important component of any person's worldview. My objective in this chapter is to offer examples of philosophical thinking about the nature of God, that is, about some of God's essential properties. Which attributes of God will be examined? I've selected two: God's omnipotence (power) and omniscience (knowledge).

Divine Omnipotence: Can God Do Absolutely Anything?

No less a philosopher than Thomas Aquinas (1225–1274) acknowledged difficulty in comprehending God's power. Thomas wrote that while "all confess that God is omnipotent . . . it seems difficult to explain in what His omnipotence precisely consists."[1] British philosopher Anthony Kenny concurs: "It is by no means easy to state concisely and coherently what is meant by 'omnipotence.'"[2]

Some people believe that any limitations, logical or otherwise, upon the power of God seriously undermine the historic Christian belief that God is omnipotent. This explains why many people think that divine omnipotence means God can do absolutely anything. But if there is anything to be learned from the classical Christian discussions of omnipotence, it is that omnipotence was always understood to be compatible with certain limitations upon God's power. There are certain things that even an omnipotent God cannot do.

Medieval theologians drew attention to some fairly trivial examples of restrictions upon the power of God. How could God be called omnipotent, for example, when he could not do some things that his creatures could do, such as walk, sit, or swim? The standard scholastic answer suggested that such creaturely acts did not mean that humans possessed

---

1. Thomas Aquinas *Summa Theologica,* trans. the Fathers of the English Dominican Province (New York: Benziger Brothers, 1947), 1:137. This and all other quotations from Aquinas in this chapter are from part 1, question 25, articles 3 and 4 of the *Summa.*
2. Anthony Kenny, *The God of the Philosophers* (Oxford: Clarendon, 1979), 91.

powers not possessed by God. Rather, human acts such as walking and sitting were possible because of a defect in human power. The ability to sin, for example, is not a power but a defect or an infirmity. The ability to walk results from having a body—in their view, also a defect. As the discussion of omnipotence progressed through the Middle Ages, Christian philosophers came to qualify the statement "God can do anything" by adding "that implies the perfection of true power." As Aquinas phrased it, "God is said to be omnipotent in respect to active power, not to passive power."

Omnipotence and the Laws of Logic

This might be a good time to reread the discussion of possible worlds in chapter 9. In that chapter, I distinguished between physical and logical possibility. If something is physically impossible, no human can perform that act in the real world, even though he might be able to do so in some other possible world. But if something is logically impossible, then it cannot be done in any possible world. Something is logically possible if its description does not violate the law of noncontradiction. Something is physically possible if some human has done it in the real world.

Most Christian thinkers have followed Aquinas in holding that logical consistency, not merely physical possibility, is a necessary condition for divine omnipotence.[3] In the case of physical possibility, something is possible for any being if he possesses the power to do it. If someone has the power to lift three hundred pounds or hit seventy home runs in one season, then those acts are physically possible for that person. Some acts, like running a mile in thirty seconds or swimming across the Atlantic, do not appear to be physically possible for any human being. Aquinas realized that nothing can be gained from analyzing divine omnipotence in terms of physical possibility. In his words, if "we were to say that God is omnipotent because He can do all things that are possible to His power, there would be a vicious circle in explaining the nature of His power. For this would be saying nothing else but that God is omnipotent because he can do all that He is able to do." Obviously, a statement like "God can do whatever God can do" is neither informative nor enlightening.

The more promising approach to an explanation of divine omnipotence, Aquinas thought, lies in the second type of possibility, logical possibility. Something is possible in the logical sense if it does not violate the law of noncontradiction. As Aquinas put it, "Everything that does not imply a contradiction is numbered among those possibles in respect of which God is called omnipotent; whereas whatever implies a contradiction does not come within the scope of divine omnipotence, because it

---

3. Aquinas *Summa Theologica* 1.25.3.

cannot have the aspect of possibility. Hence it is more appropriate to say that such things cannot be done, than that God cannot do them." Any act that is logically impossible must also be physically impossible. Squaring the circle is both logically and physically impossible. Aquinas denied that the exclusion of logically impossible acts from the sphere of divine power constituted any limitation on God's power. He regarded logically impossible tasks as pseudotasks. A being's inability to perform a pseudotask (for example, creating a square circle) cannot count against its power. Thus logical possibility, as Aquinas saw it, is a necessary though not a sufficient condition for any exercise of God's power.

René Descartes (1596–1650) and a few other philosophers have rejected the view that God's power is limited by the law of noncontradiction. Of course, language about limiting God is off the mark and indicates a serious misunderstanding of God's relationship to the laws of logic, which reflect the rationality of God's mind. Descartes believed that an omnipotent being could do anything, including that which is self-contradictory: God's actions are not limited by the laws of logic. Descartes advanced this view on the conviction, apparently, that the Thomist position dishonors God by making him subject to a law (the law of noncontradiction) that Descartes believed is as dependent on God's will as any law of physics or biology.[4] Just as God could have created the world so that it was governed by different laws of nature, so also he could have subjected the world to different logical and mathematical laws. According to Descartes, God freely decreed the logical and mathematical truths that obtain in our world (the real world for readers who remember the discussion in chapter 9 of possible worlds) and could have created a different world in which the principle of noncontradiction or propositions like "two plus two equals four" were necessarily false. Obviously, I disagree.

The first thing that should be noted about Descartes's position is that it is unassailable. Since any sound argument or refutation must begin by presupposing certain rules, it is impossible to argue against someone who rejects the most fundamental rules of reasoning. British philosopher J. L. Mackie observed that anyone holding Descartes's view

> need never be disturbed by any reasoning or evidence, for if his omnipotent being could do what is logically impossible, he could certainly exist, and have any desired attributes, in defiance of every sort of contrary consideration. The view that there is an absolutely omnipotent being in this sense stands, therefore, right outside the realm of rational enquiry and

René Descartes

Lithograph after
Frans Hals

THE GRANGER COLLECTION,
NEW YORK

---

4. In our own day, a position similar to this seems to have been held by the Dutch philosopher Herman Dooyeweerd. See Ronald H. Nash, *The Word of God and the Mind of Man* (Phillipsburg, N.J.: Presbyterian and Reformed, 1992), chap. 9.

discussion; once held, it is so unassailable that it is a waste of time to consider it further.[5]

It is unlikely, therefore, that committed believers in Descartes's position will be persuaded by any argument. Still, several points are worth making. Those who affirm that God can do anything and who also accept the authority of Scripture must deal with Scripture's own assertions that there are things God "cannot" do. As we saw earlier, God cannot lie or swear by a being greater than himself (Hebrews 6:18, 13). Scripture does not view the power of God as the unqualified ability to do absolutely anything. The catch is that such an *ad hominem* argument only points out an inconsistency in those who believe that God can do absolutely anything and who also believe the Scriptures are true. A determined irrationalist may reply that since logical inconsistency does not bother God, it does not trouble him either.

Several philosophers and theologians have pointed out the absurdity of regarding a self-contradictory description as *some thing*. British philosopher Richard Swinburne, for example, argues that those who think a truly omnipotent being ought to be able to do the logically impossible err because they regard

> a logically impossible action as an action of one kind on a par with an action of another kind, the physically impossible. But it is not. A logically impossible action is not an action. It is what is described by a form of words which purport to describe an action, but do not describe anything which it is coherent to suppose could be done. It is no objection to A's omnipotence that he cannot make a square circle. This is because "making a square circle" does not describe anything which it is coherent to suppose could be done.[6]

Mackie, hardly a friend of theism, agrees that nothing in this problem should count against the coherence of the attribute of omnipotence or the plausibility of theism:

> A logical contradiction is not a state of affairs which it is supremely difficult to produce, but only a form of words which fails to describe any state of affairs. So to say, as we are now saying, that "God is omnipotent" means "God can do or make to be X, for any X, provided that doing X or making X to be is not logically impossible" would be to say that if God is omnipotent every coherently describable activity or production is within his power.[7]

A logical contradiction can at most describe a pseudotask. And God's inability to perform a pseudotask, such as squaring the circle, cannot

---

5. J. L. Mackie, "Omnipotence," *Sophia* 1 (1962): 16.

6. Richard Swinburne, *The Coherence of Theism* (Oxford: Clarendon, 1977), 149.

7. Mackie, "Omnipotence," 16.

count against his omnipotence. As Aquinas noted, it is better to state that such pseudotasks cannot be done than to say that God cannot do them.

A supralogical God would be unknowable and unintelligible. Whatever God's relation to the laws of logic may be, it is clear that all human thinking and communication must presuppose the law of noncontradiction. "As we cannot say how a nonlogical world would look, we cannot say how a supralogical God would act or how He would communicate anything to us by way of revelation."[8] This is only a sample of the absurdities that defenders of a supralogical God must be prepared to accept.

The Paradox of Omnipotence

Philosophers and theologians who grant that God cannot do the logically impossible point out that other actions attributable to God threaten the coherence of the concept of omnipotence. Even if one grants that Aquinas was right when he said that God cannot do the logically impossible, that answer does not seem applicable to the problems that arise when we ask if God can create a stone too heavy for God to lift. The action of creating a stone too heavy to lift does not appear self-contradictory in the same way as drawing a square circle is self-contradictory. Questions about God's ability to perform actions like creating a stone too heavy for him to lift pose the theist with a dilemma. If God can create the stone too heavy for God to lift, there is something God cannot do, namely, lift the stone. And if God cannot create the stone too heavy for him to lift, there is still something he cannot do (in this case, create the stone). Either God can or cannot create such a stone. Therefore, in either case, there is something God cannot do; and in either case, we seem forced to conclude that God is not omnipotent.

In a widely discussed analysis of the paradox, philosopher George Mavrodes argues that Aquinas's original point about logical possibility can be applied to the new puzzle of the stone.[9] Mavrodes points out that in order for the critic's conclusion to follow, one must first assume that God is omnipotent. If God is not omnipotent, there is no puzzle, since the phrase "a stone too heavy for God to lift" would in all likelihood not be self-contradictory. If the argument begins by assuming that God is not omnipotent, the conclusion ("God is not omnipotent") would only repeat the beginning assumption, thus making the argument trivial. Thus the paradox of omnipotence must begin by presupposing that God is omnipotent. Once the assumption is made, however, Aquinas's argument becomes relevant. Once one grants that "God is omnipotent" is neces-

8. Peter Geach, *Providence and Evil* (New York: Cambridge University Press, 1977), 11.
9. George Mavrodes, "Some Puzzles Concerning Omnipotence," *The Philosophical Review* 72 (1963): 221–23.

sarily true (true in all possible worlds), it follows that "God cannot create a stone too heavy for God to lift" becomes a contradiction. Mavrodes concludes that the paradoxes of omnipotence fail "because they propose, as tests of God's power, putative tasks whose descriptions are self-contradictory. Such pseudo-tasks, not falling within the realm of possibility, are not objects of power at all. Hence the fact that they cannot be performed implies no limit on the power of God, and hence no defect in the doctrine of omnipotence."[10]

In a subsequent article, Harry Frankfurt sought to defuse a possible objection to Mavrodes from any critic who, like Descartes, should reject the law of noncontradiction as a delimitation of the power of God. As Frankfurt notes, even if the follower of Descartes is correct and the law of noncontradiction does not define the limits of God's power, nothing very significant follows. In fact, we only have a new way of resolving the paradox of omnipotence.

> Suppose, then, that God's omnipotence enables Him to do even what is logically impossible and that He actually creates a stone too heavy for Him to lift. The critic plays into his hands.... For why should God not be able to perform the task in question? To be sure, it is a task—the task of lifting a stone which he cannot lift—whose description is self-contradictory. But if God is supposed capable of performing one task whose description is self-contradictory—that of creating the problematic stone in the first place—why should He not be supposed capable of performing another—that of lifting the stone? After all, is there any greater trick in performing two logically impossible tasks than there is in performing one? If an omnipotent being can do what is logically impossible, then he can not only create situations which he cannot handle but also, since he is not bound by the limits of consistency, he can handle situations which he cannot handle.[11]

Suppose a theologian concludes, however, that the question Can God create a stone too heavy for God to lift? must be answered in the negative.[12] Suppose this theologian figures something in the doctrine of omnipotence must be given up but wants to surrender as little as possible. Could God's infinite power with regard to lifting be retained while limiting only slightly God's power with respect to creating? Following an example developed by C. Wade Savage, we might imagine one being (y) who cannot lift a stone heavier than seventy pounds. If some other being (x) cannot create a stone heavier than y can lift, then obviously x's power

---

10. Ibid., 223.

11. Harry G. Frankfurt, "The Logic of Omnipotence," *The Philosophical Review* 74 (1964): 263.

12. The discussion in this paragraph follows C. Wade Savage's "The Paradox of the Stone," *The Philosophical Review* 76 (1967): 74–79.

to create is limited. But suppose that y can lift a stone of any weight; in other words, imagine that y's lifting power is unlimited. Then it follows that if x cannot create a stone too heavy for y to lift, x's power to create is not limited. What then has our theologian surrendered?

> Is it the unlimited power of God to create stones? No doubt. But what stone is it which God is now precluded from creating? The stone too heavy for Him to lift, of course. But ... nothing in the argument required the theologian to admit any limit on God's power with regard to the lifting of stones. He still holds that to be unlimited. And if God's power to lift is infinite, then His power to create may run to infinity also without outstripping the first power. The supposed limitation turns out to be no limitation at all, since it is specified only by reference to another power which is itself infinite. Our theologian need have no regrets, for he has given up nothing. The doctrine of the power of God remains just what it was before.[13]

It seems clear then that the so-called paradoxes of omnipotence can be handled in the same general terms as Aquinas's dictum that omnipotence does not extend to things that are logically impossible.

Can God Sin?

The discussion about the relationship between omnipotence and logic makes it clear that omnipotence does not include the ability to do everything. There are limits even to what an omnipotent being can do. Some medieval thinkers raised another possible problem with respect to omnipotence. They wondered if God can sin. Suppose we grant that an omnipotent God can do anything that is logically possible. Sinning is an act that is both logically and physically possible; humans do it all the time. How then can God be omnipotent if he cannot sin? Both Anselm (1033–1109) and Aquinas appear to have advanced similar answers to the question. "But how art Thou omnipotent," Anselm asked,

> if Thou art not capable of all things? or, if Thou canst not be corrupted and canst not lie.... how art Thou capable of all things? Or else to be capable of these things is not power but impotence. For he who is capable of those things is capable of what is not for his good, and of what he ought not to do; and the more capable of them he is, the more power have adversity and perversity against him; and the less has he himself against these.[14]

Anselm thought the question important because the claim that God cannot sin appears to be incompatible with the assertion of his omnipotence. Anselm's suggested solution pointed out that the ability to sin

13. Mavrodes, "Some Puzzles Concerning Omnipotence," 223.

14. Anselm *Proslogium* 7, cited from S. N. Deane, *St. Anselm* (La Salle, Ill.: Open Court, 1958), 14.

results not from power but from a lack of power. Aquinas argued similarly that "to sin is to fall short of a perfect action; hence to be able to sin is to be able to fall short in action, which is repugnant to omnipotence. Therefore, it is that God cannot sin, because of his omnipotence."[15]

The point Anselm and Aquinas were trying to make is elusive and requires some effort to grasp. Some progress toward understanding their position may be gained by studying the more detailed discussion of the eighteenth-century theologian Samuel Clarke (1675–1729). Clarke began by acknowledging that God "must of necessity have infinite power. This proposition is evident and undeniable."[16] Since God's infinite power cannot be denied, "the only question is, what the true meaning of what we call infinite power is, and to what things it must be understood to extend, or not to extend." Clarke regards it as beyond dispute that God's infinite power "cannot be said to extend to the working of anything which implies a *contradiction*: as that a thing should be and not be at the same time; that the same thing should be made and not be made, or have been and not have been; that twice two should not make four, or that that which is necessarily false should be true." Clarke's acceptance of the scholastic point that God's omnipotence does not extend to contradiction is based on the same reason given by Aquinas: since a contradiction is nothing, the putative power to do nothing turns out to be no power.

Clarke then notes a second restriction on God's infinite power. "Infinite power cannot be said to extend to those things which imply *natural* imperfection in the being to whom such power as ascribed." He regards it as absurd, for example, to think that a being of infinite power could use that power to weaken itself or destroy itself. Weakness or self-destruction are universally recognized to be inconsistent with the necessary and self-existent being of God. Clark then lays the foundation for his answer to the question Can God sin? Moral imperfection is a species of natural imperfection. Once it is agreed that an omnipotent God cannot do anything that implies any natural imperfection in his own being, it follows that God cannot do anything that entails moral imperfection. Because infinite knowledge, infinite power, and infinite goodness are perfectly conjoined in the being of God, Clarke argues that creative power and moral strength are distinguishable in God's creatures. If we suppose an omnipotent being (possessing total creative power) who lacks moral perfection, such a being would lack something if it could not sin. But in God's case, the inability to sin does not constitute an imperfection. Rather, it would be an imperfection if God could sin.

---

15. Aquinas *Summa Theologica* 1.25.3.

16. Samuel Clarke, *A Discourse Concerning the Being and Attributes of God* (London: John and Paul Knapton, 1738), proposition 10.

The reason God cannot sin is because he is omnipotent and because his omnipotence is necessarily conjoined with moral perfection. If God did sin, it would prove his impotence. God is capable of doing everything that is logically possible and consistent with his perfect will. As Jerome Gellman puts it, "If God is omnipotent, then He can bring about any state of affairs logically possible for an essentially perfect being to bring about."[17] "To be powerless [to avoid perversity] is to be *imperfect,* but to be unable to lie is a perfection."[18] The power to sin is the power to fall short of perfection. Since this is the opposite of omnipotence, God's inability to sin is not inconsistent with his omnipotence; rather, it is entailed by his omnipotence.

The compatibility of God's omnipotence and his inability to sin may be viewed as an extension of the claim that the law of noncontradiction is a necessary constraint on divine power. The word *God* has descriptive significance. Among other things, it includes perfect goodness. Therefore, while no logical contradiction results from ascribing a certain action like sinning to a human being, the action does become self-contradictory when it is attributed to God.

> In our civilization, and thus in our language, it would not be strictly proper to call a being "God" whose actions were not perfectly good or whose commands were not the best of moral directives. That God is good is a truth of language, and not an ethical contingency, since one of the usual *criteria* of Godhood is that the actions and commands of such a being are perfectly good.... "God is good," therefore, is trivially true in the same way as "Saints are good."[19]

No contradiction exists, therefore, between the propositions "God is omnipotent" and "God cannot sin."

Conclusion

Enough has been said to permit an answer to two questions: How should "omnipotence" be defined? Is the concept of omnipotence logically coherent?

William Rowe seems to have included the necessary qualifications when he defines "omnipotence" to mean that "God can do anything that is an absolute possibility (i.e., is logically possible) *and not inconsistent with any of his basic attributes.*"[20] Among other things, Rowe's definition

---

17. Jerome Gellman, "Omnipotence and Impeccability," *The New Scholasticism* 51 (1977): 36.

18. Ibid., 33.

19. Patterson Brown, "Religious Morality," *Mind* 72 (1963): 238.

20. William Rowe, *Philosophy of Religion: An Introduction* (Encino, Calif.: Dickenson, 1978), 9.

would rule out any problem about the possibility of God's sinning. Since "doing evil is inconsistent with being perfectly good, and since being perfectly good is a basic attribute of God, the fact that God cannot do evil will not conflict with the fact that he is omnipotent."[21] Kenny goes a bit further in his definition:

> Divine omnipotence, therefore, if it is to be a coherent notion, must be something less than the complete omnipotence which is the possession of all logically possible powers. It must be a narrower omnipotence, consisting in the possession of all logically possible powers which it is logically possible for a being with the attributes of God to possess.[22]

> It seems clear then that the concept of omnipotence is logically coherent. Even J. L. Mackie, whose opposition to theism is easily documented, acknowledges: "Once we have decided that omnipotence is not to include the power to achieve logical impossibilities—and it must not include this, if it is to be discussable—there cannot be any contradiction within the concept itself."[23] No contradiction is involved in affirming that God is essentially omnipotent.

Omniscience: Can God Know Absolutely Everything?

Theologically conservative Christians have always assumed that God has perfect knowledge about the past, present, and future. The technical word for such knowledge is *omniscience*. Suddenly, things have changed. In the last ten years or so, a number of thinkers in the Christian church have begun to deny God's perfect knowledge about the future. My objective in this section of the chapter is to examine this new development and determine whether this new way of thinking about the Christian God is defensible.

Setting Up the Problem About God's Knowledge of the Future

Divine omniscience means that God knows all true propositions and believes no false propositions. The range of God's knowledge is total. He knows all true propositions.

When any person knows something (a proposition), at least two conditions must be present. First, the person must believe the proposition in question; and second, the believed proposition must be true.[24] If Andy

---

21. Ibid.
22. Kenny, *The God of the Philosophers,* 98.
23. Mackie, "Omnipotence," 24–25.
24. While knowledge includes more than true belief, it cannot mean less. Identifying the other component(s) of knowledge has proven extremely difficult, and philosophers disagree strongly among themselves. Plato's dialogue *Theaeatetus* is helpful to read in this regard. Plato agreed that knowledge is true belief plus something else. But exactly what this something else is is difficult to say. Most of the theories that have been proposed are discussed in the first edition of Roderick Chisholm's *Theory of Knowledge* (Englewood Cliffs, N.J.: Prentice-Hall, 1966), chap. 1.

knows that today is Amanda's birthday, then Andy believes that today is Amanda's birthday. Believing a proposition is a necessary condition for knowing it. If Andy doesn't believe that today is Amanda's birthday, he cannot know it. Thus knowing a proposition implies believing it. But just as clearly, Andy cannot have knowledge of some proposition unless that proposition is true. If Andy thinks he knows p, and p is false, then his claim to knowledge is mistaken. He may think he knows today is Amanda's birthday, but he is wrong. He does not have knowledge.

If the body of true propositions known by an omniscient being includes all true propositions about what human beings will do in the future, a serious consequence for human freedom seems to arise. It is impossible for any omniscient being to hold even one false belief. Since God foreknows what Andy will do at 8:00 P.M. tomorrow, it appears as though Andy must do whatever God knows he will do; in what sense then could Andy's action be free? If God foreknows what Andy will do in the future, does Andy have the ability to do anything other than what God knows he will do? It seems highly unlikely. If Andy had the power to do something other than what God foreknows, then God could have been mistaken. God would then have held a false belief, in which case God's foreknowledge would have actually been fore-ignorance. But this is impossible. If God has true foreknowledge of what human beings will do in the future, it seems that those actions are determined. But if those actions are not determined and human beings have the power either to do something or not, then it seems to follow that God lacks omniscience.

In an earlier book, I took great pains to examine most of the major moves philosophers have made in their attempt to preserve a sphere of human freedom in the face of God's supposed perfect knowledge of what are described as future contingent events.[25] (A future contingent event is a future event that flows from human free will.) In this book, I have other objectives. For one thing, there is no need here to concede too quickly the claim that human beings possess the kind of free will that generates such anxiety in the presence of God's putative knowledge of future human conduct. It strikes me that it is far more interesting to explore what the term "free will" means and whether humans possess free will in that sense than it is to beg the question and assume that some problem exists about future free acts when it doesn't. But we'll postpone that discussion until chapter 15.

In the rest of this chapter, I am primarily interested in those religious thinkers who are so anxious to protect their view of free will that they place constraints upon the power and knowledge of God. In their view of things, if God cannot know future contingents, then the supposed

---

25. See Ronald H. Nash, *The Concept of God* (Grand Rapids: Zondervan, 1983), chap. 4.

threat divine omniscience poses for human freedom disappears. I will focus on this limitation on divine omniscience as it appears in writings of thinkers who describe their position as *open theism*.[26]

Open Theism's Attack on God's Knowledge of the Future

Five of the philosophers and theologians who seek to limit God's knowledge of certain kinds of future events are Clark Pinnock, Richard Rice, John Sanders, William Hasker, and David Basinger, all of them contributors to a book titled *The Openness of God*.[27] These authors believe it is necessary to eliminate God's knowledge of future human actions in order to preserve a sphere of human free will. Often, it seems, this belief constitutes their only reason for holding this position. Such a belief would not follow from an argument, but it is sheer dogmatism.

Clark Pinnock, a leader of open theism, does his best to make the limited God of his worldview look good: "If choices are real and freedom significant, future decisions cannot be exhaustively foreknown. This is because the future is not determinate but shaped in part by human choices. The future is not fixed like the past, which can be known completely. The future does not yet exist and therefore cannot be infallibly anticipated, even by God. Future decisions cannot in every way be foreknown, because they have not yet been made. God knows everything that can be known—but God's foreknowledge does not include the undecided."[28]

In Pinnock's view, if God had perfect knowledge of all future human decisions, they would lose significance. This is a fundamental presupposition of his open theistic worldview, and Pinnock reiterates the mantra of open theism, that divine foreknowledge "would make the future fixed and certain and render illusory the sense of our making choices between real options."[29]

Pinnock's open theism requires its adherents to alter significantly their view of God: "God," Pinnock says, "created a dynamic and changing world and enjoys getting to know it. It is a world of freedom, capable of genuine novelty, inexhaustible creativity and real surprises. I believe that God takes delight in the spontaneity of the universe and enjoys continuing to get to know it in a love that never changes."[30] Pinnock is assuming

---

26. I suppose the name is meant to suggest that given their presuppositions, the future is open rather than closed for both God and humans.

27. Clark Pinnock et al., *The Openness of God* (Downers Grove, Ill.: InterVarsity Press, 1994).

28. Clark H. Pinnock, "Systematic Theology," in *The Openness of God*, 123. Pinnock's chapter appears on pages 101–25.

29. Ibid.

30. Ibid., 124.

that a sovereign God who might have perfect knowledge of and perfect control over the world cannot love and enjoy his creation, and he shows no interest in drawing out the logical implications of a God who is capable of being surprised.

Proponents of open theism attempt to gain support for their dramatic revision of Christian thinking by claiming that their reinterpretation of divine omniscience is no more serious than the recognition in the first half of this chapter that divine omnipotence must be disengaged from logical impossibility. If the claim that God cannot do the logically impossible does not violate God's omnipotence, then their claim that God cannot know what does not yet exist does not violate God's omniscience. Just as it is no constraint upon God's power to say that he cannot do the logically impossible, so too it is no constraint upon God's knowledge to say that he cannot know what cannot be known. Unfortunately, for the open theist, the analogy fails. There are major differences in the two cases. Even if the future does not exist for humans, it hardly follows that it does not exist for God, who is an eternal being who transcends time as humans know it.[31] Moreover, while God's creating a square circle is logically impossible, God's knowing the future is not.

A Closer Look at Open Theism

I am unwilling to give open theists a victory by default on issues this important. We must ask them for some arguments. What we have instead is an unsupported claim that if God's knowledge included future human choices, then future human actions cannot be free. But throughout the history of Christianity, many Christian thinkers have rejected this entailment. There have been several attempts to show that even if God has perfect knowledge about future contingents, the human conduct in question might still be free in some sense.[32] Perhaps these attempts are unsuccessful. But until the open theist demonstrates those failures, we have to judge that he is begging one or more questions. And perhaps among the questions he is begging is the issue of human freedom. Let us not rush to judgment in all this and think that something important has been established when nothing has.

Many open theists follow a line of thinking first proposed by Aristotle. Aristotle was the first to claim, so far as we know, that propositions about the future are neither true nor false. In chapter 9 of his *De Interpretatione*, Aristotle said that any proposition about the future can be neither true nor false. Take the proposition "There will be a sea fight tomorrow." If this

---

31. My claim in this sentence is not the same as saying God is timeless. See Nash, *The Concept of God,* chap. 6.

32. For a survey of such positions, see ibid., chap. 4.

proposition about the future already has a truth value (that is, if it is either true or false today), then it seems to follow that the future is fixed. If the proposition "There will be a sea fight tomorrow" were true today, then it would be impossible for there not to be a sea fight tomorrow. For if the sea fight did not occur, then our proposition could not have been true. But since it is true, the sea fight is inevitable.

As Kenny explains, "Since many future events are not yet determined, statements about such events are not yet true or false, though they later will be."[33] The relevance of Aristotle's position for resolving the omniscience-human freedom problem should be obvious. If propositions about future, free human actions have no truth value, then they cannot be known by anyone, including an omniscient God. God's inability to know the future should not count against his omniscience, since the power to know is constrained only in cases where there is something to know. But if no propositions about future, free actions can be true, they cannot be the object of knowledge for anyone, including God. God cannot know the future because there is nothing for him to know.

The theory in question seriously limits the knowledge of God and conflicts with the Bible's account of God's ability to predict the future. If propositions about the future are neither true nor false, it is logically impossible for God to predict the future.[34] The belief that God does predict the future presumes that God knows what he is talking about. But since God does not know what cannot be known, it follows that God cannot predict the future. The most God might be able to do on Aristotle's view is make a good guess, an epistemological liability when compared with the historic Christian view about God's knowledge. The denial of truth values to propositions about future contingents has not received a sympathetic hearing from many traditional Christians. It is an extreme position that is difficult to reconcile with much that Scripture and orthodox theology affirm about God's knowledge of the future. This situation is significantly different from the logical constraint upon an exaggerated notion of divine power since in the case of omnipotence, Scripture itself recognizes the constraint.

Advocates of open theism often criticize traditional Christian thinking about God for its alleged dependence upon pagan Greek thinking. But note the irony. The accusations of a Greek influence come from people whose rejection of God's perfect knowledge of the future is based on theories borrowed from a Greek thinker, Aristotle.

When open theists deny God's future knowledge, they are not saying God is ignorant about everything in the future. God still knows that

---

33. Kenny, *The God of the Philosophers,* 52.
34. The sense of "predict" here is to foretell with absolute certainty what will happen.

the multiplication tables will be true in the future,[35] just as he knows that the law of gravity will continue to obtain. He knows what will happen if any human being steps out of a tenth-story window; he doesn't happen to know now, before the event, which human being might choose to take that walk. While I will concede these points (save the last), there are other issues where open theists attempt to have their cake and eat it too.

Conservative Christian theologian Millard Erickson, a frequent critic of open theists, sometimes gives them a free ride. Summarizing beliefs advanced by Richard Rice, a leader of open theism, Erickson explains that some in this group believe that "the future is partially definite, not totally indefinite. Many of the things that will occur in the future are the result of past and present causes. Since God knows the past and present exhaustively, he can know the things that result."[36]

While this seems acceptable, Erickson continues his summation of open theism by saying, "In addition, God knows what he is going to do in the future."[37] This claim is much more complicated than Erickson seems to realize. How can God know what he is going to do in the future, when God's own future acts are a response to future human free actions that he cannot know? In all of the open theist rhetoric, the fact that there is nothing about the future for God to know has been lost or obscured. The fact that propositions about future contingents have no truth value has been forgotten. The open theist closes the door to divine foreknowledge but then proceeds to act as though God can know things about the future after all.

Still summarizing the views of Rice,[38] Erickson writes: "Thus, the fact that [God] does not know the future in detail does not mean that he is completely ignorant of it." Something is wrong here. The detailed future about which God can have no knowledge is far more extensive than Rice and other open theists are willing to admit.

The facts are these: According to open theists, God can have no knowledge about future human contingents. Why? Because any alleged proposition about such human choices possesses no truth value; it can be neither true nor false. God cannot know these things because there is nothing to know. There is something seriously wrong, then, when an open theist begins to suggest that his constraints upon divine knowledge are not as severe as some might think. Either God knows future contin-

---

35. However, if our open theist also happens to be a postmodernist, he might be less confident about God's future knowledge about the multiplication tables.

36. Millard J. Erickson, *The Evangelical Left* (Grand Rapids: Baker, 1997), 97.

37. Ibid.

38. See Richard Rice, *God's Foreknowledge and Man's Free Will* (Minneapolis: Bethany, 1985), 50–60. I am following Erickson's summary of Rice's beliefs because it is more compact and easy to use than are Rice's statements.

gents or he doesn't. If he doesn't, then any part of the future resulting from human free choices is also closed to God. Either God knows future contingents or he doesn't. If he knows as few as one future contingent, then the door is open for him to know more; perhaps it is open wide enough for God to know all future contingents. My advice to open theists is please don't cheat and talk in ways that suggest God can know some future contingents.

Erickson continues his summary of Rice's views: "In addition, [God] knows the range of possibilities of a person's actions, and what will be the consequences of each of these possibilities."[39] I am not confident that the God of open theism can know the possibilities of human future actions along with the consequences of those actions. Let me explain why.

Can the God of Open Theism Know What Future Human Beings Will Exist and What They Will Do?

Keep in mind that we are dealing with a theological system that says future human free actions cannot be the object of God's knowledge. It is not my fault that open theists cannot or do not wish to see the logical implications of their position. So let us do their job for them.

Reflect just a bit—perhaps not too much and not too long—upon the act of human procreation. Most of us tend to believe that participation in the act of procreation within marriage includes some decision making, some acts of free will.[40] Since this is so, then all future instances of human procreation count as future contingencies.[41] That means that propositions about those future acts are neither true nor false, and this means that no one, including God, can have any knowledge about either those future activities or their consequences. Even the God of open theism knows that if a man and woman have sex at the right time, a child will be conceived. But open theists concede that God does not and cannot know which women will marry which men. God can guess, especially in the case of a wedding that is occurring in God's present experience.

As support for my claims in this part of my argument, consider the following statements by open theist David Basinger:

God does know all that will follow deterministically from what has occurred [in the past], and can, as the ultimate psychoanalyst, predict with great accuracy what we as humans will freely choose to do in various contexts. God, for instance, might well be able to predict with great

---

39. Ibid.

40. Any supposed counterexample can be handled with a little thought. A person being raped is not a voluntary participant. But the rapist is.

41. I believe the force of my argument is just as devastating for the open theist if we change the word *all* to "many" or "most."

accuracy whether a couple would have a successful marriage. But since we believe that God can know only what can be known and that what humans will freely do in the future cannot be known before hand, we believe that God can never know with certainty what will happen in any context involving freedom of choice. We believe, for example, that to the extent that freedom of choice would be involved, God would not necessarily know before hand[42] what would happen if a couple were to marry. Accordingly, we must acknowledge that divine guidance, from our perspective, cannot be considered a means of discovering exactly what will be best in the long run—as a means of discovering the very best long-term option. Divine guidance, rather, must be viewed primarily as a means of determining what is best for us now [in the present].[43]

Basinger even admits that his God "can be positively wrong."[44]

Because putative knowledge of future humans is an example of future contingency, and since the God of open theism cannot have knowledge about future contingents and their consequences, it follows that God can have no present knowledge of which human beings will come into existence in the future. According to this line of thinking, it is impossible for the God of open theism to know the existence or the identity of any future human beings. I insist that this is a logical entailment of the open theist position. Before you and I were conceived, God had no knowledge of our future existence, nor could he have. For an open theist to deny this entailment is to repudiate the entire foundation for his rejection of divine foreknowledge. Also embarrassing at this point is that this entailment of open theism is contradicted by the Christian Scriptures that open theists profess as their ultimate authority in faith and practice.

First Peter 2:9 tells us, "But you are a chosen people, a royal priesthood, a holy nation, a people belonging to God, that you may declare the praises of him who called you out of darkness into his wonderful light." The apostle Paul teaches that God "chose us in him [Christ] before the creation of the world to be holy and blameless in his sight. In love he predestined us to be adopted as his sons through Jesus Christ.... In him we were also chosen, having been predestined according to the plan of him who works out everything in conformity with the purpose of his will" (Ephesians 1:4–5, 11). According to Paul, God not only knew us before we existed but also knew us and chose us before the creation of the world. This doesn't sound like the God of open theism, does it?

Returning to open theism's implied claim that God could not know that future human beings like Henry Ford, Thomas Edison, and the

---

42. Basinger has already admitted that God cannot know things like this.

43. David Basinger, "Practical Implications," in Pinnock et al., *The Openness of God,* 163.

44. Ibid., 165.

people who invented television and computers and airplanes would exist, we have another embarrassing consequence: since God could not know these individuals would exist, he also could not know the consequences of their free activity, namely, the future existence of planes, trains, automobiles, computers, television sets, and so on and so forth. Is this absurd? I think so. Do such absurdities flow from the premises of open theism? They do. Is this so absurd as to suggest the importance of repudiating open theism's idea of a finite God? I believe so.

But there are other implications that may be even worse. Just as the God of open theism cannot know which future human beings will exist, neither can he know which future humans will become Christian believers, will receive his salvation, and will be blessed with eternal life. In other words, this kind of God is still waiting to learn the final composition of his church.

And finally, think back to this God's conundrum at the time his Son was dying on the cross. At that moment, the finite God of open theism had no way of knowing if even one human being would accept his Son as Savior. This poor, impotent deity faced the possibility that the suffering of his Son upon the cross would bring about the salvation of no one. Hasker says as much when he admits the possibility that there could have been "no church, and a key element in God's plan would be frustrated. As things stand, to be sure, this has not happened, but it could have happened; that it has not is attributable to nothing but 'God's luck.'"[45] Compare Hasker's sad statement about the existence of God's church being a product of luck or chance with the words in 1 Peter 2:9 and Ephesians 1 quoted above.

As a final consequence, it seems obvious that a God who cannot know the future cannot control the future and cannot bring his will to pass in the future. As Erickson observes, "If God does not coerce humans, but allows them to exercise their free wills, even to contravene his will, what assurance is there that God's cause will ultimately triumph? Hasker seems to suggest that if necessary to ensure the victory of God, God can intervene to override the human will.[46] If this is the case, however, then the difference between their view and the classical one is not one of kind but of degree. It is not whether God coerces, but how frequently he does so, and presumably, on their terms, either is undesirable."[47]

---

45. William Hasker, "A Philosophical Perspective," in Pinnock et al., *The Openness of God,* 153; Hasker's chapter appears on pages 126–54. While it might appear that Hasker is only putting the view of the church's existence as a matter of divine luck on the table for consideration, his failure to offer a serious reply strongly suggests it is a problem that he is stuck with.

46. See Hasker, "A Philosophical Perspective," 142.

47. Erickson, *The Evangelical Left,* 107. Erickson could also have quoted Basinger from the same book: "God does retain the right to intervene unilaterally in earthly affairs. That

At what point in 1992, for example, could we say that God knew that Bill Clinton would win the presidential election? Note that God could not have foreknowledge of this event because it was a collocation of the supposedly free decisions of many millions of people in the privacy of the voting booth. Perhaps we could say that God finally knew the outcome by 10:00 P.M. on election night.

Can the God of open theism know in March of any year which American and National League baseball teams will meet in the World Series seven months later? The answer must be no. How could such a finite God know this in the case of thousands of games, the outcomes of which are dependent upon millions of situations affected by human free choices, such as the decision to throw a curveball at a particular target at a particular speed? Without wishing to appear irreverent, at what point in the course of a single baseball game could this God even know the final score? The answer is, only when the fat lady sings.[48] Even with two outs and two strikes on the batter, there would always be the possibility of this God being surprised by a home run. Let me be frank. When I think about this view of God, I often find myself in a situation wanting to pray for this God. I would probably do that, except under the circumstances, I'm not sure who I should pray to.

Can one lay out a scenario faithful to the Bible that explains how a God who is essentially ignorant about future contingent events can control the future? Is it surprising to learn that no open theist has ever attempted to produce such a scenario? Is it surprising to learn that no open theist has considered the problem?

Hasker has made an interesting admission. "To be sure," he writes, "God could have created a world in which he would have full foreknowledge of every detail, simply by creating a world in which everything that happens is fully controlled by his sovereign decrees. But it seems to us [open theists] that God found such a world less desirable—less appealing to his creative goodness—than a world that contains genuinely free creatures."[49] What an incredible thing to say, after all we have learned about the theological implications of open theists' denial of divine foreknowledge. In lieu of any arguments for their position, they advance their view because they like it better than the alternative. This is a surprising ground on which to develop a theological system.

---

is, we believe that freedom of choice is a gift granted to us by God and thus that God retains the power and moral prerogative to inhibit occasionally our ability to make voluntary choices to keep things on track" (159).

48. Baseball lore contains several opinions about when a game is over. Baseball player and amateur philosopher Yogi Berra once said, "A game is not over 'til it's over." Baseball sportscaster Joe Garagiola once said a game is not over 'til the fat lady sings.

49. Hasker, "A Philosophical Perspective," in Pinnock et al., *The Openness of God*, 151

Conclusion

My objective in the second half of this chapter has been to reveal some of the implications of an increasingly popular interpretation of God's property of omniscience, namely, that God cannot possess knowledge about future contingent events. It is important to note how proponents of open theism never refer publicly to the entailments I have noted. Perhaps they have failed to see these implications. It's difficult to know which situation would be worse, learning that they have yet to see where their assertions about their finite God lead or learning that they continue to push their campaign of limiting divine omniscience while fully conscious of the implications of their position.

OPTIONAL WRITING ASSIGNMENT

Write an essay in which you seek open theist answers to the implications this chapter claims to find in that position. If you cannot find good answers, sketch an alternate view and support it with reasons.

FOR FURTHER READING

Millard J. Erickson, *The Evangelical Left* (Grand Rapids: Baker, 1997).
Ronald H. Nash, *The Concept of God* (Grand Rapids: Zondervan, 1983).
Clark Pinnock et al., *The Openness of God* (Downers Grove, Ill.: Inter-Varsity, 1994).

Chapter Fifteen

Metaphysics:
Some Questions About
Indeterminism

The other day I reminisced about my first couple of years in college. I focused on the sessions we used to have in the dorm after some of the guys had come back from picking up pizza. One of the perennial topics of those friendly arguments was the issue of free will and determinism. We never did settle anything then, and I'm not sure I'm going to settle anything now. But perhaps another brief look at the determinism-indeterminism issue can help my readers get past some of the blunders we used to make in those dormitory discussions. One reason why so little progress seems possible is because of people's failure to define some key terms and their difficulty in seeing why certain commonly held beliefs are so counterintuitive once some rather elementary points are recognized.

The issue of determinism versus indeterminism belongs to two of the five worldview topics introduced in chapter 1: metaphysics and anthropology. While I have selected the topic as the subject of this book's one chapter on metaphysics, it is impossible to keep the discussion from overlapping into important issues affecting our understanding of human beings.

I have little interest in arguing for a fully developed version of determinism or indeterminism. Accomplishing such an ambitious goal is too much for a short chapter like this. Instead I look at the position that the majority of people hold on this issue and raise some questions that are usually ignored. View my work in this chapter as an attempt to get people to notice and then question features of the majority opinion (indeterminism) that are too problematic to ignore. Perhaps on some other occasion I can assume a similar role with the minority position (determinism).

Determinism Versus Indeterminism

Determinism is the belief that everything that occurs in the universe is caused by prior states of affairs. There is and can be no such thing as an uncaused event. *Indeterminsm* is the belief that at least some events occur without a prior determining state of affairs. Indeterminists may believe that some or many or perhaps all events happen without some predetermining cause.

We have already encountered two ancient versions of determinism and indeterminism in the metaphysical theories of Democritus and Epicurus. In the atomism of Democritus, everything that exists and every event that occurs is the consequence of purposeless interaction between mindless, material atoms. While the combinations of atoms are chance events that occur without plan or design, nonetheless the motion of the atoms and the change in their motion after striking other atoms are determined by prior states of affairs. There was no room for indeterminism or human free will in Democritus's universe. Of course, it would be a serious mistake to assume that all forms of determinism must resemble the mechanistic materialism of Democritus. As we also saw in chapter 2, Epicurus believed that the only way he could make room in his materialistic universe for the human pursuit of pleasure and happiness was for humans to have at least a tiny sphere of independence from mechanical determinism. Thus arose his doctrine of the swerve or declination of the atom, perhaps the most famous example of an undetermined event in the history of ideas.

Compatibilism Versus Incompatibilism

Compatibilism is the theory that in ways that may be impossible to comprehend, determinism and human free will are compatible in the sense that both can exist in the case of human actions. *Incompatibilism* is the theory that it is impossible for determinism and human free will to be true at the same time. If humans are indeed free, determinism must then be false. There must be at least some events that are uncaused. A compatibilist believes that freedom and determinism can be reconciled in some way; an incompatibilist believes they cannot. Major Christian thinkers like Augustine, Martin Luther, John Calvin, and Jonathan Edwards did not repudiate human freedom, as is sometimes thought. They defined the notion of human freedom so that it is compatible with determinism.

External Causes Versus Internal Causes

Many causes that influence or determine human behavior are external to us in the sense that the cause is outside of our thoughts, emotions, or intentions. As an example, think of some person pointing a gun at another individual, thus forcing him to do something he does not want to do. Other influences upon our behavior occur inside of us. Examples might include certain beliefs, prejudices, emotions, desires, and wants. Many philosophers are willing to describe choices affected by internal causes as free while behavior that results from external coercion is not.

The Liberty of Indifference Versus the Liberty of Spontaneity

Human beings may be said to be free in two different senses. *The liberty of indifference* explains human freedom as the ability either to do something or not. Understood in this sense, Jones's decision to watch the television news on channel 4 rather than on channel 5 is free if and only if it is completely indifferent (undetermined) which channel he turns to. In order to be genuinely free in the sense of indifference, a person must have the ability either to do something or not. *The liberty of spontaneity,* by contrast, explains human freedom as the ability to do whatever the person wants to do. On this second view, the question of the person's ability to do otherwise is irrelevant; the important issue is whether he is able to do what he most wants to do.

The liberty of indifference is an incompatibilist definition of freedom, while the liberty of spontaneity is a form of compatibilism. If liberty is understood in terms of indifference, Jones's decision is free if and only if he is either free to watch channel 4 or not to watch channel 4. But if liberty is understood in terms of spontaneity, Jones can still be free even if his decision to watch channel 4 is determined. Jones may have been hypnotized and told to watch only one station; or his set may be broken so it receives only one station; or someone holding a gun might threaten his life if he turns to any channel other than 4. But whatever antecedent events might cause Jones to watch channel 4, it is possible that it is also the channel that he most wants to watch. As long as his act is an expression of what he wants, then his action is free even if his wants are themselves determined, or so say advocates of the liberty of spontaneity. There can be different ways of understanding the liberty of spontaneity. For example, some people limit this kind of freedom to certain types of internal causes.

If human freedom can be adequately explained in terms of the liberty of spontaneity, then men and women would remain free even if their decisions and their wants were determined in some sense. God would see to it that his creatures want to do what he has determined them to do.

Because the term "liberty of indifference" can be rather unwieldy in certain contexts, I will frequently substitute an equivalent expression, the libertarian view of free will.[1] According to this view, if I am confronted by a choice between doing *A* and not doing *A,* I have the power to do either, and whichever choice I make is up to me.

What Is the Will?

Many people seem to believe that there is a separate part of us that weighs our alternatives, deliberates, and then tips the scales in one direction or another. As I write this chapter, local television stations have been playing a commercial in which the Devil and an angel give counsel to a man driving a car. After listening to both sides, the driver smiles, makes his choice, and drives his car down a steep hill. Lots of people

---

1. I use "libertarian" here in a sense totally different from its use in political philosophy. It is also important not to confuse "libertarian" with "libertine," which has inescapable connotations of immoral behavior.

associate their will with the driver in this commercial: there's a little man or woman somewhere inside of them that weighs the alternatives and then pushes the button that results in their action.

One thing that makes it difficult to make progress on the subject before us is the fact that so many people use the term *will* to refer to some part of our being. The stomach digests food, the lungs absorb oxygen, and the will makes decisions. One can spend a very long time seeking an argument to support this belief. Suppose we stop thinking about the will as a part of us. Let us suppose that the word *will* refers to the function of choosing, without any additional claims as to how that function works or what it might be. As we go through each day, we make choices.[2] Does there have to be a part of us that makes those choices?

What Is Free Will?

On the libertarian view of freedom, the human will is autonomous, which is another way of saying it can act independently of determining causes or influences, whether they be external or internal. According to philosopher Gordon H. Clark, "Free will has been defined as the equal ability, under given circumstances, to choose either of two courses of action. No antecedent power determines the choice. Whatever motives or inclinations a man may have, or whatever inducements may be laid before him, that might seem to turn him in a certain direction, he may at a moment disregard them all and do the opposite. This definition or description, however, is what I believe to be the common notion of free will."[3]

According to libertarians, all of us must have at least some occasions in life when our will can negate those influences and make its choice in spite of them. "Free will" connotes the human power to make these decisions without their being caused by prior conditions.

If free will means that people facing incompatible choices have the ability to select either one, we have to wonder if this is a power humans possess. Is it true, as Clark asks, that a human's "choices are not determined by motives, by inducements, or by his settled character"?[4]

Problems with the Uninfluenced Will

Please note therefore that indeterminists understand free will to mean that it is up to me whether I respond to influences or resist them. A free will may either follow influences or resist them. But once a will is affected by prior influences or causes, it is no longer free. This is the libertarian view of free will.

---

2. Please notice that I am not denying that people make real choices.
3. Gordon H. Clark, *Religion, Reason, and Revelation* (Philadelphia: Presbyterian and Reformed, 1961), 202–3.
4. Ibid., 204.

Try to form a mental picture of a human will, whatever it is, that has the power to act totally uninfluenced or uncaused by any prior condition, state, thought, feeling, emotion, or whatever. Then ask yourself, how does this kind of uncaused action differ from pure chance? In this regard, R. K. McGregor Wright asks an important question: "The most serious problem here is that this sort of spontaneity[5] is indistinguishable from a chance event. We need only ask, 'What causes the will to choose one way rather than another?' If it is *not* caused, it is purely random. If it *is* caused to act, then it is not free from causation. It makes no difference to this argument whether the cause is internal to the personality or impinges from the outside." [6]

Consider a situation in which your left arm is subject to a series of unpredictable, uncaused motions. Sometimes your left hand clenches into a fist and moves upward in ways that bring it in contact with the jaw of another person. But you have nothing to do with such motions. At other times, your palm remains open while your arm moves horizontally such that it slaps the face of another person. Once again, at none of these times is the motion of your arm caused. Rather, under the described conditions, the movement of your arm happens by chance. The movement of your arm is as spontaneous[7] as the unpredictable, uncaused swerve of Epicurus's falling atoms. If my actions are uncaused, my conduct is unexplainable.

The picture arising from my example of uncaused behavior is not a picture of free choice or responsible conduct. As philosopher Richard Taylor states, "The conception that now emerges is not that of a free man, but of an erratic and jerking phantom, without any rhyme or reason at all."[8] If parts of my body move in an uncaused way, the movements cannot be my conduct. If movements of my body can be described as my behavior, then I must have some control over them. But uncaused motions are under the control of no one.

If an indeterminist insists that the actions of the will are uncaused, he seems committed to the belief that what he describes as manifestations of free will are chance, random acts. If he acknowledges the will is caused, he is admitting some type of determinism.

Most of us believe that our choices reflect something of our character. This is an important conviction to maintain. A person of good character will tend to make good choices while a person of bad character will not. However, the problem of viewing human behavior as random, chance events introduces a gap between what we do and what we are

---

5. It is important to be able to use the word *spontaneity* in this context. But this usage must not be confused with the liberty of spontaneity defined earlier in the chapter.

6. R. K. McGregor Wright, *No Place for Sovereignty* (Downers Grove, Ill.: InterVarsity Press, 1996), 47.

7. I am using "spontaneous" here differently than in the term "the liberty of spontaneity." In this case, the emphasis is upon the action being uncaused.

8. Richard Taylor, *Metaphysics* (Englewood Cliffs, N.J.: Prentice-Hall, 1974), 51.

(character). When the behavior of Mr. Jones reflects his character, then to some extent his conduct is predictable or unsurprising. But imagine a person whose character is unknowable because whatever he does freely ends up being completely random and unpredictable. How would such a person be different from someone who is insane? A totally spontaneous will can have no connection with character. If I am a participant in a chance event, I cannot be held responsible.

My choices are supposedly caused by my will. Does anything cause or influence my will? Desires, motives, wants, emotions, and arguments look like good candidates. If the causes of my choices had been different, then the results would have been different.

Free and responsible behavior must be conduct that can be causally traced back to my inner states. Erratic and impulsive behavior and random behavior is neither free nor responsible. As Wright observes, "The very idea of responsibility depends on causation. Therefore the freewill theory destroys responsibility rather than supporting it."[9]

Suppose we concede there are times when the human will is uncaused. How can such a will, Wright asks, "ever *begin* to act at all? If the will is 'neutral' at first and not predetermined to act one way rather than another, what causes it to act at all? If it starts out neutral, how does it ever get off dead center? If it is said that the will is 'induced' or 'led' or 'drawn' or 'influenced' to act, we must insist that these are merely words for different types of causation. We are forced again to face the problem of what it really means for the will to be free from causation. Either it acts purely by chance, or it seems that it does not act at all. This, of course, completely obliterates the possibility of growth in holiness."[10]

Can the action or direction of the will be influenced by moral persuasion and reasoned argument? If so, does this not mean that these influences represent causes affecting the will? If evidence or arguments have no causal effect upon the will, why bother with evidence and arguments? But, if an argument has the power to push or pull me in the direction of some decision, how does this movement differ from a cause upon the will?

Some Comments on the Theological Side of the Issue

The determinism-indeterminism debate within the Christian faith divides people into Calvinists and Arminians; discussions of possible differences within each camp belong more properly to a different kind of book. Calvinists tend to regard the will as free insofar as it manifests a person's character. Calvinists insist that God never forces the will to act in ways that violate its nature. They deny that God ever uses mechanical forces to lead people to violate their nature, thus treating them as puppets.

---

9. Wright, *No Place for Sovereignty,* 48.
10. Ibid., 49.

It is hardly surprising that Calvinists and Arminians disagree over various biblical passages that may appear to teach a libertarian view of freedom. Two biblical passages that are often discussed in this context are Revelation 22:17 and John 3:16. In the King James Version, Revelation 22:17 reads as follows: "And whosoever will, let him take the water of life freely." It is easy to interpret these English words as an endorsement of a libertarian view of free will. However, a literal reading of the Greek says "the one wishing, let him take." The word *will* does not appear in the original language. What is not discussed in the text is what leads some people to this state of wishing. The Calvinist says that people reach this state as a result of God giving them that desire. The word *freely* in the text means that the water of life has no cost. As Wright explains, "It is not the human will that is free in this verse but the gospel."[11]

In the case of John 3:16, the King James Version reads: "For God so loved the world, that he gave his only begotten Son, that whosoever believeth in him should not perish, but have everlasting life." What misleads people in this translation is the word *whosoever,* which seems to suggest that anyone might qualify. But there is no word in John 3:16 that means "whosoever." The New International Version eliminates this confusion by translating the clause in question as follows: "whoever believes in him shall not perish but have eternal life." The relevant issue before us in this dispute is why some people believe and why others don't. While Calvinists and Arminians have their competing answers, the text itself does not support an indeterminist position. In order to find some theory of free will in the Bible, the verses appealed to would have to show that the will is uncaused in one way instead of another, either by external causes or internal influences. To find that in the so-called free will passages in the Bible would require reading more into the text than the text itself says.

Summary

At the start of this chapter, I made it plain that I have no interest in playing the role of the dogmatist regarding this highly complex issue. In my thinking, indeterminism has become a kind of official doctrine for most people in this day and age. However, I believe, a large part of the appeal of indeterminism is the difficulty of getting people to dig below the surface, to recognize that things are not always as they seem, and to understand the way in which undefined or badly defined terms disguise serious problems. In short, I want to help people to think more clearly about issues that go unrecognized and undiscussed in most attitudes toward the debate between indeterminism and determinism. I have attempted to show that what seems to be the common understanding of the human will may be confused and that

---

11. See ibid., chap. 9.

this confusion carries over to the common understanding of what free will is thought to be. The belief that a free will is autonomous and independent of any causal influence leads to consequences that are destructive of the kinds of human liberty and responsibility that constitute the major reason why so many people are attracted to indeterminism.

The question is whether any human choices are ever uncaused and uninfluenced. My objective in this part of the chapter is to lay out a theory of human behavior that is influential in the philosophy of economics and relate it to the discussions of this chapter. I will then offer several examples of real human choices that might appear free in the libertarian sense until they are analyzed from the perspective of the theory I've presented. I do all of this in order to encourage my readers to apply the theory to their own choices. I believe this kind of analysis will help most of us to see the subtle, often unrecognized influences upon our choices.

Influences upon Our Choices

A Personal Scale of Values

It is interesting to plug some material from the philosophy of economics into our examination of human free choices. Economics studies the ways in which people attempt to satisfy their wants with the resources at their disposal. It is concerned with how people choose to bridge the gap between what they have and what they want. Because our resources are never sufficient to satisfy all of our wants, we have to make choices about how to use our resources so as to supply the wants that we judge to be most important to us.

As human beings seek ways to get the most out of their limited resources, they are forced to rank their available alternatives. This ranking will reflect the individual's personal order of values. In other words, the options sensible people consider at any given moment must be attainable. At this moment in my life, buying a five-million-dollar house in Santa Barbara, California, is not a live option. I probably would enjoy living in such a house someday, but I will never have the money, and I have important obligations in Orlando, Florida, that take precedence over a fantasy home on the West Coast.

Everyone has a scale of values by which his needs, wants, and goals are ranked in order of the importance and urgency he attaches to them.[12] Even though we may be unconscious of the process, we all engage in a

---

12. A reminder: I am discussing economics and human behavior from a descriptive point of view. Nothing I say entails any kind of relativism in ethics. It is one thing to recognize that different people have different scales of values, that is, place differing values or attribute different degrees of importance to different options. It is something quite different to contend that there are no standards independent of human preferences and desires that report how we *ought* to evaluate our options.

constant ranking of the relative value to us of things we want but do not possess and of things we possess but might be willing to trade for something else.

Not only do value scales differ from person to person, but also the value scales of individual persons are constantly changing. As people's interests, wants, and information change, their preferences change. The things that a person puts forth the greatest effort to secure at any given moment are those that rank highest on his personal scale of preferences at that moment and in those circumstances.

Students of a particular school of economic theory[13] know that whenever people are acting, that is, behaving in ways that reflect conscious thinking and choices, their actions are always a function of several factors: (1) the unavoidable fact of scarcity in life; we can never have everything we want; (2) the need to make choices, because we cannot have everything we want, we must choose among available options; and (3) the subjective ranking we place upon the choices open to us. Whenever people act (as opposed to responding to stimuli), they are always choosing the option that ranks highest in their personal scale of values at that time.

In cases where it is impossible for someone to have both A and B, a person's choice will reflect the relative value he places upon A and B. People's actions, choices, and decisions, then, are a reflection of their value scales at the moment of choice. Their choices are made in order to help them secure the options that accord more closely with their values.

Consider three college students, all of whom have the same three options as the top three alternatives in their scale of values at some particular moment. Suppose those options are (1) watching a Chicago Cubs game on the last day of the 1998 regular baseball season in order to see if Sammy Sosa can catch Mark McGwire in the home run race as well as seeing if the Cubs make the postseason playoffs; (2) reading several chapters of this book and otherwise studying other course material for an exam they'll take tomorrow; (3) going to Pizza Hut with their favorite date.

Suppose our three students, whom we'll call A, B, and C, rank their three options in the following ways: A's rankings are (1), (2), and (3); B's rankings are (3), (2), and (1); and C's rankings are (2), (1), and (3). If this theory of human behavior is correct, A, B, and C will choose the alternative that ranks highest for them at the moment of decision. It is important to remember that changes in conditions and time can affect one's rankings. If it's the bottom of the eighth inning, Sosa will not bat again and has not hit a home run, and the Cubs are behind by ten runs, stu-

---

13. I am referring to the Austrian school of economics. For a fairly detailed account of this approach, see Ronald H. Nash, *Poverty and Wealth* (Richardson, Tex.: Probe Books, 1992).

dent A might well turn off the television and study. If so, that would prove that option (2) then ranked highest in A's scale of values at that moment.

Let us now consider two events in which I participated.

Example One

Ordinarily, I enjoy eating breakfast at a Bob Evans restaurant. I usually order fried eggs, over medium, with crisp bacon, wheat toast, and coffee. When I'm able to eat at a restaurant before noon on a weekday, this kind of breakfast at a Bob Evans often ranks highest in my personal scale of options. But on a recent Friday I entered a Bob Evans, and while I was waiting for the waitress, I surveyed the food on the plates at adjoining tables. The woman to my left had a big stack of pancakes plus a side order of that great bacon. The fellow behind me had the bacon and eggs. But when the waitress came for my order, I requested a bowl of oatmeal. As if that weren't bad enough, I asked her to hold the brown sugar; I would use artificial sweetener. A bit later, the waitress noticed tears dropping into my oatmeal and asked if my breakfast was all right. A week later, I walked briskly into the same Bob Evans, and without even looking at the menu I ordered my bacon, eggs, toast, and coffee. There were no tears that day.

If some indeterminist knew me well enough to know how highly I usually rate that breakfast and that restaurant, how might he explain my behavior? I can imagine an indeterminist claiming that my conduct proves indeterminism. It does so by showing how the human will can resist powerful influences and make choices contrary to those influences. On the first Friday in question, Nash exhibited great moral courage and steadfastness, resisted his lust for bacon and eggs, and proved himself to be an autonomous moral agent. Ah, for such blissful ignorance. It is time that you know the rest of the story. My behavior on that first Friday does not support indeterminism.

Let's revisit my choice of oatmeal for breakfast. What I didn't state earlier was the fact that the following Friday I was scheduled for one of an ongoing series of blood tests. About a week before each of these tests, I begin altering my eating habits. Some might think I'm trying to fool my doctor so he won't prescribe new medication or perhaps give me a stern lecture. If that were true, I might well be guilty of behaving irrationally, in one sense of the word. But my action would still be rational in the sense that I was behaving in a way that would help me reach an important goal. My action a week later when I ordered my usual bacon and eggs reflected the fact that I had had my blood test and could celebrate the good results.

What's the point? My refusal of bacon and eggs on the first Friday and my choice of oatmeal was not an action in which I selected an option that ranked lower on my scale of values. I'm not sure anyone can do that. At that time, what ranked highest for me was getting a good score on the upcoming blood test. The blood test ranked higher for me at that moment than my desire for bacon and eggs. If the test of a free choice is either being free from any causal influence or having the power to resist a powerful influence in favor of a lesser influence, my choice of the oatmeal was not an instance of free will. The ranking of the options in my scale of values had changed and, as we always do, I selected the one that ranked highest at that moment.

Example Two

Several years ago a friend and I found ourselves at the John Wayne Airport in Southern California, waiting to board planes that would take us back to our homes on the East Coast. Being a rational person, I would be changing planes in Dallas, en route to my home in Orlando. I assumed that my friend would be doing the same. To my surprise, he told me that he would be making his connecting flight in Minneapolis. Not wishing to appear impolite, I decided not to ask him why he was doing something so irrational. But I hoped my friend would make his connection, since he would find the Minneapolis airport suffering from a midwinter blizzard.

If any reader believes that my choice of Dallas as the city for changing planes was a free, uncaused, uninfluenced, spontaneous movement, it was not. Flying through Dallas was the shortest and quickest way home. I was not going to change planes in Minneapolis or Chicago in the middle of the winter.

But what about my friend? Changing in Dallas was also the shortest and quickest way home for him. I can imagine some indeterminist thinking that while poor, weak Nash was following his desires in flying through Dallas, his friend's action demonstrated the truth of indeterminism. His friend exhibited the inner strength and resolve to resist the impulses that conquered Nash and chose freely. Really?

I must confess that it took me an hour or so to figure out what lay behind my friend's decision to fly through Minneapolis. As I said, I didn't want to appear impolite and ask him why he was behaving so irrationally. As I pondered my friend's peculiar behavior on my own flight to sunny Dallas, I remembered that he used to live in Minneapolis. Is it possible, I thought, that he retains a strange obsession with Minneapolis, such that he breaks out in hives unless he visits the place every so often?[14] I ruled that out. Were friends going to meet him for a brief visit at the airport?[15] Since the city was suffering through a blizzard, that seemed unlikely. Then I saw the light!

---

14. Please note that this explanation would explain his choice in terms of a cause.
15. Note that this would be another cause.

During all the years my friend had lived in Minneapolis, the airline he had to fly most often was Northwest. A rational man such as he undoubtedly had a frequent-flyer account with Northwest. The explanation for his choice was now obvious: he had to change planes in Minneapolis in order to add mileage to his Northwest account. He ranked that incentive high enough in his personal scale of values to incur other costs, such as the possible inconvenience of bad winter weather in Minneapolis. When people are offered incentives that match their present ranking of values, they will likely select options that reflect those incentives. In my friend's case, he chose Northwest Airlines over American or Delta. In my case, I chose oatmeal over eggs and bacon.[16]

Example Three

Unlike my first two examples, which describe actual events and real choices, my last example is hypothetical. But it illustrates an answer to a potential objection some might raise to the theory of human choices we're considering. Imagine a critic who happens to be a personal friend reacting to my theory in the following way: "Nash thinks that humans always choose that option that ranks highest in their personal scale of values. I'm going to trap him in a way that will prove his theory false."[17] My friend knows that I know the priority he gives in his scale of values to fried chicken wings at a local restaurant. If it's lunchtime and he can possibly get to that restaurant, he'll be there and gulp down all the chicken wings he can in twenty minutes. Unaware of the trap he is setting for me, I accept his invitation to lunch at this restaurant because he has promised to pick up the tab. (In other words, my decision to go with him had a cause.) As we wait for the waitress, he goes through the motions of studying the menu. I chuckle to myself because I expect him to order chicken wings. When the waitress asks for his order, he peers over the top of the menu with a triumphant gleam in his eyes and says, "I don't want chicken wings today. Bring me some liver and onions."

With the menu gone, I can now study his body language, and I sense that something is going on. Because I know that he hates liver and onions, I know that liver and onions will never occupy any place in any of his scale of choices. An indeterminist would assume that what has just occurred is an instance of free will triumphing over desire. My friend has supposedly made an autonomous, uncaused, uninfluenced decision. Being a more reflective person, I know otherwise. I squint and ask him if his choice of food is some kind of experiment. Unable to hide his glee

---

16. Once again, I am not teaching ethical relativism. I am describing some of the conditions that exist when any person makes a choice.

17. Question: Which one of our worldview tests do you suppose this criticism would exhibit?

any longer, he blurts out that he has falsified my theory that humans always select the option that ranks highest in their scale of values. "How so?" I ask. "You know that when I'm in this restaurant, the food choice that *always* ranks highest for me is chicken wings and the food choice that *always* ranks lowest for me is liver and onions. You have just seen me defeat your theory. I did not choose the option that ranked highest for me. Therefore, your theory is wrong. I overcame my desires, I resisted my wants, and therefore proved that I have free will."

Before I tell you what was wrong with my friend's analysis, see if you can identify the error. Don't read any further. Just close the book, close your eyes, and think. Did my friend's behavior prove what he said it did?

Here is why his conduct confirmed my theory. At the moment he ordered liver and onions, the highest ranked alternative in his scale of values was neither chicken wings nor liver and onions. The highest alternative for him at that moment was not food. Rather, it was proving my theory to be wrong. He didn't choose liver and onions because he wanted them. He chose the liver because he falsely believed that choice would disprove my theory and would support his indeterminism. He chose the way he did because of the influence of a powerful desire to prove me wrong. But his action only supported my theory. His decision was not the result of free will.

What's All This Got to Do with Indeterminism?

The indeterminism we're examining in this chapter explains free human choices as decisions that are uncaused or uninfluenced by prior circumstances or states of affairs. I believe that any of us who understands fully the context in which our choices occur will be able to see the causes and influences at work in every instance. It might be easy to imagine an indeterminist employee of Northwest Airlines who completed my friend's ticket purchase and later, during a short pause, thought how nice it was that my friend's voluntary, free, responsible selection of Northwest over its competitors accidentally, randomly brought extra income to the business she works for. But she would be wrong. My friend's choice was not undetermined. It was caused by external considerations (the airline's frequent flyer program) and internal considerations (his desire to get miles).

When I teach economics, I go into all of this material and then say the following: Human beings always select the option that at that moment ranks highest in their personal scale of values. Now we could ask how various options reach the top position in our personal scale. I don't think there is any mystery. The reasons are many and varied. Was my selection of an American Airlines flight connecting in Dallas an act of free will? If free will means the liberty of indifference, the answer is no. There were influences and causes behind my decision. Similar causes and influences lie behind all of our choices; we simply fail to recognize those causes on many occasions.

Some Questions

If you see the point to my discussion, do you believe, when *you* make decisions, that there are more influences at work than you recognize? Perhaps your position on this would be helped if you would keep a diary for a week or so in which you record your most important decisions and identify as many operative influences as you can. This latter point can be accomplished by noting in your diary the highest ranked alternatives in your scale of values at that moment. Let me suggest that if there's a conflict between what you identify as your highest ranked alternative and the choice you made, your analysis was faulty. But give it a try.

What accounts for changes in our scale of values? Lots of things. Not even my friend who eats twenty chicken wings at noon is going to drive back to that restaurant an hour later and desire more chicken wings. On the day that my friend behaves in that way, I suggest he seek help from a counselor. If my friend has the stomach flu some day, that will alter his eating habits. But these examples deal with trivial matters. There are more important considerations.

Suppose some kind of unethical or immoral conduct ranks high in a person's scale of values. But then this person's character undergoes a significant change. Perhaps he has a genuine, moving, and sincere religious and moral conversion. Won't that result in a change in his scale of values? The world is full of people who hated going to church and reading the Bible and listening to sermons and living moral lives who have suddenly been transformed. Even religious indeterminists concede that those changes in character can be wrought by God. Of all of the possible influences upon our character, our scale of values, and our decisions, let's not ignore the fact that God can change a person's scale of values. This is a central teaching of the Christian faith. Let's not ignore the fact that God can lead a person to place faith in and obedience to God at the top of a scale of values.

This might be a good time to reread the material about the liberty of spontaneity: a person is free when he or she chooses those things that are most important at that time. If God alters a person's wants, motives, and desires, thus resulting in that person's decisions, dare we say that the person's choices are not free?

How do we change a person's conduct? Answer: Change his or her scale of values. How do you change your personal scale of values if it includes conduct that you're ashamed of? Answer: Your conduct won't change until your character changes. Religious conversion often affects a person's scale of values. In the case of Saul of Tarsus, prior to his conversion, persecuting Christians ranked highest on his scale. After his conversion, serving Jesus Christ ranked highest. In chapter 1, I mentioned Mickey Cohen, who wanted to become the first Christian gangster. The fact that his life did not change in response to what obviously was a less than life-changing religious conversion is reason enough to doubt the sincerity of his conversion. Forget the idea of a little man or woman sitting somewhere inside of you and pushing a button or tilting a scale at the moment of decision. Our decisions reflect the personal ranking of live options in our life at that moment.

One Last Look at Compatibilism

A proper evaluation of compatibilism would require too lengthy a detour at this stage of the book. Critics of the theory frequently resort to an analogy of a man imprisoned in a locked room. As long as the prisoner wants to remain in the locked room, he is free. At least this is the claim of those who defend the liberty of spontaneity. But to claim that the imprisoned man is free in a broader sense seems to stretch the meaning of "freedom" far beyond the bounds of ordinary usage. But as the proponent of compatibilism can reply, on what grounds are we prepared to show that the bounds of ordinary usage are correct in this case? The attack on compatibilism, including its appeal to the stretched meaning of "freedom," begs the question.

Perhaps the most common attack against theological compatibilism maintains that the position entails that God is ultimately responsible for the evil in the world. The issues raised by this objection are topics of perennial debate in the history of philosophy and exceed the space available in this chapter. The problem is well and fully discussed elsewhere.[18]

---

18. The writing on this subject is extensive. For one who maintains the inability of Christian determinists to absolve God of moral responsibility for the world's evil, see Anthony Kenny, *The God of the Philosophers* (Oxford: Clarendon, 1979), 86–87. For a counterargument from a Christian determinist, see Clark, *Religion, Reason, and Revelation*, 204–6. Clark thinks that all talk about holding God accountable or responsible for what he does is incoherent. If God is the sovereign Lord of the universe, there is no one or nothing to which he is accountable besides himself.

OPTIONAL WRITING ASSIGNMENT

Select either indeterminism or determinism as your position. Ignore the issue of whether this is a free choice. Write a short essay to a friend explaining why you hold the position that you do. Make certain that you define carefully what you take to be the key points in your position.

FOR FURTHER READING

Gordon H. Clark, *Religion, Reason, and Revelation* (Philadelphia: Presbyterian and Reformed, 1961).

Ronald H. Nash, *Is Jesus the Only Savior?* (Grand Rapids: Zondervan, 1994).

Ronald H. Nash, *Poverty and Wealth* (Richardson, Tex.: Probe Books, 1992).

Ronald H. Nash, *When a Baby Dies* (Grand Rapids: Zondervan, 1999).

Richard Taylor, *Metaphysics* (Englewood Cliffs, N.J.: Prentice-Hall, 1974).

R. K. McGregor Wright, *No Place for Sovereignty* (Downers Grove, Ill.: InterVarsity Press, 1996).

Chapter Sixteen

Ethics I:
The Downward Path

A fter I decided on the content of this chapter and realized that all of its topics deal with approaches to ethics that lead people in the wrong direction, "The Downward Path" seemed a good title. Once that was settled, titling my second chapter on ethics "The Upward Path" also made sense, since each topic in chapter 17 discusses approaches to ethics that will lead people in what I regard as the right direction. The titles also lend a measure of closure to the book, tying the information here to material in part 1.

In this chapter I examine five mistaken approaches to ethics, several of which happen to be popular, especially on college campuses and in the nation's capital. The topics I cover are, in order, ethical subjectivism, ethical relativism, situation ethics, hedonism, and utilitarianism.

Ethical Subjectivism

E thical subjectivism is the belief that whenever people say something is morally good, they mean they like it or approve of it. The key to understanding this position and then grasping its failings is seeing that moral judgments, on this view, refer not to the objective good or evil of actions but instead to inner, subjective feelings on the part of the speaker. People who declare an action is right or wrong are doing nothing more than asserting that they, the speakers, feel positively or negatively toward the action. In the view of such a person, the claim that "partial-birth abortions are immoral" means nothing more than that the speaker disapproves of the practice. The counterclaim, that "partial-birth abortions are good," must mean nothing more than that the speaker likes or approves of the practice. There are five paradoxical consequences of this theory.

(1) On this theory, a person is always correct when making ethical judgments. The only way to be wrong is to make a mistake about your own feelings, and since that is hard to do, every ethical judgment is true. Since debates over abortion get intense at times, I should think that pro-choice advocates would eschew ethical subjectivism, which carries the conviction that the moral judgments of pro-life advocates are also always correct. I have never met a pro-choice or pro-life person willing to make that kind of concession. Therefore, anyone who believes that even one

person who holds a conflicting moral opinion is objectively wrong, cannot, if he is consistent, be an ethical subjectivist.

(2) All moral actions are good and bad at the same time. The reason is that people who think they're involved in a moral disagreement are only describing their own subjective states. If Jones says, "Capital punishment is wrong," and Smith says, "Capital punishment is good," there is no real disagreement. Jones is saying nothing more than "I dislike capital punishment" while Smith is saying nothing more than "I like capital punishment." The fact that ethical subjectivism entails that both people in a moral dispute are right ought to disqualify the position from serious consideration. It is also important to note that many people inconsistently hold to ethical subjectivism in the case of some moral issues (sexual conduct is a frequent example) and abandon it in other cases. That is not the behavior of a reflective person.

(3) No two people ever disagree over moral matters. This follows logically from the discussion in (2). Imagine a case where Smith says, "I have blue eyes," and Jones objects by saying, "No, I have brown eyes." There's no more disagreement than if Jones had said, "I like broccoli" and Smith said, "I don't like broccoli."

(4) No two people ever mean the same thing when they make ethical judgments. Imagine two White House advisors who both say, "Telling the truth is bad." Each person is describing his own subjective state. Neither person is saying the same thing.

(5) Ethical subjectivism turns apparently significant moral judgments into either vacuous tautologies or contradictions. Consider a person who says, "I like to get drunk, but I know it's wrong." In ethical subjectivism, this kind of utterance turns out to be a contradiction, to wit, "I like to get drunk, but I don't like to get drunk." Or take the case of a person who says, "I like to do what is right," which on subjectivist terms reduces to the vacuous claim that "I like to do what I like to do."

Since all readers of this book should by now be experts on using the *reductio ad absurdum* argument, the absurd consequences implied by ethical subjectivism should lead us to look elsewhere for an adequate moral theory.

Ethical Relativism

Ethical relativism is the belief that conflicting moral beliefs can be true at the same time in the same sense. These conflicting moral beliefs may exist in the case of two or more individuals or in different cultures (cultural relativism) or in different historical epochs (historical relativism).

Many attempts have been made to undermine the claim that there is an objective moral law that is the same for all human beings. Theists should be encouraged by the weakness of these countermoves. For example, some attempt to argue that human moral consciousness results from learning or conditioning, which would undermine the presumed objectivity of objective moral laws. Philosopher Ed Miller notes one serious weakness in this line of thinking. He writes that the fact

> that something is learned is hardly evidence against its objective truth and validity. We learn that two plus two equals four, and that war is bad, and we learn all kinds of things which we believe to be nonetheless true. Is there, in fact, anything that we claim to know that we have not learned in one way or another? And though people may disagree about their interpretation of "good," it does not follow from this that there *is* no objective good. We may just as easily conclude from the fact that people often disagree in their interpretations of the world that the world does not exist, or from the fact that some people cannot see that two plus two equals four that perhaps it doesn't.[1]

So far as objective truth is concerned, nothing follows from the fact that two individuals or two cultures disagree over the morality of a particular action any more than that their disagreement over a nonethical issue might be thought to imply the absence of any objective truth in this nonethical case. When person A says the world is flat and person B claims the world is round, it hardly follows that there is no objective truth about this issue. Similarly, when person A says that abortion on demand is morally acceptable and person B says it is wrong, it does not follow that the morality of the practice is relative. In both cases, we are dealing with beliefs: A believes the world is flat while B believes otherwise. As we know, there is an objective truth on this issue; therefore, one person's belief is correct and the other's is not. Likewise, ethical disputes involve conflicting beliefs. Even in especially difficult cases where we may have trouble knowing which belief is correct,[2] it is difficult to see what would justify the conclusion that in ethical disputes no beliefs are objectively true.

Equally implausible are attempts to explain moral beliefs in terms of the supposed evolution of instincts or social feelings. According to C. Stephen Evans,

> The moral order does not seem to consist of any such things [i.e., instincts and feelings]. It is not an instinct, because it is itself the standard by which we judge our instincts to be good and bad. And it is not merely a social impulse or feeling. People who have dulled their consciences often are in fact obligated to do things, yet have no such feelings of obligation whatsoever. On the other hand, people with tender

---

1. Ed L. Miller, *God and Reason* (New York: Macmillan, 1972), 87.

2. There are times when neither of two competing beliefs might be true because there is a third alternative. But so long as the law of noncontradiction obtains, there can never be a time when both competing beliefs are true.

consciences often *feel* obligated to do things which no reasonable person would claim they really ought to do. Feelings and real obligations can't be identical.[3]

Paradoxical Implications of Relativism

As is the case with ethical subjectivism, ethical relativism gives rise to a number of paradoxical consequences.

(1) If we accept ethical relativism, then no moral code can be better than another. We have no grounds for criticizing other people. As Scott Rae points out, "The relativist cannot morally evaluate any clearly oppressive culture or, more specifically, any obvious tyrant.... The relativist cannot pass judgment on someone like Hitler, who oppressed a minority with the permission, if not approval, of the majority, since no moral absolute that transcends culture exists to which the relativist can appeal as a basis for that judgment."[4] If there are no transcendent, objective grounds for moral criticism, no side can be more right than another.

(2) If we accept ethical relativism, there can be no such thing as moral progress, either for individuals or for larger social groups. This would mean that the end of slavery in the United States was not a sign of moral advancement. Nor could it ever be possible for a human being to become a better person. Genuine moral progress cannot exist in a universe without there being some transcendent and objective moral standard by which we can judge progress.

(3) If we accept ethical relativism, moral effort becomes meaningless. Why strive to become a better person or bring about a better society if moral progress is impossible (2)?

(4) If we accept ethical relativism, then no human is better than any other.

(5) If we accept ethical relativism, then we are wrong in believing that moral reformers are possible. As J. P. Moreland argues, if relativism is true,

> then it is impossible in principle to have a true moral reformer who changes a society's code and does not merely bring out what was already implicit in that code. For moral reformers, by definition, *change* a society's code by arguing that it is right if and only if it is in the society's code; so the reformer is by definition immoral (since he adopts a set of values outside the society's code and attempts to change that code in keeping with these values). It is odd, to say the least, for someone to

---

3. C. Stephen Evans, *The Quest for Faith* (Downers Grove, Ill.: InterVarsity Press, 1986), 47. An excellent account of the relation between the objective truth of moral judgments and the subjective feelings that often accompany such judgments can be found in Mortimer J. Adler, *Six Great Ideas* (New York: Macmillan, 1981), chaps. 9–14.

4. Scott B. Rae, *Moral Choices: An Introduction to Ethics* (Grand Rapids: Zondervan, 1995), 91.

hold that every moral reformer who ever lived—Moses, Jesus, Gandhi, Martin Luther King—was immoral by definition. Any moral view which implies that is surely false.[5]

(6) If relativism is true, then all choices are equally good. If all choices are equally good, even intolerance toward other beliefs can be morally correct. Why then should anyone practice tolerance?

Once again, the kind of argument known as *reductio ad absurdum* can come to our aid if we retain our ability to think. Why can ethical relativists not recognize the absurd consequences of their position?

Other Objections to Ethical Relativism?

As we know, many people cling to a kind of ethical relativism in which different groups or cultures or nations are entitled to hold conflicting moral beliefs. But there is a serious problem in linking relative ethical standards to different groups: Where do we draw the moral boundaries? Moreland illustrates the difficulties with such a claim:

> It is difficult to define what a society [or moral group] is, and even if that can be done, it is difficult in many cases to identify the morally relevant society. Some acts are done in more than one society at the same time. Suppose there is a community of fairly wealthy, sexually liberated adults who hold that adultery is actually a virtue (since it is a sign of escape from sexual repression). Now suppose there is a community ten miles away which is more conservative and has in its code "adultery is wrong." If a man from the first society, Jones, has intercourse with Mrs. Smith, a member of the second society, at a motel halfway between the two societies, which society is the normative one?[6]

Furthermore, Moreland contends, some moral agents can belong to more than one group or society at the same time.

> Suppose Fred is an eighteen-year-old college freshman who is a member of a social fraternity and a member of a Baptist church. His social fraternity may hold that it is morally obligatory to get drunk at parties, the university may hold that such acts are not obligatory but are at least permissible, and the Baptist church may hold that such an act is morally forbidden. It is hard to tell which society is the morally relevant one. So these objections point out that even if we have a clear notion of what constitutes a society (and this is a difficult task), we still have the problem that some acts are done in more than one society by people who belong to more than one society.[7]

---

5. J. P. Moreland, *Scaling the Secular City* (Grand Rapids: Baker, 1987), 243.
6. Ibid., 242.
7. Ibid., 243.

Some acts are always wrong. The war crimes committed by the Germans and the Japanese during World War II were wrong, regardless of what their social codes were at that time. The atrocities committed in the areas of the former Yugoslavia are immoral, regardless of what social codes may exist in that region. The killing of babies is wrong, regardless of possible sentiment to the contrary.

There are lots of ethical relativists in the world. But it is difficult to imagine a supposed set of claims more problematic than the belief that all moral claims are true.

Situation Ethics

More than thirty years ago, a professor of ethics at Episcopal Seminary in Boston named Joseph Fletcher published a book titled *Situation Ethics*.[8]

Fletcher's position was picked up by many other religious liberals in the English-speaking world. The theory became popular because it talked about love while effectively allowing people to do almost anything they wanted; all they had to do was find a way to say that their actions were "the loving thing to do." The theory also became popular because it came in a religious package that allowed people to think they were being religious even as they continued to act as rebels against God's moral law. Some leaders of the movement falsely claimed Augustine as a forerunner of their view, for he had once said that humans could love God and do as they please. But what Augustine meant was miles removed from the moral relativism of situation ethics. When Augustine talked about loving God, he meant loving the pure and holy God of the Bible who had revealed his will, including the Ten Commandments, in the words and propositions of Scripture. Augustine would have delivered an anathema against the purveyors of situation ethics.

Situation ethics asserts that Christian ethics imposes no duty other than the duty to love. In determining what we should do, the situationist declares that Christians should face the moral situation and ask themselves what is the loving thing to do in this case. There are no rules or principles that prescribe how love will act. Indeed, each loving individual is free to act in any way he thinks is consistent with love as he understands it. The point to situation ethics is that Christian ethics provides no universal principles or rules. Nothing is intrinsically good except love; nothing is intrinsically bad except nonlove. One can never prescribe in advance what a Christian should do. Depending on the situation, love may find it necessary to lie, to steal, even presumably to fornicate, to blaspheme, and to worship false gods. The only absolute is love. Regrettably,

---

8. Joseph Fletcher, *Situation Ethics: The New Morality* (Philadelphia: Westminster Press, 1966).

"love" is a word that has no specific content in the vacuous dictums of the situationists.

A proper response to situation ethics will begin by pointing out that love is insufficient in itself to provide moral guidance for each and every moral decision. Love requires the further specification of principles or rules that suggest the proper ways in which love should be manifested. Because human beings are fallen creatures whose judgments on important moral matters may be affected by moral weakness, love needs guidance from divinely revealed moral truth. Fortunately, Christians believe, this content is provided in the moral principles revealed in Scripture.

Hedonism

As we learned in part 1, hedonism is the belief that pleasure is the highest good. Hedonism has appeared in several forms, two of which are seen in the important difference between egoistic hedonism found in the ancient world and altruistic hedonism that became prominent in the late nineteenth century. If we believe that pleasure is the highest good, we have to decide whose pleasure is most important. An egoistic hedonist is going to think that his pleasure takes precedence, while an altruistic hedonist is going to care about the pleasure of others or, to be more specific, the pleasure or happiness of the greatest number of people.

Egoistic Hedonism

Another important distinction within hedonism divides egoistic hedonism into two movements: namely, the crude, sensual hedonism of a man named Aristippus (435–356 B.C.), whose life overlapped the lives of Socrates and Plato, and the more sophisticated hedonism of Epicurus (341–271 B.C.).

Aristippus and Cyrenaicism. Aristippus was a minor figure in ancient Athens who led a movement known as Cyrenaicism. The Cyrenaics not only believed that a person's own pleasure was the highest good but also emphasized the primary importance of bodily pleasures. Do not worry or think about the future, they said. Get all of the bodily pleasure you can get in the present. Cyrenaics lived by the motto "Let us eat, drink, and be merry, for tomorrow we may die." Things don't change much. The world is full of people who live by that motto.

Epicureanism. Even though Epicurus believed the pleasure of each individual was the highest good, he offered perhaps the best critical examination of crude, sensual hedonism. Everyone living the life of a hedonist ought to examine the beliefs and arguments of Epicurus.

Epicurus agreed with the Cyrenaics that pleasures differ only in quantity, never in quality. As we know, some pleasures are more intense than others. Pleasures differ not only in intensity but also in duration; some pleasures last longer than others. The pleasures of the body may be more intense, but they tend to be fleeting. Think of how many times you've had a great meal in the evening, but come sunrise, the memory of last night's meal cannot satisfy your hunger of the moment. Up to this point, there was basic agreement between Epicurus and Aristippus.

Epicurus began his movement away from Aristippus and Cyrenaicism by recognizing that if pleasure is the highest good, then the greatest evil must be pain. And since pain has the potential of canceling out pleasures, the wise hedonist will be as interested in avoiding pain as he is in achieving pleasure. What kind of hedonist chooses actions that produce 100 units of pleasure and 250 units of pain? Epicurus's answer: only a foolish hedonist would engage in such behavior. Wise hedonists will settle for less pleasure in exchange for less pain.

Epicurus also emphasized the difference between the pleasures of the body and those of the mind. Pleasures of the mind might include the pleasures we receive from listening to great music, observing great art, or watching the sun rise over the Grand Canyon. I can't speak for you, but last Thanksgiving's dinner, as good as it was, hasn't given me any pleasure since the day I ate it. But memories of happy times with my grandchildren or visits to the Louvre in Paris or performances of *Les Miserables* or experiencing that sunrise over the Grand Canyon continue to give me pleasure. Yes, the pleasures of the body can be overwhelmingly powerful, but they are short-lived, while the pleasures of the mind, though they are less intense, live on. As Epicurus might have said, "Hedonists of the world, unite! Pay more attention to the pleasures of the mind."

One reason for this attitude is that the pleasures of the body always carry the danger of producing pain, the greatest of all evils. This is so in at least two ways. For one thing, it is impossible to enjoy a bodily pleasure without first experiencing some want, need, or desire, each of which is a form of pain. For example, during my first year of teaching at a state university, the papers carried the story of a college freshman who reportedly made the *Guinness Book of Records* for drinking the most consecutive bottles of Coke. I think he drank more than twenty bottles in five minutes. How much pleasure do you suppose he got from all that carbonated soda? You cannot enjoy the pleasures of drinking unless you're thirsty. And thirst is a kind of pain. The reason we fail to recognize this is because none of us allows our thirst to go unsatisfied for more than a few minutes. Where's the water fountain? Where's the Coke machine? Where's the fruit juice? And so it goes.

It is also impossible to enjoy the pleasures of eating unless you're hungry. Many of us remember a Paul Newman movie titled *Cool Hand Luke*. It's the movie that's famous for the line "What we have here is a failure to communicate," a fact that may make it the first public appearance

Epicurus

Roman copy of Greek work of 3d century B.C.

THE GRANGER COLLECTION, NEW YORK

of deconstructionism. It's also the film in which Luke, the Newman character, accepts a challenge to eat fifty hard-boiled eggs within ten minutes. Do you think Paul Newman enjoyed eating those eggs? You cannot enjoy the pleasures of eating unless you're hungry. And hunger is a kind of pain. If you doubt that statement, try to go three or four days without eating anything.

To summarize Epicurus's position thus far, the wise hedonist will be as concerned with avoiding pain as with attaining pleasure. While the pleasures of the body are stronger and more intense than pleasures of the mind, they have some disadvantages. For one thing, as we've seen, enjoying bodily pleasures requires one first to experience degrees of pain such as thirst or hunger. But there is a second disadvantage to bodily pleasure: overindulgence in the pleasures of the body produces pain. The more overindulgence, the more the pain. Surely all of us can testify to the truth of this observation.

Epicurus parted company with the Cyrenaics in another regard. He warned his hedonistic followers not to live just for the present moment. The wise hedonist takes the long view. He lives for tomorrow, for the future. Epicurus had no use for hedonists who live by the mantra "Eat, drink, and be merry, for tomorrow we may die." Since the odds are strongly in favor of your being alive tomorrow, do not be a fool and engage in behavior that will produce long-term pain that will far exceed the short-term pleasure. If you are such a fool, the odds are good that the day will come when, like people I've known, the infections cannot be overcome, your liver will be ruined, your heart will fail, or your mind will be gone. Spend some time interviewing an AIDS patient and ask how much fun he's had during the past week. So far as the pleasures of the body are concerned, Epicurus taught, live a life of moderation. Don't overindulge in any bodily pleasures, or they will come back to haunt you.

Finally, Epicurus recommends the pleasures of the mind to us. While mental pleasures are much less intense than bodily pleasures, they last much longer than physical pleasures and avoid the bad side effects of irresponsible bodily behavior. Epicurus's advice is play it safe, practice moderation, and not do anything stupid.

Epicurus, the most famous hedonist in history, has presented a powerful case against the kind of crude, sensual hedonism so popular in our society. And he did so without once quoting the Bible.[9]

Does Epicurus's version of hedonism deserve our respect? I think not. Plato and Aristotle had delivered serious objections to hedonism generations before Epicurus was born. Keep in mind that what we're evaluating is still the simplistic identification of pleasure with the good. Plato

---

9. For obvious reasons, Epicurus could not have quoted the Bible.

noted that pleasure and the good cannot be identical. If the claim of identity were true, then there could be no such thing as a bad pleasure. Pleasure and the good cannot be equivalent. Aristotle explained that pleasure is only one component of a happy life (*eudaemonia*).[10] While this implies an admission that pleasure is important, it counters those who say that pleasure is identical with the good. The best way to attain pleasure is to forget it, Aristotle said. The way to get pleasure is to lose yourself in other activities, and suddenly you'll discover that you're enjoying yourself. Since the path to pleasure is to pursue and attain other things, this counters the belief that pleasure is the highest good.

Altruistic Hedonism

Hedonism experienced a revival of sorts in the work of Jeremy Bentham (1748–1832) and John Stuart Mill (1806–1873). Bentham repeated the ancient claims that pleasure is the highest good and that pleasures differ only in quantity. Because Bentham believed that pleasures differ only in quantity, he urged people to seek the happiness of the greatest number of people. Incorporating more and more people within the circle of hedonism was a guaranteed way to increase the total quantity of pleasure being produced.

Jeremy Bentham

Engraving based on painting, oil on canvas, by H. W. Pickersgill, 1829

THE GRANGER COLLECTION, NEW YORK

Eventually this way of thinking came to be known as utilitarianism. More recently, the name *consequentialism* has been used. The point to this latter name was the fact that the goodness of an act was deemed to lie solely in its consequences, namely, the tendency to produce the greatest amount of happiness for the greatest number of people.[11] Because my primary interest lies in the hedonistic side of utilitarianism, I will skip other issues raised by the utilitarian thinkers, save for a few comments later in the chapter. What concerns me here is Bentham's belief that the quest for the good life will lead us to maximize the quantity of happiness in the world, where happiness is understood as pleasure.

Scottish essayist Thomas Carlyle (1795–1881) charged that hedonism is a pig's philosophy. His point was that if pleasure is the highest good, then that highest good is as attainable by a dirty pig playing in the mud as by a prince, a professor, or a poet. Stung by what he knew was a devastating critique, Mill wrote a short book titled *Utilitarianism* that introduced a major change into the theory of hedonism.

Prior to the appearance of Mill's book in 1861, proponents of hedonism had insisted that pleasures differ only in quantity. Pleasures may be stronger or weaker, but they cannot be higher or lower; pleasures can-

---

10. Notice that Aristotle rejected any attempt to equate happiness (the good life) with pleasure.

11. There are both hedonistic and nonhedonistic versions of utilitarianism and consequentialism.

John Stuart Mill

not differ in quality. Mill sought to change that by arguing that some pleasures can be superior to others in quality. In Mill's famous words, "It is better to be a human being dissatisfied than a pig satisfied; better to be a Socrates dissatisfied than a fool satisfied." In order to avoid a moral philosophy that would degrade humans by lowering them to the level of the pig, he argued that some pleasures are qualitatively superior to others.

To update some of Mill's examples, an advocate of Mill's position might contend that the pleasure derived from reading Shakespeare is qualitatively better than the pleasure received from reading a cartoon strip such as "Hagar the Horrible" or "Peanuts."[12] The pleasure derived from watching a ballet is superior to that received from watching your favorite team win the seventh game of the World Series. Mill did not realize that when he introduced a qualitative difference of pleasures into hedonism, he was setting the stage for the destruction of hedonism. Understanding why this was so is an important step in the maturing of one's philosophical skills.

Under the quantitative analysis, if the only good is pleasure, then the only way to make a pleasure better is to increase its quantity. One must not introduce qualitative considerations. But contrary to hedonists before him, Mill argued that a pleasure can be improved by altering its quality. This was a mistake on Mill's part. Consider the following analogy. Suppose someone claims that money is the highest good and then adds that money earned teaching philosophy is better than money earned robbing banks. If money is the highest good, it doesn't matter how you acquire it. All that does matter is getting more. Once one introduces qualitative considerations, he has crossed the line so that money is not and cannot be the highest good. The reason this is so is because there is now a standard higher than money. Since that newly introduced standard enables us to pass judgment on two piles of money while ignoring quantity, money is no longer the highest good. The standard by which we judge some piles of money to be superior to others, without regard to quantity, is the higher good.

Mill's dilemma can be formulated as follows:

Premise (1): If a utilitarian ignores qualitative differences among pleasures, then he advocates a pig's philosophy, and if he affirms qualitative differences among pleasures, then in principle he is abandoning hedonism by elevating some standard above pleasure.

Premise (2): Either he does or does not affirm qualitative differences.

---

12. So as not to break the thread of argument, I comment about another feature of Mill's position in this footnote. Some people would disagree that reading Shakespeare produces a superior quality of pleasure than reading "Peanuts," a fact that raises the question of whose judgment determines which pleasure is higher. Mill believed that the best judge in such matters was a person just like him.

Therefore, either the utilitarian advocates a pig's philosophy or abandons hedonism.

In the work of Bentham and Mill, *utilitarianism* referred to the position that consequences always are the primary determinant of the morality of an act. For Bentham and Mill, the most important consequence is the tendency of an act to produce the greatest happiness or pleasure for the greatest number of people. This view, which came to be known as *hedonistic utilitarianism,* was savaged by philosophers in the decades following Mill. The basic line of attack was to show that an exclusive dependence upon pleasurable consequences led to embarrassing results. The arguments often took the form of comparing two scenarios, as the following examples illustrate.[13]

Imagine two worlds. In world one, leaders of a nation seize the property of a minority of citizens and send them to concentration camps where many are tortured and killed. Let us suppose that the suffering of these people produces significantly more pleasure for the majority in that society than would have happened without the theft of property, the persecution, and the imprisonment and the killing of innocent people. In world two, the citizens of the country treat all citizens justly, but for some reason the amount of pleasure or happiness in world two falls short of that produced in world one. The hedonistic utilitarian would have to say that on his grounds, world one is ethically superior to world two.

Critics of hedonistic utilitarianism kept tossing examples like this at the hedonists like hand grenades. By the time British philosopher G. E. Moore (1873–1958) published *Principia Ethica* in 1903, utilitarianism had begun to turn in a nonhedonistic direction. The nonhedonistic version of utilitarianism practiced by Moore and others came to be known as *ideal utilitarianism*. Its basic thesis was that we should always act in a way that produces the greatest amount of goodness, not simply pleasure. For several decades, many people believed that this was the kind of emphasis on consequences that would work. But this view also was clobbered, often through the use of contrasting scenarios in which the ideal utilitarian position ended up supporting unjust situations.

For example, consider world three, in which only guilty people are accused, tried, and convicted, whereas in world four there are times when authorities knowingly and intentionally accuse, try, and convict innocent persons. Suppose the authorities in world four do this only in rare instances and only when, in their judgment, convicting innocent people serves the public good. Something much like this could have happened

---

13. All that is required for these arguments to succeed is for the descriptions to be logically possible.

in the case of the infamous London killer known as Jack the Ripper. Between August 7 and November 10, 1888, operating within a square mile of slums in London's East End, the unknown killer murdered as many as fourteen drunken prostitutes by slitting their throats and eviscerating them. One theory as to the murderer's identity is that he was a mentally disturbed nephew of Queen Victoria who was finally institutionalized. After he was committed, the killings stopped.

Suppose the London authorities believed that it would harm the public good if the queen's nephew were accused of the crime and that it would help the public good if another mentally deranged person, this one a poor resident of the London slums without any family, were tried and convicted. Such an act would satisfy the desire of the people of the city for justice and for an end to the killings. This would be a significant accomplishment for the small price of punishing an innocent person who could not defend himself.

According to ideal utilitarianism, the greater quantity of goodness produced thereby in world four would make it ethically superior to world three. This is one example of the kinds of paradoxes people raised to embarrass ideal utilitarianism. A century later, it is extremely difficult to find anyone interested in defending hedonistic or ideal utilitarianism as it was taught between 1860 and 1920. A different kind of utilitarianism known as rule utilitarianism has its advocates, but interested people will have to pursue that subject in other books.[14]

I don't have time to go into detail on these theories except to say that all the king's horses and all the king's men cannot put consequentialism back together again. The position has been badly beaten up in the twentieth century. While consequences of our actions are often important, they can hardly be the only thing we should consider in determining the morality of an action.

---

14. It is customary in this connection to distinguish between act utilitarianism and rule utilitarianism. Both Mill and Moore were act utilitarians who appealed to consequences to determine the morality of individual acts. Rule utilitarians appeal to consequences as a way of justifying the rules by which a society will be governed. In the view of many, rule utilitarianism ultimately stumbles over specific cases that violate basic moral intuitions.

OPTIONAL WRITING ASSIGNMENT

Assume that a friend of yours prides himself on his tolerance and open-mindedness. One reason he wants you to know that he has become an ethical relativist is because he believes you're too rigid and too intolerant because of your belief in transcendent and objective moral standards. After careful study of this chapter, write an essay laying out how you would answer your friend.

FOR FURTHER READING

Joseph Fletcher, *Situation Ethics: The New Morality* (Philadelphia: Westminster Press, 1966).

William Frankena, *Ethics* (Englewood Cliffs, N.J.: Prentice-Hall, 1973).

William Lillie, *An Introduction to Ethics* (New York: Barnes and Noble, 1964).

Alasdair MacIntyre, *A Short History of Ethics* (New York: Collier, 1966).

Scott B. Rae, *Moral Choices: An Introduction to Ethics* (Grand Rapids: Zondervan, 1995).

Louis P. Pojman, *Ethics: Discovering Right and Wrong* (Belmont, Calif.: Wadsworth, 1990).

Chapter Seventeen

Ethics II:
The Upward Path

If the failed positions discussed in chapter 16 represent the downward path in ethics, what are the basic components of what I call the upward path? I begin by noting several distinctions introduced by a British philosopher, Sir David Ross, in the 1920s. His insights can serve as a starting point for what I hope to accomplish in this chapter. With that behind us, I will begin to focus on such concepts as justice, law, virtue (character), and love.

Right Acts and Morally Good Actions

By this distinction Ross meant to draw attention to the fact that any moral behavior can be viewed from at least two perspectives: (1) Is the moral behavior fitting, is it the right thing to do? In the case of right or wrong acts, we are considering the "outside" of the act. The rightness of an act has nothing to do, Ross said, with the agent's reasons for performing it. An act's rightness is determined solely by whether it was or was not the correct, the fitting, the proper thing to do. To help a little old lady across the street is the right thing to do (providing that she wishes to cross the street). But one can do all sorts of right acts for the wrong reasons. And so this led Ross to the second part of his distinction, morally good actions. (2) An action is morally good if the agent's motives or intentions are good. Here we are considering the "inside" of the action.

Given the distinction between right acts and morally good actions, four possibilities exist:

(1) A deed that is a right act and a morally good action.
(2) A deed that is a right act and a morally bad action.
(3) A deed that is a wrong act and a morally good action.
(4) A deed that is a wrong act and a morally bad action.

To qualify as an example of (1), a deed would have to be both the fitting thing to do and be done from a proper motive. An example is when I, prompted by a good motive, give money to a worthy charity.

To qualify as an example of (2), my deed would have to be the right thing to do but be tainted by a bad motive. Suppose I'm walking along the beach, and I hear that a person is caught in a riptide and is being dragged out into deep water where he might drown. Even though I'm a good swimmer and could easily rescue the person in danger, I decide to continue walking and enjoying the day. But then suppose I hear that the person in trouble is famous and wealthy. Suddenly motivated by the possibility of financial gain, I jump into the water, grab the celebrity by the hair, and pull him to shore. While I did the right thing, my bad motives contaminate my deed. Naturally, it is better to save a drowning person than not. But motives do count.

To qualify as an example of (3), my motives would have to be pure even as I perform the wrong act. Suppose I sincerely intend to make a friend happy by bringing him and his wife gifts. However, I'm unaware of the fact that events in both of their past lives result in my friends misinterpreting the reason for my gifts. Both people end up with hurt feelings.

To qualify as an example of (4), my motives would have to be bad even as I perform the wrong act. Suppose I want to hurt someone and accomplish that objective by telling a lie.

If I were to ask you to identify the most preferable kind of deed, I'm sure you would select type (1). But then suppose I ask you to select the next best kind of behavior; which would you select, and why? This could make for an interesting class discussion.

Justice

Near the end of chapter 16, we saw how utilitarian or consequentialist theories of ethics run afoul of the notion of justice. Any ethical theory that justifies unjust behavior deserves criticism. While many people talk about justice, few have a clear understanding of what justice is. And that failing on their part often encourages new forms of injustice. For this reason, the so-called upward path that we're following in this chapter should include some analysis of the notion of justice.

The Classical Analysis of Justice

The ancient Greeks, most notably Plato and Aristotle, believed that justice always involves giving people their due, that to which they have a right. The reason why a person may be due something varies with his or her situation. A hypothetical person named Jones would be due something in each of the following cases:

(1) If Jones does better work than any other student in the class, she is due the best grade.
(2) If Jones is the first to finish a race, she is due the prize.
(3) If Jones is promised something by Smith, Jones is due the fulfillment of that promise.
(4) If Jones's property is stolen or damaged by Smith, Jones is due whatever reparation is required to restore what she lost.

The what and why of any person's due cannot be reduced to a single formula of the form "to each according to her _____." Many attempts have been made to complete this phrase with terms like ability, need, and achievement. But each of these criteria would fit some situations and not others. However much the determination of a person's due varies with the situation, it seems clear that the nature of justice involves each person having or receiving that which she is due. However complex the total analysis of justice may become, any adequate inquiry must retain this ancient insight.

The Universal and Particular Senses of Justice

One of the great merits of Aristotle's discussion of justice was his attempt to distinguish the more important meanings of the word. As Aristotle saw it, a person can be said to be just in two different senses.[1] The first of these, *universal justice,* is coextensive with the whole of righteousness, with the whole of virtue. A person is just in the universal sense if he possesses all the proper virtues, if he is moral, if he keeps the laws, which Aristotle thought should accord with virtuous behavior. A soldier who runs away from the enemy during a battle is unjust (unrighteous) in the universal sense. So too is a husband who is unfaithful to his wife or who fails to provide for his family. The just human being in Aristotle's universal sense is the person who acts virtuously toward others.

The Bible also utilizes this universal sense of justice. It is present in Genesis 6:9, where Noah is described as a just man who is perfect in all his ways. In Ezekiel 18:5, the just man is defined as one who does what is lawful and right. In fact, the vast majority of biblical allusions to justice appear to be examples of justice in this universal sense.[2] Attention to this fact is important because many who are anxious to find biblical support for leftist political programs quote many of these passages about justice.[3] Read carefully, however, the texts are irrelevant to these purposes.

A person is just in the universal sense if he is virtuous and keeps the laws of his country (Aristotle), if he keeps the commandments of God (the Old Testament), if he is kind and charitable, if he provides for his family, if he helps the poor; in other words, if he manifests the virtues normally associated with being a moral or righteous person. The reason Aristotle referred to righteousness as universal justice is because this is the kind of behavior we have a right to expect humans to exhibit regard-

---

1. Aristotle's examination of justice is found in book 5 of his *Nichomachean Ethics.*

2. See 2 Samuel 23:3; Job 29:14–17; Psalm 82:3; Proverbs 20:7; Jeremiah 9:24; Isaiah 26:7; Micah 6:8; 2 Corinthians 9:8–10, and so on.

3. For a book full of examples, see Ronald H. Nash, *Why the Left Is Not Right: The Religious Left, Who They Are and What They Believe* (Grand Rapids: Zondervan, 1996).

less of their station or situations in life. A different sense of justice is called *particular justice* because humans can manifest it only when they occupy particular situations in life. Universal justice is justice as righteousness; particular justice is justice as fairness.

The Major Kinds of Particular Justice

In the case of particular justice, people are just if they treat others fairly, if they do not grasp after more than they are due. Aristotle distinguished three kinds of particular justice.

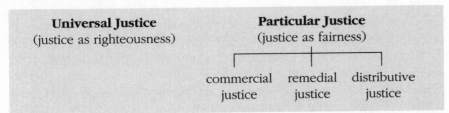

Figure 17.1

Interpersonal relations involving economic exchanges raise questions of *commercial justice*. When people exchange goods and services, questions arise as to whether the exchange is fair. Passages of Scripture like Leviticus 19:36 and Proverbs 16:11 that oblige merchants to have just scales and weights seem directed to this type of justice.

Instances where some wrong must be made right under either criminal or civil law are occasions for *remedial justice*. Cases where an innocent individual is found guilty or where the punishment for an offense is too severe or too lenient are instances of injustice in this sense. Exodus 23:3–6 is one of a number of biblical passages that speaks to issues of remedial justice.

Finally, questions about *distributive justice* arise in situations where some good or burden is apportioned among human beings. Such situations are encountered frequently as, for example, when a parent divides the dessert among the members of a large family or a woman divides her estate among her heirs. As the term is often used in contemporary writings, *social justice* is viewed as that species of distributive justice concerned with the distribution of burdens and benefits within society as a whole, a distribution that is usually controlled by political authorities.

The Relation Between Justice and Equality

As before, the writings of Aristotle are a good place to begin an exploration of the relationship between justice and equality. For Aristotle, the basic principle of all just action (in the particular sense of justice) is summarized in the statement that *equals should be treated equally and unequals unequally*. Injustice always exists when similar people are treated differently or when dissimilars are treated alike. Chaim Perelman has referred to

Aristotle's formula as the Formal Principle of Justice.[4] While the formal principle is, many believe, a necessary condition for any just action, its admirers are quick to admit the deficiencies of the principle. For one thing, it is not a sufficient principle of justice. That is, conformity to it will not guarantee justice. For example, a society might decide to treat all members of a particular class alike but badly, something Hitler's Germany did during World War II. Equal treatment of equals can be unjust if the criteria by which people are grouped into classes are discriminatory and irrelevant to their claims to justice. The most serious weakness of the so-called Formal Principle of Justice is the absence of a criterion to identify which of the many ways people can be compared are relevant to questions of justice. If one is assigning grades in a philosophy class or deciding the winner of an election, the factors that should count in each case are both different and fairly obvious. It is unlikely that a young man's inability to write a good philosophy essay will disqualify him from membership on a football team whereas weighing only seventy pounds might.

Something else must be added to the formal principle to complete the picture of justice and identify the relevant respects in which similarities require similar treatment. Aristotle believed that human equality and inequality should count only in instances where the similarity or difference is relevant to what is being distributed. While the parentage of a flute player is not relevant to the distribution of flutes to orchestra members, musical ability is. It is not enough to add up the ways in which human beings are equal or unequal. One must count only those respects that are relevant to what is being distributed. Aristotle's formal principle leaves open the possibility of discriminatory treatment. Similar people in similar situations should be treated alike. But the presence of relevant differences also mandates different treatment. Left unstated in Aristotle's account is a principle to identify which differences should count as grounds for unequal treatment.

Material Principles of Justice

In an effort to supplement the formal principle, some philosophers have sought a *material* principle of justice that would supply criteria for justifying dissimilar treatment. A number of these proposed material principles are clearly inadequate. For example, many possible bases of unequal treatment are unacceptable because they are factors for which no one can claim responsibility or credit. This consideration has been used to rule out all attempts to ground a distribution on criteria like sex, race, height, or eye color. Other possible criteria for unequal treatment like

---

4. Chaim Perelman, *The Idea of Justice and the Problem of Argument* (New York: Humanities Press, 1963), chap. 1.

wealth, power, and social position have been challenged because they depend upon earlier distributions which themselves may have been unjust. Critics of such a view hold that no theory of distribution can be acceptable that is based upon some feature that may have resulted from unjust human action. They think a person's sex, race, wealth, power, or social position should not be used as the basis on which he or she receives a larger or smaller share of what is distributed.

The most promising candidates for a material principle of justice are well-known. They include such factors as ability, past achievement, effort, need, merit, and desert. Depending on the context, the application of any of these criteria might be correct. If it is medical care that is being distributed, the health needs of the patient are relevant. If a parent is distributing praise to her children, the deeds or effort of the child are relevant. The distribution of wages is often pertinent to a laborer's work. Great difficulties result from the attempt to elevate any one of these principles to the exclusion of the others. No single, all-embracing material principle of distribution can be adequate. Sometimes need is relevant, but not always. Sometimes, but not always, merit should count.

Some religious thinkers advance need as the ultimate material principle of justice. Robert K. Johnston claims that the biblical definition of justice is "to each according to his or her needs."[5] The Bible nowhere says such a thing; Johnston is reading his own ideology into the Bible. Johnston criticizes other norms of justice as secular in origin, as an intrusion of secular ideologies into what should be an exclusively biblical position. It is ironic that his own formulation of justice, which he insists is not derived from a secular ideology, is a paraphrase of one offered by Karl Marx.

The unsoundness of all attempts to push something like need as the exclusive principle of material justice always fails. Sometimes inequalities based on need are just, but many times they are not. A just distribution of grades for a college course should have nothing to do with whether a student needs a particular grade, as many football players used to plead in my university courses. In the case of a college grade, the just grade should be assigned on the basis of what the student has earned, not what he needs. The notion of need is ambiguous. People need things for many different reasons. A student may feel he needs a particular grade in order to stay on the football team, in order to graduate, in order to continue on the dean's list so as to qualify for a scholarship, or to increase the student's self-esteem. However much sympathy such needs may generate, they should not be relevant in cases like this.

Many believe, perhaps rightly, that a good society will not allow certain fundamental and essential human needs to go unmet while a surplus

---

5. Robert K. Johnston, *Evangelicals at an Impasse* (Atlanta: John Knox, 1979), 98.

exists. Unfortunately, need is too elastic a concept to serve as the precise standard required for distributive justice. Needs have a way of being generated and expanded as people become accustomed to former luxuries. If need is to function as one of the several material principles of justice, society must find some way to identify the essential needs in a given situation. It is also unclear whether the efforts of a society to meet such essential needs should be described as justice or charity.

Summary

What should we learn from a study of classical discussions of justice? (1) Justice occurs in situations where people receive their due. (2) Distributive justice occurs in situations where equals are treated equally and unequals are treated unequally. (3) But this knowledge won't get us very far until we discover some principle that will tell us the relevant respects on which equal and unequal treatment should be based. (4) Several clearly inappropriate material principles of justice were identified. (5) The criteria that may be appropriate are many and varied. No one of them will work in every case. (6) While much about the notion of justice remains unclear, it is certain that justice and equality are not equivalent. Sometimes equal treatment is just; often it is not. Frequently, justice will require that people be treated differently. But in all the circumstances of life, we should seek to treat people fairly, a fact that requires us to seek the relevant ways in which different people are alike and dissimilar.

Law

Chapter 7 in part 1 contains important material on Thomas Aquinas's accounts of the natural law and God's revealed law. This would be a good time to review that material in connection with this chapter. Natural law provides general moral guidance but needs to be supplemented with more specific content from special revelation.

Many human experiences seem to point to the existence of moral laws or standards of behavior. Our failure to do something that we believe we ought to do may lead us to feel guilt. The failure of others to perform certain duties toward us may produce feelings of resentment or anger or sorrow. Whenever we dare to suggest to someone else that his conduct is wrong, we are doing more than appealing to our own moral standard. Moral criticism like this would make no sense unless we also believed that the other person knew about the same moral standard. It is interesting to note that the person whose moral conduct is being criticized seldom denies the existence of the moral standard. That is, such people seldom try to argue that there is nothing wrong with cheating, stealing, or lying. Such people attempt rather to find some way of showing that what they did doesn't violate the principle or at least is a justifiable exception to the moral standard.

C. Stephen Evans points out that

> this standard, this "law" if you will, is therefore not simply a description about how people behave. It is a prescription about how people should behave, though one they are constantly violating. So morality is not simply a law of nature like the law of gravity. It doesn't describe how things in nature go on, but how human behavior ought to go on.[6]

An important feature of this moral law is what we take to be its objectivity. By comparison, the laws of mathematics are objective (not subjective) in the sense that their truth is independent of human feelings and desires. When we deal with objective truth, it does not matter whether we like it; it is true—and that's all there is to it! In a similar way, the moral law is independent of our feelings and desires. As C. S. Lewis explains, "There is nothing indulgent about the Moral Law. It is as hard as nails. It tells you to do the straight thing and it does not seem to care how painful, or dangerous, or difficult it is to do."[7] The moral law doesn't care whether we like it, whether we want to obey it, or whether we're disposed to do it. It informs us that this is our duty, now do it!

I do not want to leave the impression that the case for the objectivity of moral laws rests solely on the weakness of arguments against objectivity. "If we did not believe," Ed Miller writes,

> that there is an objective and unchanging foundation of moral values and ideals, then we would never bother to make such judgments, at least not seriously. On the contrary, that we continue to exercise moral judgment, not only in reference to ourselves but also to others, is clear evidence that we do, in fact, take such judgments as counting for something and being ultimately and objectively significant. In this way, it may be argued, it is self-contradictory (practically speaking) to make judgments of moral value and to deny at the same time that there is any objective basis of morality. What can be more comical than someone who spends the day fanatically and passionately crusading for the eradication of certain evils, while in the evening he delivers cool lectures on the relativity of all ideals?[8]

The belief in the existence of an objective and universal moral law qualifies as a rational belief. For anyone who recognizes this fact, the next natural step is to ask what is the source and ground of the moral law. British philosopher Hastings Rashdall summarizes the answer to this question:

> We say that the Moral Law has a real existence, that there is such a thing as an absolute [i.e., objective] Morality, that there is something absolutely

---

6. C. Stephen Evans, *The Quest for Faith* (Downers Grove, Ill.: InterVarsity Press, 1986), 45.

7. C. S. Lewis, *Mere Christianity* (New York: Macmillan, 1960), 37.

8. Ed L. Miller, *God and Reason* (New York: Macmillan, 1972), 90. Note Miller's use of the test of outer experience.

[i.e., objectively] true or false in ethical judgments, whether we or any number of human beings at any given time actually think so or not.... We must therefore face the question *where* such an ideal exists, and what manner of existence we are to attribute to it. Certainly it is to be found wholly and completely, in no individual human consciousness.... Only if we believe in the existence of a Mind for which the true moral ideal is already in some sense real, a Mind which is the source of whatever is true in our own moral judgments, can we rationally think of the moral ideal as no less real than the world itself. Only so can we believe in an absolute standard of right and wrong, which is as independent of this or that belief in God ... is the logical presupposition of an "objective" or absolute Morality. A moral ideal can exist nowhere and nohow but in a Mind; an absolute moral ideal can exist only in a Mind from which all Reality is derived. Our moral ideal can only claim objective validity in so far as it can rationally be regarded as the revelation of a moral ideal eternally existing in the mind of God.[9]

Which worldview best explains our consciousness of an objective moral order? Christian theism must be considered a leading candidate.

Virtue and Character

It is important what we do. It is also important what kind of people we are, a fact that moves us into the territory of virtue ethics. This would be a good time to review the important material about virtue and character in the chapters on Aristotle, Augustine, and Aquinas in part 1. Other information about the importance of character appears in my treatment of human choices (chap. 15). As stated earlier in this chapter, it is not enough that we do the right thing. As important as performing the right act is, we should also make sure that our deeds are morally good actions in the sense that they reflect morally good motives, something that seems unlikely in the case of people who have not been attentive to their character.

Love, Law, and the Christian Ethic

The fact that all human beings carry the image of God (one of Christianity's more important worldview beliefs) explains why human beings are creatures capable of reasoning, love, and God consciousness; it also explains why we are creatures capable of moral behavior. Of course, sin (another of Christianity's presuppositions) has distorted the image of God and explains why humans turn away from God and the moral law; why we often go wrong with regard to our emotions, conduct, and thinking.

Because of the image of God, we should expect to find that the ethical recommendations of the Christian worldview reflect what all of us at the deepest levels of our moral being know to be true. As Lewis pointed out,

---

9. Hastings Rashdall, *The Theory of Good and Evil* (Oxford: Clarendon, 1907), 2:211–12.

ETHICS II: THE UPWARD PATH

Christ did not come to preach any brand new morality.... Really great
moral teachers never do introduce new moralities; it is quacks and cranks
who do that.... The real job of every moral teacher is to keep on bringing us back, time after time, to the old simple principles which we are
all so anxious not to see.[10]

When one examines the moralities of different cultures and religions,
certain differences do stand out. But Lewis was more impressed by the
basic, underlying similarities.

Think of a country where people were admired for running away in battle, or where a man felt proud of doublecrossing all the people who had
been kindest to him. You might just as well try to imagine a country
where two and two made five. Men have differed as regards what people
you ought to be unselfish to—whether it was only your own family, or
your fellow countrymen, or everyone. But they have always agreed that
you ought not to put yourself first. Selfishness has never been admired.[11]

According to the Christian worldview, God is the ground of the laws
that govern the physical universe and that make possible the order of the
cosmos. God is also the ground of the moral laws that make possible the
order of the cosmos. God is the ground of the moral laws that ought to
govern human behavior and that make possible order between humans
and within humans.

Christian theism must insist that there are universal moral laws. In
other words, the laws must apply to all humans, regardless of when or
where they have lived. They must also be objective in the sense that their
truth is independent of human preference and desire.

Principles and Rules

Much confusion surrounding Christian ethics results from a failure to
observe the important distinction between principles and rules. Let us
define *moral principles* as general moral prescriptions, general in the
sense that they are intended to cover a large number of instances. *Moral
rules* will be regarded as more specific moral prescriptions that are appli-
cations of principles to more concrete situations.

The difference between principles and rules contains advantages and
disadvantages. One advantage of moral principles is that they are less subject to change. Because of the larger number of instances they apply to,
they possess a greater degree of universality. One disadvantage of any
moral principle is its vagueness. Because principles cover so many situations, it is often difficult to know exactly when a particular principle
applies. Rules, however, have the advantage of being much more specific.

---

10. Lewis, *Mere Christianity*, 78.
11. Ibid., 19.

Their problem concerns their changeability. Because they are so closely tied to specific situations, changes in the situation usually require changes in the appropriate rule. For example, Paul warned the Christian women of Corinth not to worship with their heads uncovered. Some Christians have mistakenly regarded Paul's advice as a moral principle that should be observed by Christian women in every culture at all times. But a study of the conditions of ancient Corinth reveals that the city's prostitutes identified themselves to their prospective customers by keeping their heads uncovered. In the light of this, it seems likely that Paul's advice was not a moral principle intended to apply to Christians of all generations but a rule that applied only to the specific situation of the Christian women of Corinth and to women in similar situations.[12]

I recognize that the distinction I am drawing here suffers from some degree of impreciseness. This is due in part to the fact that the difference between principles and rules is sometimes relative. That is, Scripture presents a hierarchy of moral prescriptions, beginning at the most general level with the duty to love. This duty to love is then further broken down into the duties to love God and love man (Matthew 22:37–40) and then still further into the more specific duties of the Decalogue (Romans 13:9–10). Yet more specific duties spelled out in the New Testament, such as the prohibition against the lustful look and hatred, are further specifications of the Ten Commandments (Matthew 5:21–32). The distinction between principles and rules suggests that whenever a more specific scriptural command is derived from one more general, the more specific injunction is the rule and the other is the principle. It is possible to read 1 Corinthians 13 in this way. First, Paul proposes love as a moral duty binding on all humans. Then he proceeds to provide more specific rules about how a loving person will behave; for example, he will be kind and patient.

Based on our distinction between principles and rules plus a careful study of the New Testament, several conclusions can be drawn. (1) The New Testament gave first-century Christians plenty of rules. But the rules cover situations that may no longer confront Christians, such as Paul's injunction against eating meat offered to idols. (2) The New Testament does not provide contemporary Christians with any large number of rules regarding our specific situations. The reason for this should be obvious. The rules were given to cover first-century situations. A first-century book that attempted to give moral rules to cover specific situations in the twentieth or twenty-first century would have been unintelligible or irrelevant to readers in the intervening years. What moral help could the first-century

---

12. Even if my particular interpretation of 1 Corinthians 11 is challenged, my point can be made in terms of other New Testament passages. See, for example, Paul's remarks in Romans 14 concerning Christians' eating meat that had been offered to pagan gods.

Christians in Rome or Ephesus have derived from such moral rules as "Thou shalt not make a first strike with nuclear weapons" or "It is wrong to use cocaine"? (3) At the same time, some of the New Testament rules apply to situations that have existed throughout time. Passages dealing with acts of hating, stealing, lying, and the like continue to be relevant because the acts are similar. (4) But often what many people miss is the importance of searching out the moral principles behind the New Testament rules. These principles are equally binding on humans of all generations. A careful consideration of the Bible's first-century rules can enable us to infer the more general principles behind them, principles that apply to us. It may be unimportant today whether Christian women keep their heads covered, but it is important that they avoid provocative dress and behavior. Though few Christians in our generation are bothered by pagan butchers who have offered their wares as a sacrifice to false gods, we can profit from the principle that we should do nothing that causes a morally weaker person to stumble.

In spite of all this, life often confronts us with ambiguous moral situations in which even the most sincere among us can agonize over what to do. There are times when we do not know enough about ourselves, the situation, or the moral principle that applies to be sure we are doing the right thing. As many of us know, weakness of character can also hinder moral decision making.

In the unambiguous situations of life, Scripture teaches, God judges us in terms of our obedience to his revealed moral law. But how does God judge us in more ambiguous situations where the precise nature of our duty is unclear? God looks upon the heart, Scripture advises. We are judged if we break God's commandments—this is certain. But in those cases where we may not know which commandment applies or where we may have incomplete knowledge of the situation, God's judgment will take into account not merely the rightness of our act's consequences (something that we ourselves are sometimes unable to determine in such ambiguous situations) but also the goodness of our intentions.

OPTIONAL WRITING ASSIGNMENT

Consider the following statement: Justice always means treating people equally. Write an essay either defending or criticizing this claim. Make sure you utilize material from this chapter in your essay.

FOR FURTHER READING

Charles E. Curran and Richard C. McCormick, eds., *Readings in Moral Theology,* vol. 7, *Natural Law and Theology* (New York: Paulist Press, 1992).

Paul Helm, *The Divine Command Theory of Ethics* (New York: Oxford University Press, 1979).

C. S. Lewis, *Mere Christianity* (New York: Macmillan, 1960).

Ronald H. Nash, *Freedom, Justice, and the State* (Lanham, Md.: University Press of America, 1980).

Ronald H. Nash, *Social Justice and the Christian Church* (Lanham, Md.: University Press, of America, 1992).

Scott B. Rae, *Moral Choices: An Introduction to Ethics* (Grand Rapids: Zondervan, 1995).

Chapter Eighteen

Human Nature:
The Mind-Body Problem
and Survival After Death

I often tell students that we know more about objects millions of miles away in space than we know about the thing that is closest to ourselves, namely, our *self,* or soul or mind. The question before us in this chapter amounts to asking What am I? Am I just a body, or am I more than my body? And whatever I am, will death end my existence, or are there good reasons to believe in conscious personal existence after death?

It doesn't make much sense to address the issue of survival after death until we first gain a clearer understanding of the human mind or soul and its relation to the body. I will identify seven different theories about the mind and body, six of which will be represented on a chart. The seventh position, sometimes known as central-state materialism or mind-body identity theory, must be covered separately because of the difficulty of diagramming the position. Before the chart makes its appearance, a few words of introduction are necessary. For example, the chart refers to what are often called mental and physical events. I use the star (*) as a way of indicating mental events and the plus sign (+) to refer to physical events. When I talk about physical events, I mean things like playing a piano, pushing a table, raking leaves, throwing a baseball, riding a bicycle, drinking a Coke, combing my hair, and things like that.[1] By a mental event, I mean things like discovering the sum of nine times sixty-four, sensing a pain in my big toe, remembering a joke, having a bad dream, or thinking about the perfect circle. Mental events include such activities as thinking, believing, intending, sensing, wishing, imagining, and so on.

A physical activity requires that any other physical objects related to the event or activity must exist in the physical world. If the physical activity we're considering is pushing something, there must exist something

Seven Theories About the Mind-Body Problem

---

1. For the record, some unkind people would, in my case, regard combing one's hair as an imaginary act, thus placing it, for me at least, in the domain of mental events.

like a lawn mower or an automobile or a table for me to push. It is impossible to push a nonexistent object. However, it is not necessary that the objects of mental activities exist in the world. Mental activity can take as its object something that does not exist. I can think about things like unicorns, Tinker Bell, and the Wizard of Oz. Mental activity is sometimes intentional while physical activity is never intentional. And now my chart:

Figure 18.1

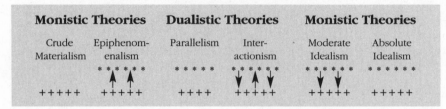

My chart necessarily ignores many other options, one of which (mind-brain identity theory) I will cover separately. Also, please note that I treat epiphenomenalism as a form of materialistic monism, even though some regard it as a type of dualism.

The six theories fall into three major categories. The two positions in the middle are forms of *mind-body dualism,* that is, they affirm the full and complete existence of both body and soul or mind. The two positions to the left of my chart are forms of *physical monism*. Physical monists either deny the existence of soul or mind or reduce it to body. The two positions on the right of my chart are forms of *immaterial monism*. Immaterial monists do to body what physical monists do to soul, that is, either deny its existence or reduce it to mind.

Absolute Idealism

Absolute idealism denies the existence of body. While a position like this seems far-fetched to contemporary men and women, it had several proponents in the nineteenth century, one of whom was a German philosopher named Arthur Schopenhauer (1788–1860). Schopenhauer, a pantheist who thought of himself as a western proponent of religious ideas from the orient, published his theory in *The World as Will and Idea* (1818). According to Schopenhauer, "The world is my idea. The world is an illusion. Beneath appearances, we are all one and the same." At this moment in the history of ideas, there does not seem to be any good reason to spend more time on this theory.

Crude Materialism

This theory's denial of the existence of mind and mental events is experiencing a revival. Since *crude materialism* denies the facts of human introspection, it purports to solve problems that have troubled humans for thousands of years by denying what we all know about the contents of our minds. One famous proponent of crude materialism was the German thinker Ludwig Feurbach (1804–1872). If crude materialism were true, I could discover that I have a pain by observing my behavior; I could in principle discover when you have a pain by observing your behavior. When we say that people are in pain, however, we do not mean they are behaving in a certain way. There is no contradiction in stating that Mr. Smith is suffering from pain even though he does not behave as though he is.

Epiphenomenalism and Moderate Idealism

The next two theories moving from both the right and the left are mirror images of each other. The positions labeled on my chart as *epiphenomenalism* and *moderate idealism* acknowledge the existence of mental events (as in the case of the first) or physical events (per the latter) but treat them as ephemeral byproducts either of body (as with epiphenomenalism) or of mind (as with moderate idealism). For epiphenomenalism, there are such things as thoughts, beliefs, and pains. Surely my readers know the difference between something's stimulating nerve endings in a leg and the consciousness of pain that is in the mind. According to an epiphenomenalist, when the brain (part of the body) dies or ceases to function, mental events cease to exist. According to the moderate idealist, all physical objects are nothing more than ideas in the mind of some perceiver.

Moderate idealism was taught by the eighteenth-century British philosopher George Berkeley (1685–1753). In his system, what most of us regard as the world of bodies and other physical objects is a collection of ideas that exist first and foremost in the mind of God who, we could say, loans these ideas to our minds. Berkeley regarded his form of idealism as a serious objection against any form of materialism. If there is no such thing as matter, it will be hard to be a materialist. He also thought his idealism offered an important set of reasons for believing in God. After all, if there is no divine mind to act as a home for the collections of ideas that we take to be real entities, then things like cars, chairs, and trees would come in and out of existence, depending upon whether any human was perceiving them.[2]

In spite of serious difficulties, epiphenomenalism still receives more respect than it deserves. Epiphenomenalism does not deny immaterial mental events or consciousness. But it denies that mental events can influence physical events. There is a causal relation between body and mind, but it is not reciprocal. Physical events can cause mental events, but mental events can never cause physical events. Human minds can have no effect on the course of events. As Thomas Huxley, one of the best-known proponents of epiphenomenalism, has stated,

---

2. Berkeley is an interesting thinker whose arguments merit serious consideration but not at this time and not in this book.

All states of consciousness in us, as in [animals], are immediately caused by molecular changes of the brain-substance. It seems to me that in men, as in brutes, there is no proof that any state of consciousness is the cause of change in the motion of the matter of the organism. If these positions are well based, it follows that our mental conditions are simply the symbols in consciousness of the changes which take place automatically in the organism; and that, to take an extreme illustration, the feeling we call volition is not the cause of a voluntary act, but the symbol of that state of the brain which is the immediate cause of that act. We are conscious automata ... [3]

If epiphenomenalism is true, it cannot be true. In other words, it is a good example of the kind of logically self-defeating theories we noted in chapter 8 of this book. Philosopher J. B. Pratt has examined this weakness of the theory:

To say that a thought is even in a minute degree a co-cause of the following thought would be to wreck [epiphenomenalism]. In the process known as reasoning, therefore, it is a mistake to suppose that consciousness of logical relations has anything whatever to do with the result.... We may happen to think logically; but if we do, this is not because logic had anything to do with our conclusion, but because the brain molecules shake down, so to speak, in a lucky fashion. It is plain, therefore, that no conclusion that we men can reach can ever claim to be based on logic. It is forever impossible to demonstrate that any thesis is logically necessary.[4]

Epiphenomalism denies mind any active role in nature or history. Mind has no causal power with respect to the body. This means, among other things, that deliberations of the mind can neither prove epiphenomenalism true nor lead people to accept it. Moreover, plenty of evidence suggests that the causal relation goes in both directions, that it is reciprocal, that mental events can and do cause physical events.

To bring this brief account of materialistic and idealistic monism to an end, materialists believe the existence of body is a necessary condition for the existence of mind, while idealists believe the existence of mind is a necessary condition for the existence of body.

Mind-Brain Identity Theory

While *mind-brain identity theory,* also known as central-state materialism, does not appear on my chart, it is a widely accepted version of materialism.[5] It differs from crude materialism in asserting the existence of mind but

---

3. T. H. Huxley, *Method and Results* (New York: Appleton-Century-Crofts, 1893), 244.
4. J. B. Pratt, *Matter and Spirit* (New York: Macmillan, 1922).
5. See Herbert Feigel, "The Mind-Body Problem in the Development of Logical Empiricism," in *Readings in the Philosophy of Science,* ed. Herbert Feigel and May Brodbeck (New York: Appleton, 1953); J. J. C. Smart, "Sensations and Brain Processes," *The Philosophical*

differs from dualism with regard to the nature of mind. Mind-brain identity theorists do not deny consciousness, nor do they deny a causal role for mental events. The human mind is not a mysterious immaterial thing; it is nothing more than the human brain attached to the central nervous system. Incidents of consciousness are physical occurrences inside the brain. The theory claims that every apparent mental event is identical to some event within the brain. Talk about mind does not have the same meaning as talk about brain processes. People can talk about their minds without understanding that their language refers to the brain, a part of their body. They have to discover that the mind and brain are identical, just as people had to discover that a bachelor and an unmarried man are identical.

When identity theorists are challenged by the apparent implausibility of identifying mind and brain, they respond by making a distinction between the meaning of a statement and its referent. Two words can have different meanings yet still refer to the same thing. Consider, for example, the terms "evening star" and "morning star." For thousands of years, observers of the heavens defined the terms differently.[6] Today we know that both terms denote the same object, namely, the planet Venus.

Several noteworthy objections have been raised to mind-brain identity theory. For one thing, philosopher Jerome Shaffer explains, "it makes sense to ask of a neural event where it occurred in the body (even if the answer is that it occurred in no local place but throughout the nervous system), whereas it makes no sense to ask where in the body the thought occurred. Since two putatively different things can turn out to be one and the same only if they have the same location, it cannot be the case that thoughts and neural events are identical.... We rarely, if ever, feel sensations in our brain."[7] While physical events have location, mental events do not. How can two such different events be identical when they do not occupy the same space?

Shaffer notes another objection when he writes that identity theory cannot explain the fact that one essential trait of mental events is "the privileged position of the subject with respect to his own mental events. If they were ordinary physical events, why should the subject be in a position to report their occurrence without having to make the observations or inferences the rest of us would have to make? That [mental events] can be known, but not in the way physical events can be known suggests that they are not physical events."[8] The fact that we have privileged access to

Review 68 (1959): 651–62. For a critique, see Jerome Shaffer, "Mental Events and the Brain," *The Journal of Philosophy* 60 (1963): 160–66.

6. One was the brightest heavenly body seen in the early evening; the other was the brightest in the early morning sky.

7. Jerome Shaffer, "Mind-Body Problem," in *The Encyclopedia of Philosophy*, ed. Paul Edwards (New York: Macmillan, 1967), 5:339.

8. Ibid.

our mental events strongly suggests they are distinct from physical events. Many believe that difficulties like these are sufficient to disqualify the identity theory as a plausible theory.

Dualism

As we have seen, the basic question in the mind-body problem concerns whether a human being is composed of one thing or two. In the intellectual atmosphere of the moment, the dominant position among academics is some type of materialism or physicalism. However, dualism is making a comeback, even though many secularists thought the dualist position died and was buried a long time ago. We come now to the two forms of dualism in the middle of the chart. We can dispense with mind-body parallelism rather quickly.

Mind-Body Parallelism

Mind-body parallelism is usually associated with the seventeenth-century philosopher Baruch Spinoza (1632–1677). Spinoza's theory affirms that both mental and physical events exist but that no causal interaction between them occurs. It is helpful here to think of parallel railroad tracks that never meet. On one track occur mental events, while all physical events are confined to the second track. Every time either a mental or physical event occurs, a corresponding event appears on the other track. Spinoza's explanation of this was based on his claim that mind and body are attributes or aspects of one more fundamental substance. In the case of Spinoza, this one substance was a pantheistic God.

Mind-Body Interactionism

The last remaining position on the chart is mind-body interactionism. As the term *mind-body interactionism* suggests, our second type of dualism teaches that both mental events and physical events exist and that causal interaction can and does occur between them. That is, physical events (a kick to a shin) can cause a mental event (pain), and mental events (such as concentrated thinking about a lemon meringue pie) can cause a physical event (salivating). Another sign of physical influence upon mind appears in the fact that physical fatigue or injury can hinder mental processes. Not only can mind act causally upon body and body act causally upon mind, but also mental and physical events can exist without causal influence from the other sphere of activity. One example of a mental event uncaused by physical events would be a person's adding a column of numbers. An example of a physical event with no relation to mental events would be a person blinking his eyes or turning over in his sleep. The most obvious problem with mind-body dualism is figuring out how two very different entities such as a physical body occupying space and an immaterial mind can causally affect each other.

Mind-body interactionism is often associated with the thinking of René Descartes, a French rationalist (1596–1650). Descartes can be blamed for a common caricature of interactionism called "the Ghost in the Machine."[9] This distortion of interactionism has led many to view the human body as a machine with a ghostlike soul peering out at the world through the human eyes. Christian theists have a stake in avoiding any view of the human person that might appear to support this metaphor. C. Stephen Evans points them in the right direction when he writes that to speak of a person's soul

> is not to speak of a ghost residing in a person. It is to speak of the person himself (or herself)—that essential core which makes us persons. Christians are very clear that we are meant to be embodied. In this life and in our ultimate intended state after death, personhood is expressed in bodily form: it is incarnated. But our personhood can survive the death of our present bodies. The power of God, which gives us life now, can continue our conscious, personal history in a new body.[10]

Any satisfactory solution to the mind-body problem must take account of the fact that the mind has a significant relationship with the body (brain). Neither body nor mind can be absorbed into the other. A major blow to the head can cause a loss of consciousness. Artificial stimulation of parts of the brain can affect consciousness. We are a unity; we act as a whole. Some mental states can affect the body. Stress can bring on ulcers; anxiety can paralyze limbs.

The Major Objection to Interactionism

Over the past century and a half, a variety of objections have been raised against mind-body interactionism. While few of them have had much staying power and thus deserve no attention here, nonetheless the general perception among intellectuals is that mind-body interactionism has been discredited, has been hurt so badly that no sensible person treats it as a live option. I recall during my years as a graduate student in philosophy watching other students and professors roll their eyes upon learning that they were in the presence of not only a dualist but also an interactionist.[11] Those were the years (the late 1950s and early 1960s) when many acted as though all one had to do to dismiss interactionism was toss out the phrase "the ghost in the machine." Those old objections, which can easily be found in many introduction to philosophy texts published before

---

9. Descartes is also famous for his suggestion that the point of contact between the immaterial soul and the physical body lay in the pineal gland located at the base of the brain.

10. C. Stephen Evans, *The Quest for Faith* (Downers Grove, Ill.: InterVarsity Press, 1986), 123.

11. There were a few exceptions back then, including C. J. Ducasse, by that time an emeritus professor of philosophy at Brown University. But Ducasse was hardly a Christian theist.

1990, impressed people solely because they fed into the antidualist bias of the day.

The major objection to dualism that is still standing concerns the alleged impossibility of two such different things as mind and body interacting. The qualitative difference between mind and body is too fundamental for us even to conceive a reciprocal relationship. How can an immaterial soul without any physical properties cause changes in a material body possessing no mental properties? How can an immaterial soul cause a body to move? How can a physical body give rise to a mental event like pain in the mind? Obviously, such things cannot happen. Therefore, mind-body interaction is impossible. In the words of British philosopher C. D. Broad, humankind's inability to explain how interaction between two such disparate things as mind and body "is supposed to show that, however closely correlated certain pairs of events in mind and body respectively may be, they cannot be causally connected."[12] Broad's answer reveals how weak the objection is: "One would like to know just how unlike two events may be before it becomes impossible to admit the existence of a causal relation between them. No one hesitates to hold that draughts and colds in the head are causally connected, although the two are extremely unlike each other. If the unlikeness of draughts and colds in the head does not prevent one from admitting a causal connection between the two, why should the unlikeliness of volitions and voluntary movements prevent one from holding that they are causally connected?"[13]

While skeptics continue to claim that mind and body cannot interact, we continue to be aware of the causation that occurs between them. Many mysterious events seem that they should not occur, but they do. It was once thought inconceivable that humans could fly or live on the underside of the earth. While we all acknowledge the force known as gravity, none of us understands it or can explain it. There are many cases in life where we know that one thing causes another, even though we don't know how. As J. P. Moreland explains, "A magnetic field can move a tack, gravity can act on a planet millions of miles away, protons exert a repulsive force on each other, and so forth."[14]

Considerations That Support Dualism

If there are only two live options, some form of physicalism such as the mind-brain identity theory or dualism, then the discovery of one thing true of mental events that is not true of physical events disproves physicalism.

---

12. C. D. Broad, *The Mind and Its Place in Nature* (London: Routledge and Kegan Paul, 1962), 97.

13. Ibid., 98.

14. J. P. Moreland, "Basic Questions About Human Nature," in *Christian Perspectives on Being Human*, ed. J. P. Moreland and David M. Ciocchi (Grand Rapids: Baker, 1993), 76.

Physical and mental events possess significantly different features. Physical substances have weight, are located in space, are composed of chemicals, and, in the case of the brain, have electrical features. However, my own thoughts and other mental events do not.

Another difference between mental and physical properties appears in the fact that mental properties are self-presenting, which is to say that we are aware of them directly. My mental events are directly present to me. My awareness of them is not mediated by anything else. They are in my consciousness immediately. All of this is related to issues of private access (I can know the contents of my mind while you cannot) and incorrigibility.[15] These differences strongly indicate that mental states cannot be equated with physical states.

The Christian View of the Human Person

The following quote from Peter Kreeft and Ronald K. Tacelli serves to tie together many of the important points presented thus far:

> Christians believe that the human person is a mysterious unity of matter and spirit. There is a part of us that is extended in three dimensions and takes up space; this we call "matter." But there is another facet of the unity we are which cannot be thought of in that way; this is the part of us we call "spirit." Scripture says that God breathed life into lifeless matter, and that image of breath and life is most appropriate to the nature of spiritual being. The human spirit animates matter, gives it vital energy and gathers it into a living organic unity. That is what God created it to do. Thus Christians believe that a human spirit exists for a body; it was made to exist in matter as its life-giving principle. This means that all those parts of human life that seem most essentially spiritual, like knowing and choosing, also involve the body; the spirit experiences *through* the body. And so human life involves a most intimate relation between these two sides of our being: matter needs spirit to bind it into a functioning unity; spirit needs matter to release its potential for pursuing and enjoying all the goods, moral and intellectual, proper to a human life.[16]

The kind of substance dualism defended thus far holds important implications for another significant question about the human self: What is the ground of a person's identity before death and after death? Evans makes an important point when he writes,

The Continuing Self and Human Identity

> The identity of a human being is not found merely by looking at the body as a physical object. I am who I am because of my thoughts, feelings,

---

15. See chapter 12 of this book.

16. *Handbook of Christian Apologetics* (Downers Grove, Ill.: InterVarsity Press, 1994), 234–35. The authors use "spirit" as a synonym for soul.

actions, memories and other rich elements of consciousness, which form my personal history. Even in this life I am not simply a physical object: the atoms which compose my body are constantly changing, yet my "person" remains. Christians have traditionally affirmed this truth that we are more than physical objects by speaking of people as *souls* and *spirits* as well as *bodies*.[17]

Let me underscore some of the points made in this paragraph.

The first point is the question of human identity through the three score years and ten that most of us are given. During seventy years, it is estimated that the molecules of a human body undergo a complete change ten times. If I have no soul or mind, if I am nothing but a body, how can I be identical with the baby, with the third grader, with the high school student, with the college graduate, with the father, with the grandfather, to mention just six episodes of my sixty-two years? One of life's ultimate questions that few people think about outside of a philosophy classroom is personal identity throughout time. Am I the same person who experienced so much over so many years that are now just memories? How can I be praised or blamed for what I did ten years ago unless I am a continuing self? If physicalism or materialism is true, how can I be the same person?

According to Moreland, "substance dualists hold to a literal, absolute sense of personal identity and physicalists and property dualists hold to a loose, relative sense of personal identity that amounts to a stream of successive selves held together by resemblance between each self in the stream, similarity of memory or brain, similarity of character traits, and/or spatial continuity."[18] Advocates of substance dualism, the fact that my self or soul or mind is an immaterial substance distinct from the body, insist on a literal sense of personal identity. In their view, I am the same person, I am identical with the person who was born, went to Parma High, graduated from Brown and Syracuse universities, taught at Western Kentucky University, and is now teaching at Reformed Theological Seminary. The fact that I have memories of all the experiences of those years presupposes that I am the same person.

Our privileged access to these memories of the past, my consciousness of the present, and the case I can make for a continuing self during all of the changes my body has undergone during my lifetime constitute important arguments for dualism and for the belief that I am more than my body.

I am conscious of my self, the center of my consciousness, as something that is different from my body and also different from my mental experiences. I have a direct awareness that I am different from my body

---

17. Evans, *Quest for Faith*, 122.
18. Moreland, "Basic Questions," 70.

and my mental events. I am the person that has my body and that has my mental life. As Moreland puts it, "I am the owner of my experiences and I am an enduring self who possesses all of my experiences through time."[19] All this shows, Moreland continues, "that I am not identical to my experiences (or my body in whole or in part), but I am the thing that has them. In short, I am a mental substance. Only a single, enduring self can relate and unify experiences."[20]

The word *I* refers, Moreland contends,

> to my own substantial soul; it does not refer to any mental property or bundle of mental properties I am having nor does it refer to any body described from a third person perspective. *I* is a term that refers to something that exists and *I* does not refer to any object or set of properties described from a third person point of view. Rather *I* refers to my own self with which I am directly acquainted and which, through acts of self awareness, I know to be the substantial possessor of my mental states and my body.[21]

Consider another problem with the claim that my personal identity over time is related to my body. Suppose my bodily appearance changes. How do I know the different appearance belongs to me? Kreeft and Tacelli provide the answer:

> Surely because of a self-consciousness that retains its identity throughout these bodily changes, which makes memory possible, which holds together the varied fabric of sensible experience and makes it all one, makes it *yours*. Here is the most radical center of personal identity. It cannot be understood in bodily or material terms, but it is very real. Without it, we could make no use of bodily criteria to identify anyone or anything; for without it, there could be no acts of knowledge and, therefore, no acts of recognition. That much is clear. It is not clear how souls are individuated, how God identifies them, or how they can identify and communicate with each other. But we have no need to know these things. We know that we are just the persons we are. We know that the self-identity allowing this knowledge is not describable in material terms and therefore cannot be understood that way.[22]

Therefore, the existence of an immaterial continuing self or soul is needed to ground personal identity over time. The human body cannot provide the necessary ground for this identity.

And what shall we answer when people ask how souls retain an identity when separated from the body between death and the resurrection?

---

19. Ibid., 68.
20. Ibid., 68.
21. Ibid., 69.
22. Kreeft and Tacelli, *Handbook of Christian Apologetics*, 234.

If the criteria to identify and distinguish different persons belong to the body, there would be no way to distinguish between one disembodied soul and another. If this were so, there would be no way to identify such souls. Obviously personal identity is an essential part to life after death and to judgment after death. Once again Kreeft and Tacelli provide help. What follows, they ask, when bodily criteria cannot be used to identify disembodied souls?

> Merely that we cannot identify disembodied souls as we now identify living human beings. It does not follow that these souls cannot be identified or that they have no identity. The objection seems to demand that we provide bodily criteria to identify or distinguish disembodied souls. The demand is absurdly unfair. The criteria by which we have habitually identified living human persons could not be applied in altered circumstances—for example, after the death of the body. Everyone admits that. But are these criteria the only ones possible? If the objection assumes this, then it sorely begs the question. It must demonstrate that no others are possible. And of course it cannot show this, for even now, while we live on earth, criteria other than bodily ones are involved in identifying persons.[23]

Belief in some form of substance dualism, that *I* am an immaterial soul that owns my experiences, my mental states, and my body, is a necessary condition for personal identity both in this life and the life to come. Abandon mind-body dualism and there is no basis for our belief in continuing selves existing over time.

Is There Conscious Survival After Death?

Human beings do not want to admit that death means the termination of our existence as conscious persons. We want an answer to the problem of death and the possibility of life after death. If there is no answer to the question posed by death, if there is no hope beyond this life, then we must attempt to make peace with that fact. But our examination of materialistic accounts of human beings hardly gives us reasons to despair. Since a naturalistic worldview closes the door on any possibility of survival after death, anyone who is a naturalist must approach life with the conviction that someday everyone he or she loves and everything he or she values will cease to exist for him or her. However much they may long to survive death, consistent naturalists must treat the appearance of this desire as a superstitious relic of a preenlightened period in their lives or in the life of the species.

And so naturalistic presuppositions do rule out any hope of personal survival after death. But a more basic question comes to the surface at this point. Why would anyone choose to be a naturalist? As we saw early in

---

23. Ibid., 233–34.

this book, there are plenty of reasons to look elsewhere for an adequate and rational worldview. We have found good reasons to consider favorably an alternative worldview that teaches we live in a universe in which personal survival after death is possible.

To be fair, let us look one final time at the indisputable facts about the significant extent to which mental activity seems closely linked to a living, functioning brain. I quote William Rowe:

> The evidence we have indicates that our mental life is *dependent* on certain bodily processes, particularly those associated with the brain. We know, for example, that damage to various parts of the brain results in the cessation of certain kinds of conscious states—memories, thought processes, and the life. It seems eminently reasonable to infer from this that consciousness is dependent for its existence on the existence and proper function of the human brain. When at death the brain ceases to function, the reasonable inference is that our mental life ceases as well.[24]

There is no point in pretending that this is not a serious problem for anyone who believes that human consciousness can continue after physical death. However, at least two lines of reply are available.

First, as Rowe himself indicates, the theist may be able to ease this problem by pointing out how the objection

> depends on a *false analogy* of the relation of the mind to the body. If we think of the mind as a person enclosed in a room with only one window, we can readily understand the dependence of mental functions on the body without having to suppose that with the death of the body the life of the mind must cease. For while a person is enclosed in the room, experience of the outside world will *depend* on the condition of the window. Board up the window partly or completely and you will affect tremendously the sorts of experiences the person in the room can have. So too, when the human person is alive in a body, changes to that body (particularly the brain) will have considerable effect on the sorts of mental experiences the person is capable of having. But perhaps bodily death is *analogous* to the person gaining freedom from the enclosed room so that he or she is no longer dependent on the window for experience of the outside world.[25]

Rowe continues by noting it is possible that at death

> the mind loses its dependency on the bodily organs such as the brain. The mere fact that the mind is dependent on the functioning of the brain *while it (the mind) is associated with a living body* is no more proof that the mind will cease functioning at bodily death than is the fact that the

---

24. William L. Rowe, *Philosophy of Religion: An Introduction* (Encino, Calif.: Dickenson, 1978), 141.
25. Ibid., 151.

person is dependent on the window *while she or he is in the room* prove
that when the room and window are no more the person will cease having experiences of the outside world.[26]

This alternative analogy helps us see how the human mind can
exhibit the kinds of dependence on the body with which we are so familiar while leaving open the possibility that familiar forms of consciousness
may continue after the body, including the brain, has died. Rowe is not
sure he wants to recommend this analogy, however. For one thing, "the
evidence seems to show that the relation between our bodies and our
mental life is enormously more intimate and complex than that between
a human being and a room in which he or she happens to be enclosed."[27]
I agree with Rowe's comment. The analogy does not explain everything
we would like it to, but few analogies do when the subject before us is
something as complex as the nature of the human self. In this case, the
analogy is not supposed to solve our problem but only make it easier for
us to understand how the human mind can often exhibit dependence
upon the body without being reducible either to the body or to its functions. We should never underestimate how far nonreflective people can
be led by claims that beg the question.

But Kreeft and Tacelli want to push Rowe further than I do. They
write that even if Rowe's objection were true, "it would not follow that
nothing survives bodily death. What would not survive is the instrument
by which the self gains access to the material world and builds up a
wealth of human experience. That is no minor loss. But neither does it
exclude the possibility of life after death. Therefore, in order for this . . .
objection to work, it must assume the truth of materialism. Either the self
is *identical* with the material brain and its motions, or the self is wholly
produced by them."[28]

Nor should anyone forget how important the body is in the New Testament view of a human being. The doctrine of the inherent immortality
of the human soul and the claim that the ultimate destiny of that immortal soul lies in its being freed from dependence upon a despised cor-
ruptible body belong not to the New Testament but to the philosophy of
Plato. When the New Testament describes the final destiny of the believer,
it speaks not of a Platonic disembodied soul but of resurrection![29] It
should be clearly understood that I am not questioning the conscious
existence of humans between death and the resurrection and final judgment. But we need to keep reminding people of the significant differ-

---

26. Ibid.
27. Ibid.
28. Kreeft and Tacelli, *Handbook of Christian Apologetics,* 229.
29. See 1 Corinthians 15:54, 56–57.

ences between Plato's view of life after death and the position described in the New Testament. Even Rowe wants to dissociate the biblical position from Platonism. As Rowe explains, the Christian view teaches that

> the body is not simply the prison house of the real person, the soul. Instead the person is generally viewed as some sort of *unity* of soul and body, so that the continued existence of the soul after the destruction of the body would mean the survival of something less than the full person. On this view, a belief in the future life of the full person requires the reuniting of the soul with a resurrected body.[30]

The New Testament emphasis upon the resurrection of the body carries an important implication that is often overlooked by people who believe, for whatever reason, that human beings must be understood in materialistic or physicalist terms. Even were such a materialistic view of the human person warranted, it would not provide grounds for dismissing the New Testament view of survival after death. Because our ultimate destiny is linked to the resurrection of the body, no one can use his or her commitment to a materialistic or a physicalist view of the human being as an excuse for rejecting the biblical position. Such a materialism would be incompatible with the theories of Plato and Descartes, but that's a different matter.[31]

The task for the Christian thinker is showing people that the Christian doctrine of survival after death is true and is linked necessarily to resurrection. In another book, I defend the possibility of miracles and then present some of the evidence that suggests that at least one resurrection, albeit the resurrection that turns out to matter most, happened.[32] The New Testament leaves no doubt about the fact that this resurrection—the resurrection of Christ—holds important implications for our survival after death. If the Resurrection never happened, the apostle Paul makes plain, Christians are in trouble.[33] But, Paul continues, "Christ has indeed been raised from the dead" (1 Corinthians 15:20), and his resurrection is only the beginning. Paul describes Christ's resurrection in terms of an agricultural metaphor: he is the firstfruits or the first gleaning of what will be a more complete harvest later. His resurrection guarantees the resurrection of all believers. The certainty of our future resurrection rests upon his resurrection.

But now, it appears, we're almost back to where we were at the beginning of this book—back to the subject of competing worldviews

---

30. Rowe, *Philosophy of Religion,* 141.

31. I am arguing hypothetically here. I do not believe there is any reason to accept a materialistic or physicalist view of the human being.

32. See Ronald H. Nash, *Faith and Reason* (Grand Rapids: Zondervan, 1972), chaps. 16–19.

33. Read all that Paul says on the subject in 1 Corinthians 15. In connection with the point just made, see 1 Corinthians 15:12–19.

and the effect they have on our thinking about such matters. It is interesting to see, therefore, that Rowe, an atheist, recognizes clearly that the strongest argument for survival after death "rests on the belief that the theistic God exists. If we begin with this belief as a foundation, a quite formidable argument for human survival can be built. For according to theism, God has created finite persons to exist in fellowship with himself.... Consequently, if it is reasonable to believe that the theistic God exists, it is certainly reasonable to believe in life after death."[34] If belief in the God of the Bible can be placed legitimately in the foundation of one's noetic structure, it is reasonable to believe in survival after death. If it is reasonable to believe in the Christian worldview, it is reasonable to believe in one of the major tenets of that worldview, namely, that God will keep his promises to believers regarding eternal life.

Christian theism does more, therefore, than provide a conceptual framework in which survival after death is possible. It goes further and promises eternal life to humans who meet certain conditions. As Jesus said, "I am the resurrection and the life. He who believes in me will live, even though he dies; and whoever lives and believes in me will never die" (John 11:25–26). Needless to say, if Christian theism is true, the person who spoke these words was God incarnate and conquered death in his own resurrection from the dead.[35]

Kreeft and Tacelli ask an obvious question that is less than obvious for many people: "What would be the most convincing evidence for life after death? Skeptics would probably reply: Only if we could put our hands into the wounds of a dead man who had risen again and showed himself to us, could we be absolutely sure. Only then would we have a 'sure and certain hope of the resurrection' (in the words of the old Christian Burial Service). Even this evidence, however, will not convince one whose will is set and whose mind is made up."[36]

Christ did rise and was seen and touched (1 John 1:1–3). Christians are assured of life after death not just through argument but also through eyewitnesses. The church is that body of witnesses, the chain of witnesses beginning with the apostolic eyewitnesses to the Resurrection. "Thus the Christian's answer to the most skeptical question of all, 'What do you really know about life after death, anyway? Have you ever been there? Have you come back to tell us?' is "No, but I have a very good Friend who has."[37]

---

34. Rowe, *Philosophy of Religion,* 150.

35. See Ronald H. Nash, *Is Jesus the Only Savior?* (Grand Rapids: Zondervan, 1994), chap. 5.

36. Kreeft and Tacelli, *Handbook of Christian Apologetics,* 255.

37. Ibid. For a detailed examination of arguments and evidence for the resurrection of Christ, see Nash, *Faith and Reason,* chap. 19.

OPTIONAL WRITING ASSIGNMENT

This chapter argues that all that is necessary to disprove a physicalist or a materialistic view of a human being is to identify one feature of mental events that is not shared with physical events. How many such features can you identify?

FOR FURTHER READING

Stephen T. Davis, ed., *Death and Afterlife* (New York: St. Martin's, 1989).

C. Stephen Evans, *Preserving the Person* (Downers Grove, Ill.: InterVarsity Press, 1977).

John Foster, *The Immaterial Self* (London: Routledge, 1991).

Gary R. Habermas and J. P. Moreland, *Immortality: The Other Side of Death* (Nashville: Thomas Nelson, 1992).

H. D. Lewis, *The Elusive Mind* (New York: Humanities Press, 1969).

J. P. Moreland, *Scaling the Secular City* (Grand Rapids: Baker, 1987).

J. P. Moreland and David M. Ciocchi, eds., *Christian Perspectives on Being Human* (Grand Rapids: Baker, 1993).

J. B. Pratt, *Matter and Spirit* (New York: Macmillan, 1926).

Richard Swinburne, *The Evolution of the Soul* (Oxford: Clarendon, 1986).

GLOSSARY

Many terms in this glossary have several meanings. I offer only definitions that are relevant to their use in this book.

absolute idealism • The theory that the universe exists only as ideas in the mind of a pantheistic deity.

accident • In Aristotle's philosophy, an accident is a nonessential property. A nonessential property is one that may be lost without changing the essence of the thing in question. One example of an accident or nonessential property is color. (See *essence*.)

active intellect • In Aristotle's philosophy, the active intellect is the part of the mind that abstracts the universal element from sense information received by the passive intellect.

actuality • In Aristotle's philosophy, the opposite of *potentiality*. The actuality of a substance lies in its form. The actuality of any substance is the realization of one of a substance's potentialities.

aesthetics • The branch of philosophy that focuses on beauty, especially in art.

agnosticism • A theory that holds that humans cannot obtain knowledge about some subject-matter.

altruism • The belief that humans should seek the well-being of others. The opposite of egoism.

analogy • A similarity between two things, as in the claim that an ocean liner is like a floating city. Aquinas claimed that language used about God cannot have precisely the same meaning it has when applied to created beings; it can only be analogous. When a predicate such as "love" is applied to God, it can only mean that God is like the love that humans are familiar with.

analytic philosophy • A way of doing philosophy preferred by many recent British and American philosophy that applies philosophic analysis to particular problems while tending to ignore the older practice of constructing philosophic systems.

analytic statements • A vacuous or noninformative statement, such as "All bachelors are unmarried men."

antirealism • In postmodern thought, the belief that it is impossible to establish a correspondence between objectively given "reality" and the thoughts or assertions of any knowing person. (See *realism*).

a posteriori • A term that refers to claims that are dependent on human experience. The opposite of *a priori*.

a priori • A term applied to propositions and principles that are known by reason alone, independently of sense experience. The opposite of *a posteriori*.

atheism • In its broadest sense, the denial of the existence of any God. In a more restricted sense, it is the denial of the existence of a personal God.

atomism • The belief that the basic building blocks of the universe are indivisible pieces of matter moving through empty space.

Averroism, Latin • The adoption of several anti-Christian beliefs of the Muslim philosopher Averroes by medieval professors in such institutions as the University of Paris. The beliefs included a denial of creation and personal immortality.

basic belief • A belief that is taken to be rational without support from any other belief. The opposite of a nonbasic belief. (See *foundationalism*.)

becoming • Undergoing change.

being • An existent not subject to change, flux, or motion.

cardinal virtues • In Plato and later philosophers, temperance, courage, wisdom, and justice.

category • (1) In Aristotle's work, a predicate; a basic way of thinking about any subject; (2) in Kant's system, any of twelve a priori principles of the human understanding that function as necessary conditions of experience.

cause • That which occasions or brings about a given effect.

Cause, First • In Aquinas, an important term for God, the first and ultimate cause of everything else that exists.

change • In Aristotle, the movement from potentiality to actuality. The process by which any existing thing loses some property and acquires a new property.

choice • In the view of many, an act of will in which humans decide among different alternatives. Philosophers disagree over whether the will is undetermined or "free" in such choices or whether the choice reflects our strongest desires.

coherence theory of truth • A theory that tests the truth of a proposition in terms of its consistency with other information we have.

compatibilism • The belief that free will and determinism are compatible with each other. The opposite of incompatibilism.

contingent being • Any existing thing whose nonexistence is possible and whose existence depends upon something else. The opposite of a necessary being.

contingent truth • In the language of possible worlds (see chapter 9), a proposition that is true in some possible worlds and false in others. In common parlance, a proposition that happens to be true in the real world but could be false. The opposite of a necessary truth.

contradiction, law of • The proposition that A cannot be both B and *non-B* at the same time and in the same sense. It is impossible for a proposition to be true and false at the same time and in the same sense. It is impossible for some existent to possess a property and the complement of that property at the same time and in the same sense.

correspondence theory of truth • The belief that a proposition is true when it correlates with the way things really are.

cosmological argument • One of a family of arguments for God's existence that attempt to prove that the universe is contingent and must therefore be caused by a noncontingent or necessary being, God.

deconstructionism • The relatively new theory that it is impossible to know the meaning of language. Meaning is subjective, never inherent in a text.

Demiurge • Plato's finite maker of the universe.

determinism • The belief that every event has a cause.

dualism • An explanation of some aspect of reality in terms of two. For example, mind-body dualism (as in Plato) attempts to explain human beings in terms of two ultimate features, mind and body.

emanation • A term used by Plotinus to explain the major levels of reality (mind, soul, body) as an eternal flowing forth from the being of God. One example of emanation is the relationship between the sun and its rays.

empiricism • The belief that all human knowledge is derived ultimately from sense experience. (See *rationalism.*)

Enlightenment, the • A term generally applied to a period of European history running roughly from the seventeenth to the start of the nineteenth century. This period was characterized largely by an elevation of human reasoning over revealed truth.

entelechy • In Aristotle's philosophy, the state in the development of any substance when it actualized its most important potentiality, when it fully realized its essence. For example, the entelechy of an acorn is a mature oak tree.

epiphenomenalism • The theory that human consciousness is a product of physical events and has no causal power of its own.

epistemological relativism • The theory that all beliefs are true.

epistemology • The study of the origin, structure, and validity of knowledge.

essence • The nature of a thing; the collection of properties that cannot be removed from something without destroying it. For example, the essence of a ball is roundness.

ethics • The study of such moral concepts as right and wrong, goodness, duty and obligation.

evidentialism • The belief found in W. K. Clifford that it is wrong always and everywhere to believe anything on insufficient evidence.

eudaemonism • A term applied to an ethical system that regards *eudaemonia* (sometimes translated as "happiness") as the highest good. Aristotle's ethic was a version of eudaemonism.

ex nihilo • In the Christian worldview, the belief that God created the universe "out of nothing."

faith • For Augustine, that which we believe on the testimony of another. As such, faith is a precondition of knowledge. The term is also used to mean a trust or commitment to a person or belief in the presence of some warrant.

final cause • The purpose for which something exists; God's reason for creating the universe.

form • For Plato, the proposition that a form is an eternal, nonspatial, nonphysical ideal that exists independently of the world of particular things. For Aristotle, a form is the essence of some substance that exists as a part of that substance. For Augustine, the forms discussed by Plato subsist as ideas in the eternal mind of God.

foundationalism • The theory that human beliefs are divided into basic beliefs and nonbasic beliefs. Since basic beliefs do not require support from other beliefs, they constitute the foundation of a properly structured system of belief.

free will • A common term for the theory that humans have the power to make choices independent of human causal influences upon those choices.

future contingent • A future human action that results from that person's choice. According to proponents of "open theism," God cannot know future contingents.

hedonism, ethical • The belief that pleasure is the highest good.

humanism • A worldview that denies the existence of the supernatural and regards humans as the most important thing in the universe.

identity theory • The theory that mental events and physical events are identical.

immutability • An attribute of God that is interpreted in two ways. In the strong sense of the term, God is deemed to be incapable of change in any way. In the weak sense, God cannot change with respect to any of his essential properties.

indeterminism • The theory that human choices can sometimes be independent of prior causes. The opposite of *determinism*.

innate ideas • Ideas that are present implicitly in the mind from birth. Such knowledge is *a priori*, that is, independent of sense experience.

interactionism, mind-body • A theory that holds that both mind and body exist and can have a causal influence on each other.

irrationalism • Ar term with many meanings. One used in this book is a description of any belief or beliefs that violate or denigrate the law of non-contradiction.

justice • Treating equals equally and unequals unequally (Aristotle).

kenosis theory • An interpretation of the Incarnation that asserts that when the eternal Son of God became a man, he surrendered one or more of his divine attributes.

liberty of indifference • The theory of human freedom that insists that humans have the power to choose freely between competing alternatives; the presumed power either to choose to do *A* or not to do *A*.

liberty of spontaneity • The theory that humans are free when they are able to choose what they most want to do at the moment.

logical positivism • A school of philosophy popular from the 1920s and afterward that may well have not a single representative today. Famous for its so-called Verification Principle, it asserted that only two kinds of propositions have meaning, namely, meaningless tautologies such as "All roses are red," and propositions that can be verified by sense experience. Unfortunately, its basic thesis failed its own test and was itself meaningless.

Manicheanism • The pagan worldview Augustine adopted in his youth. It taught the existence of two gods, one good (light) and the other evil (darkness).

materialism • The theory that only matter exists.

mechanism • The theory that the universal is a machine admitting of no design or purpose.

metaphysics • The study of ultimate reality.

middle knowledge • The theory that God knows not only everything that has happened and everything that will happen, but also everything that could happen under every conceivable set of circumstances.

mind-body dualism • The theory that both human minds and bodies exist independently of each other.

monism • A theory that attempts to explain something in terms of unity. Contrast with *dualism*.

moral law • A term usually taken to be a reference to an absolute, unchanging moral principle.

motion • In Aristotle's system, a term that connotes change, an actuality of some potentiality.

mysticism • For Plotinus, the belief that God can be encountered through a subjective, nonrational, ineffable experience.

naturalism • A worldview that denies the supernatural, anything existing "outside" of the natural order. The universe is self-explanatory.

natural law • An unchanging, objective moral law that stands above and apart from the activities of human lawmakers.

necessary being • An eternal being whose existence is not dependent on anything else; the opposite of a contingent being. God is a necessary being.

necessary truth • A proposition that is true in every possible world. The opposite of a *contingent truth*.

Neo-Platonism • A modern name given to the theories of Plotinus and his followers.

noetic structure • The sum total of a person's beliefs plus the relationships among those beliefs.

noncontradiction, law of • The proposition that *A* cannot be both *B* and *non-B* at the same time in the same sense. For example, a proposition cannot be both true and false at the same time in the same sense.

noumenal world • For Kant, the real but unknowable world.

Nous • The Greek word for mind or intellect; Plotinus's name for the first emanation from God.

omnipotence • An attribute of the Christian God; God's power to do whatever is logically possible for a being like God.

omniscience • An attribute of the Christian God; God's perfect knowledge of the past, present, and future.

ontological argument • For Anselm, an attempt to establish the existence of God through reflection about the nature of God's being.

One, the • Plotinus's name for his God.

open theism • A revival of an older theory (going as far back as Aristotle) that denies God's perfect knowledge of future contingent events.

panentheism • Another name for *process philosophy;* the belief that God and the world are co-dependent, often expressed by saying that the world is God's body and God is the soul of the world.

pantheism • The belief that God and the world are one.

paradigm • An habitual way of thinking or acting. Worldviews are composed of many paradigms.

parallelism, mind-body • The theory that teaches that while mental and physical events both exist, they never interact causally.

passive intellect • According to Aristotle, the part of the intellect that receives information from the senses.

percepts • For Kant, the raw material of human knowledge. Before information from the senses can become knowledge, it must be acted upon by the categories of the understanding.

physicalism • The belief that everything that exists is material or reducible to matter.

possibility • The power or ability to change.

possible world • A way the real world could have been; a complete state of affairs.

postmodernism • A vague term that many people use as a name for various features of contemporary Western culture, including its irrationalism. In a philosophical sense the term embraces many concepts of deconstructionism.

potentiality • The power to become something else. The opposite of *actuality*.

pragmatism • For a number of American philosophers during the twentieth century, the theory that a belief is true if it works.

predicate • For Aristotle, one of several ways of thinking about any subject.

preexistence • A theory that teaches that human beings existed in some form prior to their birth into this life.

preformation theory • The theory that the cognitive faculties that make human knowledge possible were given to us at birth. This human rational endowment bears important similarities to eternal ideas in the mind of God.

presupposition • A belief that is assumed, that is believed without proof.

Prime Mover • For Aristotle and Aquinas, the ultimate cause of the universe.

process philosophy • A system of philosophy that views God as a finite, changing being who did not create the world and who cannot know the future.

process theology • A theological system based on process philosophy that claims to be an acceptable alternative to historic Christian theism.

proof • An argument that convinces someone that its conclusion is true. Unfortunately, many people are persuaded by arguments that contain false premises or that are logically fallacious.

property • A trait, attribute, or characteristic of something. (See *accidence* and *essence*.)

proposition • In simplest terms, a sentence that has meaning and that is either true or false.

Pure Form • For Aristotle, a term that refers to God. He described God as Pure Form because his God possessed no potentiality.

reincarnation • The theory that human beings have existed in earlier lives and will live again after this death.

soul • For many philosophers such as Plato, the immaterial part of a human being. For Plotinus, the second emanation from God.

rationalism • The theory that some human knowledge does not arise from sense experience.

realism • The theory that affirms the existence of some thing, fact, or state of affairs. The opposite of *antirealism*.

reason • (1) The laws of logic; (2) human reasoning. Obviously, much human reasoning violates the laws of logic.

Reformed epistemology • The theory that a belief can be rational even if it is not, or cannot be shown to be, self-evident or incorrigible or grounded upon a such a belief.

relativism, epistemological • The belief that conflicting beliefs are true.

relativism, ethical • The belief that conflicting moral beliefs are true.

revelation, general • God's revelation through nature and conscience independent of the Bible.

revelation, special • God's communication of truth to selected individuals.

skepticism • The theory that no one can know anything or that no proposition is true.

subjectivism • A theory that human beliefs about truth or morality are true when we like them or have positive feelings about them. In contrast, a claim or moral principle is objective if its truth is independent of human preference and desire.

substance • For Aristotle, any given thing that exists.

tautology • A true but uninformative proposition, as in "All spinsters are unmarried ladies."

utilitarianism • The theory that the morality of an act lies in its consequences.

virtue • A positive trait of human character, such as honesty, kindness, and courage.

way of analogy, the • For Aquinas, the first of two ways of attaining knowledge about God. We can know that some attribute of God is like some property we know through our experience (such as love), but God's love transcends the imperfect and incomplete understanding we have of love from human experience.

way of negation, the • For Aquinas, the second of two ways of attaining knowledge about God. While we cannot attain complete, positive knowledge of God's nature, we can know what God is not like. This approach fails, since we can hardly know that God is not *x* unless we first know something of what he is.

worldview • The sum total of a person's answers to the most important questions in life.

INDEX OF PERSONS AND TOPICS